TOUCHING

THE WORLD

A Blind Woman
Two Wheels
25,000 Miles

Cathy Birchall and Bernard Smith

Panther Publishing

Published by Panther Publishing Ltd in 2012
Panther Publishing Ltd
10 Lime Avenue
High Wycombe
Buckinghamshire HP11 1DP
www.panther-publishing.com
info@panther-publishing.com

Additional photos

*The authors have set up a website which contains many more photos of the trip
than can be shown in this book. To see these additional photos please go to*

http://worldtour.org.uk

ISBN 978 09564975 8 1

Dedication

In memory of the people we have loved and lost

Our personal thanks go out to friends and family who supported this mad dream in a hundred small ways. Each one of you is more important than you could ever know.

If you dare to dream...

Preface

'Being blind means you see the world in a different way.'

Wandering through the everyday things of life you may well cross paths with a person using a long white cane or a lovely bundle of fur called 'a guide dog'. If this happens you will probably step to one side to let them pass before thinking, 'I wonder how they...?'

This story, in many ways, reflects on such things as throughout our long miles together on a motorcycle people would stand shaking their heads on realising Cathy was blind. You see, she belongs to the 5% of visually impaired people who have 'no useful vision'. In Cathy's case I do mean nada, zip, nothing. Across time life robbed her of what once was, leaving only recollections of a visual existence in her memory. Now she lives in a continuous rolling grey cloud that drifts across her vision swamping all before it.

With this answer, this description, this scary thought for most of us, you may well be formulating your next question:

'But if she can't see how can she come to know and write about the world?'

A fair question to pose but we might also ask why blind people 'watch' television, go to the cinema, or sit in theatres? Moreover, when they do, does this lack of sight mean they gain little or no understanding of what transpires before them? Our answer to this is contained throughout the pages of our meandering journey through this chaotic, scary, wonderful, exhilarating, delightful world.

It's important to understand that each one of us constructs a different world, despite having the same things in front of our very eyes. How is this possible? I will leave that philosophical curiosity for you to ponder, but in truth, Cathy experienced so much more of the world than just a film or a stage production as she physically and emotionally lived and breathed the story in its entirety.

With that in mind we would like to say that we never actually set out to write a book about her 'blindness' as such. Blindness is only one aspect of Cathy's life, not the totality of it; it is not 'who' she is. The title of this book was chosen long ago because we wanted to encompass her blindness as one of the THREE very different aspects to the story. To do anything else, for us, would have been to miss an important panoply of experiences and memories written deeply into us, in both similar and different ways. If we had done anything else it would have weakened the very true tale that these pages will tell.

For now, I would like to add my own thanks concerning the communication system provided by Autocom. Without their support, I would have been seriously compromised in my ability to translate vision into words, conditions into emotions, and the world into shades of everything else in oh so many different ways. Try to imagine a year of describing the world so that you can share it in a meaningful way with another person as it sits before your eyes in ways you've never before thought of recounting. Now you are me.

Because of this experience I became a better person in fundamentally different ways. No greater thing could I have asked for. Now, before we go on:

'You are standing alone on an empty beach. The sky above you is the brightest blue...'

Bernard Smith

Acknowledgements

This book would not have happened without Bernard's tenacity and single mindedness. I say this, as never did he waver from the story we set out to tell. Indeed, I believe it is a rare person who would have attempted such a feat as guiding a blind person around the world. Throughout it all he endured my foibles in long suffering patience and, generally, with good humour (apart from in India, as you will find out). No words can ever truly express my gratitude to him for opening up this marvellous planet so completely to me.

It is also important to acknowledge the role of both Autocom Communications (www.autocom.co.uk) and Dolphin Computer Access (www.yourdolphin.com). Both companies provided vital equipment for me in terms of my blindness. Without their freely given assistance, it would be true to say that everything would have been so much harder as a blind person. I can never thank them enough for their assistance.

We would also like to thank sincerely Rollo Turner from Panther Publishing who took the time to read and understand the story we wanted to tell. You see in this world of celebrity culture it is sometimes hard to hear ordinary people amongst all the clamour. However, when Rollo read the manuscript he 'got it'. Importantly, he believed in it. For that simple understanding which so eluded many others, we are truly grateful. It made everything else so much easier.

My final thoughts go out to all the people who followed our journey across those long miles and sent their support through the wonderful virtual land of cyber space. Sometimes it was the thoughts and prayers of friends we have never met that got us through some very hard and very scary days.

Contents

Introduction

As a small child I had no idea my eyesight was anything other than normal. My world consisted of shifting shadows and indistinct images, which I exuberantly interpreted in the way a child does. It never occurred to me other people could see more than virtually nothing when darkness fell. Objects such as lampposts or bins on the pavement were all merrily clattered into as passing people probably thought me distracted or clumsy.

Throughout my early years I climbed indistinct trees, played with my indistinct friends, and made my way through time in the way of children. Growing older with my sight, or lack of it affecting me more, I was often left sitting on schoolyard walls. Meanwhile my friends played netball, hockey, or simply ran around as youngsters do in playgrounds everywhere. Thus I sat and listened, sidelined by what I could not see in a chaotic, frantic, beautiful playground. Excluded, marginalised, and often alone, I was betrayed before I was ever born, by little cells in my eyes programmed so that they would never work properly.

In class teachers would tell me off for copying from friends' books, making me feel a failure: small and stupid from an early age. Their disappointment fed the belittlement of me although looking back I do not blame them now. The teachers were, by-and-large, good people who simply did not recognise or understand as I peered so hard at a board I would never see. The same was true of books whose pages shifted the more I concentrated on them, revealing little more than fuzzy shapes. Thus, I struggled in the twilight of even the brightest classroom as I continued to sit on walls while everybody else ran around with excited voices.

Eventually, after years of exclusion, at age 14 I was transferred to a school specifically catering for children who were blind or partially sighted and it felt like I'd arrived home. Home in the sense that for the first time in my life people understood, truly understood. In many ways it was the best thing that ever happened to me. No longer were there feelings of being 'different' or 'excluded'. No longer was there a need to sit alone on school walls. Now I could take part completely as, in many ways, my sight was 'good' compared to many of my classmates who had no sight at all. 'Are you a total or a partial?' became many of my first introductions to the new people around me. Hardly a politically correct question in our modern times. But then again, over my life, I have often found that political correctness has often been driven by people who can see, rather than those who cannot. Visually impaired people themselves tend to be much more irreverent about sight loss.

Two years passed in my new-found home as I adjusted to living through the traumas and angst of adolescence but I enjoyed every minute of my life. Then the day came when I had to leave and re-enter mainstream education at 16 and all the same old difficulties reappeared. Again, misery descended in twilight classrooms with teachers who lacked the specialist equipment and knowledge which would have given me any chance of progressing.

It was during this time I met Peter, the person who would become my husband. Falling head over heels in love with a man 11 years older hardly enamoured me to my family but I did not care. He was the love of my young life and, at 22 years old, I walked down the aisle to become his wife.

Ecstatic and blissful, we threw ourselves into renovating houses and the years passed happily despite my family's misgivings. We worked to build up the small transport company we owned and all through this period my sight continued to deteriorate. The level of decline was hard to appreciate as the incremental steps were so small.

With the deterioration of my sight reaching the critical point, a realisation dawned quite unexpectedly one day: I understood that no longer was I able to travel independently. In fact, I had not been able to do so for many years. The complete loss of my sight had quietly slipped past me, somehow, in my happiness of our life together. The same thing had happened to my independence without me ever realising it.

Thus my first guide dog, Petra, appeared and she proved to be my pathway back out into the world I had withdrawn from. I still wonder at the timing of her arrival as not long afterwards, an earthquake shook my darkness when Peter was diagnosed with leukaemia. It was to claim his life at the age of 52, leaving me alone in my blindness after nineteen years of happy marriage.

Some of you may know that grief is a funny thing when it strikes, as it seems overwhelming and never ending. Each day feels the same as previous ones as pain wraps itself around you. Tossed between self-pity, anger and absolute misery, the spiral took me down deeper and deeper to a place where there was no perception of light, no good times, no happiness, no warmth, no anything. It became a numbness, cutting me off from life itself. Much like everybody else who has been through this, I was convinced it would never get better.

Over the long months I slowly emerged from this place and, as is often the case, it happened with a profound realisation. It involved fundamental truths, a real understanding about what and who I was and where I now found myself at 41 years of age, with no qualifications and no training in very much at all. Nineteen years had flashed past working with Peter, handling accounts, receipts, and a hundred other little things around the business. Now I had nothing. It was all gone, swept away, destroyed by his cancer. I could see nothing and there seemed no future for me. This perception of my value at that time, of my worth as a person, was something that shook me to the very core as I judged my own value like never before.

During the subsequent years I turned to college to alter everything I was, everything I felt about myself. As I threw myself into learning I would walk miles with Petra to catch buses and trains. Many times these journeys would take two hours each way purely to get to a one-hour class at college. However, I persevered as I knew nobody was going to give me anything. And I hated being dependent on state handouts. I wanted to, I needed to stand on my own two feet and the only way for me to do this was to become something different. I had to become a new person and slowly over time the qualifications gradually notched up as I reached higher and higher.

Then the day came when I put on a mortarboard and donned a long black gown to cross a stage with Petra guiding me in my graduation as a teacher. To this day I can still hear the applause and whistles of my classmates; they knew what it meant to me. Importantly, without those years I would not be where I am to truly begin this story of being the first blind person to cross the world on a motorcycle. You see, this story's true beginning occurs near the end of those lonely years when I met one particular person.

What happened at that point was instantaneous, immediate, and it left me with no doubt, no hesitation or possibility of misunderstanding. It was as if my eyes saw a flash of certainty for the first time in my uncertain world of seven lonely years. Everything inside me shouted it was about to end and it was the first time I met Bernard. Thus our stories are, in many ways, as much about his personal journey as about mine and when we sat down to write about all that happened in crossing the world we were interlinked naturally, without it being contrived or forced.

Even though we have two different starting points due to his sight and my blindness, our paths entwined together on the pages by the very nature of the people we are. In many ways, we hope this contributes a richness to events as you will find a reality to the words and experiences which were written in rooms all over the world as events actually occurred. The words themselves often display our real emotions and experiences because they were often still raw and sharp when committed to the page, whether exhilaration or fear, anxiety or joy. Their inclusion was important to us in that rawness as any book we produced needed to be 'real'. It had to tell the story of what it means to travel alone through unfamiliar places.

The journey we set out to embark upon on an old bike started, in many ways, long before we ever met. While it had started in Bernard's imagination decades earlier, for me it started the day of our meeting and over our two years of planning. Throughout all the time we spent on the road I soon learned how everything always seemed possible to him. It was a fact that was always clear and consistent in his thinking. Often it would come out forcefully when barriers were encountered, both before we left and as we travelled.

In many ways embarking on such a journey is all about accepting and knowing that many things are possible despite how things may appear. I knew this to be a fact from the seven years on my own. However, neither of us had truly appreciated how true this would prove to be when you are in trouble and a long, long way from home.

What became apparent over our time together was a very simple truth.

All you had to do was believe.

EUROPE

IRELAND, FRANCE, SWITZERLAND, ITALY, CROATIA, BOSNIA, SERBIA, MONTENEGRO, MACEDONIA, AND GREECE

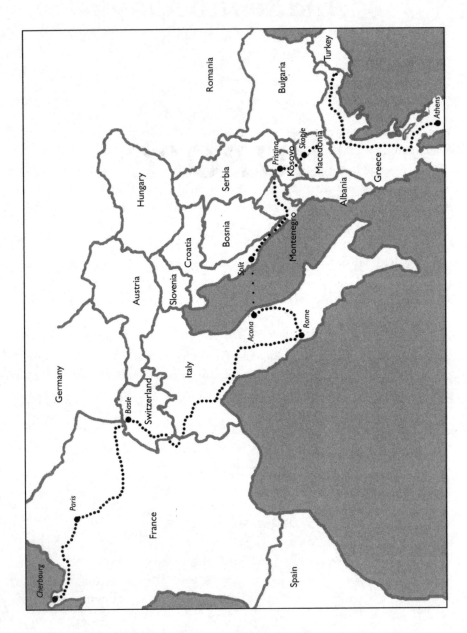

Map of route through Europe. 1 August - 28 September 2008

And so it begins

(GB) The day of departure arrives with Bernard still fussing over the bike and a hundred other things. Our heads are full of seemingly insurmountable problems as the bike is packed and repacked so many times I'm sure there must be holes in the panniers. With two hours to go he disappears into the garage to have a cigarette, which in the past often marked days of disappearing into a black hole. So it has been over months on end as a once complete bike became thousands of separate bits of metal spread across benches. Overhead lights burned deep into the night for weeks on end as it all came back together, with fewer and fewer engine parts for me to trip over each day.

The garage sits behind the house, resplendent with TV, radio, DVD player and a permanent supply of cold beer. I know it well from my many forays clutching copious amounts of coffee and sandwiches. Months drifted past before all those metal bits become our shiny red 1990 BMW R100RT motorcycle once again, known as Bertha, a name that just felt right.

As Bernard returns from repacking, again, friends and family gather for the start of our trip, which many sceptics thought was nothing short of madness – taking a blind woman around the world on a motorbike. Through a round of tearful farewells (Bernard) and hugs (everybody) we eventually lever our way onto the bike. Wobbling off down the road, no newspapers, TV crews, nor local radio beam our departure onto the airwaves, we are just two people setting off on a voyage of discovery.

For Bernard it is the chance to answer a life-long question (could he do it?) while, for me, it involves… what? Finding answers? Answers to what? The things I think I know? Really? After all, what does it mean to experience this world as a blind person? In this way, at this time, without a manual? Carrying everything we possess, my head thrums with questions, leaving me feeling vulnerable, excited and scared all at the same time as I sit wondering through our first miles.

What I am doing? Really.

Sometimes, perhaps, I wonder if the others were right. In my quiet times, often in the night when sleep wouldn't come, reflections revolved around madness, stupidity, and a whole set of words others have assigned to setting off around the world in this way. Blind. Across the whole world? Alone? Really?

Over the last two years we have heard most of those words while it simply left me wondering about 'the whole world' as a blind person. Is it to be something other than I expect? Something less or something more? How do I know? Will I recognise the question to ask, or the answer when it appears?

Are we truly, leaving behind everything we know; all the familiar things of our life, All the securities? Cut adrift from everything by shedding the stability of our anchors, the very ones we hold onto throughout our lives, it is confusing, now, to feel disconnected in this way. From all those familiar places. From all those familiar people. A whole collection of feelings jumble together in a confused mixture of emotions. Time will tell.

(IRL)We say goodbye to my mother and step-dad a hundred miles further on after another bout of repacking turns their path into a jumble sale without a sign. Just down the road our first ferry waits as Bernard tells of my mother asking him to make sure he looks after me, to bring me home safe and in one piece. It brings tears to my eyes as memories of childhood cascade from the past. Times gone by, happy, sad, and every shade in between, play out their emotions on the chalkboard of my memory, reaching forward to here and now, reminding me.

There is no doubt each of us will be confronted by such emotional demons as people have thought such an undertaking will consume us, spit us out physically or emotionally wrecked onto some foreign shore, no doubt under catastrophic circumstances. All aspects have been drawn for us so many times with the many 'what if' questions people have posed. Doom and gloom. Death, mayhem and destruction. All with us at the centre of it, of course. Perhaps it is really true we should both have taken that first aid course. You know, the one where you are taught to sew your arm back on with your Leatherman attachment. Damn – we were too busy drinking wine to attend that class. Never mind. And we don't have a Leatherman anyway.

People. The world? A world? My world? Which is it to be? Can they blur and merge into one or will they forever remain distinct and separate? Questions without answers. Answers to, as yet, unasked questions. Both will flow through our time together.

Ireland sees another round of tearful farewells to Bernard's family before setting off again, without a wobble on a completely repacked bike, feeling stable and more secure in many ways. The wind is cool and there's a feel of rain in the air, the engine throbs steadily as I listen, feeling the movement beneath me. It reminds me of our previous trips in 2006 and 2007 when we had set out to see if this was feasible. A blind woman around the world. Really? Getting to know each other on those trips we learned how things could be done as the jigsaw slowly assembled. Settling back into the experience now, it all seems so right, so familiar.

(F) A new day dawns overcast at Cherbourg. Sitting on the docks, Bernard smokes a cigarette, watching the flow of traffic before nudging into gear. Heading off on our first day on the 'wrong side of the road', our destination is Bayeux in north western France, famous for its cathedral and tapestry depicting the rise and fall of Harold, King of England. We visit the sights and continue ringing people at home, arranging things forgotten despite two years of planning.

Before long we're in Paris, and the traffic is sucking us through the Champs-Élysées and onwards to the Arc de Triomphe despite Bernard swearing that he'll ride neither. However, like being caught in the wake of a giant ship, we are pulled along in a torrent threatening to drown us in a sea of screeching metal. Happily we reach a city centre hostel unscathed.

Monday finds us in the office of French Guide Dogs with English-speaking Ange from the press office, as I explain our visit to centres around the world as part of a journey about blindness. The two of us stand cuddling gorgeous white German Shepherd puppies whose long pink tongues lick anything within range; my ears in particular. Other staff members gather as word spreads of the English Blind Woman on the motorcycle and many mention the Swiss method of training guide dogs, which I have never heard of. Such is their enthusiasm that we decide there and then: next stop Switzerland.

Blindness. Guide dogs. Both are aspects of my life. And in our visit not a motorbike or navigation system was mentioned. It was about me and, well, we all need our 'me' time don't we? Several hours later we sit wondering about people's kindness and what happens by simply having the confidence to knock on a door in a foreign country and say 'Hello'.

The ride from Paris towards Switzerland is the first day of covering real distance with a 350 mile journey into a grey wall of rain and wind. For hour after hour we're blasted sideways as the temporary shelter provided by juggernauts is gone as we pass into the space in front, only for the bike to be picked up and launched sideways again, the conditions sapping our strength.

Petrol stops come and go in our well-established routines of 'how to handle Cathy being blind'. Our routine consists of the bike stopping at a pump as Bernard gives directions and describes the surroundings. Standing up on the bike's peddles, I swing my leg over the seat to step off the bike, before waiting for Bernard to direct me towards the safest place. Usually this involves following the bike backwards to the large aluminium back box. All the time he watches as people around me do not realise my blindness as cars come and go inches away from me. Only at this point, when he is sure I am safe, does he climb off himself.

Listening, the sound pattern builds into recognisable sequences with their familiarity. Each small thing becomes numerous facets which a blind person separates to create understanding, to give meaning to events. Thus, the side-stand clicks down; the bike tilts left to take the weight; he climbs off himself; shifting upwards, the bike slowly comes back towards me as a 350 kg bike is pulled onto the centre stand. A simple thing. Click, tilt, rustle, movement, movement, clunk. After two such stops in a day of cold rain we have had enough and Bernard is starting to go quiet on me, unlike virtually the whole of the day.

Throughout our time so far weird and wonderful stories, interspersed with motoring updates, come through the intercom in strange voices as if from the captain of a plane giving altitude, directions, speed and weather conditions. They are preceded by a curious bing-bong sound coming through the speakers in my helmet before updates leave me wondering at the way his mind works. These stories are full of facts, observations and sometimes pure fantasy spilling out in Goon-like voices describing the world. Strange accents from all over the globe echo through my speakers, one minute sounding Welsh, then Scottish, or could that be Pakistani or Indian? Sometimes I just cannot tell.

The next morning, with a loud groan my companion describes feeling as if he's been squashed through a mangle, or chucked off a cliff several times. Listening to him, it seems every muscle in his body is aching. 'I'm getting too old for this,' he groans. Several more exaggerated moans occur before he falls out of bed to stumble around the room, disappearing though the door muttering 'who's idea was this?' By the time he gets back the magic of nicotine has worked its wonders and he's vaguely human again. At this point, I remind him the idea was his.

The route to the breakfast room is starting to become clear to me and my confidence in using the long cane is growing. Everywhere I'm learning and orienting quicker to the point where I'm half way through the building before Bernard has even left the room. It's funny really as it just seems to happen. The more it does, the more I need to do it and it doesn't matter if Bernard worries as I chuck myself willingly into strange places. It is something I need to do.

I'm not a natural cane user as I have been a guide dog owner for many years. The skills of the long cane are very different and it has taken two weeks so far to start to develop them even though I've always been very good at orienting myself, knowing where I am in physical space. Now this rusty skill has to be applied every day in new places and Bernard is even starting to get used to leaving me alone in a strange room. In this way I set out to locate objects by myself, building up my own internal spatial map, even if it means hitting my head on a wall-mounted TV monitor. My poor companion finds this so difficult to do, often grumbling 'can I just show you...' as I firmly push him out the door.

(CH) At the Swiss border a guard takes his time walking around the bike evaluating us before waving us through to the land of chocolate, international banking, avalanches, watches and cuckoo clocks, and tram-filled streets whose lines tug at our wheels.

Heading into the countryside we ride down a lane to a beautiful white building that flies the banner of the Swiss Centre for Guide Dogs. Climbing off the bike to the sounds of wind rustling the trees, the noise of the engine seems intrusive until it falls silent, the only sound the ticking of the cooling engine and the snapping of flags on their poles. Taking off our helmets, we do not know if they are expecting us; Paris had said they let them know. As we enter the modern building set in farmland, with a beautiful backdrop of woodlands, it is cool as we step out of the afternoon sun.

Our introductions (in French) see the receptionist rapidly disappear in a rustle of clothes and within seconds Bruno arrives and listens as I explain the purpose of our journey to him. The concept leaves him positively beaming with interest. Our introduction launches us into a four-hour demonstration of the most amazing training regime of dogs.

Exploring the centre, I find four-week-old puppies are surrounded by toys of all sorts, different tactile floors, wall markings, zebra crossings and road signs. Mobiles hang from the ceiling, from the walls, making the whole centre feel very much like a children's nursery. Bruno explains to me how they recognised the Labrador's (the most used breed for guide dogs) inherent tendency to constantly scan the ground for food. Trying to overcome this natural behaviour from an early age, they cover walls with 'interesting' things for the dog to look up at. At times they even lower the dog's meal down from the ceiling. Thus, over time, the dog naturally looks upwards as an awareness develops of all things above them.

On the street, meanwhile, this translates into overcoming 'Rover's' inherent tendency to happily scan the floor for last night's discarded kebab or bag of chips. Inevitably this results in suddenly being yanked left or right like some cartoon character as a kind person has left half a sausage roll on the pavement, with your dog's name on it. At times they have been known to miss head height obstacles which they have merrily trotted under, only to leave the blind person lying flat on their back after an unexpected face-height encounter with a solid object; not recommended I can assure you. It can definitely leave you cursing all fast food takeaway outlets and the Labs' love of food!

Everywhere in the grounds different textures for paws, different sounds to distract ears disturb the air as children's wind wheels spin noisily on fences, filling silent spaces with distracting sound. Bruno helps me explore a big bath-like structure full of plastic tennis balls that the puppies do not initially like due to the shifting instability under their feet. He paints vivid pictures of child-like behaviour, after time and experience, with dogs launching themselves into the arena to scatter brightly coloured balls everywhere in their play. Thus if a dog can feel physically in control of its own balance then psychologically it will feel more confident, more secure in its own abilities.

Descending down into the bowels of the building behind the nuclear blast doors of the compulsory nuclear shelter required for every structure in Switzerland, we find puppy mazes with ever-changing floor surfaces. Thus, if ever there is an international fit of nuclear pique then at least blind people will have plenty of (Swiss-speaking) dogs with which to restock the world.

After hours of touring the site we have to resist many of the gifts Bruno tries to shower on us. Fleeces, T-shirts, pullovers, baseball hats, umbrellas, books, DVDs and leaflets are piled up for us and Bernard chooses his Swiss Guide Dog stickers, displayed on both panniers before we set off back across the border.

The bike hums softly through the foot pegs all day as I start to tune into the feel of the thousands of mechanical bits and pieces whirling around, up and down, round and round. Creating their own symphony, I am aware of their distinctiveness against the backdrop of the tyres going over different road surfaces as 180-degree bends through Swiss mountains fill the early hours. Mad German-plated bikes flash past, diving past us around corners in a wall of noise as they accelerate hard before braking at the last minute. Their rush to pass the inconvenience of cars and trucks blocking their path contrasts with our thumping along gently, separated from their urgency, from their madness in many ways.

Coming to a small town on the border with France, we park and stretch our limbs. A nearby hotel nestles beneath power lines which disappear up the steep sides of the valley where an evening meal consists of a bubbling, flame-heated pan of cheese, mushrooms and cognac. Within this mix I must stab pieces of bread on a metal skewer before guiding it to my mouth. It is all very interesting to do as a blind person I can tell you.

Through the border the next morning, we descend into the seven-
mile-long Mont Blanc tunnel towards Italy as Bernard tells me of the
1999 fire which killed 41 people, of the tale of Pierlucio Tinazzi, a motorcyclist
who entered the tunnel time after time to assist people. He died on his fifth
attempt and a plaque commemorates his extraordinary bravery. His BMW was
later found melted into the tarmac.

With the newness of everything the sombre mood soon lifts and we pull
into a lay-by for me to use my talking phone to let people know we are alive
and well. On discovering that my voice software isn't working, my mood dives
southwards and for the next hour we try to get it to work, but to no avail. Feeling
cut-off from accessible communication, I am denied a sense of autonomy and
control. Importantly, the phone contains a list of emergency contact numbers
should Bernard ever be incapacitated. After an impassioned call to my sister in
England, two hours later my talking phone makes a miraculous recovery after
various buttons are pressed and reset in strict order. Bernard's laughter fills my
helmet as we set off.

Tunnels hewn through the Italian mountains thunder to the sound of
Bertha's exhausts before we eventually arrive at Vercelli, at 7pm. It's early but
Bernard has a rule about travelling on this journey. Actually, he has many rules
but one is applicable here and now. Once the light starts to fade, we get off the
road and find a pillow for the night. It's an €82 pillow but we're tired and also,
there's a garage. Little did I know that the garage was a subterranean labyrinth
involving descent down what feels like a corrugated ski-slope full of three-
foot-high speed bumps set 8 inches apart. Thus, we end up very shaken – but
not stirred. Later Bernard scratches furiously from a zillion bites of the Italian
nightlife, which avoid me completely. The sound of scratching lulls me to sleep.
It's the last thing I hear.

The same scratching sound greets me in the morning, along with vivid
descriptions of the lumps and bumps now infesting him, and I must admit his
head does feel somewhat lumpy, a bit like bubble wrap. This comparison fails
to impress him. Nor does my lack of compassion for his extreme discomfort as I
soon learn he has developed the insect-bite equivalent of man-flu. Being kindly
and supportive, I offer to help him write his last will and testament. Hopefully
he'll have time to finish it before he turns into the elephant man. Miraculously
his head even fits inside his helmet despite the earlier protestations that it would
need a bumpelectomy for this to be possible.

Starting the day trying to stay off the Autostrada (motorways) to save
money, we change our minds at the first gridlocked Italian town and select the
Sat Nav unit's 'Avoid Traffic' function. This takes us down single-track farm

paths with cavernous potholes big enough to swallow the bike without trace. After several miles we head back onto the euro-swallowing motorway; relief and speed become apparent with the rapidity of the miles covered.

> *Bernard – If you've ever driven on an Italian motorway, you'll know either there are no speed limits, or the Italians ignore them completely. It's either one or the other. They also have a wonderful tradition of overtaking and then cutting in so close you swear they are collecting wing mirrors (left side). On many occasions, it appears they want to park their cars on our petrol tank as they come so close it would be possible to share strands of pasta on a fork, like two lovers, through open car windows.*

At each stop we now consume gallons of water as the heat is profound, even driving at 70 mph. It's worse for Bernard as he sits behind a large fairing with his feet beneath the hot cylinders, getting the full force of the engine heat. Climbing off dripping with sweat at each stop he gulps water, constantly replenished to get us through, before apologising (in French) to Italian women as he clumps into the toilets to assist me. It makes me laugh and it's a common occurrence but there is little we can do; separate disabled facilities are rare on this journey.

Hotel searching begins in earnest at 6pm in Viareggio with my head filled with descriptions of the 'beautiful' people driving Lamborghinis and Porsches, and frolicking in the streets scantily clad. Bernard's eyes seem to dart between looking at the cars and the nearly naked (female) bodies. Swearing he is looking only so he can describe what they are (nearly) wearing, somehow I do not believe him. 'Watch the road,' I urge, reinforcing my message by digging him in the kidneys with pointed fingers.

The first hotel leads to Mr Indignant starting to refine his 'No, no, you do not understand, not buy, just use for one night'. The hotel staff seem less than amused at his comment but he acts innocent, sticking to his 'No, not rent floor of hotel, just one room for one night!' Alternating between this and his next question involving, 'Best price?' I want to leave as quick as possible but down the road they want as much again and we give up. Turning away from the sun-worshipping, sports-car owning people, we travel onwards.

Even though it's getting dark and we're tired there's little choice but to continue as Bernard assures me something will turn up; it always does, we just have to wait. Sure enough, 20 km later, an affordable hotel appears and with it comes relief at the end of a very long day as sleep comes easily and quickly.

Our destination is a convent in Rome where the nuns do a little side number in bed and breakfast but the heat of the day turns oppressive, heavy, leaving our mouths dry when we breathe in. All I can do is take little sips of water to keep it moist as sweat dries instantly, leaving me clammy and looking forward to a shower. Meanwhile Bernard is quiet for long periods, admitting the heat and straight white lines are somnambulistic. With little to keep him interested on this long straight road, it is like riding into a furnace with his feet feeling like two boil-in-the-bags inside his motorcycle boots.

To pass the time he describes cars pulling alongside to read the bike's panniers before accelerating hard away. This is repeated hour after hour as curious Italian drivers translate the English on the bike which declares, 'A Blind Woman, Two Wheels and 25,000 Miles'. The day drifts past in petrol, drink and toll stops.

Rome, and the traffic closes around us, sweeping us along much like in Paris with cars and bikes zipping past on left and right. Some are so close I feel the wind of their passing as we ride on roads of ancient cobblestones. Cars and bikes screech to a halt in 'last minute braking' and scooters zip between the traffic with their exhausts sounding like wasps trapped in a tin can. The convent is full when we arrive and like Joseph and Mary there is no room at the Inn. A hundred metres away around the corner Bernard sets to engaging in the international game little known to the British: bargaining. Not for him any form of 'passive acceptance' in handing over money without flinching in the 'stiff-upper-lip' fashion. Wheedling, joking and smiling his way through the encounter, he chips away little by little until no better price can be extracted. Standing in the foyer with sweat dripping down onto the immaculate marble floor he tries one last-ditch effort: 'Does that price include evening meal?' The woman laughs, so the assumption is no.

The next morning, clutching our scribbled directions (in Italian) towards the metro (underground), we find the system shut down as some poor soul has 'Kissed the train' (committed suicide) which, it seems, is very common. When this sad event occurs, Rome takes to the buses while complaining bitterly over the inconvenience.

A man adopts us for the bus journey while insisting on describing all the main features of the city as Bernard furiously tries to keep track of road names as the bus zips along. During the journey, he shakes hands so many times as the next stop is 'his', only for him to change his mind. It may well be he stayed with us to make sure we got to our destination – the Vatican – without getting lost. With the whole bus watching, we say our 14th farewell to him and climb off.

St Peter's square is quieter than expected and wandering through the tomb of St Peter with descriptions flowing to me of everything around us, a heated exchange occurs between several tourists. The guards will allow no pictures or videoing. Voices are raised as they aggressively state, 'I put you out if you take picture!' Walking on to leave them arguing in the centre of the compassionate Catholic world the Basilica feels 'cold' to me, with little real atmosphere. This is probably a function of the marble encasing the whole building, leaving everything feeling very 'clinical'.

The metro has reopened by the time we reappear and the train reveals French college students with loud-voiced teachers frantically trying to keep track of their charges in the crushed conditions. Sitting wedged among them, Bernard tells me of similar trips he used to take, of how teachers grow eyes in the back of their heads with the passing of years in order to avoid losing pupils. 'Sorry Mrs Jones, but the last time I saw your daughter was…' Of how he gave it all up, left teaching, and still missed it in many ways.

At the Coliseum, Bernard encourages me to have a hands-on exploration of a Roman soldier, despite my obvious reluctance for groping a complete stranger, in broad daylight, with witnesses filming everything. So it is that people pass by before turning back to watch (and photograph) as I explore the uniform, the significance of each item being explained by the wearer. Joining the entry queue for the Coliseum with my face slowly returning to its normal colour, an American tries to convince us to take a tour to shorten the 40 minute wait in the shuffling queue, for a price. We ponder before deciding what are 40 minutes in the realm of being away a year? Thanking him, we edge forward and 10 minutes later we're at the front and entry is free anyway due to my blindness.

Moving around the Coliseum many of the guides propel their charges at a brisk pace, charging through the amphitheatre while recounting the same information Bernard gleans from his guidebook. Making our way back after graphic descriptions of bloodshed, slaughter and mayhem, the evening passes to the gentle hum of the air conditioner as freshly washed clothes dry on the balcony in the warm night air.

The next day we make our way to the Italian Federation of the Blind but our loud knocks on the door and ringing of the bell get no response. Even Bernard's size 10 boots make no impact and eventually he gives up. And with only a little encouragement from me, he takes me shopping instead. Well what can I say, a girl in Rome and no shopping? Are you serious?

Shop after shop brings descriptions of clothes as I feel along rack after rack until becoming the owner of two little Italian numbers (one in white and one in black). Despite all his moaning about the clothes I already have with me, he gives in easily. Retiring to the rooftop garden later on I feel the warm night air as a breeze swirls across the rooftops. Sitting drinking Italian red wine listening to the peal of the church bells we count down our time in Rome as tomorrow we head for Ancona and the ferry to Croatia.

Bernard — The road out of Rome to the Port of Ancona is a nightmare as every conceivable Italian driving tradition is displayed. I swear I can hear my heart pounding through the intercom as I try to get us out of the city in one piece while people undertake, overtake, and nearly go over our heads. Eventually escaping this chaos, the temperature rises the further east we travel until I feel sun blasted. Meanwhile the lower half of my body sits in a furnace with the engine heat and things get worse with the approach to Ancona as a traffic jam stretches miles into the distance, moving at little more than walking pace. Eventually the source of the problem is passed as a hugely embarrassed German driver stands by the side of his broken-down Mercedes.

Arriving at Ancona like two baked potatoes, the queue of Italian cars waiting to board the ferry to Croatia tells us how the country has now become a big holiday destination, contrasting with the 1990s when the region tore itself apart with bullets and tank shells. As the only north Europeans in the queue, an officer approaches us, realises I am blind, and waives the rule declaring all pillions must walk aboard.

The deckhands however are not amused at our appearance on the bike together, shouting, 'Off, off' to which Bernard replies 'Bugger' in a quiet voice through the intercom. Speaking to the shouting deckhand, saying, 'Madame is blind' in both English and French he misses the vital Italian sentence for the same thing. This sends the deckhand into a frenzy of hopping about like a demented bee shouting, 'Blind? Blind? I no understand Blind, off, off!' waving furiously at the bike while pointing at me. Perhaps there are no blind people in his country, or maybe English or French sounds as incomprehensible as Japanese to a Lithuanian deckhand working on a Croatian ship. Whatever, he harangues us violently and the experience leaves me shaken.

Bernard — Take no notice of anybody but me Cath. Calm down, everything is fine. You take your time and do everything as we normally do. Take no notice of Mr Head About to Explode here.

I climb off cautiously, move to the back of the bike, as the side-stand comes down my hands are shaking at the fury in the voice still confronting us. Ignoring the shouting voice, my companion assures me I am safe, how I should not worry about the sounds of cars and wagons thundering onto the deck as I stand clutching my cane. His hand issues reassurance through its touch on my shoulder, before adding mischievously:

'Mr Potato Head can stuff himself, everything is fine.'

The sounds of the bike being shifted and strapped into place penetrate the surrounding din but by the time I arrive in our cupboard (sorry cabin) I am not feeling well at all. All day I've felt aches developing, feeling hot, sick and shivery in cycles. Within 20 minutes I am deep beneath every piece of bedding there is in the cabin, hot and cold flushes racing through me. The sound of the ship and the hum of turbines fill my ears as the 12 hour crossing of the Adriatic Sea to the Port of Split begins. The rattling of cabin fittings was the last thing I heard before passing out.

Bernard – Cathy has a high temperature, feeling very hot to the touch and soon she's asleep under the mountain of duvets I pile on top of her. As she rests I explore the ship and change our money into Croatian kuna, allowing me to buy 200 cigarettes for a fraction of the price I'm used to. I decide I like the country before even setting foot on its soil.

Like all people entering foreign countries, my first Croatian is soon learned by entering the universal language of 'Please' and 'Thank you' with much gusto. Thanking everybody for everything, I wander the ship as I cannot sleep although I feel tired, excited, nervous, all at the same time. Returning to our cabin to check Cathy's temperature her eyelids flutter open to say hello. Feeling cooler, I ply her with more paracetamol and water before she drifts back to sleep again.

Wandering the decks alone in the darkness, a fantastic light show appears as an Adriatic lightning storm strikes while I sit drinking coffee with a Croatian seaman at 3am. All around us people are asleep on the floor, wrapped in blankets and mats. The air is cool indoors but a warm breeze immediately hits when I step out onto the deck to an explosion of stars. The profound blackness makes them appear candle-like, each one winking against the black sky. Millions and millions of them against a perfect backdrop.

I stand on the bow of the ship looking upwards as the waves crash past. From somewhere comes the thought that Cathy has never seen the night sky. It's such a simple thing isn't it, to be able to look at the stars? Yet it is something she will never be able to do.

I immediately realise how depressing the thought is. I usually, and quite deliberately, hold such thoughts away from me. It does no good to dwell on such things.

My earlier excitement is suddenly gone, overwhelmed by my train of thought.

You see I do know. I do understand. It's one of those things I can never give her. No matter how much I would want to. It can never be. It's the way it is. But it doesn't help. It probably never will.

Neither the stars nor my face will she ever see.

Unbidden and unwelcome, tears fell as I looked upwards at the star-filled sky.

Balkan surprises

(HR)The next morning I feel less fragile as Bernard leads me back to the car deck where deckhands now magically appear to guide me to the bike with no arguments about blind pillions walking off the ship. Pulling slowly towards a police checkpoint, within seconds we are waved into Croatia.

I do not want to spend too long on the bike today but the first hotel receptionist responds condescendingly at our polite request for the costs for one night. Looking us up and down before answering, 'Well first I have to check if a room is available.' Lo and behold one is, for €150. Ushering him out before one of his 'HOW MUCH!' rants begin, we push on looking for somewhere not seeking to pay off, as he sees it, the Croatian national debt; years of civil war can do that I suppose. By mid afternoon, after a few hours of gentle progress along the coast we find the Hotel Merlot.

Dawn sees us following the road to Dubrovnik before veering away from the old walled city towards Montenegro where 4 km before the border we see a garage. Four Harley-Davidsons are on the forecourt along with their bearded, denim-jacketed, Swedish riders on a three and a half-week tour of Bosnia, Croatia and Montenegro. Sunburnt, they joke about the temperatures being somewhat different than they're used to and they tell us about the roads ahead, suggesting we skip Albania as bandits are targeting travellers. We accept their advice as, after all, if these four men are concerned about travelling through Albania then there must be something to worry about.

(MNE)A short ride takes us to the border with Montenegro where lines of vehicles move slowly forward until a guard's voice demands our documents, locked in a pannier. Climbing off, Bernard retrieves them but it's soon obvious there's a problem as we don't have a 'Green card' (an insurance bond). The guard gets impatient. Aggressive. Impatient and aggressive at the same time, telling my companion to move (bugger) off and clear the border. However, when he realises I cannot see 'The Transformation' occurs.

Appearing from his hut in a flash, gentle hands take mine to guide me to a bench where I can sit as the bike slowly follows him. 'Safe here, safe here,' he assures me, patting my hand. With a final pat on my arm he concludes, 'No problem, you here, is OK. Safe.' Patiently explaining to Bernard where the paperwork has to be resolved, his footsteps recede. And the ranting resumes. The bellowing permeates an upstairs office where Bernard is relieved of a small number of euros for the insurance levy to enter Montenegro. Soon back downstairs, the bellowing guard waves in our direction, giving Bernard a big thumbs-up from his position. We return happy signals back in his direction. Falling into bed later at a nearby guest house, we ponder his reactions, his perception of my need, my vulnerability, and his ability to seek to soften that insecurity. All blind people feel this, at one time or another. Give or take. Plus or minus. Sometimes it takes so little to reduce the impact.

Drifting into sleep, the silence is shattered by dogs barking on the hill above, lasting most of the night and complete with howling doggie harmonies. We bury our heads under our pillows to muffle the sound but in the morning we feel rough. After breakfast the massed ranks of locals line the veranda with paparazzi cameras firmly pointed in our direction. Everybody waves us off as the first English ever to stay there. It feels very strange to be seen off in this way after only one night.

At Lepetane we pay the princely sum of €1.50 for a 15 minute ferry crossing that sees us crammed in among the cars with no room to breathe. Like a rugby scrum, the disembarkation fray spits us out onto the jetty where we head for Budva, Cetinje, then onwards to Podgorica. Every time Bernard pronounces the town names they sound different; often I have to check if he is actually talking about the same place mentioned earlier. You'd be surprised how many vocal variations he can generate with a name like Podgorica. Our route follows the major arterial road, a decision taken before we ever left the UK: we want to minimise the risks wherever possible. Stay on the major routes.

We head east, passing the road north to Belgrade, sweeping along the tarmac joining Montenegro to its former capital before gaining a peaceful independence in 2006 after the turmoil of the 1990s. The road towards Montenegro is mountainous and tortuous, the tarmac winding through valleys, with gorgeous scenery and sheer falls to the side. We travel slowly, carefully, through the rapid switchbacks with their uncertain surfaces. Passing through numerous tunnels, the sound of the bike echoes against the hard rock surfaces and I gauge their sizes by the echo bouncing back. They are dark according to Bernard, particularly so after leaving the bright, bright, light of the day. Somewhat worrying sentences come from him such as, 'Where's the road gone?'

I notice that Bernard seems tense, on edge, and as we down drinks at a later stop he admits something feels wrong. The weight of the bike and concentration level required on these roads is worrying him. When we encounter really bad road conditions in later countries, such as India and Pakistan, will he be able to manage the bike?

Leaving this thought for later, he sets off to find a Montenegro badge at the nearby garage, returning minutes later to where I sit in the shade. Like an excited two-year-old, he recounts the attendant presenting it to him as a 'gift for traveller'. All his cares seem to have disappeared as we remount the bike. It is funny how such a small thing can alter his mood but, in many ways, I am still learning about him. His moods, his worries, everything in between the complexity he sometimes presents, has to be learned about, slowly, patiently.

The receptionist/waiter at the hotel we find hours later reminds us of Manuel from Fawlty Towers. He greets us with such enthusiasm when we fall in through the door after a frantic day of mountain riding where 200 km feels like 600 leaving us both glad the day is over. Collapsing onto the bed, the mountains show through the large windows of our room.

England seems so far away as a thunderstorm sweeps through the valley the next morning, with streams descending the steep sides to the swollen river behind us. Lightning flashes across the heavens in bright streaks blasting through the sky and ferocious thunderclaps roar as rain hits the floor, bouncing upwards 6 inches.

Our friend Manuel (or Slobodan, his real name) could not be more attentive. Soon picking up all the little things being blind means in terms of placing cup handles the right way, or indicating where things are on the table and so on, he is a real treasure and such a lovely guy. His English is as good as Bernard's Serbian and it's hilarious when they try to communicate. Once the minefield of breakfast is traversed, we set off to find a pharmacy as I'm still not feeling well. Bright blue skies have appeared after the earlier pyrotechnic displays.

No one speaks English, French, or even Franglaise and Bernard resorts to pantomime in explanation concerning my coughing and sneezing, and washing (his non-existent) hair. Cleaning imaginary teeth and using face wipes, I can only laugh and imagine. In the end, the shop fills with people watching the mime show but they don't seem to get it. Eventually the poor girl lifts the counter and motions for him to hunt her shelves for the necessary items. Arriving back at the hotel, I dose up and disappear under duvets for several hours of restless sleep.

Bernard – After Cathy has curled up, I unpack the bike and consider what to send home to further lighten the bike. The car park is littered with everything we have, spread out in nice neat bundles. Rows of this and that. Bits and pieces. Essential and mega-essential items. I consider every item, its merit, its worth in terms of space and weight. Hours later Cathy is awake. Asking her opinion, soon the box is filled with inessential things. I agonise over only one item – my second bike manual – but decide to send it home. Strapping everything onto the seat I set off to the post office in Kolasin, to send our second parcel home in under four weeks.

The post office is empty when I walk in and place the box on the counter where blank and puzzled staff – all smoking despite a plethora of no smoking signs – stare at me. After about 10 minutes of frantic gesturing in English and French and my two phrases of Serbian (please and thank you) it dawns on me the parcel is not acceptable, not being wrapped in brown paper... Ahhhh, big problem, they don't sell brown paper... or parcel tape.

'OK, where?' I point to all four points of the compass.

'Scorpio,' they conclude after a hurried discussion in Serbian.

'Pardon?' I think the puzzled, universally understood, frown is apparent.

'Scorpio!' comes through loud and clear in three-part harmony, along with a whole subtext signifying 'you stupid boy'.

I ponder with the same mystified expression on my face.

One of the women waves for me to follow her through the building, past the toilets, through the storeroom, turning right to the back door. Clutching the box under my arm, the back door opens and her hand waves in vague directions while repeating the term 'Scorpio' several times. I practice my Serbian 'Thank you' like a native as the door closes behind me, leaving me with no idea where I am supposed to go.

Twenty minutes later I find 'Scorpio', a T-mobile shop with a sideline in brown paper and parcel tape. The box is soon on the shop floor where it's chased around much to everyone's amusement. They stand in the doorway scrutinising my every move, waving to their friends to come over and watch as well. Fifteen minutes later I think the consignment is bombproof, covered with copious amounts of brown paper and parcel tape. Thanking everybody in the shop at least twice in my fluent Serbian, I head back to the post office.

Now, not that the staff duck when I reappear but I'm sure they argue about who is going to deal with me before one of them passes the necessary Serbian post office forms. €40 disappear over the counter to cover the cost of both parcel and 15 Vatican City postcards as I shake hands with all the counter staff, still practising my Serbian for thank you (which sounds like hwhala by the way). I exit into the sun and as the door closes behind me, I can hear laughter. Perhaps they weren't laughing at me. But I'm not so sure.

By the time I'm back at the hotel Cathy is on the verge of ringing the British embassy in Belgrade to report me missing. All in all though, it just seemed to be another day in downtown Montenegro doing a simple transaction.

We share evening drinks with a wagon driver who mourns the shattering of his country in 1990. Recalling the warring ethnic states and the hatred that spread all around him he told us how he was 'not a Serb, a Croat or a Bosnian, but a Yugoslavian'. His voice contained both pride and regret at the eventual division of what once was a single country. The owner joins us and tells of being taught to fish by his father and grandfather in the river Plasnica, just behind the hotel. His grandfather had fought the Germans as a Partisan during WW2 when the inhabitants of these mountains tied up thousands of Germans. Chasing them through the ranges all around, both sides had played their dangerous game of hide and seek.

The hotel itself (Djevojacki Most or 'Maiden Bridge' in English) is on the river and takes the name of a small stone bridge built over it by his grandfather. As a child fishing there, he had decided to build a hotel on the site where the Germans and Serbian Partisans exchanged prisoners during the war, a film being made about it in 1976. Looking around the hotel he waves his hands saying, 'And I did it.' It is good when a dream comes true.

In the morning we realise that six weeks have drifted past and we have taken to asking each other 'What day is it?' or 'How long have we been away now?' A sense of dislocation from the rhythms of everyday life has crept in, surrounding and sealing off our previous existence of work, home and sleep. Our 'before' time, or life, as it was now seems bizarre. In many ways we are starting to feel like gypsies, always on the move.

Before long the whole hotel 'clan' gathers for the big farewells and Sloba or Petrovic Slobadan (to give him his proper full name) our faithful and humorous waiter/manager/runner of everything proudly presents us with as a gift of a Serbian (SRB) sticker. Alex (the hotel owner) notes that it will not be well received in Kosovo (our next country) where its appearance will lead to the locals 'poking your eyes out', due to the events occurring in Kosovo between Serbians and Albanians.

It's a humorous exchange between the gathered Serbians over the sticker but I can well understand Bernard's reticence about it being on the bike at all as we eventually pull away complete with both Serbian (SRB) and Montenegrin (MNE) stickers for our trip into Kosovo. As Montenegro is predominantly Serbian we are now doubly defined by the stickers.

In the nearby mountains the road edge is defined by the sheer drop on one (our) side as tunnels come thick and fast, short, long, cold and warm, with the road winding ever higher upwards. We're soon at the Montenegro border as we re-enter the inevitable game of 'where are you going to, where have you come from (Montenegro?)' for the 21st time on our trip.

Everything grinds to a halt, as all the guards leave the cars and trucks to look at Bertha. Circling the back of the bike, they come back smiling at our SRB and MNE stickers (proudly) displayed. Soon we are all friends as handshaking all around seems to act as the trigger for the soldiers to fiddle with the bike's switches, like excited school children.

Familiar with this behaviour, Bernard leaves the bike in gear and hits the engine kill switch. Thus, people can blow the horn and flash the indicators, but no longer can they catapult us forward by starting the engine. It also negates revving the engine until it sounds like it's about to explode. It still seems strange to me that grown men should behave like this but I suppose 'boys will be boys' in whatever country, and no matter what language.

Disagreement breaks out between the surrounding voices as many want to wave us through and only one insists we get off. Up to now nobody realises I am blind until Bernard does his usual mimic signs (point to eyes and covers them with hands waving 'No sight') to let them know. A plainclothes official understands immediately, firing off a string of words. Everybody moves back to give me the space to climb off. Fortunately, I do so without kicking anybody with my reinforced boots.

The long cane is duly popped with its distinctive 'click, click, click, click' and I start to walk towards the office with Bernard. Within seconds the sound of 'No, No, just you!' comes as he is forcibly stopped by a hand in his chest. Guiding me back to the bike, Bernard places my hand on the back box before telling me of the queue, of how he'll be able to see me the whole time. The funny thing is I do not worry, as he does, about being alone. I'm at an international border crossing; what could possibly happen? Still reluctant to leave me, a plainclothes official indicates he will stay as he waves Bernard off to do the paperwork. With a final 'I can see you the whole time' my companion disappears.

Within seconds, a voice beside me asks, 'You England?' I turn towards it, confirming this. A soft whistle replies, 'Have come long way'. Approaching me very gently, he takes my hand and places it on the back box before saying, 'must go, stay here, safe for you here'. I smile and thank him to the sounds of his disappearing footsteps as I know this simple action meant he had some awareness of being blind in an open space. Perhaps he had simply mimicked Bernard's behaviour of earlier on? Thus, he'd given me a physical object with which to locate myself. It showed how people can be so very gentle, demonstrated so many times during our border crossings so far. No matter where we've been, it always seems to be true.

While the time at this border has given me a really interesting insight into men and their attitude to machines, for me it will always be remembered for the gentleness of the short-sleeved man, of how he gently guided my hand to the back of the bike. It spoke volumes about human nature and it was louder than any bike engine.

(SRB) Riding away from the border the roads are rougher than anticipated and for long periods Bernard is quiet as the tarmac has deep channels dug into it which constantly rip the front wheel sideways, causing the bike to suddenly veer to one side. Within a short distance the road splits in two directions, with no indication on the map of the new bridge stretching across the river, veering off somewhere. Ahead another checkpoint flies the Serbian flag, denoting an exit from Serbia we think. Which way? We go straight, assuming that beyond this checkpoint is the United Nations controlled region of Kosovo. As such, we will soon be entering the 'no-man's land' between this disputed region which led to the United Nations launching air strikes against Belgrade (the capital of Serbia as it is now).

Inching forward slowly in preparation for another crossing (the third in under an hour) the two policemen on the border smile as we pull up. Within seconds they wave us through into a strange area with nothing on the road. When I say nothing, I mean absolutely nothing; not a person nor animal can Bernard see. Riding through this twilight world, I hear of some of the things he knows of this area where so much death, destruction and relocation of people characterised the disintegration of the former Republic of Yugoslavia.

The euphemism 'ethnic cleansing' was coined to encapsulate this disintegration of the country, seeing Croatians, Bosnians, Serbians and Albanians all seeking to push their neighbours off 'their land'. It is hard to reconcile our experiences with this period of their history. Having met so many of these people on our journey, it leaves us pondering about the same event occurring in England with the Scots, Irish, Welsh and English all killing each other. I know historically they did. But we grew out of it mostly. Now try putting it into a contemporary timeframe - neither of us can imagine it.

Soon we enter areas containing enormous concrete roadblocks as heavily fortified United Nations areas appear. Riding at barely walking pace, we slowly negotiate barriers, including steep concrete down ramps in the road itself before drawing up at a final barrier. Waved down by the Kosovo police, it is immediately apparent the female police officer does not understand English but within seconds a United Nations officer appears, asking our destination. 'Athens' Bernard answers as we learn of the special transit pass required, which will take only a few minutes to sort out. Pulling over under the full view of machine gun posts, we climb off the bike as passports are taken for processing.

As we unzip our jackets to settle down for the wait, an armoured troop carrier comes thundering up the road followed closely by two white UN 4x4 vehicles. Screeching to a halt in a cloud of dust feet away from us, soldiers leap out from everywhere to set up a cordon around the crossing. Photographers appear from one of the vehicles and snap, snap, click, click, sounds occur all around to the sound of French voices as Bernard describes the tall, very handsome, and very senior, French officer who strides towards us.

The cameramen capture the officer shaking our hands, introducing himself in a flurry of words ending with, 'Do you need anything at all?' Thanking him, we let him know nothing is needed. 'The French camp is completely at your disposal. If you require anything, water, food, anything at all, please let us know.' Snap, snap, snap. The cameras capture all as he talks to us.

Bernard takes the opportunity to ask whether the SRB and MNE stickers on the bike will present any problems for us. 'Foreigners nobody bothers about. Now if you were Serbian or Albanian it would be a problem, but for you no.' Thanking him for his offer of assistance, he wishes us well on our journey. Disappearing, but still surrounded by the 'click, click, click' of photographers, we stand waiting. Within ten minutes our passes appear and we are free to continue.

(Kosovo) Much like the entry to the border, the outward journey is surreal in the passing through a land where nothing moves, be it vehicle or person. Coming round a bend, a squad of soldiers sit in the shade waving at us. Returning their waves we disappear up a road of unlit tunnels and we go from bright sunlight into the darkest night. Within seconds of entering one a startled exclamation comes through my helmet as the bike is wrenched, violently, to the side as a roaring sound fills my ears. It is that quick. That sudden. The blink of an eye, and then we are out of it as Bernard explains what transpired.

Bernard — We entered the darkness and suddenly, in the totally black surroundings, two men are kneeling in the middle of the road facing me. In the pitch black of the tunnel they are kneeling burning white lines on the road with no light but the blaze of the tool turned on a fraction before I ran over them. No warning signs, no high visibility jackets, nothing. Two Kosovo mothers must have been saying their prayers for their sons that day.

The houses in this part of Kosovo all fly the Serbian flag. It is draped over every building, it flies from every telegraph pole, from every electrical pylon; it is absolutely everywhere. Passing through the region we often rapidly slow down and I know we are entering yet another UN position, to move forward at walking pace, weaving around the various obstacles designed to stop cars crashing through checkpoints. The Swiss flag flies high above the early ones as men look down at us from the heavily protected watchtowers, waving us through without ever stopping.

It is now that I start to understand that the UN presence is probably more to protect the Serbian community as they have moved from majority to minority at the stroke of a pen on a map. From being in the driving seat when ethnic cleansing began, they now watch helplessly as the majority forge forward to form a link with Albania. This feeling is further reinforced as the UN checkpoints fall behind to reveal houses now flying the Albanian flag. Never again did the Serbian appear.

The path south grows worse and the bike starts to weave across the road as Bernard searches for the best surface in hypnotic movements swaying from left to right. The road is bad, and our teeth chatter. There are long periods of silence as, in the middle of describing something, Bernard will suddenly stop mid-sentence while he works out where to put the bike. We never go above 40 mph and for long stretches our pace is even slower.

My lasting impression of this landscape is of burnt-out homes littering the environment, a place where bulldozers have pushed off roofs, leaving families with nowhere to live. Forced to leave after generations of occupancy, I try to envisage the human misery surrounding such an act; it is so hard to imagine. Putting myself in this position – suddenly people come and tell me to leave my home. Right now. I am no longer welcome. Then my neighbours – whom I have known all my life – bring a bulldozer. The end is placed against my roof. It pushes. Watching these events in my head, clouds of dust rise as children cry, unknowing, not understanding what they are seeing. I can't shake the image. The Serbians we have met on our travels? The kindness experienced? It is hard to put the two events together in my head.

The images of shattered buildings full of shell and bullet holes remain powerful reminders of people's inhumanity to their fellow beings, all of whom want only the same basics of freedom, a sense of security for their family. I suppose, like a phoenix rising from the ashes, the consolation (if any is to be had) concerns the signs of reconstruction, which are everywhere. New houses have been built right next to the shattered homes, left standing precisely as they were when events unfolded. They seem to act as permanent reminders of how quickly things can go wrong between peoples with a shared history.

Passing through miles of this landscape the realisation dawns how the areas first we crossed did not show these ravages, this brutality of intent. I question Bernard about his descriptions, his omissions, his protecting of my nature, and he assures me the recounted images were as they appeared before him, nothing was missed out. Thus, all the damage existed beyond the Serbian area and, perhaps, it confirmed the 'They will poke your eyes out' jokes made on leaving Serbian Montenegro.

Approaching the capital, Pristina, there is construction everywhere as all corners of northern Europe seem to have a presence in terms of multinational companies 'helping' the Kosovan people. The flags of Germany, France, Italy, America, Switzerland and Ireland fly above towns and villages as convoy after convoy of UN military vehicles pass us going the opposite way, back to bases for the night after being on patrol, we think.

The road to Pristina is nothing more than a hardcore underbelly causing cracking and crunching of tyres, with shifting and twitching of the rear end of the bike making it a very unnerving experience. The road is being widened and it seems there will be three lanes in and out of Pristina, linking it to Macedonia with its good road network down to Greece. For now, it appears the Kosovans are looking south rather than north for their development. History. Old grudges in the here and now.

Soon we start looking for our pillow for the night and before long, a hotel appears and we cross three lanes of hardcore to exit hard right. Bernard is relieved as it had been hard, hard, work on the bike. The way he drags his legs upstairs to reception tells me so.

The hotel looks relatively modern and on enquiring (in English) about a room, the response comes back in German. He tries French; only to be met with German again. Trying again English, the response is in German, again. Now the only thing Bernard knows in German is counting and ordering a beer, and so, reduced to the fine art of pantomiming, he imitates sleep: two hands, palms together, complete with snoring sounds.

The receptionist is puzzled by Bernard but then again, a lot of people are so there is nothing new there. However, the receptionist quotes 'Tenty euro' which we assume is German for 20 as our smiles indicate we will have it as Bernard loves a bargain. Whistling a happy tune up to the third floor; 'it always seems to be the third floor' he grumbles by the third trip at the end of a hard day.

Late at night it starts to dawn on me that this hotel is something more than anticipated. A television blares away in another room but I initially think nothing of it, apart from that the person must be hearing impaired, as Bernard falls asleep within seconds. I lie awake listening to sounds of laughing and giggling filling the air until eventually the TV stops and I slip into sleep.

At midnight loud laughing rips us both from a deep exhausted sleep.

Grumbling, Bernard climbs out of bed, hunting for earplugs within the mountain of gear he's scattered around the room. With much rustling and thumping he undoes various bags and pannier locks while fumbling for keys in the dark. Sinking back into bed with earplugs inserted he is sound asleep again within seconds. Meanwhile I lie awake listening. Analysing sounds from throughout the building. It is not long before all the pieces start to fall into place.

From the numerous television sets echoing loudly through the air comes the sound of grunting and groaning as I start to ponder if the programmes could truly be about weight lifting. Soon other sounds start to penetrate the air, those of passion and energetic, frantic, sex. When I say sound, I actually mean a wall of it. All around me. In stereo. Nay, more like quadraphonic. Meanwhile Bernard sleeps on.

I honestly think somebody must be having a baby next door due to the sudden outbreak of throaty bellowing coming through the thin wall separating us, like an elephant in labour. Loud thumps nearly shake me out of bed at one point. It causes the walls to start vibrating and the lampshades to tinkle on the bedside tables. I'm not sure if the passing traffic causes the windows to rattle but I have increasing concern for our well-being; caught in the middle of this seismic disturbance as the room shakes from the pounding above our headboard. Meanwhile Bernard sleeps on.

The baby is delivered next door to the full crescendo of a female voice shouting, 'Oh Yes, yes, yes' (at least that is what it sounded like, although this is Kosovo). Like a relay race, the baton is passed over to the room at the foot of our bed and again all the noise is female. Not a peep is heard from the male. Nada, nothing, zip. The only sound indicating this is not a solo activity is the sound of slapping. Heavy, heavy, slapping. Not a little tap, a tweak, a mere precursor to some form of light-hearted slap and tickle of the amorous kind. What I mean is a CAPITAL SLAP. You know, the sort normally associated with arrest for assault in most countries. Here, it appears, it is a normal fun activity for two like-minded people.

After it seems to me the poor person receiving such a slapping must be unconscious, the same even louder 'having a baby' (female) sounds split the night air. The tone of the voice is plainly designed to egg her companion on and, to me, it indicates quiet may very well soon descend upon us. Sure enough, with a final ear-splitting scream, all goes quiet. And Bernard sleeps on.

I lie awake. Surely sirens will announce the arrival of the police due to the ferocity of that final scream? Without doubt, some dire deed has been performed, requiring a coroner's report? A trial will ensue, we'll be called as witnesses. Well, I will anyway. I mentally write my statement and remember the time while waiting for the heavy knock on our door. No police arrive.

In the resulting silence I think to myself, 'Thank god that's over.'

Within minutes the silence turns out to be merely a pause, a pitstop, a period of refreshment and a time to change drivers.

Lighter footsteps leave the room at our feet and two female voices talk in the corridor before being joined by a man's voice. Then the door slams at our feet and the coffee break is over as the whole scenario replays to even throatier exultations from our enthusiastic female performers. Meanwhile Bernard turns over. Spreading himself across the bed I hang on as he nearly pushes me onto the floor.

It is during the third (or fourth?) birth I begin to replay our arrival here, along with the descriptions given to me of the environment.

1. The receptionist seems completely puzzled by our need to sleep. This was despite turning up in motorcycle gear covered in layers of road dust.

2. There are no females in the hotel as far as Bernard could see. All were men.

3. Our room had a king-sized mirror on the wall beside the bed. Now most girls appreciate a good mirror but this one is just too big to brush your hair in, even if you could see it, which I can't.

4. The only bedding is a thin sheet and it is not that warm in Kosovo.

So it is I reach the conclusion that the 'Tenty Euro' requested by the German receptionist has purchased a room in a German/United Nations/Kosovan brothel. It is a startling realisation but here I am. And all the time Bernard blissfully sleeps on.

In the morning – after a fitful night's sleep – he just laughs off my deduction.

'Don't be daft, it's just a hotel, you're imagining things.'

Taking off for his morning constitution (meaning smoke) he returns sheepish. Unlike the previous evening when he had tiredly dragged himself up and down the stairs, he actually pays attention. Looking about on the multiple trips up and down to repack the bike, it turns out that every room is empty and already remade: 8am and the place is deserted. He even notices the industrial-sized condom machine the size of a dinner table, mounted on the wall by the stairs and passed at least eight times the previous evening. This from a man who can spot gravel on a road at a hundred yards. Setting off with our newfound realisation to find breakfast, the same German receptionist from the previous evening assures us none is served until at least 11am.

The girls are having a late morning after a heavy night.

I suppose it is not surprising really.

There are no embassies here

The road onwards alternates between brand new highway and other sections that feel like a giant rake has scored the whole road into deep channels. They grab the bike and for hours and hours Bernard constantly corrects our line. In the distance a valley is covered with a pall of dense black smoke released from small factories. Dry dust blows off the verge, creating little whirlwinds on the road. The valley is long and flat in the approach to the mountains where, after passing through the smoky dome, we soon spot the border out of Kosovo.

The guard smiles and takes our passports, complete with UN passes while asking, 'You coming back through?' to which Bernard replies, 'No, to Athena, Athens.' He smiles and stamps our passes, removing them from our passports, before we enter back into the twilight world of no-man's land towards the Macedonian border. Within a few hundred yards the queue for Macedonia appears and we edge forward to the post itself where a voice says, 'Green card'.

Bernard – When he asked for the Green card I knew there was a problem. The Green card is the insurance bond, or certificate, issued for the motorcycle and our UK insurance company doesn't issue them. As in Montenegro, we now have to purchase insurance for Macedonia. Handing him everything I have, he fingers the papers before repeating, 'Green card'.

Giving him my best 'I don't understand' look, I point to the sheaf of documents in his hand. He gets annoyed with the queue building behind us. 'Green card' is barked at me once again. I smile, shrugging my shoulders. Sitting, waiting, knowing perfectly well what he wants, I don't have one. Fingering the papers, all the while getting wound up at Johnny Foreigner, I try to defuse the situation by pointing to one side, indicating should I pull over there? He nods and I edge the bike out of the stream.

Before long a female officer joins us and the whole Green card issue is replayed again, and again, and again. 'Big problem,' she says. 'No Green card, no entry.' Putting on my most endearing face (yes, I do have one), I ask how this can be done? We would be SO grateful for her help. Truly, truly grateful. 'No Green card, no entry,' she repeats. Time to change tack. 'Where can this be done?' I point up the road asking, 'Here?' I ask again pointing down the road 'there?'

She thinks before saying, 'Not here,' looking adamant. I am getting stressed now as everything I've read says I can get it at the border – as in Montenegro. I try again.

'Perhaps there is a tax or a charge I can pay? There must be way you can get it done here? Please, you can help us?'

She waves at us to follow and at this point she realises Cathy is blind. So it is THE CHANGE occurs.

'May be expensive...' Personally I take this to mean we are getting somewhere as we approach a small window. 'If is needed, is needed,' I reply.

Our documents disappear through a hatch where a woman tries to read the English V5 registration document before transferring the details onto Macedonian paperwork. As this happens she says 'Very brave journey.' Pointing to Cathy, I say 'Very brave' before pointing to myself saying 'Very foolish'. She laughs.

Euros disappear through the hatch, before magically teleporting into a scrap of paper indicating we can now enter Macedonia.

(MK) An immediate change is apparent to Bernard. The road is good and the countryside is significantly different having crossed the border, as the highway reveals quiet vineyards, neatly kept and green, compared to the scrap yards and massive rebuilding programme we'd experienced in Kosovo. The whole country somehow feels cleaner and fresher. It certainly smells that way as no longer are we passing through pollution domes.

Heading for the capital Skopje our speed increases until we are whizzing along at 70 mph, and it feels good to be really on the move again. It does not last long, though, as the roads deteriorate and the dust blows on our approach to the capital. Traffic lights appear, the first seen for some time now and with them, beggars. They descend on us in their rush to bypass every other – local – vehicle. Hands outstretched for money, or miming putting food into mouths, one girl shoves a baby at Bernard, imploring him for cash. The baby has the biggest pair of brown eyes Bernard has ever seen and he tells me for a second – just a split second – they look at each other and connect. He cannot explain how, why, or truly in what way. The only words he can find are 'we knew each other'. Then the feeling was gone. Just like that.

The people become increasingly desperate as the lights change to leave them behind but the whole scenario is replayed, constantly, at each set of traffic lights where we are instantly surrounded by unkempt, lank-haired people, all miming various aspects of need. At every stop we become a magnet for the same people with the inevitable washing of car windshields, not something we really need. But they do try. With our windshield. Drifting into the car park of a hotel in this dust bowl of a city, they want more for a room than in Paris or Rome. We keep going.

Before long we join a motorway network with charges of €1 for mile after mile of good road, contrasting with the per metre charges in France and Italy. Miles later the bike chugs onto reserve and a service station leads us to two Dutch lorry drivers who tell us of their trips to England, their love of Liverpool ('so friendly') and a dislike of London ('not friendly and full of traffic'). Climbing into their rigs, with horns honking, they leave us to finish our drinks.

Empty motorways are consumed as we thump along while looking in vain for a hotel and I discover the joys of 'traditional toilets' in this part of the world (a hole in the floor inside a cubicle). Declining the pleasure, it is postponed for as long as possible. Several further stops all reveal the same layout. There is nothing to do but grin and bear it.

Travelling on the side of a mountain for many miles, temporary traffic lights control the crossing of viaduct after viaduct spanning huge gorges. While waiting, people get out of their cars, light cigarettes, and talk to each other, all of us baking in the sun, while those in cars with air conditioning sit smug and cool.

Soon I can feel the bike drifting to the right round a sharp bend and I know we're coming off the highway to arrive at the Hotel Vardar, complete with tree-lined terraces and a cool breeze to sweep away the day's heat. After a meal we collapse into bed at 10pm after deciding to stay another day, which soon passes sitting on a hill watching a forest fire consuming trees miles away as fire engines scream past on the road below us. The wind sweeps the inferno away from a small town on the mountain opposite and, after several hours, everything is brought under control. Plumes of white smoke trail high into the air to fill the sky as the smell of burnt timber reaches across the distance.

(GR) We are only a few kilometres from the Greek border and once through, we're back in the European Union. The bike hums happily as more empty motorways stretch out before us. The wind picks up and starts to blow us around the road as I discover a dislike for the wind; whether walking or on a bike. You may have come across the phrase 'Blind man's fog' and when you rely really on your hearing so much, it really is. On the bike it can be very unsettling as gusts blast you several feet sideways before everything comes back under control. This happens time after time after time until you feel a little seasick with the rapid and violent, unexpected, movements of the bike.

Bernard finds his Greece sticker (GR) at a garage and whistles happy tunes as he places it on the bike along with the MK sticker of Macedonia. Through miles and miles of empty roads we hunt our pillow for the night before finding the Hotel Gonatas Beach. Here a lovely elderly couple greet us in a strange and humorous mixture of Greco-English and misunderstandings and confusion before they realise I am blind. Heleni tells how her 'heart is hot and heavy' with the fact I am unable to see, going off to the garden to specifically pick scented flowers for me, presented as a gift along with a bible to take on our travels.

Waking early to startlingly immaculate road surfaces glistening under the sun, it gets noticeably hotter the further south we go as Greek drivers – when they do appear – all drive in the 'anything less than 160 kph is not manly' mode. At one point a startled yelp comes from Bernard as a motorcycle passes us at 160+ kph on the inside; just as Bernard is about to change lanes.

Bernard – It was so close. I checked my mirrors and was just about to start moving to the slow lane when, bang, he was there and gone. I could not believe how fast the bike was travelling while undertaking. At that speed, there would have been no chance of missing us at all. Things like this remind me how close things are sometimes, of how a fraction of a second can change everything.

Approaching Athens I can feel the traffic building and, unfortunately our arrival is at 5pm just as it was getting 'interesting' (as Bernard calls it). Navigating through traffic giving no quarter, pandemonium reigns as the fight begins to cross Athens towards a youth hostel plucked from a *Rough Guide* entry. However, the description in the guide is nothing like what we find on arrival, as everything – apart from breathing – seems forbidden. You cannot wash clothes, bring food or drink or anything at all, into your room and none of the hot taps work. However, we are tired and need somewhere to start in Athens so we acquiesce to the raft of restrictions taking up a whole wall at reception.

The narrow road outside is covered with graffiti declaring Basque separatists as heroes and the decision is made to remove anything not fastened to the bike. The hostel is full of young Australians and Americans loudly proclaiming their knowledge of the world as they step from plane to plane, and city to city, in their gap years. Sitting like two old fogies in the corner, we think of the wonders of youth, when we all seem to know so much. Sitting listening to the conversations all around us, it leaves us feeling OLD, in some ways like grandparents. After drinking and demolishing our pizza (brought in from outside, of course) a hasty retreat is beaten to our room to fall asleep to the sound of Athens traffic deep into the night.

In the morning our embassy trail begins with Pakistan, although after bashing through the complete mayhem of Athens traffic to the other side of the city, the locals all happily tell us there are 'no embassies here'. We go back along the same route as Greek drivers blast their horns at everything in sight, at us quite a lot, or so it seems.

Cars race from light to light and motorbikes weave through the traffic, at speed, with only inches to spare between themselves and buses, cars and trucks. Bernard grudgingly admires their skill in navigating through such narrow gaps, while thinking it suicidal. From his descriptions, perhaps it's no wonder Greece has the highest rate of accidents anywhere in the EU.

Heading for the Iranian embassy, numerous people assure us once again 'There are no embassies here' as we park up to walk the district. The people are right; there are no embassies APART from the one with the 100 foot flagpole flying the Iranian flag. In all fairness, it must have been hard for them to see the flag through the sprouting antennae and massive satellite dish sitting behind huge steel gates and compound wall.

After spending two hours to get here it turns out to be closed but Bernard pushes the buzzer anyway. We're greeted in Arabic (or Farsi?). In his best English voice – reserved for times like this – Bernard asks about visas and minutes later an official appears at the gate, through which the conversation is conducted.

'You need invite to enter Iran,' he answers to everything we ask, no matter what variation we take. Wondering if this sentence is taught at the Iranian Diplomatic School for dealing with Foolish English People we get nowhere. Turning away we arrive back at the hostel deflated after traversing awful traffic with the overall outcome being the Pakistan embassy has gone AWOL and the Iranian party is by invite only, wearing suitable attire if you are female of course. Thus it becomes apparent our stay in Athens will be far longer than anticipated. Meanwhile, neither of us is enamoured with our current accommodation for one simple reason.

You see, as a blind person the layout of accommodation is important in order to be independent. Signing into the hostel we had asked straight away if the rooms were en suite. 'Of course' we were told. And they are, apart from the toilet, which is out the door, halfway down the corridor, past several other doors just by the stairs. It's also true that there's a cold water sink in the room and a shower (with no holder for the showerhead). But there is no toilet. It's down the corridor and shared with 10 other people. This inevitably means I need Bernard's assistance to get there and back. Now Bernard is a lovely patient person who takes everything in his stride but waking him at 2am to guide me to the toilet might stretch our relationship just a tad.

While looking for other accommodation we find a street bar nearby called The Red Indian, with a Greek owner who has a serious affinity for all things 'American Indian'. Driving a bright red jeep, wearing fringed clothes, beads, bangles and large cowboy hat, he sits on the pavement outside his café watching the world go by. After a couple of drinks in downtown American Athenian Indian Land, several hotels are located in the vicinity and a deal struck with a manager of the local City Plaza Hotel. Our new home has hot water, a proper shower, and is only three blocks away from the hovel, sorry hostel.

A celebratory drink is called for with our Stetson-wearing friend who sends over several rounds of complimentary drinks. By the time we leave Bernard is, shall I say, somewhat unsteady on his feet. Weaving down the street he assures me that his motion results from the amount of street furniture in his way. He seems, however, quite unable to explain his slurred voice but to give him his due, he did try. Making our way back thankfully unscathed, he promptly wakes up two hours later proclaiming, 'It's the heat, it knocks me out', denying Mr Heineken had anything to do with it.

After the paucity of the hostel, our new three-star hotel seems plush by comparison with the roof garden's fantastic view of the Acropolis. Bernard draws word pictures to allow me to appreciate the sights across the city. The population of Greece is about 11 million and the city houses 6 million of them within the vista seen from the roof. Our fifth-floor room is clean and spacious and he now has a lift to fill up with bike gear and a new room to trash. Once again, I'm independent and can move around our room to my heart's content. This small act leaves me feeling good to have this freedom back again.

We plan to approach the Indian embassy (open 9–11 for visa applications) before moving on to the Pakistani (9–1 for visas). Stopping at an autobank to withdraw even more money, we reflect on how Athens eats euros like a monstrous bottomless pit. It constantly mugs your pocket as we come to understand that existing here is like drawing breath at high altitude, with never enough being available.

The metro is a crush of people being either considerate or kicking my stick out the way to get on the train where you sit awash with moisture. Walking the mile to the Indian embassy, a large queue has already formed but within seconds the door opens and a hand waves us forward. People step aside as a ripple of understanding concerning my blindness opens pathways previously closed. Reaching the front, we climb stairs clutching a slip of paper bearing the number 4.

The first-floor office has two windows, one for Europeans and one for Indian Nationals. Taking a seat, number 4 is not called. Ten minutes later Bernard notices forms on a box on the counter which need to be completed first and 20 minutes pass before we go to the window for the first time. There a young woman looks completely nonplussed when Bernard hands over the – nearly completed – paperwork and there is much pencil chewing.

'Why did you not apply in England?'

Explaining the difficulty of timing a round-the-world motorcycle trip to any great precision when considering the distances involved leads to increased levels of pencil chewing. The masticated pencil eventually descends to our papers and a flurry of crosses are driven through our carefully completed applications. Anything we were not sure of ends up with crosses before she asks for a letter from each of us explaining why we had not applied in the UK. Pushing two pieces of paper under the window we are dismissed back to our seats to write the same thing twice (one for each of us). After tackling all the criss-crosses on our applications, we are beckoned forward again.

This time a flurry of pencil ticks – rather than crosses – means we are winning. Carefully checking every answer with the diligence of a chief examiner leaves us sure the Indian authorities would be proud of their daughter's meticulous examination of our papers as she presides over our future like an Empress who can bestow wondrous gifts.

Asking for copies of our passports, she carefully examines each before they are stapled to the first form (definite progress is being made). Letters are minutely examined before being stapled to the first forms (round two, making real progress now). Our photographs soon join the forms, now full of staples (round three to us). Peering at us deeply while chewing her pencil, she disappears into another office.

Bernard is hopping from foot to foot with anxiety as he is definitely getting excited with the 'clunk, clunk' of the stapler indicating India is before us. Ten minutes later she comes back with another form asking for the same information already given. Another 20 minutes pass back in our still warm seats before presenting two beautifully, identical, scripted forms.

Ticking her way through everything with her busy pencil, the satisfying 'clunk' indicates they are acceptable to our governess of the Indian Empire. The fee of €134 (ouch) is handed over, and we know the problem has been all but cracked. Asking for our passports (getting excited now), the myriad layers of forms are placed inside them along with our stapled pictures. Bernard starts hopping from foot to foot as he describes how she is writing a receipt for the passports:

'Are you keeping the passports?'

'Yes' our protector of the empire says, scribbling, without looking up.

I gently mention they are needed for the Pakistani embassy. She looks up at us for a few seconds before asking, 'When bring them back here?' Bernard's feet can be heard drumming throughout the office.

'How long will you need them? When will the visas be ready?' he asks.

'Cannot give date without passports,' she says while smiling sweetly.

'If we keep passports, you collect visa in eight days.'

'EIGHT DAYS' Bernard groans 'Just to put a stamp or sticker in it? Can't this be done when we come back to pick up the visas?'

'Cannot give date without passports, if you take passports, cannot give date for visas.' Catch 22. Trapped. Game set and match to Indian Bureaucracy.

Having no choice but to leave our passports, Bernard sits on a wall outside muttering as it becomes our bench. The click of the cigarette lighter signifies the calming influence of nicotine. 'Damn... blast...' and the loud exhale of toxicity follows as talk turns to our options. It is important to note at this point that Mr Organised (as he can be) has digital copies of all the important documents, including our passports. He also has photocopies of everything ever likely to be asked for so all is not lost. In fact, he has copies of copies of everything. It's the way he is.

Setting off through the Athens heat, the Pakistan embassy is found miles before ever seeing it as it is no exaggeration to say the queue is MASSIVE. I know it with the large exhale followed by 'Oh my God, is that the queue...? Bloody hell.'

However, Bernard has the bit between his teeth now as he guides me to the front where he innocently asks 'Is this the Pakistan embassy?' Having already described the huge flag flying over the embassy I smile inwardly as it is such a gentle enquiry the armed security (three of them) reply 'yes, it is, how can we help you?' Our explanation leads to an invite to follow them to a lift rising to the second floor where, when the door opens, a rugby scrum is occurring. The noise of raised voices rebounds around the corridor while our destination, the large teak door on our left, has a bell. The door opens into an air-conditioned office full of leather chairs and couches and 'Hamid' joins us.

Explaining our journey to him, and our route through Pakistan, the same response comes back as at the Indian embassy 'Why did you not apply in the UK?' Again, we tell of the problems of timing, distances, and the limited life of visas. 'It cannot be done, you are two foreign nationals without Greek address. You have to apply in your home country.' Bernard's crestfallen voice indicates this will be so hard for us as we already have the Indian (nearly) and Iranian (not at all) visas and time is running out on us. The final plea in his voice asks the ever effective 'Is there anything you can do to help us?' statement he uses at critical moments.

Hamid ponders. 'Only the two of you?' We nod like bookends as he disappears into another office. Settling onto a couch for an indeterminable wait, fifteen minutes pass before he ushers us into an office where a large swivel chair is occupied by somebody several rungs higher up the food chain.

The official asks me questions about my blindness, about how hard it is to be always in a strange environment, thinking it must be very difficult for me sometimes. I relax and explain you get used to it along with the fact I learn very quickly – if given the chance – to find my way around new places. Taking a deep breath he looks at us before explaining what we want is 'very difficult' for a foreign national. Asking where we live in the UK, he instantly knows our nearest Pakistani embassy is in Manchester. 'It may be possible,' he goes on, saying how he will fax the embassy to seek clearance for the visa from them. Forms are duly completed and at this point we explain our passport predicament, waved away as 'Not a problem' due to the photocopies we have. Promising an answer inside two days, an hour later we are outside with everything completed. Astonishing really, considering what everything read and heard about visa applications for Pakistan.

As we leave, Bernard notes dozens of Pakistani/Indian people sitting on the pavements magically clearing a path, like the Red Sea parting for Moses. Friends pull companions out of the way as we make our way for a celebratory milkshake at a nearby café, no expense spared. After all the frustrations of visa applications two have been cracked in a single morning, leaving us feeling good, really good, for the first time in days. Now all we can do is wait.

While waiting we track down the major Greek visual impairment organisation, set up in 1946. The Lighthouse for the Blind of Greece operates under the umbrella and supervision of the Ministry of Health and Welfare and from which it draws some of its funding. Setting off on the bike to locate The Lighthouse, a receptionist is completely puzzled by our arrival and language before quickly ringing for somebody to come and see us. Over the next few hours we are shown around the centre by Zoe, one of the staff at the centre, although this only occurs after the Director realises we are not after donations of money for the journey in a hilarious confusion of language.

We learn of the theatre where shows are staged, the gymnasium, Braille and audio production facilities, of music classes, language courses, ceramic workshops and computer courses. It also becomes apparent that blind people in Greece work for fifteen years before retiring in order to 'recycle' the jobs within the disabled workforce. To facilitate this, the Greek government ensures disabled people are financially secure when they retire and many at the centre confirmed this.

Visiting the tactile museum, the staff kindly open it up especially for me and I spend a wonderful hour exploring the historical statues and ancient artefacts of Greece. Examining reproductions of the originals, located in the Louvre in Paris and in the museums of London, Zoe tells us how many had been plundered by other nations throughout history. I also had the chance to examine the layout of the Acropolis to appreciate the size and scale of the sacred rock as my fingers gleaned understanding while roaming around a scale model.

Zoe answered candidly about our observation of not seeing blind people out and about in the capital, telling us how Athens is actually very dangerous for blind people: 'rule-free' driving and the seemingly optional red traffic lights ('I might stop, but then again I might not') causing great difficulty. The lack of awareness is truly profound. People constantly look as we pass by and there is little or no understanding of the white cane. Bernard has found it very, very tiring guiding me through the streets. Cars are parked on junctions and across zebra crossings, while motorbikes adorn the pavement. It would be impossible to navigate or learn a route independently. A guide dog would get dizzy trying to find a way through before collapsing into a vet's arms whispering, "I want to retire on health grounds".

In the meantime the Greek government has spent a fortune on a wonderful tactile method to cover pavements with a channel-like system which, with a long cane, leads you to front doors and to lifts at, for example, the metro system. In many ways it should be easier than in the UK but what defeats it is the profound culture of 'the car' and street furniture. Parked motorbikes and cars, as well as tables, chairs and street stalls cover the tactile routes until they become meaningless; there seems to be no understanding of what they're actually there for. On our return to the hotel, we experience a very sobering encounter showing us how vulnerable a blind person is.

Coming out of a shop Bernard is watching the steps down onto the pavement (I stress, onto the pavement), telling me, 'Two down' (to denote the number of steps), when we start to move. Suddenly a motorbike rips past and I am slammed backwards into the doorway. There's a startled yelp from my companion as the motorbike misses his left leg by inches. I cannot repeat the stream of profanities coming from Bernard, but I did ask how some of them would be physically possible in terms of the man and his motorbike. Angry? He is beyond angry as the motorbike rider stops, looks back, and takes off, still on the pavement. It just goes to show how insecure you would be in Athens on your own as a blind person. Our journey was nearly terminated with a trip to the hospital or the police cells for Bernard on a charge of assault.

The days pass with our small observations as Bernard's father (Jim) flies in to join us in our wait for Visas. When he does appear the 1am heat leaves him gasping on the roof garden under the night sky sipping a cold drink. Over the following days, whether walking up the Sacred Hill to the Acropolis, passing underneath Hadrian's Gate, or standing before the Temple of Zeus, his camera snaps everything in sight before Bernard asks if there is any possibility of there being 'just a little Japanese in him?' I suppose, much like many people who spend their whole life working and paying bills, time drifts past us without the realization of just how much has gone by. Then one day we realise with the opportunity to be somewhere completely different. With that opportunity appears a need to imprint the memories into both our heads and photo albums.

Visiting the Acropolis and having used the tactile model at the Lighthouse Centre, the whole experience becomes much more acute in terms of putting the site into perspective. However, my abiding memory of this day is the comment by Jim as he says in a wondrous voice: 'I cannot believe I'm standing here. After reading about such places for my whole life, I'm here. I'm stood on the Acropolis.' He is mesmerised by standing on the same rock where it is said that St Paul once stood when he gave sermons to the Athenians. It is probably one of the abiding moments of his trip.

We take in the changing of the guard at the Parliament building as the elaborate and stylised 'performance' is acted out to the massed ranks of video cameras and the click, click, click of cameras all around me. The officer in charge of the ceremony waves Bernard and I forward. He crosses to one of the tall handsome soldiers, whispers something in his ear, then indicates I should move close to the immobile statue so Bernard can take my picture. I whisper 'Thank you' while standing beside him and Bernard swears a tiny smile appears on his face, gone in a flash. The picture shows no trace of it. But Bernard knows it was there and I do not doubt him.

Evenings find us sitting on the roof garden under the night stars as a jug of wine is delivered to the table and here we met Gordon from Scotland, who regaled us with stories of his trips through the region driving heavy goods vehicles (HGVs) along with spectacular motorcycle crashes that he's seen, just what we need to hear. However, we learn a lot of useful information about the roads in Turkey, the driving habits, and places to stay as we talk far into the night. Gordon is the soul of kindness and generosity and many such evenings are spent in his company (along with his colleague Davie) as they tell us of their work in the petrochemical industry.

In the blink of an eye a week passes and Bernard's dad disappears through the airport security gates. Hotel evenings now leave us feeling like regulars with the barman Manuel no longer asking what we drink, but merely arriving with them at our table.

During this three-week period the internet Visa Agency used for our Iranian Visa applications eventually tell us how they can be picked up at Erzurum (1800 miles away in the far East of Turkey) once they have been cleared by the authorities. Since our boredom threshold has long been surpassed sitting still, and with that final piece of the Visa jigsaw now firmly in place, we can move on as both Indian and Pakistan Visas now sit safely in our passports.

The thought of leaving cheers Bernard up, even accounting for the prospect of driving in the traffic which he has come to loathe. Coming out to the bike, he finds a hundred cigarettes sitting in the front fairing with a note from Gordon stating, 'Use half a packet to solve a minor problem in Turkey, a full packet for something more serious and at least two packets to get you out of jail! Always remember, if in doubt FOLLOW THE WAGONS.'

The road to Turkey

Istanbul is 1,200 km away and it dawns on me this single figure, this distance, my knowledge of it, all now measure how far I've travelled, mentally, physically and emotionally. 1,200 km? It used to sound so, so, far away. But now? It's not so far anymore. From the tip of my home country to the furthest point southwards? It's not far. Not really. Realising how the days are long gone when distance seemed to matter, when it was counted by hours instead of days, or countries, now the word 'only' creeps in. It's only 1,200 km. It will take us 'only' three days. Only. Worlds change. Perceptions accept new meanings of time, scale and distance.

The bike feels like home the instant I'm on it. Everything is comfortable, familiar, secure in all ways and even the traffic is light for some reason and we have no problem finding the dual carriageway system leading out of Athens. As we ride along the big topic of conversation turns to tyres: change them in Istanbul or not? The current ones were new in England and they have completed only 7,000 km with a life expectancy of about 13,000–14,000 km for the rear, due to the weight on the bike, with the front lasting longer. We need to decide whether to change them both at the same time.

Heading north out of Athens, calculations show the distances involve the journey through Turkey to be about 2,500 km with the same mileage in Iran. There will be a further 2,000 km in Pakistan and roughly the same in India. By our calculations, this accounts for 9,000 or 10,000 km more before a change is possible as it would be difficult to change them in Iran, as there are no large-capacity motorcycles in the country. By the time we get to India the canvas will be showing through the tyre tread, leading to a likely stream of punctures. In the end it is an easy decision. At Istanbul we change tyres and these will take us through to India. It is also true that it is better to live by the principle: 'Get things when you can as five miles down the road they may not be available.'

The days pass and miles are covered until the bike coughs and splutters onto reserve after sequences involving 250 km of sitting on dual carriageways at 120 kph; we need to cover mileage. The three-and-a-half weeks kept us static too long, leading to an overwhelming sense of needing to be further on, always further on, and the price is paid in terms of petrol consumption.

Covering 1,086 km to the Turkish border over two days, all the familiar patterns re-establish themselves and at 4pm it's time to search for somewhere safe for the night. We find somewhere, pull up, go in, negotiate prices, unpack the bike, shower, find something to eat and fall into bed before getting up in the morning and reversing the whole process. Splashing through our first rain for weeks we become aware of the weather changing around us as. It increases our need to push on through the heavy rain that pelts us. Soon the border with Turkey appears and the whole familiar 'Bernard stressing' pattern comes back.

At a café on the Greek side of the barrier Bernard de-stresses with a couple of cigarettes and a cup of coffee before tackling the process. We meet Adam who is travelling to India on a 125cc motorcycle having passed his test only two months before; Bernard considers him hardcore. Forget 1200cc bikes with aluminium-clad boxes hanging from expensive machinery full of bling, bling. To live your dream, grab an e-Bay 125 bargain, buy some ex-army bags, roll everything you have in bin liners, strap them on with bungee-straps and off you go. Simple. 'Like the old days,' according to my sidekick.

Exiting the Greek side with a cheery wave and a cursory look at our passports, heavily armed Greek and Turkish soldiers separate the two countries as everybody waves and smiles at our passing. Travelling at little more than walking pace in case anybody waves us down 'with their big guns' (Bernard), soon the 'entry' side of the bridge appears where multiple barriers and checkpoints block our way, each one dealing with our documents. Waved to one side, we hold the whole queue up as Bernard, again, has left our vehicle registration documents locked in the bottom of the pannier. Back on for another 50 metres before another barrier stops our progress as we are sent to another building for motorcycle insurance.

Thus time passes, coming and going, backwards and forwards. To the same windows, different windows, one checkpoint, another checkpoint, each packed with people merrily stamping everything in sight. After an hour of this, our way is clear to climb onto the bike just as another motorcycle turns up, an ex-pat English living in Cyprus.

His bike is a real homemade affair with ammunition boxes for panniers and homemade petrol tank which my hands trace, finding the weld lines, homemade metal fairing, and numerous metal boxes crammed with belongings. Whereas Bernard has bought stickers to show the lands passed through, deep screwdriver scratches have bored the names into his windshield. My fingers find the long list of places and our decision not to go through Albania was borne out by his experience of atrocious, barely passable roads. With a cheery wave, he sets off to start the process of entering Turkey as we pass the final checkpoint and are truly in Turkey. The Middle East beckons.

TURKEY

THE GATEWAY TO THE EAST

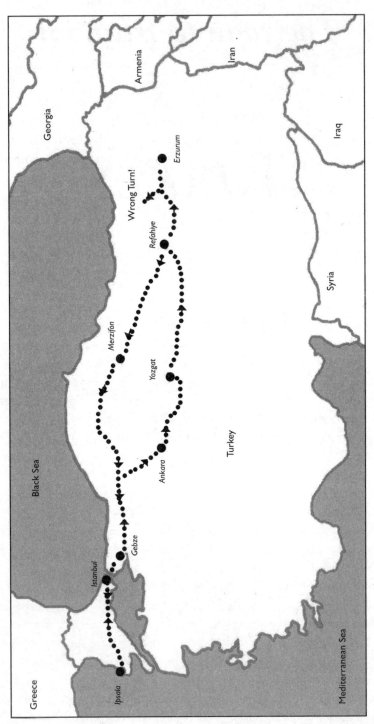

Map of the route around Turkey! 28 September - 29 October

The road to Istanbul

TR Sometimes just the name of a country inspires nervousness and it's easy to feel nervous in crossing from the certainty of Europe to the uncertainty of Turkey. Throughout his life, Bernard has read countless books whose pages have been filled with dire events written about by those who've travelled through this huge country. While musing on this, we settle on an overall perception which has slowly crept into our mental world. Our reality has been forged by this, rather than a fantasy full of dark events and catastrophes. People are people. Everywhere. All the time. In many ways, this thinking is now a constant we understand and accept.

Travelling with our companion Adam on his 125cc motorcycle, we keep our speed down to allow for the little engine's struggling ability to climb hills. Small towns and scattered houses appear for hour after hour. Pulling over for petrol the locals scowl at the GR (Greece) sticker on the bike but they smile when they realise we aren't Greek. A short while after pulling away, we part company and wave farewell. It leaves me feeling sad. Company. Shared experiences. It felt good to have his company, even if only for a brief period where communication can go beyond pantomime.

Continuing east reveals nothing but burnt landscape, with little to break up the monotony. With a plan to stop west of Istanbul before dark and enter the city in the daylight next day, the gods simply laugh at us, as blackness spreads into the sky. For the first time, Rule 1 is seriously broken (Don't drive at night) along with Rule 2 (Never enter a strange city in the dark). Yet, before we know it, the ring-road system of Istanbul pulls us in.

Cars fly past us in the dark as we try to find a base, any base, visible from the main route. The light has gone and pitch black falls frighteningly quick and a serious decision is needed: do we come off the main route and be more vulnerable on side streets? Decisions. After agonising, the road pulls us forward for a little longer. Kilometres pass as nothing appears. Meanwhile the temperature drops significantly and the coldness eats slowly into me.

Stopping at a petrol station, attendants surround us telling us that the nearest hotel is 14 km away. True, at that point a sign appears, but there is no way to it. So we come back down the motorway and frustratingly it appears again, with no apparent exit. It is cold, so cold now. I shiver inside my vented suit. Hunger, worry, both impact on my thinking. My only consolation is I know 'him up front' is feeling just as bad, if not worse. There is no point in complaining. Hang on. Something will turn up. It always does. You just have to wait.

Chanting to myself, we pass flyovers beneath which people sit, huddled against the cold. In the darkness others climb down embankments towards us when Bernard pulls off the highway to light a cigarette. Sitting on the bike generating warmth by the absence of cold air passing through our suits, suddenly he stamps out his cigarette on seeing several men coming towards us. Feeling nervous sitting in the dark, vulnerable, rapidly he pulls away to leave them behind. The ghost of everything ever read spooks him. Istanbul in the blackness.

In the end, we leave the main route as we are getting nowhere. Sparked by the tiredness setting in for us both he pulls off the highway to puff his way through the problem. I sit. Quietly. Wanting it to end, to feel warm, safe, secure, I sit waiting for him to think his way through the darkness, the situation. Suddenly he leaps off the bike and rushes over to a taxi which appears, convincing the driver to lead us to a hotel, with bright yellow hazard flashers lighting the way. Ten minutes later we sit outside the Hotel Anibal in Gebze. Never have I been so relieved in my life. I am so cold, so hungry, and uneasy, more than ever before and yet it feels driven by stupidity. True, perhaps. But during the drive around the town an overwhelming feeling of 'something is going to happen', some catastrophic event, struck me. Hard. An accident, leaving us at the mercy of all he has told me of Turkey. The other Turkey. The one not full of nice people wanting to help. Wrapped up in tiredness and frustration our plight had seemed so large, so inevitable, so serious.

Receiving a hugely warm welcome from the hotel staff, we stumble in through the door and within a very short time tension drifts away from me as I fall fast asleep in the warmth. Was I really being stupid? Imagination does wondrous things to the paranoia sometimes coming from blindness.

Perhaps those selfsame gods who so mocked us the previous day took pity on their poor subjects. Alternatively, they had a sense of humour as a few doors away is a Michelin dealer and within two hours they track down suitable tyres and have them delivered. Bernard, meanwhile, sets to taking the wheels off Bertha under the amused and critical eyes of the staff who are impressed with the range of tools appearing from all over the bike. They love the two 'torpedo tubes', our two stainless steel spaghetti holders mounted in the fairing just above the cylinders. Tools appear from everywhere.

Bernard – It's really funny as they gather round and finger every one of them.
At one point, though, my heart is in my mouth as the front wheel is already

off, sitting on the pavement and the back is about to come off. Before I can say anything two of them grab the back of the bike and lift it, standing the front on the forks. The back end comes five feet off the ground and the rear wheel falls out of the frame. Only then do they realise how precarious it all is as one runs off to get an axle stand to jam under the frame. Health and safety? Working practices? Errrr, no, not really. Neither really feature as the bike is left in the middle of the pavement, with no wheels, with only one axle stand holding the whole thing up. 'Is OK, is OK,' they smile as I flap about it falling over.

Clutching the two wheels Bernard sets off in a van from Gebze to Istanbul where the tyres will be fitted by a motorcycle dealer. Several hours later he returns to tell me of the two-hour white-knuckle drive there and back, witnessing four crashes (two each way) in the heavy traffic.

Bernard – It's the scariest car drive I have ever had with the van hurtling along the dual carriageway like an Exocet missile as the driver floors the accelerator at every opportunity. No matter what was in front – cars, buses, lorries, grannies crossing the road – this man was on a mission. He is going to complete it no matter what, even if he kills us. People leap out of the way as he aimed for every gap, or near gap, he could see.

All the time Turkish music is blasting from the stereo and he grins enthusiastically (maniacally?) at me, honking and beeping everything out of his way. He actually passed an ambulance at one point, hammering along with its siren wailing and I was never so relieved to get out of any car in my life. When we reach the bike shop I smoke three cigarettes before anyone can get any sense from me. The same was true when I forced myself back into the car for the trip back. I feigned sleep for part of the way. I just couldn't watch anymore.

It's funny really, but even with all these events, in one day everything has been accomplished. After travelling thousands of miles to turn up in a strange city without knowing the language, two new tyres sit on Bertha after only a few hours of effort. Resplendently shod in gleaming new rubber for the onward journey across the Turkish mountains we have heard so many stories about, she is now ready.

You cannot really come to Turkey without going to downtown Istanbul as it would be like going to Paris without the Eiffel tower, or Rome without the Vatican. So we pass a day travelling by packed bus 50 km each way to the city. Like everything else on this journey, it is slightly more complicated to get to the significant locations. Nothing ever seems to be simple.

Yashar, the hotel manager, escorts us to the bus stop like two schoolchildren where lengthy instructions are given to the bus driver (along with eight lira) about how to look after us. He stresses nothing untoward must happen. We are 'his guests'. Meanwhile other passengers watch the exchange, listening to every word, every instruction. As we move down the small bus to find seats, everybody gives us a thumbs up, rippling down the bus like a small wave as stacked crates, suitcases and wrapped presents are climbed over. Clambering off the bus an hour later, with 30 people indicating our stop, we discover two metro trains and a tram are required to get to the district of Sultanahmet.

Three hours after leaving the hotel, finally, we find the Blue Mosque, so named due to the 20,000-odd blue tiles adorning the interior. But within seconds of our appearance people descend on us in droves. Like sheep dogs, they try to shepherd us towards carpet shops where tea waits while all promise fantastic prices on that 'must have' rug. Even telling them of our motorcycle has no effect, nothing deflects their eagerness. In chorus they all reply 'No problem, no problem, we ship to your home country'.

Escaping carpetless, we explore the mosque where hundreds of tourists mill about with freshly washed feet. Standing for a little while, this pleasure is forgone as even with washed feet, our motorcycle boots would have led to a state of emergency being instigated by the biohazard team of the Turkish Army. Instead, we walk the main courtyard as Bernard describes the entrances and six minarets, for which it is famously known, along with its tiles. Walking the short distance to the Palace, it's closed for the holidays occupying three days at the end of Ramadan, as is the nearby Grand Bazaar.

There are numerous stalls outside the Palace walls and I learn the layout of the Blue Mosque through a detailed ornament which my fingers explore, tracing minarets, courtyards, the ornate entrance, before everything is put together in my mind. Laughing at belly-dancing costumes, Turkish hats, pointed slippers and artefacts, only now, do I truly feel the gateway to the East.

We find pin badges showing the Turkish flag with its distinctive moon and star as a young woman comes out from behind her array of wares. Standing closely looking at me, she asks in carefully formed English 'Blue eyes?' I look in the direction of the voice as Bernard tells me she is peering intently at me.

'Yes.'

'Very beautiful colour,' she enunciates carefully, before moving off.

Walking down to the bay and drinking cold drinks, we listen to the everyday sounds of laughing families at play and to the sounds of the mosque calling the faithful to prayer. It is haunting. Beautiful. A sound which worms its way in while leaving a sense of peace and contentment.

The bus trip back through the darkness follows congested, gridlocked roads, as people have been visiting families and friends at the end of Ramadan.

It seems very much like Christmas as people carry gifts and children ride new bicycles.

Friends and families greet and hug each other at the roadside. The bus progresses with sudden stops on the motorway to pick up and drop off passengers from under bridges, from hard shoulders all along the route. Our stop two days before near one such bridge, and Bernard's uneasiness, now seem so silly to him. Ruefully he admits his decision was based on fear and ignorance, now making him feel small, stupid and overly cautious. 'A fine intrepid world traveller I make,' he says, 'jumping at my own shadow.'

While he ponders his own reactions at each successive stop, I understand the weight sitting on him for our safety. 'Always better to be cautious,' I answer. With each stop, something is reinforced in him. This single journey changes him as he learns what it means to draw 'facts' from observations with only one piece of evidence. One event. One circumstance.

The driver's assistant approaches, battling to make himself understood until we realise the bus doesn't go back to the hotel. We are left in the darkness, 2 km away, unsure of which way to go. Bernard has the bike's Sat Nav with him with the hotel's location programmed in, and we follow the small screen through the blacked-out streets. People appear from doorways. Nightlife sounds floods the air. Discreetly, Bernard checks the screen but there is only the vaguest information as we have no detailed maps on the unit.

'Walk confidently,' he whispers, 'as if we actually know where we are going.'

'So we're not two lost tourists walking through the back streets of Gebze, in the dark, me with my white cane, you clutching a Sat Nav unit under your jacket?' I innocently enquire.

'We're not lost,' he notes. 'We're just not sure which way we're going! Besides Cath, we blend in perfectly. Totally inconspicuous, despite your white cane glowing like a light sabre from a Star Wars movie.'

He makes light of our situation walking through dark side streets, stepping over rubbish and piles of masonry, and soon the hotel sign shines in the distance. Arriving, a sense of achievement warms us, as Yashar leaps out of his chair in the foyer, declaring his worry at us being away for over ten hours. Reminding us that we are his guests, he feels responsible for us, like a mother hen with its 'youngsters'. Being so pleased to see us, he disappears behind the bar to return with complimentary drinks. We are too polite to refuse.

'You need invite to enter Iran'

It's nearly lunchtime before we leave the hotel the following day as all the staff want to say goodbye. After many, many farewells we pull out and, for the first time, Bernard heads the wrong way onto a dual carriageway. He knows instantly. Stopping, he turns the bike slowly inch by inch before setting off exchanging cheery waves with all the beeping cars. Blasting off the hard shoulder like an object fired from a catapult, Bertha's front wheel paws the air like a stallion unleashed.

Cars pull alongside and drivers and passengers frantically wave in passing, one group leaping up and down inside the car with excitement, blowing the horn in greeting as they weave close beside to take in details. At our first petrol stop I need to brave the toilets, which I dread in many ways but now it's more complicated. We're in the world of Islam and men walking into women's toilets? Mmmm, perhaps not. It was made very clear to Bernard that he was not welcome, not needed and should get out, and he retired diplomatically and rapidly. And a very nice Islamic woman attendant guided me from cubicle to washbasin, to the soap on the wall, before passing paper towels to dry my hands.

I'm not sure how disabled people manage this process in Greece and Turkey as there have been no separate facilities and the disabled toilets always seem to be *inside* the men's or the women's. Not a lot of use if you are blind and your guide is of the opposite sex. There have been some very 'interesting' (Bernard calls them 'traditional') toilets along the way, which proved to be difficult to manage as a blind person. Often consisting of nothing more than a hole in the floor with places on either side for your feet, there you squat to perform your ablutions; and there are no handrails. While I dread the visits, and I really do, Bernard cheers me up no end as it seems there will be worse to come.

Returning to Bertha, a crowd gathers and questions come thick and fast concerning where we are from, how much for this, for that, how many miles today, tomorrow, ever, where we are going. Their response to the word 'Iran' consists of much air sucking in the universal 'big problem' sound.

'Iran very dangerous,' they all chorus.

'Not safe for you in Iran,' they go on, 'they rob and steal from you. Not like the Turks. Turkish people honest. Iranians are thieves.'

We do not have the heart to tell them the Greeks said the same about themselves (honest) and their Turkish neighbours (dishonest). Everybody is duly thanked for their kindness regarding the information, the weather, the strong coffee, and even their football team. Yes, we will follow their advice. Definitely. Without doubt. Thank you. Yes, we will be very careful. No, I understand, don't trust anyone.

In our simple understanding we keep to ourselves how the nature of Islam is of the Prophet insisting on generosity to travellers as to do less is to be less in the eyes of the Quran. Thus far, in our limited experience of Muslim people, there has been nothing but openness and kindness.

Two nights in a stunning location in the mountains north of Ankara gives Bernard enough time to fiddle with the bike and to meet staff from the Iranian embassy in Ankara, who just happen to be strolling past in the car park. Offers of assistance come for our onward journey with explanations of how an authorisation code issued from Tehran will mean everything when we get to Erzurum. This response reassures both of us. But, he continues, 'When your wife is in my country she must be as my wife is,' pointing to a lady standing, waiting, behind him, complete with headscarf and demure dress.

Bernard tells me later he nearly responded, 'In my country we let women wear the burka even though it is alien to us.' Thankfully he bit his lip, reached into the pannier, and pulled out two headscarves bought in Athens. It brings a smile from our Iranian officials who then introduce the males of the group; the females wait dutifully behind them. Bernard tactfully introduces himself, shakes hands with all the males (men and children) before mischievously introducing me. No handshakes are offered.

The road south winds through hills and valleys with light traffic, the hum of the engine keeping us company until it's time to seek refuge. Bouncing through a section of roadworks, waving to all the workmen, a few kilometres later we turn back towards them, returning to a hotel seen earlier by the roadside. It's closed for refurbishment and the workmen watch us pass a third time while leaning on their shovels, laughing.

Pulling into Yozgat we find an 'Otel' that is 'nearly' finished. The food is 'nearly' hot, as is the water itself. The toilet 'nearly' flushes without leaking. Well, actually, the floor floods every time it is flushed. This is discovered quite by accident on the first occasion as my feet suddenly received a free wash. Worst of all, the shower 'nearly' works.

Gordon, our wagon-driving friend, maintained that Turkey is a land of everything being 'nearly' right, but never quite. The final act, or job, is never quite completed with 'nearly' being deemed close enough. His other expression stated that, 'anything is possible in Turkey… for a price' although we have yet to hear that ominous phrase.

While all this is true, the drivers of Yozgat stop their cars as we cross the road. No matter where we are, the traffic grinds to a halt. It's a far cry from Greece, where people will run over you in order to gain those precious few seconds. The Turkish drivers wait patiently as Bernard places his hand on his heart while giving a little bow to indicate 'thank you'. It's a typical Turkish gesture he's taken to using where language does not suffice, and the gesture ('you are welcome') is returned.

Not a car horn is blown. There are no signs of impatience, people merely stop and stare at us. Inquisitive, curious, puzzled, all these terms seem to suffice to describe the stares; neither threat nor cause for concern can Bernard find. Apparently, we seem so different. I wonder if it is the cane? The motorcycle suits? Perhaps it is the slowly – used to be so white – turning colour of our skin? Aliens in another land.

The journey across the middle of Turkey takes three days (seven days from Athens) in a land where we met many lovely people everywhere along the way. All expressed kindness, in a hundred similar little ways. It mattered not where we stopped, nor for how long or why, wherever we stopped people gathered. The roads themselves, which we had heard so much about, are varied. Nowhere were they as bad as anticipated as an enormous road-building exercise is under way, spurred on by the promise of EU membership. It really is a fantastic, huge, impressive undertaking stretching for hundreds of miles, but some sections are so bad that Bernard would stand up on the foot pegs to keep the bike balanced through the worst of it.

It rains on and off some days as we try to keep ahead of black clouds, the rain threatening to disintegrate the surface of dust and red clay into red mud. Importantly the surface often stays dry in front of our wheels and the road from Zara to Refahiye is as variable as any others we have travelled so far in Turkey: one moment good road surface, the next none. Cars blast past without slowing down, pelting us with stones, chips, machine gunning the fairing with the clatter as clouds of dust envelop us, taking minutes to dissipate, leaving Bernard with dangerously little visibility. Cars approaching us launch the same debris directly at us; whiteness descends like fine old London smog.

Dropping down through the mountains of red, gold and green, it seems like a child's painting where the brush has been loaded with too much watery paint, causing streaky runs down the canvas. So it is with the hills and mountains, gorgeous colourful collages stream through my mind as Bernard paints pictures with the touch of his words. By 4pm the familiar sign for 'Otel' appears and 250 miles of dust and debris lie behind us. It is a welcoming sight of an easily understandable and recognisable petrol station with attached accommodation. Familiar. Comfortable. We could just as easily have been pulling into any European service station so common are all the cues to Bernard.

The shop window shows Turkish tea sets and jewellery beside knives long ago banned from open sale in the UK as moral panic swept the country concerning our descent into a 'knife culture'. However, in Turkey you can buy knives that would drop a horse from 30 feet away. I'm reminded of the film *Crocodile Dundee* and the comment 'You call that a knife? This is a knife!' Actually feeling these things, I'm sure his was merely a toothpick, something to take the stone out of a horse's hoof. And nobody bats an eyelid. It is the way it is. A knife is a tool for everyday living. Nothing more. It is the person who holds it that determines everything.

Sitting inside we see a crowd gathering around the bike and several point to us. Do we really stand out that much? Perhaps it is the redness of our faces from the constant sun making us obvious? Of course we stand out; there is no escaping it. There are no discreet hiding places. There is no respite from the stares, no 'blending in' or disappearing act to be pulled. Obviously, I am less conscious of it than Bernard, who feels minutely examined. The bike is a beacon, a flag, a spaceship which attracts people from all over. The same is true for us. There can be no hiding place. Nor do we want one.

The final day towards Erzurum sees us on the bike by 10am under a perfect blue cloudless sky. Tyres have been checked, petrol filled, nuts and bolts examined, all in the daily act of checking Bertha. The sun is shining and brightness permeates my own perception of the landscape as everything vibrates as Bertha pounds, rattles, and bangs her way east up the mountains towards our destination.

For mile after mile we climb up 2,000 metres (7,000 feet) through continuous pothole-filled 180-degree turns through the dust. Our spines take a pounding across knee-shattering roads before resting, surrounded by a profound silence. Listening, the only interruption is the click of the lighter which sounds like a gunshot against the nothingness as the numbness gradually fades from our bodies, enabling us to climb back on.

After 288 km the Turkish Army garrison town of Erzurum appears after more hours of spinal pounding and it feels like the Holy Grail of a destination. A significant location. An 'end', in some way as the town signifies a demarcation line.

Dense traffic soon surrounds us, bearing Turkish flags spread across car roofs, bonnets, and on boots. Every window in the town is adorned with the crescent and moon flag as roads are blocked off with heavily armed police. Soldiers stand on every corner, scanning the crowds nervously.

We learn from a bystander of our arrival into emotional demonstrations surrounding clashes between the Partiya Karkerên Kurdistan (PKK, Kurdistan Workers' Party) and the Turkish forces in the south of the country; seventeen young soldiers lost their lives and many were from Erzurum. A Nationalist feeling is sweeping the town and feelings are running ominously high, as there is a significant Kurdish population in the area.

'Get out of Dodge' is the best advice we give ourselves by heading for Palandoken, on the outskirts of this boiling pot of emotion. There are many hotels and we soon find one, cool in temperature, a tiny electric fire throwing out mournful heat, and young in staff. The staff are on work placements from the school next door, eager to please and nothing is too much trouble. Several help to carry our gear to our room and Bertha is driven up the long ramp and parked outside the front door.

It becomes our base for the twice daily visit to the Iranian consulate where, over days, we find that having a code authorising entry to Iran means... well little really. It certainly does not enable us to get our visa. Every day we meet with the same sentence coming through the glass partition: 'Maybe tomorrow.' We sit and wait for hours every day: 'Maybe tomorrow.' Always the same: 'maybe tomorrow.' The chairs are hard and uncomfortable and Bernard watches his reflection in the mirrored glass where a tiny semi-circular hole allows communication. To actually see the person on the other side he has to crouch down low, as if bowing, half kneeling to communicate. Sometimes the staff appear after two hours of waiting only to issue the two-second dismissal. 'Maybe tomorrow.' Days pass trying to understand. What is happening? Phone calls are made to Tehran and Athens before finding out.

An email eventually arrives from the visa company, telling us the code is valid only for Athens, 1,800 miles (2,896 km) away. For the code to be issued here we need to reapply (through them of course). It does not matter that they told us, before leaving Greece, that we could pick up the visas in Erzurum. Naïvely ringing the Iranian embassy in Athens, Bernard asks them to fax the authorisation through to Erzurum but the consul tells us they do not have a fax in their office. Bouncing off the brick wall of bureaucracy, Athens confirms both authorisation codes are there, yes we have been cleared to enter Iran, no they cannot be faxed, emailed, telephoned or teleported to Erzurum. We have to go back to Athens to pick them up. Personally. We get nowhere and ponder our options. There appear to be only two:

1. Return to Athens (fly to Istanbul, stay overnight, fly to Athens), stay there for up to three days and then travel back to Erzurum, leaving the bike and everything here while still paying for the accommodation; or

2. Start again by applying direct to the consulate in Erzurum for our visa. The consul tells us it will take about seven to ten days to process.

After many cigarettes (Bernard) and a many tears (me) we start again, reapplying through the consulate and waiting the seven to ten days it will take. The reasons are simple really, tragically so. In the end, it should be much quicker than riding to Athens and back. Logic tells us. It shouldn't be a problem as we've already been cleared to enter Iran. Logic tells us. The flights to Athens turn out to be ruinously expensive. Logic tells us. Thus, there seems little choice but to pray the weather will hold as new photographs, fees and applications are completed, all the time realising my white stick is having no impact at all.

The first photograph Bernard hands over the counter of the consulate is of me without a headscarf. It is met with nervous uncomfortable shuffles. Long brown hair stares out of the image. He then hands them a very fetching one of me in my regulation headscarf. Smiles all round. They are obviously pleased. I must look very fetching. Now all we can do is wait.

For days we walk the streets of Erzurum, past the army barracks where young soldiers wave 'hello' from lonely sentry boxes. Nodding at people outside cafés and on the pavements, conversations stop as we pass. Crossing roads, cars stop, people step out of our way, we become 'regulars' to a town with 90% unemployment, with the only brisk business being conducted by shoeshine boys who furiously polish while the men are in the mosque.

We come to know the road crews who do in one night what would take months in England. Here there are no lines of traffic cones standing forlornly for weeks on end. No machinery stands silent gathering dust, rusting with the passage of time, neglected, unused. Men drink coffee picked up from pavement tables, or spend the day talking as life drifts past, unhurried, slowly, patiently. Bernard describes the ruins of buildings, the decrepit surroundings before turning to the similarities of people, where others see only differences. To him the shops are full of girlie pink beds and women look at clothes while the men play draughts or chess in the coffee shops; he speaks of children laughing or crying while parents play or scold. Universal themes of existence as the call of the mosque resonates, and most things stop when it does.

Shopping for headscarves, Muslim women take me gently by the hand, teaching me to wear them appropriately while my shadow watches as they argue among themselves about which is best for bright blue eyes and long, unadorned hair. He is the only male in the shop and laughs as they wrap and unwrap scarf after scarf. Eventually everybody nods approvingly at the 23 lira price tag attached to the one chosen.

Eating kebabs for days on end until we can stand them no longer, we switch to pizzas as there is little else to choose from. Throughout the wait, people on the pavements continue to come to a standstill at our appearance but we merely smile and walk on by. The soldiers carry on waving and Bernard thanks their acknowledgement of our existence by placing his hand on his heart.

The weather gets colder and the tiny single-bar electric fire battles pitifully against the cold air. Some evenings there is no choice but to retire beneath bedclothes until sleep overcomes us as the hotel cannot turn on the heating until a specific date due to government restrictions. Palandoken meanwhile prepares itself for the arrival of rich Eastern Europeans who fly in when the snow comes. Everybody tells us it will happen by November, only weeks away.

'First comes the rain, then the snow,' everybody tells us.

Bernard, meanwhile, frets about the mountains we must pass through filling up with whiteness, making them too dangerous to attempt. After seven days the consulate's 'maybe tomorrow' still resounds as more days pass with no news, nothing to do, and nowhere to go. The cold descends, the rain starts, and the shops do a roaring trade in umbrellas and we contribute. 'First comes the rain, then the snow' becomes our mantra as my sidekick nervously checks weather forecasts daily on the internet, then spends the rest of the day anxiously peering up at the sky. Our window is closing unless we move soon. Emails from home are one of the few things to look forward to and each is devoured. Sometimes they are read over and over again as we remember the people who have sent them.

Frustration gives way to overwhelming boredom as time drags on and I haven't felt well for days, descending into a world of weakness, listlessness and shivers. Narrowing it down we think it's probably due to taking the antimalarial drug Lariam, which takes several weeks to be fully effective, by which time we hope to be in the 'red' malarial zones of southern Iran. The stated side effects seem to match the way I feel. Weak, cold, listless... bored.

Bernard, meanwhile, has other issues which necessitate multiple trips to the toilet as he mutters 'better now than on the road' before rushing off to leave me once again. This is compounded by a developing infection which leaves him coughing, with fire in his chest, treated with antibiotics bought over the counter from a chemist.

To fill time Bernard posts on motorcycle websites where he asks if anybody knows where a beer can be bought in the east of Turkey? It seems unlikely to me, being a devoutly Muslim area, but he lives in hope. Sure enough, several responses come back from people who have taken the same route and offers of sympathy pour our way as the Las Vegas of the East it is not. Soon we can bear prohibition no longer and Bernard is despatched for a serious round of wine hunting in the darkness of downtown Erzurum.

Bernard – I set off full of confidence lasting all of 20 minutes as I drive up and down roads with no off-licence in sight. Nothing. In desperation, I head into a shop and approach the shopkeeper. I wait for it to empty before whispering the dreaded words for wine 'sarap?' and beer 'bira?'. He looks around the empty aisles furtively before pointing down the road, the one I've been up and down for 20 minutes. In exasperation I reach onto the counter, draw an X on a piece of paper and point to the pair of us. He understands immediately. Looking around once again he draws a line to two letters written on the paper, P and O.

'Post Office?' I ask, looking at him.

Shaking his head, he reacts like a scalded cat when the door suddenly opens and whisks the notepad off the counter. A man enters and grabs a loaf of bread before heading for the till. Like two criminals, we both look away shiftily, waiting for him to disappear out the door. From somewhere in my brain a connection is made with the reappearance of the notepad and the words 'Petrol', then 'Benzene?' pop into my head. Nodding vigorously, he breaks into a smile, puts his thumb to his mouth, sucks on it, and whispers 'sarap' while drawing a little x on a side street next door to the PO written previously. Bingo.

Grabbing his hand and shaking it effusively, I run back to the bike, leap on it and head down the road looking for the petrol station called PO. It's on the corner, opposite the mosque. Right turn and down the road a blacked-out shop window beckons me. It is then I notice the small ESEF (Turkish beer) logo. I laugh to myself. Turning round, I stare at the front of the mosque.

The location is incongruous, ridiculous really, but I thank the liberal aspects of Turkey's attitude to something which, if you do not flaunt it, is discreetly available. Leaving the shop ten minutes later, I feel like I've visited a sex shop, some seedy place where 'favours can be bought', where 'naughtiness' abounds. Our naughtiness is a bottle of wine and several bottles of beer, all carefully camouflaged in a black bin bag.

Bertha's back box becomes the depository for my ill-gotten gains, and I pack them carefully. The hilarious thing is that everyone knows what the black bin bag conceals, what the shop is selling. It's understood and recognised without being condemned.

Pulling up, back at the devoutly Muslim hotel, I leave everything on the bike and head upstairs to retrieve a backpack in which to conceal the booty. Downstairs once again I look round self-consciously before rapidly stuffing the bottles in, making sure they do not clink as I walk past reception to our room.

'Hail the conquering hero' seems to be the appropriate response Bernard requires and I happily supply his ego needs while savouring the taste before suddenly being startled. A sound causes him to, nearly, drop his drink as he flies over to the huge cast iron radiator sitting by the windows: 'Bloody hell, the pipes are hot!' he laughs. Sitting on the ridged radiator with his drink, the creaks and groans signify the onset of winter with the rush of hot water through long dormant pipes, even though we have been freezing for a long time already. It is the harbinger of the district preparing for the arrival of snow boots and skis. Soon the radiator is too hot to sit on and we go to sleep to pinging and gurgling sounds.

More days pass and invites appear from the school next door when people realise we are both teachers. Sitting in the staffroom people introduce themselves and ask if we would like to teach some of the English classes; the students have never heard a 'native' English speaker. One hands Bernard a long cane on entering the first classroom, to be 'used if you need it'. Putting it on the desk, he tells the class it will not be needed, unless somebody wants to challenge him to a sword fight; then they are to call him Obi-Wan-Kenobi.

Before long several Turkish teachers sit watching as he fires up like Robin Williams on amphetamines, like Billy Connelly on the finest Scottish Malt as laughter resounds in the classroom. Included in their ranks is the resident 'religious teacher'. He sits impassively, watching the ensuing mayhem as students realise learning can be 'fun' and fun involves, inevitably, laughter. It was interesting to listen as I have never experienced his classroom teaching before. There is a 'buzz' in the room and I can feel it.

Rapid-fire interactions, interlaced with examples, anecdotes and numerous other ways of conveying knowledge come from the textbook he was handed, the basis of the lesson. The interactions range from argumentative and challenging to gentle. I think the Office of Standards for Education (OFSTED) would have been proud. He even managed to gently close down a teacher who had an irritating habit of finishing sentences for the students themselves, rather than helping them towards an answer. When a student asks Bernard about speaking English 'poorly' he comments on their self-consciousness:

'Never forget, the purpose of language is to communicate. You and I are communicating are we not? Never be frightened of making mistakes. It's what we learn from them that matters.'

Talking with the teachers later, it's obvious that the normal structure of the classes was completely thrown into chaos by Bernard as the conversation drifts from teaching to daily life until the inevitable subject of Iraq and Afghanistan emerges. It seems Tony Blair has been quoted as saying Iraq needed to be attacked due to its (Islamic) religion. 'Absolutely no possibility he said that,' Bernard counters, 'He may be a lot of things, but he is not stupid.' They appear mollified by the answer, they too think it would be stupid. Still they claim to have read it in the press. 'Never believe everything you read in the press' Bernard goes on 'It is a dangerous way to discover the "truth" of anything.'

The conversation moves onto the Turkish system of education, the pressure teachers are placed under not to fail their students. If they do, it can be expensive for the parents and many stories are told of tearful parents begging them not to fail their offspring, how grades become meaningless. Everybody nods in agreement at the concept that without failure there can never truly be success. Listening to the stories of their experiences in the Turkish education system it echoes many of Bernard's thoughts of education in the UK itself: incessant drives for everybody to pass everything. And if this doesn't happen? Somehow it must equate to the teachers' fault. Somehow.

Questions fly about Britain's involvement in Afghanistan and Iraq while the religious overseer sits watching, but never taking part. Bernard tells me later it is obvious he can understand everything but that he never uttered a word. People have told us how some Muslims will not speak English, considering it the language of Christianity and the crusades. So long ago? Yet still, it seems, they cast a shadow over the here and now for some people. Such thoughts, attitudes, 'beliefs' are beyond our comprehension.

It would be like the West completely ignoring a complete culture, language, artefact or philosophy purely because they originate from 'Islamic' beginnings. To such people we would say knowledge enlightens people and language is an important key to understanding itself; it sweeps away misunderstandings when used by reasonable people. Reasonable people? Discuss. What entails being reasonable? We hope it resides in our 'law givers', our 'will of the people' expressed through stable political systems. Maybe. But then again: 'Sometimes politicians do not reflect the will of the people, it is the same in every country I believe. Perhaps it is also true of Turkey?'

Bernard asks carefully as they ruefully admit, so it is in their country. We think a draw is declared on the matter.

The day leads to an invite to visit the house of one of the teachers but the evening is spent with the male teacher (Farteh) as his wife (Asia) cannot meet Bernard; it is 'forbidden'. His two children are also conspicuous by their absence. Farteh himself returns to the subject of British involvement in Afghanistan and Iraq – time and time again – as his wife stays hidden in the kitchen with the children. His mother obviously does not really understand the word 'forbidden', when she suddenly appears through the front door, bustling straight into the room where we sit. Farteh is not amused at her appearance but cannot do much about the lovely women she turns out to be as he translates while she sits beside me, joining in on non-political aspects of life in our two countries.

'I cannot do anything with her, she is my mother,' he says throwing his hands up in mock horror as she is being 'very naughty'. All the while his wife sits in the kitchen as Bernard asks about her absence. 'It cannot be,' Farteh responds. 'Our religion forbids it, it is a rule to protect women from men,' he announces. Who I wonder? Bernard? Really? Does he seem that dangerous? That lecherous?

The conversation traverses many aspects of their lives, of the 'shame' in putting parents into a 'senior house' (old age home); of the duty to look after parents, as they had themselves been looked after when they were young. Of how the flat they live in cannot be bought until he pays 3,000 lira in back taxes to the government. Bernard latches onto the admission, teasing him about his earlier statement how 'good Muslims must pay their taxes'. A sheepish silence falls on the conversation at the contradiction sitting before us.

During the evening Bernard disappears down the stairs to have a cigarette with Farteh as his minder. Within seconds of the front door closing his wife, Asia, appears, gently reaching for my hand. I feel her head beside mine as we touch temples on both sides in greeting. Talking to each with no real language we can understand, two people sharing time and space until the doorbell rings, causing her to shoot out of the chair and back into the kitchen. The doorbell was Farteh's signal; Bernard is reappearing, make yourself scarce from the potentially marauding Westerner. She did so quickly.

The next day, the familiar door of the consulate is opened by its smiling policeman who no longer asks for identification and leads us to the same worn seats. The same indeterminate wait stretches before us as Bernard takes out his copy of the Quran and starts reading to me. So it has been for several weeks as he thought it might help our progress through the region if we know, understand and appreciate aspects of such a diverse religion. An hour later a well-known face waves us forward and we sit before the reflecting glass for our world to be ripped apart in the mirror of bureaucracy. The apologetic official breaks the news I can enter Iran but will have to travel alone as Bernard's application has been refused.

Bernard starts laughing at the news. 'Very good joke my friend,' he replies. Since we had arrived three weeks ago and have visited twice a day – everyday – throughout the intervening period we are nearly friends with the consul. The official states he has been refused due to 'not having an invite to enter Iran'.

The words echo across time and distance as, once again, we stand outside the steel gates in Athens listening to the 'crash course in diplomatic language for dealing with Foolish English People'. It makes no sense to us as I do not have an invite either, apart from a very nice headscarf. 'But how can she go alone?' Bernard asks, 'she is blind and you know we are on a motorcycle.'

The official shrugs his shoulders.

We ponder about giving me a crash course in riding a bike but think this may not be such a good idea as our journey would be very short, as we told a very well known publicist in England when asked: 'Will Catherine be riding the ride?'

Bernard had laughed as he answered: 'Catherine's blind.'

'Yes we know that, but will she be riding the bike?' he asked again.

'It would be a very short journey if she did, we might make the first corner if we were lucky!'

Perhaps the Iranian authorities think more of me? Who knows?

Bernard asks if the Iranian authorities will give me a driving licence as well so that I can ride the bike?

The official shrugs his shoulders.

Sitting in disbelieving silence, the consul indicates Bernard can always reapply again and wait another ten days for an answer. It is now the 22nd of October and it's been raining on and off for several days. Rapidly going through all the best advice involving historical data on weather patterns and local knowledge, all agree the mountain passes will be too dangerous for us to travel. We're at 7,500 feet altitude and will need to climb higher on the journey. Shaking our heads to clear our thoughts, we ask how it can be so that a blind woman can enter but her guide and driver cannot.

The consul shrugs his shoulders again in response, merely saying, 'It is Iran.'

Nothing more, nothing less.

A bureaucracy and a country summed up in three words indicating, 'It made no sense.' The same events are unfurling for two Australians who have recently turned up, Chris and Wes, who are trying to get home on their 500cc Honda. Over the days they too travel the same merry-go-round of applications using the same company initially, only to be let down in the same way. 'It is Iran.'

Leaving the consulate we head for Turkish Airlines to find a way to Pakistan by flying over Iran. The manager is truculent with us after hearing our predicament, saying the Iranians are right.

'You can come into my country but Turkish people cannot enter yours, you refuse them permission. Britain also interferes in our Kurdish problem and so the Iranians are right. Meet like with like.'

Bernard cuts him off before he can go further.

I can feel him like a simmering pan of water about to boil over with events. 'So you are saying that Turkish Airlines cannot solve this freight problem?' The manager goes quiet. Picking up the phone it turns out Erzurum has no equipment to handle the bike. The only realistic option seems to be a flight from Istanbul to Karachi in Pakistan, meaning 1,800 km ride back to the capital.

A final throw of the dice is performed by ringing the British embassy in Tehran as it seems our final, last-ditch, effort to enter Iran by road. Speaking to Sandra, an embassy official, she cannot understand why there is such a problem with the visa. Promising to look into the matter with the visa company, Bernard tells her she should be able to recognise Mr Hamid by the shame written across his face and the big car parked outside his office. Laughing, she promises to talk to the Iranian Ministry of Foreign Affairs while pointing out relations are 'a little strained at the moment'. It seems there is nothing like a financial embargo and ongoing argument about nuclear power to create divisions between two peoples. As always, such things draw in the little people. Like us.

Hanging up, we sit and wait. Two days pass. The rain starts to fall. In earnest. Everybody looks up at the sky.

'The snows are coming.'

Back to Istanbul

There is no time left as the temperatures drop further. Much further. Frost covers the ground and moisture crackles beneath our feet. Packing the bike, we have three hard days of riding to Istanbul. Pulling out of the town we pass the now familiar roads and places. Military convoys have formed, full of young soldiers in large transporters carrying tanks and field guns. They're heading south to the Kurdish areas where violence has been spreading for days, news channels showing stark images of the boiling violence. Waving to the young men clutching their weapons, we wonder if they are the same friendly faces who had smiled at us from within their sentry boxes. Waves come back from beneath their steel helmets. Soldiers. Always the first to pay the price of politics, of diplomacy going wrong. The folly of intelligent people running out of words.

On good roads, Bertha surges forward, attracting the attention of the very nice Turkish police. With the bike appearing over the horizon like a red missile, while being tracked by a shiny laser device, people gather round to aid in translating the Turkish for 'hand over your money'. Bernard is surprised at the size of the fine, and is shown several documented tickets, all officially completed on the same day, before reluctantly handing over our diminishing funds.

The second day of our dash back to Istanbul involves the very nice driver of an unmarked police car showing Bernard the onboard camera footage of Bertha passing him. 'It looks really good Cath,' he states, before asking for a copy of the footage. Unfortunately nothing is achieved apart from another roadside ticket. The size of the fine leaves Bernard clutching his chest and eventually the officer understands we do not have this amount of money. Thus he allows us to depart clutching an orange ticket that is supposed to be paid somewhere.

In his final fling at understanding, the officer even tried mouthing each Turkish word slowly due to our obvious hearing defect before giving up completely. Filling out his papers, they're handed over and everybody is satisfied. Justice has been done. Importantly justice has been seen to be done so everyone is happy. The officer waves us off knowing full well the matter remained indecipherable to us.

After three hard days we reach the outskirts of Istanbul, fighting the horrendous traffic tooth and nail across the city towards the airport. Settling into a hotel, Bernard contacts air freight but achieves nothing due to language difficulties. He rings Heathrow Airport (thank God for a laptop and Skype). Air freight there can't believe we're ringing them to find a freight company in Istanbul, but it works and things happen very quickly from that point. The local freight company cannot do enough for us, running us between customs, flight offices, our hotel and without this help from our contact Cem it would have been much, much harder.

Over the following days, the process is a nightmare for Turkish Customs. Cem leads us from office to office as he tries to resolve the problem of shipping a bike to Pakistan. At one point interviews take place with the head of Customs as explanations are sought as to why such an unusual shipment is occurring. All the time Cem virtually bows and kneels before officials like a court supplicant, as this has never been attempted before as far as anybody knows. However, everything is completed and official approval is eventually gained, involving several inches of signed paperwork. Leaving the bike dismantled and as tiny as possible, the hotel greets us tired and hungry late in the night.

The next morning we find the carpenter has built the most enormous garden shed for Bertha, and consequently the freight costs have increased by a third. The customs officers have already sealed the crate with very impressive twine for export and moved it to the secure compound. From here it is be despatched on a night flight to Dubai, then onwards to Karachi. Our flight is tomorrow. It was an expensive mistake to make and one we will not make again; in future we'll stay until the crate is built.

Piling up mountains of Turkish lira on a hotel coffee table with notes containing far too many zeros, we watch nervously for the imminent arrival of the drugs squad. Instead of physically counting the pile it would have been far simpler for Cem to reach for a ruler and measure the height. It all leaves us wishing it were more 'adventurous', rather than depressing.

After weeks of turmoil, tears and uncertainty, our evening flight to Karachi is before us and Bertha is already in Dubai. We feel relieved but also disappointed and angry. Never before have we felt more alone, more depressed, more anxious about what we're attempting. The world feels very big at this moment and we feel small, very small. Trying to combat the changing logistical issues, petty bureaucracy and uncertainty, the emotional journey leaves us tired beyond anything ever before encountered.

We never expected to land in Karachi. It wasn't planned or expected.

Although we knew that circumstances could change and were mentally prepared for that, it feels like we've been clobbered sideways, time-wise and financially. Blown off course beyond expectation, we seek information from all possible sources.

We can find no reference of anyone ever having done this route before, travelling alone straight up the middle of the country by motorcycle; none can be found. This doesn't mean it hasn't been done, but there seems to be no information anywhere, unlike for our previous planned route. We do know that the military or police escorts deemed necessary are not set up for it, as they are for the traditional routes. While this may turn out to be true, it doesn't frighten us, although it probably should.

Much like everything else so far, we have little doubt in being able to overcome whatever the days ahead reveal. Deep inside, however, it leaves me insecure. Insecure in the way of a blind person. Emotionally it feels like taking a step without knowing how far my foot will come down before it makes contact with something solid.

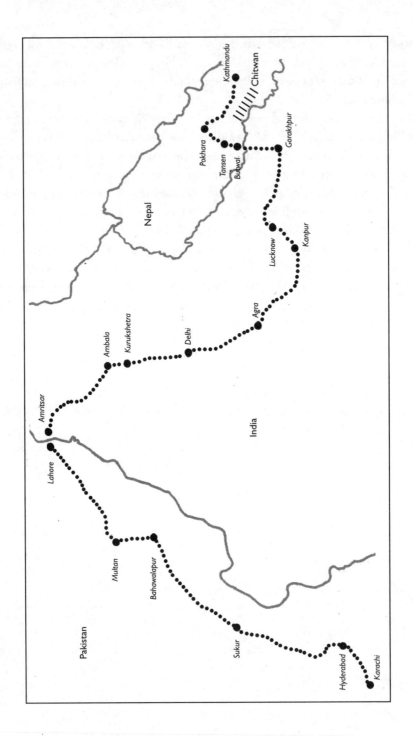

Map of the route through Pakistan, India and Nepal.
29 October - 3 January 2009

ASIA

PAKISTAN, INDIA AND NEPAL

Culture shock and Bertha's return

(PK) Heat. Waves and waves of heat. It envelops us stepping off the plane five and a half hours later in Karachi Airport at 3.30am with a four-hour jump forward in time zones. Wrapping itself around us like a hot space blanket, I have to remind myself it's 3.30am and not midday.

Outside the terminal people stare in stupefied silence. With our appearance voices trail off until suddenly we are descended upon from all directions as Bernard lights his first cigarette for over eight hours. The sound of his lighter is interrupted by taxi drivers arguing about who will relieve us of our money and it was the first time Bernard saw the 'Santa Claus gleam' in their eyes. Two 'tourists' with their, likely, thick wallets.

We are both culture shocked and completely worn out and feel intimidated as people jostle and hassle us. People grab at our cases, the trolley, our sleeves, all seeking to guide us towards beat-up taxis. Normal rules have gone. Furiously trying to get to grips with events, little except for growing frustration is achieved through our foggy brains.

The growing crowd soon attracts airport security, who solve the problem by bustling us into a beat-up taxi complete with springs sticking through worn-out seats. Within seconds it heads down dusty roads, leaving us praying it will lead to a hotel. Feeling stressed, tired, uncertain, the car bounces down potholed roads, weaving around the worst so as not to destroy any remaining suspension on the near derelict car.

By the time second gear is reached, the driver tells us how poor he is, of how his family is starving. Then comes offers of heroin and hashish, both for a 'good price'. Bernard declines the offer.

'All Westerners want drugs, yes? What drugs you like, I find if not have, I get for you.' Again, his offer of Nirvana is politely refused, despite passing several brick-sized packages over his shoulder for Bernard to inspect. 'No thank you.' Polite refusals again.

'You must want, yes, I have many drugs, what you like, I get?'

It goes on constantly as he becomes more and more desperate in wanting to 'help us' with our drug-related needs. The bombardment is incessant, constant, urgent, becoming more and more forthright until Bernard can stand it no longer.

'That hotel there!' he suddenly says.

'No, no, Sir, I take you to very fine hotel, is further, but not much.'

'Yes I'm sure it is not much further. Thank you. That one, there. Pull over.' Bernard insists.

Reluctantly, the cars drifts to the right and armed guards leap to their feet at heavy barriers barring further progress. Approaching the car cautiously, they relax on seeing two foreigners as the driver talks through open windows while mirrored trolleys slide underneath the wreck to check for bombs. The boot is opened to reveal our cases while the space beneath the bonnet is checked for suspect devices other than an engine. Pronouncing themselves satisfied, the gates lift, allowing us to drive onwards with everybody peering in through the windows.

Arriving at the entrance, the driver wants the equivalent of ten days' wages and gets really angry when Bernard offers the previously agreed fare. He aggressively remonstrates with Bernard, before rapidly changing tact, offering huge discounts for the glove box full of drugs. To finish the transaction Bernard offers the driver a hundred extra as he tells us of his 'great offence' before insisting how he will now only accept the earlier agreed price. 'Fair enough,' Bernard says, giving him the lower amount. And so the matter ends as we enter what feels like a sanctuary. Our introduction to Pakistan leaves us shell-shocked.

The hotel will not allow the two shambling wrecks to book in at 4.30 in the morning unless they pay the full day which starts at 8am. Stunned at our introduction and feeling totally worn out, two seats in the foyer become our home for three and a half hours until 'the day' begins. Welcome to Pakistan.

The next afternoon we begin the process of trying to retrieve Bertha and contact the forwarding agent, Ahmer, at the number given to us in Istanbul. Things do not sound good when he virtually tells us that getting Bertha out will be as much fun as Hitler looking for a tourist visa to Israel without Mossad's involvement.

The office is full of the sound of diesel generators as people have to produce their own electricity for 11 hours a day as the government produces only 6 hours' worth. The rest of the time there is nothing but the flicker of candles. A 31% price increase has left the whole country reeling with shock and people are overwhelmingly unable to pay their bills. The government helpfully responded by asking people to pay only 60% of the bill; perhaps a suggestion for British Gas in England as a way of addressing the 37% price rise since we've been away?

Ahmer calls TV stations, newspapers, radio stations, his granny and the next-door neighbour as our arrival is so unusual. 'Very special event,' he says through many different conversations as we listen, one-sided, to the curious combination of Urdu and English. A smattering of words can be understood such as 'blind woman', 'moto' (motorbike), along with 'good story'.

Ahmer is genuinely excited at our appearance and, without doubt, is linking his company to it. He tells us it is important for people to know of our arrival as it tells the world that if a blind woman can arrive on a motorcycle then, truly, 'Pakistan is not dangerous'. We don't have the heart to tell him of the bombs in Karachi destroying the main police station, leaving five people dead and scores injured. It might shatter the picture he's drawing for us. Neither do we mention the other ten bombs killing people in the north east of India as the whole region teeters on the brink of chaos. As long as he feels safe then we're happy.

Even with all the correct paperwork in place it takes days of thumb-twiddling and sitting around to get Bertha back. Entering buildings where the heat is swirled by overhead fans, men leap out of chairs to nearly run from the room with the appearance of a Western woman. At least we gain a seat quickly.

The days pass along with the likely mounting storage costs in a land where we have no real financial reference points. It is only after Bernard commandeers a hotel car and insists on being driven to the cargo depot that we discover that they have been waiting for days for the paperwork from Ahmer's company. For days. Returning to our driver, he tells us 'It is not safe' to take us into town but reluctantly agrees, while telling us of his years serving in the Pakistani Army. He will stay with us.

Good to his word, he attaches himself to our shoulders on arriving at the agent's office and Ahmer is not amused when he refuses to move from our side. Seeming unsure of what to make of Bernard's forthright approach about retrieving Bertha, paper soon starts to fly under the watchful eyes of our shadow in the corner. Further phone calls are made as interviews are arranged for Pakistani TV for later in the day as the office is left behind, with our minder providing protection close enough to warrant a marriage certificate.

The Pakistani TV crew turns up at the hotel and things do not get off to a good start as they ask Bernard, 'Does she speak?'

'I think so. He turns to me asking 'Cathy, do you speak?'

Things get worse when it becomes apparent that English is the interviewer's 39th language rather than their second. As the cameras roll on like a Monty Python sketch, people wrongly interpret each others' answers but their English is better than Bernard's Urdu.

'So how do you ride the bike, Katie?'

'My name is Cathy and I do not ride the bike, Bernard is the driver.'

'But Katie it is hard for you to see the road yes?'

'I can't see the road, my eyes do not function at all. Bernard rides the bike.'

'Goodness me, but how do you drive the bike if you cannot see the road?'

'Bernard sees the road and rides the bike.'

'So he tells you which way to go? It must be very hard?'

'Incredibly hard yes, but I manage.'

I know all of the questions are being directed at Bernard by the direction of the voice shifting and it is a relief when it finishes. 'Bring back the BBC World Service,' Bernard mutters on reaching our room. For the rest of the day my name becomes Katie as he shouts, 'Watch the pothole' or 'Cliff on the right' while he dodges shoes thrown at his moving voice. Sometimes I hate sighted people. The very least he could do was stand still.

Through the days of waiting, the worsening security situation is evident as Bernard notes the truck full of Pakistani Rangers sitting outside the hotel. Armed guards patrol inside the grounds and they become people with names, from being 'the huge guard with the Kalashnikov' to Aadil. Even when Bernard merely waves 'hello' they leap to their feet.

Others too become names, like Umar who works in the laundry, after two of my tops are fused into crinkled layers, leaving them like folded tissue paper, despite the No Iron instructions. Umar panics, begging us not to complain as he will lose his job. Waving away his worries, and the offer of his wages for the week to pay for them, we don't have the heart to tell him it would take him two months to pay for a single one. Umar touches the back of Bernard's hand in gratitude, and his reaction leaves us feeling humbled.

Days later at 1am Bertha turns up in her Turkish garden shed, much to the consternation of the guards who respond suddenly to the headlights heading towards the gates on an otherwise empty road. A squad of Pakistani Rangers leap from their truck outside and take up positions facing the approaching headlights.

Bernard – I run over to the gate as I've been expecting her but, clearly, the company hasn't told the hotel. I can see quite clearly it's Bertha and I shout 'Moto, moto', while frantically pointing to myself and the truck. Everyone nervously watches its progress towards the gate. Aadil is on duty and he looks at me searchingly with an uncertain 'thumbs up' gesture, as if asking, 'Is this OK?' The Kalashnikov looks tiny in his enormous hands and his eyes stare at me from beneath a forehead the size of a pool table. His long beard glistens in the lights as I return his thumbs up. He shouts to the Pakistani Rangers arrayed outside the gate in defensive formation; they relax, a little, as the gap between them and the vehicle closes.

The tiny truck is instantly surrounded and weapons are pointed nervously as the occupants inside, unsurprisingly, keep their hands in clear view. Anxious inspections follow with the mirrored trolleys. The bonnet is opened to peer into the confines of the engine and the crate thoroughly inspected before the gates open. So it is we find ourselves with a 700 kg crate on a flatbed with no lifting equipment amid a startling security situation. How a 330 kg motorcycle became 700 kg was incomprehensible until I felt the crate.

Shouts of 'No problem, no problem' ring in the air as the guards (apart from one) put down their automatic weapons to get to work lifting the enormous crate off the flat bed truck by sheer muscle power. The Rangers outside laugh and shout encouragement – and probably insults – at the events unfolding inside. Through much grunting, groaning, and a lot of laughing (Bernard) the job gets done and Bertha sits covered in the dust and muck of the frantic dash back from Erzurum. We're relieved to have her back. Falling into bed after many, many handshakes and with much backslapping and laughing at 3am, we're tired but contented. Outside in the darkness we hope the Guards enjoy the biggest chocolate cake the restaurant had; our small way of saying 'thank you'.

The next day the engine is filled with oil and tyres are pumped up in our eagerness to be on the move. In the middle of all the 'dirty hand' work, a film crew turns up from ARY television. After the hopeless interview conducted days earlier, the Pakistani channel wants to interview us again for transmission across the Middle East.

This time they send Sofia, whom Bernard instantly falls in love with, along with Ahmed the cameraman (whom he just likes). I can tell Sofia is quite taken with him but his ribs feel my presence as she questions him about his marital status. Their English is excellent and two hours go by in interviews before the bike is ridden around the car park in big circles getting dizzier with each circle. In the middle of it all the hotel owner appears with the senior managers, and a huge bunch of flowers for me. It's surprising really the difference a TV crew makes to your reception and subsequent treatment. Bernard successfully resisted reminding them of sleeping in the foyer for three and a half hours on arrival.

During our enforced stay in Karachi, Sandra, from the British embassy in Tehran, calls as it turns out the Iranians having looked at pictures of Bernard, decided they do actually like him. I know I am stretching the truth here but, like all good lies, it has some truth in it. Sandra was as good as her word and pursued the matter with the Iranian Foreign Ministry, making them aware of what we are doing. Once they realised there was no real threat to national security, they'd relented and offered a 'special visa' to be collected from anywhere in Turkey. Sadly, we had to tell her of already being in Karachi. We were sad at this turn of events and no one more so than Bernard, considering the 1,800 km across Turkey, then 1,800 back, plus six weeks of actually going nowhere.

Once Sofia (sorry, the TV crew) departs, Bernard turns back to solving one more problem, that of finding petrol. The staff tell him they will send a car for some.

'Is it far?' he asks and it turns out to be only around the corner.

'I'll ride there to check everything is fine with the bike,' he answers.

'Is not safe,' they all chorus together 'you need security.'

'It'll be fine, no worries,' he tells them, convincing them to open the barriers while I wait at the hotel.

Bernard – Pulling out I felt very nervous as cars stop when they see me and people on the pavements pull at their friend's sleeves as I appear. Everything feels incredibly alien, more than I'd ever anticipated. I find the petrol station, where everything grinds to a halt when I pull up. Within seconds 20 people surround me asking, 'Where is your security?' They shake their heads on realising I am alone and several run off to a nearby building. Other people emerge running towards me and soon the 20 become 40 as the same question is voiced, 'Where is your security?' I give the same answer before adding, 'Do I need it here?' The road fills with cars as occupants peer at the maroon motorcycle with the large aluminium cases and the Martian standing beside it.

The petrol station owner appears, presenting his business card as a formal introduction, before I present him with ours, a cartoon of Cathy, myself and Biscuit (her guide dog) standing beside Bertha. He doesn't know what to make of the image but politely puts it into his wallet, before inviting me to join him for tea.

Ringing his father, who appears within minutes in a large modern car, they tell me of the Pakistani state oil company, talk of the UK, Pakistan, and everyday life while sipping strong tea until suddenly through the large windows I see an open-top truck screeching onto the forecourt. Armed people leap out before heading for the office under the furious waving motions of the people near Bertha, now covered in soapsuds being 'groomed'. One enters our room and I recognise him from the hotel and an exchange occurs between my host, his father, and the heavily armed guard.

'You gone long time,' he turns to me speaking slowly. 'People worried.'

'I'm fine thank you, as you can see,' I motion to the cup of chai.

'I leave guards for you, for coming back to hotel.'

'It really is not necessary,' I answer, but he is not mollified.

One of his men takes station by the bike and one sits outside our door with his rifle across his knees. It's Aadil, the huge black-bearded guard with the shining eyes and the easy smile. Two more sit in a waiting car as Bertha is scrubbed clean and filled up with petrol under the watchful eyes of my minders. It brings home to me the world we've now entered.

Setting off from the petrol station an hour later after forcing down several cups of tea (which I don't usually drink) a car attaches itself to me. Staring in my wing mirrors it's unnerving to see so many weapons sticking out the windows on the short ride back to the hotel. On arrival, the guards gather round me.

'You big man,' they chorus with much backslapping for braving the drive to the petrol station but I feel anything but big. In fact I feel incredibly small, naïve, and more frightened than anticipated. I wonder what crossing the country will mean if something as small as going for petrol, in a major city, turns into something so big.

I return to a hailstorm of anger from Cathy at being AWOL for one and a half hours. The pressure causes us to respond badly to each other and we have a furious row, smoking several cigarettes on the veranda before I calm down. It's rare for me to respond badly, as I did here. As I suck on the cigarette, I try hard to keep my own fears under control, as it will not help us. It can only make things worse as the argument proved; we have only each other for support and cannot afford to react in any other way, no matter what.

I knew she was worried as I sat drinking tea at the petrol station. I also knew she felt the frustrations of blindness as my absence left her 'trapped' in so many different ways, sitting and wondering if I was safe. All these things I accept and understand. At the same time I sometimes feel she cannot know my own pressure. My own anxiety. My own level of fear, which has caught me by surprise. The prospect of taking a bike through this alien land, where simple transactions take on layers of complexity, leaves me with a profound sense of fear. Real fear. Heightened and honed by my own reckless imagination.

I have to look straight into these fears.

Trying to overcome them, to focus on keeping us safe, and Bertha in one piece, *fills my insides with deep-rooted feelings of inadequacy. These have grown daily as we've waited. Threatening what I think I am. Weakening me in so many different ways. As a motorcyclist. As a person. I'm learning. But the learning involves things about myself I never knew. Never wanted to know. But, overwhelmingly, it leaves me insecure and ill-prepared for the journey ahead, the one that involves pulling Bertha out of the 'safety' of the hotel. I dread it.*

During our six-day wait there are suicide bombings in Karachi and Uncle Sam fires missiles into northern Pakistan. Our nervousness grows daily as events unfold before us, and is amplified by everyone we've spoken to: journalists, TV staff, and the everyday people we come in contact with. All confirm the need for 'security' to travel. People convince us to contact the British embassy in Islamabad and the consul in Karachi. We get through to someone in the Karachi office who assures us no security is needed, which flies in the face of the concerns being expressed to us daily. We pack to leave Karachi.

The compound guards and hotel staff cannot believe we want to leave the following morning with no armed escort. Previously they would not even allow us to walk across the road to a nearby bank without escort. The 'petrol' event has made them even more nervous for our safety as furious phone calls are made to stop us leaving on our own. The hotel managers contact the local police, who contact the British embassy, who relay the message back: no security is needed. All the guards, including Aadil, turn up complete with a Pakistan sticker for the bike while still refusing to lift the barriers to let us out.

The Pakistani Rangers appear at the gate and furious communication ensues with much arm-waving and raised voices in an unfathomable language. Bernard conveys the scene to me, involving much shoulder shrugging as we sit impassively waiting with Bernard rocking the bike from side to side with the engine ticking over beneath us. Eventually, after many handshakes, goodbyes and advice, we set off into Pakistan alone with just our hopes and crossed fingers.

Our smiles soon fade as bad roads and horrendous traffic sees people stop in their tracks at the sight of a large maroon motorcycle. Beggars descend on us in the walking-pace traffic through the deeply corrugated 'road'. They pull at our arms, our clothes, the bike, as we progress at less than the speed of a turtle while the bike wobbles unpredictably. Cars pull over to watch with inquisitive looks on their faces. Then something magical happens. We smile. And the most enormous grins come back at us, accompanied by happy waves in response to our gestures of 'hello'.

Safety in movement

Clearing Karachi involves getting lost in trying to find the 'superhighway', which everybody tells us is an excellent road heading north. Passing the same military barriers three times to set off over sandy surfaces before reappearing back at the same point, the police and soldiers collapse laughing. Our third appearance at the same checkpoint was just too much for them. Climbing out of their chairs, they insist we take sweet cakes and drinks with them as they draw a map for us to find the mythical 'superhighway'; the three lane 'motorway'. Naïvely, we anticipate something easily identifiable and 'findable', anything but what we find.

Corrugated folds cause the bike to shudder and skip along the surface as huge holes appear filled in with branches and soft dirt. The road passes through the middle of villages where people saunter out into the traffic like suicidal lemmings. Camels and donkeys pulling carts appear in the 'fast' lane while pushbikes containing whole families wobble along before riding straight across the traffic towards dusty paths. Vehicles drive on the wrong side, the inside, the outside while expecting us to move into the deep sand of the verges as badly overloaded wagons pull into our path without looking. Actually, it is not they do not look, it is that they cannot; the width of their loads cover wing mirrors – if they have them.

Petrol stops become pantomimes surrounded by curious smiling people, all wanting to shake our hands as they ask the inevitable and constant question: 'Where is your security?' Heads shake on discovering we are alone, before moving onto the next question concerning our 'home country'. 'Ireland' Bernard confidently declares as the wars in Iraq and Afghanistan make our presence 'sensitive'. 'What are your thoughts on George Bush?' comes at us throughout the day as American missiles land in the north. Bernard spits into the dirt beneath his feet. Smiles appear all around as 'Ireland very good country'. It is declared so many times I think we should apply for naturalisation to the land of permanent rain.

Cold drinks beckon at a truck stop where the highway patrol homes in on us and we spend an hour talking with officers trained in England, who loved the country but hated the cold. They tell us of their time in France on police exchanges (loved the weather but not the country) and of how it is safe for us to travel as long as we are off the road by dark. 'Then is a different matter,' they confide in us.

Pulling away from the truck stop, within miles 100 years turn back in time as the road changes to potholes and rubble, as people live under tarpaulins in absolute poverty. The small town comes to a complete and utter stop as we ride within deep corrugations where trucks have compressed the road into two channels. People walk alongside, staring, as Bernard paddles his feet along the track made by vehicles sinking into the surface and Bertha's exhausts scrape along as her wheels bury deep inside foot-wide trenches.

'Jesus,' Bernard's voice comes through the intercom, 'this is not good.'
Bernard – I feel intimidated, out of my depth like never before. No matter how much I think of the underpasses of Istanbul, my own reactions, I feel the same way. Again. Only worse. Much worse. You could disappear here. Completely. And nobody would ever know. The roads, the conditions, being so far off the normal radar, make us vulnerable. Hugely so. Even smiling at the people walking alongside does not help. All they do is impassively stare back. Sullen. Unsmiling. There are no smiles or grins, no offers of handshakes or conversation. I wonder if I look the same to them. Am I seeing what they see? Could it be they are mirrors, reflecting back my own image? Mirrors of my own language, my own feelings. I smile again.
Nothing.
A small hand wave.
Nothing.
It's a huge relief to find my way out.
I can breath again.
Miles further on we return to the highway, working out the loop I've taken through the town without realising it. Road signs are rare and travelling under these conditions means suspending everything you think you understand. About driving, about navigating, or even what you think you know about yourself. Suddenly you find this is very little, verging on nothing. Nothing at all. And it shakes you. Really shakes you. Harder and more completely than you could ever believe. More than you would think could ever be possible.

After ten and a half hours of sitting under a blazing sun covering 480 hard kilometres Sukkur appears and with it, darkness. Entering the blacked-out town, a dead camel lies in the road minus its legs, hacked off to provide somebody their evening meal. Weaving around the carcass people walk past unconcerned as the search eventually shows a 'Motel' sign which turns out to be an eating house. Fortunately one of the staff jumps onto his 50cc bike and guides us through the traffic to a 'hotel'. By the time Bernard is on his third trip up with our belongings several armed police have arrived. The questions begin, starting with a sentence we have come to know, to expect.

'Where is your security?'

They are obviously confused by our presence, along with the fact we are alone. For the next half hour they are mystified as to what to do with us.

Our photographs are taken (for security) by a very nice officer (Asi Abdul) and little do we know how everything will change with this simple act. Maybe it should have been obvious. After all, when two armed police are stationed outside the entrance to the building all night you should really understand that something is amiss. Shouldn't you?

But when truly exhausted, so far beyond tiredness by a further million miles, even ordering food from a menu consisting of mainly 'Do not have' options becomes a feat of mental endurance. Working our way patiently through the menu, we eventually find the 'Do have' selection of Chinese meals. Sometimes it is nice to have a certain sense of familiarity with 'local cuisine'. At least Bernard could now read the menu.

In the morning we are not allowed to leave until a police escort arrives. I am grateful for this initially as my mouth takes some time to recover from the hottest omelette on the planet. Picking it for breakfast, never did I suspect it to be loaded with chillies. And I do mean loaded. Somewhere among the chillies there were eggs, I think. Tears run down my face as Bernard wipes away his own from laughing. Anyone who has ever suffered the assault of 'the chilli' will know you are caught in the 'damned if I do' and 'damned if I don't'. Do I drink water? I chose the 'damned if I do' option as several jugs are delivered to the obvious amusement of staff.

As the morning passes my mouth returns to something akin to normality without having to reach for a hosepipe to dowse the fires from hell. Meanwhile Bernard pours over maps, stressing over covering the next 480 km to Multan before darkness. Eventually an open-top truck arrives with more armed police on it than we have ever seen in one place.

So begins an eight-hour journey following armed teams across 220 km with each stage taking us about 75 km before we're waved past. There we find another vehicle waiting. In these vehicles people clutch metal sticks which throw out small bits of metal designed to rip through bodies, to kill people. Protection. For us? Do we really need it? Really, really? Are they serious? They must be for somebody else. Surely. Perhaps we've strayed somewhere where important people are to pass. That's it. We've just become caught up in their passing. Important people will be along soon. People who matter, on the great scale of something. But slowly we come to understand.

All this effort, all this manpower, the thinking, the planning, is all for a blind woman and sighted companion who sit on an eighteen-year-old bike. Then it dawns on us. People are worried. They live here, this is their land, under their rules and they are worried...

Throughout the journey, the police wave good-naturedly to Bernard as we ride along. Stops for leg stretches do not occur and Bernard takes to riding the bike smoking cigarettes, much to the amusement of our advance guard. Bottles of water are passed backwards and forwards from me to him as the miles go by in ferocious heat. The bike slowly changes from maroon to white as it passes through the dust cloud of our escorts. Police officers wrap clothes around their faces to protect their lungs from the billowing white clouds as we sit enveloped in them throughout the day.

Hours later, everybody tells us we are in a really a 'dangerous' area. It is so dangerous the Punjab Elite Anti-Terrorist Squad are to take over for the 100 miles north to the city of Multan. Bernard stands listening to instructions from the commander as everything is carefully explained: how to drive, speed (no faster than 100 kph?) distances from their vehicle (3–4 metres at most) and what to do if anything happens (follow their lead).

In contrast to the police vehicles so far, the anti-terrorist vehicle will take station behind us on the journey. They tell Bernard how, if necessary, they will pass *if anything occurs* and he is then to stay within the 3–4 metre area *no matter what*.

'*If anything happens, stay close.*'

With this final warning, their truck bristling with weapons, we set off with sirens howling.

Petrol stops take on a new meaning as a cordon is set up and people stare nervously at our arrival; nobody in and nobody out until we are on the move again. Unlike the previous day where inquisitive people would suddenly appear from all directions with smiles to break the distance between people, now it is harder. Still smiling and shaking hands, Bernard finds people nervous, they watch seven armed men shutting down entry to the petrol station until Bertha leaves. One young man looks terrified when we appear as he hand pumps petrol. Suddenly he beams in happiness as Bernard offers his hand to say hello.

Approaching one of the toll sections, the team hammers past as two bodies leap from the still-moving vehicle to kick barrels barring our way. Bemused soldiers leap from chairs in the shade at the sound of the siren. With the route clear in front our minders jump back onto the moving truck and wave us to follow closely through. At their signal, we assume the 'in front' position they require. 'Safety in movement' becomes their priority as they charge through situations without ever stopping the wheels of their vehicle.

The sun starts to drift down in the sky as it becomes obvious daylight is not long for the heavens and Multan will not be reached before dark. At a hurried stop our escort suggests stopping for the night in Bahawalpur to which we readily agree as Bernard is completely worn out. They lead us to a secure army compound where a small hotel sits within high walls surrounded by troops but there are no rooms available. Meanwhile dozens of heavily armed soldiers gather at our arrival until officers shoo them back to their positions as they work out what to do with us.

Bernard — We pull into the compound and I have nothing left as I struggle with the bike in an overwhelming exhausted sense of 'I'm finished'. The road conditions, the stress of close protection riding for hours on end, has mentally finished me. When I realise there are no rooms, my head drops and my eyes close in resignation.

Heading for the washroom, I plunge my blackened face into a sink of cold water before staring at the stranger in the mirror who does not want this anymore. Not now, not tonight, not ever. I ask the mirror if it's really supposed to be like this. After all the dreams, all the years of waiting, all the books of tales, is it really like this? I wait for an answer but all that comes back from the black-streaked face is silent agreement that we both want it all to end. Enough. Now. Please.

My body is giving up on me, dangerously so, as the riding is so hard, with so much concentration needed and it is unremitting. Out here there are no nice road surfaces, no understandable rules, no street lights to keep you safe from the things that lurk in the dark. They're going to get me. Eventually. I know. As I stand looking at the frightened person I have become I know there is no choice. There never seems to be any lately. It has been taken away from me in ways I am coming to understand. I have to do this.

'You do what you have to do,' the voice echoes as it has done so many times before through the countless miles.

Leaving the compound we head back into the black town with new security vehicles front and back, protecting us from the things they fear. In the darkness. Travelling at 15 kph as they are frightened of losing us, the slow speed wears me out even more. It causes Bertha to bounce through the deep potholes suddenly appearing from underneath the vehicle in front. Heavily corrugated surfaces rip us all over the road where a little more speed would make everything much more manageable. I am not even running on reserve anymore.

I am completely flat.

Bernard is quiet and I know he is struggling. Frustratingly there is little I can do but squeeze his sides in support and encouragement. Twenty minutes later downtown Bahawalpur appears with nervous troops shepherding us towards the misnamed 'Luxury Hotel'. Sitting near a roundabout with an incongruous missile as a centrepiece, it is a reminder that Pakistan is a nuclear power. Within minutes, Bertha magically disappears underneath a large white sheet, like a child's game of 'You can't see me!' Meanwhile the side of the road jams with curious people looking at her tent-like structure.

Inside, armed guards spread out as we eat with two sitting feet away in an empty 'restaurant' as later two more sleep outside our room where we toss and turn restlessly, listening to every noise, every footstep. Sleeping like two frightened schoolchildren, every noise is a harbinger of death, doom or destruction. We lie awake whispering, beating ourselves up over the stupidity, our stupidity. The ridiculous nature of what we feel. Is it ridiculous? Is it all merely a product of our overactive imaginations? Are we truly imagining the danger as two men sit outside our room in a chair with guns across their knees. Adventure? No, not really. I feel scared. Scared listening to the night sounds, to the scrape of chairs outside our door, to the footsteps of people passing by, to the muffled voices. Saying what? Who are they? What do they want? Us? A million questions with no answers or perhaps ones that I could never understand anyway. Everything seems beyond me to appreciate, to know why this is so for people who need guns to solve something, anything. Streams of thought cascade helplessly inside me for hours and I feel as tired and worn out as before I went to bed in search of non-existent sleep.

Dragging ourselves down for breakfast, more armed police watch us as a crowd gathers outside in the road. The police pass on their nervousness as people press in from all sides when we eventually appear. Even more officers arrive as Bertha crawls through the pressed bodies, surrounded by a walking police cordon until the escort trucks can gather enough speed to leave behind the walking officers.

Coughs and splutters echo through the intercom as our lungs start to say hello to the permanent air of dust that has surrounded us since arriving in Karachi. Nowhere has it been more so since setting off across the hundreds of miles following trucks, escorts and jeeps. They all throw up this constant cloud that we must pass through for hour after hour.

In the middle of sentences coughing starts while the other waits patiently for it to cease. Meanwhile the air hangs lifeless, with not a breeze from any direction. Even riding does not help as it clings to us in a heat wave, trapping listlessness into every part of our bodies. People trudge along the roadside, stopping to watch our passing, some waving, some staring as the circus rolls by.

Petrol stops involve people descending from everywhere as the big top rolls into town, while Bernard tells me he can see them wondering, 'Who are these people? Are they important? They must be very wealthy.' Many silently mouth the wording on the side of the bike 'A Blind Woman, Two Wheels, and 25,000 Miles' before turning to their friends and, we assume, translating. They smile. Pakistan seems to be the land of smiles, of curious people, of people who want to spend moments with us, to share words. Fortunately, this is helped by many, many people speaking English. Towns, villages and single tarpaulin-covered homes lay scattered through the land as the trip passes under a sky covered by a constant heat haze, blocking the sun behind a permanent yellow tinge.

Our eventual destination of Lahore is too big a jump for one day at nearly 480 km so the decision is made to make the short 100 km ride to Multan to have a rest day. The escorts hand us over to other vehicles waiting patiently at deserted lonely areas and our speed varies widely.

One escort driver crawls along at less than 30 kph before the handover passes us to Michael Schumacher who wants to find out how fast Bertha can go on a good section of road. He gives up at 120 kph as his engine starts to bellow black smoke. Realising the unequal struggle, no doubt he watches Bernard in his wing mirrors nonchalantly smoking cigarettes. The guards in the back of the truck egg Bernard on with waves, saying 'yes, yes, faster, faster'. As Bernard smokes cigarettes and drinks from the bottle of water they turn to their driver, saying, 'Give it up, the boss will kill us if we wreck the truck.'

Entering Multan the traffic closes around us and nervousness reaches a whole different level as 'Safety in movement' becomes impossible. Hemmed in all around with traffic on all sides, it makes Paris, Rome and Athens all appear to be little more than desolate wastelands. Even with sirens wailing like banshees while bullying a route up the wrong side of the road we become hopelessly snarled up in traffic. All the time they wave to Bernard from the back of the truck: 'close up, close up.' We drive so close I can smell their exhaust fumes.

Bernard – It's the scariest riding I have ever done, travelling this close to a vehicle in front in dense traffic. The police constantly wave at me 'closer, closer' as we plough through the mayhem. It soon becomes obvious why they insist on us staying so close because if ANY gap appears it instantly disappears. It can be a car, a bike wobbling into the gap with several people on it, a tractor, donkey,

cart or human lemming, but something will fill it. People step into the road as
cattle saunter along and vehicles pull out of side roads without looking. And so
it goes on. I stare into the open back of the truck, trying hard to peer through its
windshield in order to stand any chance of stopping if they slam on their brakes,
which they do a lot. It's obvious the police are acting as a cushion to keep us safe
and, with some concentration, it's possible to ride this close, to stay relatively
safe; in fact, it's safer than being swallowed up by the traffic swarming around
us. Nevertheless, it's scary and I have to suspend all rules concerning 'distance
and braking' as there are no reference points for driving in Pakistan. You have
to leave most things you know behind as they do not work here.

The police threaten, intimidate and harass people out of their way and one
poor rickshaw driver pays the price for not moving fast enough. An officer
leans out of the passenger door and slaps him. Hard. Hard enough to nearly
turn the three-wheeled taxi over as it lurches sideways dangerously. The
shock in his eyes is visible to Bernard, who is plainly upset at the event. 'We
caused that, it's because we are here,' he says quietly. We are uncomfortable
at being the cause, or reason, for him to be dealt with in this way. Perhaps
it is the remaining thin veneer of Western views still covering our thoughts?
We are conscious of it being stripped away, little by little as time progresses.

Arriving in Multan relieved and worn out from the humble 60 miles
covered, we have been riding for over four hours. The waiting staff move
lines of prayer mats facing Mecca to make room for Bertha as she is lined up
to face towards the Kibble (Mecca). Right now, we will take all the help we
can get.

The following morning finds us waiting for another escort. Nearby, a
well-dressed man sits reading documents, watching as people ask if we will
pose for photographs with them. Eventually he puts his papers down.

'What is the white stick for?'

So begins our introduction to Advocate of the Supreme Court Mr Dogar,
famous for the constitutional crisis in 2007 brought about by the former
military ruler and President Pervez Musharraf. After a long period of
wrangling, the President had eventually declared emergency rule across the
country before suspending the Constitution itself. Serious stuff. At the same
time, a State of Emergency was declared and the Supreme Court chief justice
was sacked. More serious stuff. Troops subsequently went into the Supreme
Court building, arrested all the judges, placed them under house arrest, and
took over all state-run media outlets. Things are now getting somewhat out
of control for many people as all independents were forced from the air,
leaving many people reaching for their guns.

After tidying up his court papers and some time talking about blindness, my life and experiences, he passes his business card over with an invitation to visit his home when we reach Lahore. It is only when he leaves that people tell us we've been talking to one of the most famous people in Pakistan. We hope that our 'ambassadorial' duties were well performed with our learned friend.

The staff, again, will not let us leave until the police arrive, which they eventually do. Having tried to sneak off several times, any approach towards Bertha is met with much arm waving, gesturing and animation. As on previous days, we follow armed police trucks across 368 scorching kilometres towards Lahore, constantly shadowed by vehicle after vehicle. It goes on and on for hours. There are no stops, no rest, no leg-stretching or loo stops as dust clings to us, and our coughing gets worse by the hour. It now keeps us awake at night. Every night. Barking and spluttering. Spluttering and barking. New days bring nothing but tiredness and no respite as it continues throughout the day.

Passing through endless barren, baked landscapes, people work in the yellow heat haze, turning over dry ground as dust clouds rise from their work. Makeshift tents and fabricated 'homes' line the fields where people live in abject poverty, clothes grey from the constant blowing dust. Groups of people sit in the dirt of the roadside watching as we roll by and many times it seems the stares are directed towards the police, rather than ourselves. To Bernard the looks appear sullen, resentful or suspicious.

Over the days the lead pace vehicle sets the speed, determined by whether the 'handover' is waiting for us to appear; if not we grind slowly onwards. Arriving at one point, no escort waits. Our minders spread out near a Highway Patrol vehicle whose occupants have been trained in either the UK or Turkey, radar guns aimed down the road. Rupees are flying left, right and centre as vehicles arrive in a hurricane of dust within the unmarked 70 kph zone. Two patrol officers come over to pass time as their colleagues continue to trap the unwary.

The commander explains to his colleagues how Britain is blessed with white lines to denote a divided road, how people stay on 'their side', wait patiently, and wave for others to pull out, of the general politeness of drivers operating under 'rules'. They shake their heads in amazement at the fact that blowing the horn in England may be a warning but is usually used to denote anger. Here in Pakistan, everybody blows their horn. For anything. For everything. Eventually all you hear is a constant wall of honking noise. It can mean, coming through, move over, I'm here, pull out, don't pull out, my child is about to be car sick, or 'Hey, nice dress'.

In the end, it all becomes meaningless.

A crowd gathers and one of them is dispatched for cold drinks, magically appearing minutes later complete with straws as the commander listens to the warning of an immanent arrival at over 100 kph. It will cost the driver 750 rupees (€7.50), an enormous amount in this country where people work for sometimes less than 100 a day. The car pulls over in a massive cloud of dust and 'important' people get out with handshakes all around. Their faces get longer when they realise there is no escaping the fine, despite their freshly pressed, very white linen clothes.

Our talkative commander tells us of his time in Manchester, Glasgow and the Lake District, of his dislike of the rain and cold but of liking England, of his high regard for the British Police. The watching crowd grows to over 50 people as Bernard offers him an American cigarette. Half a packet disappears as several officers help themselves while people look on from the sidelines until Bernard wanders over to them. Standing in their dusty grey clothes, his packet is offered and several reach for the contents as smiles break out all around when he lights them all.

Eventually our escort appears and we are thrown back into the mayhem of following trucks full of armed people who watch anything, everything, nothing. Throughout each day so far, a hand will suddenly appear through the side window, waving us forward, past them, an indication to pass and follow the next vehicle toddling along in front.

Approaching the outskirts of Lahore, the same thing happens in the fading light and bewilderment comes through the intercom when there is no vehicle to follow. Travelling several kilometres, expecting to see the familiar sight, it slowly dawns on us that there is nothing, and no one, to follow. The light is falling and the sun disappearing as we realise something is wrong. After several days of constant protection, and of being led to destinations, it comes as a shock to find ourselves alone. There are no directions, no idea of which way we should go. Waiting in front of us is the chaos of Lahore.

'Is it likely to rain?'

Darkness and Lahore. The worst three hours and the worst conditions. Ever. And then some. And then some more. The beeping of horns fills the air and traffic clings to us on all sides as we try to find a hotel, any hotel. Stopping to ponder our options attracts crowds within seconds, making us feel vulnerable in the darkness with our Christmas-tree bike standing out wherever it stops.

Bernard pulls over on a corner as traffic comes at him from everywhere. Lighting a cigarette he sits silent. No banter fills my helmet. No descriptions. Nothing. Just silence. And breathing. I can feel his thoughts through the silence, through the tense silence; he does not think it is possible to ride the bike under these conditions; his confidence is vanishing before me as he shivers, and not from the cold.

I sit quietly, waiting as he works through his emotions. It is not time for him to hear, 'You can do this' or 'you have no choice'. He needs time. Time to work through his uncertainty, his fear in being surrounded by traffic coming from everywhere. It appears on the right side, on the wrong side, cars with no lights, pushbikes, rickshaws, horses, donkeys, camels, pedestrians; all hem us into a space smaller than the bike and all at less than walking speed. After several cigarettes, he speaks again:

'I have no choice do I, it has to be done?' I very quietly say, 'Yes.'

He presses the starter and Bertha sings into life. The sound of deep breathing comes through the speakers in my helmet and the bike surges forward.

Bernard – We fight our way through traffic which gives no quarter. If you give an inch something will take it from you. It's a place where cars go through red lights without a thought, causing hard and desperate braking. It's a place where people step off the dust into the dark road without a care as traffic thunders along inches from the vehicle in front. Unlit camel-drawn carts suddenly appear from the darkness as cars and bikes pull out of side roads without looking to see if anything is coming. Vehicles race past us, then pull in nearly taking out the front wheel as I wonder why the roads are not full of bodies. Despite the frantic madness, within the mayhem, I start to see a rhythm. A glimmer of light in a world of darkness, a style needed to survive, a way of getting through this alive. 'Give no quarter.' Let nothing have space and shout 'this is my space' as loud as you can with the hammering of the horn.

Imperiously assume everyone is going to get out of your way. 'Move NOW! I'm coming through. Get out of the Goddam way, otherwise I'll road rage you TO DEATH. Be sure of it. Shift. Now.' Keep the wheels rolling. Please God keep them moving, don't stop them at all.

Slowly but surely progress is made. From metre by metre to street by street. Asking people for directions fills me with fury as they send me in wrong directions all over the city. More darkened streets, more chaos, more everything. Eventually we reach a hotel and gratefully pull in through the security gates (and guards) before climbing off the bike.

Trudging into the hotel black-faced from pollution and dust, two coal miners have arrived fresh from the pit while all around us teem the best dressed of Lahore. Parading through the reception in their finery, we stand filthy, with dust falling from us with any movement at all. Destroyed, but glad to have survived. As luck would have it (and we certainly needed some), the hotel has the ONLY LEGAL bar in the country. Falling inside, both of us sit numbly for a long time. Sitting on the table is my first wine for nearly two weeks. Shall we say I had several glasses.

The next day dawns, finding us exhausted, coughing and weak. So weak. The fumes, pollution, dust, have all made sleep hard as we wake each other constantly. Incessantly. It feels like I have swallowed cotton wool, all the time trying to cough it up, but to no avail. Our chests are sore and breathing comes hard. Unable to even breathe easily, it is obvious we cannot ride any more. Not yet and only when able to breathe properly will the border to India be crossed.

During our rest period, we visit the famous Wagha border ceremony where twelve-foot-tall Indian and Pakistani Rangers perform a ritual every night at the lowering of their respective flags. It is a fabulous mixture of martial preening and good-humoured baiting of the opposite side's soldiers. The Pakistani Rangers, in their jet-black uniforms, stand face-to-face, toe-to-toe, with their khaki-uniformed Indian counterparts as the crowd bays support. Both sides are wound up by flag-waving cheerleaders, exciting and encouraging nationalistic fever. Both sets of troops high step and stamp their way towards each other to conduct the ritualised performance: the ritualised 'My Dad is bigger than your Dad'. To the delight of the crowds on both sides the gate between the two countries slams shut, but with boisterous good humour.

The days pass with me being fitted for saris while talking to many people who have had their visa applications ripped up in front of their eyes in the

British embassy. The comment, 'You do not want to go to the UK,' is the only explanation offered after waiting for several days. We meet French and American embassy officials from Islamabad on immaculate BMW motorcycles who have travelled south to Lahore to play golf for the weekend. Their bikes sit outside the front entrance covered in dust sheets and hotel staff offer to hide Bertha similarly. When Bernard asks if it is likely to rain, the staff say no.

'Why would we cover it then?' he asks.

In all innocence, they reply 'to keep the dirt off'.

Bernard describes the caked appearance of Bertha to me, then starts laughing. Soon the staff join in the laughing, realising how funny their offer is as we stand looking at our bedraggled bike. 'Is fine, is fine, very safe,' they assure us pointing to Bertha. Of this we have no doubt as the hotel has anti-crash ramps to stop car bombers and metal detectors constantly checking everything. A small – heavily armed – army of people patrol the grounds constantly which, in some ways makes us feel safe. In other ways it leaves us feeling uncomfortable. Vulnerable. A target. It is a very strange mixture of feelings.

As people come to know of the 'English Blind Woman on the motorcycle' many stop to ask our thoughts concerning America firing missiles into the north of Pakistan; they wonder how the Americans would like it if Mexico or Canada did the same thing to them?

Talking with people who shake their heads at our travels, the word 'brave' constantly appears in their thoughts on our route. It is not something we think. It is not something we feel. Sometimes, we feel much less than brave and are not frightened to admit it. Often we take refuge in our belief that 'people are people' and a smile and a handshake can overcome many of our worries. There is a very old saying that, 'A stranger is just a friend you have not met yet,' and it is very true and it is a thought shared with the people we meet.

After some days our hacking, racking coughs are gone and Bertha is packed and made ready to leave again. The ritual checking is done: spanners deployed on loose nuts, cables checked, tyre pressures adjusted; then luggage is strapped down into long familiar places. To the massed ranks of hotel staff and guests who line up to take photographs, we exit the fortress to re-enter the pandemonium which awaits us. Forcing our way towards the border, the surface dissolves into 70 km of dirt tracks which the locals helpfully spray with water to keep the dust down. It might help with our coughing but it turns the surface into a gluttonous mess devoid of any real traction. The bike slaloms, slips and slides through sections of mud not yet baked by the blazing sunshine as we sit with new scarves wrapped around faces to protect us from lungfuls of the white dust. Suppressed coughs and splutters echo through the intercom as buses packed with people head to the same border crossing at Atari.

In India we'll face new challenges: staying alive in the traffic generated by over one billion people. It is also the home of the dreaded Indian wagons, the Tat trucks, so named after Tatra, the largest truck manufacturers in India. These have been the downfall of so many foreign motorcyclists who came home by air ambulance, if lucky, following a visit to the joys of a local hospital.

Sometimes they have not been lucky, not lucky at all.

Crossing our fingers, toes, and everything else, we head further east.

'The British used 1,650 bullets...'

(IND) Pulling into the Pakistan Customs compound, Bernard describes two motorcycles bearing Polish registration plates with owners climbing to their feet to tell us of sleeping here for two days. They're grounded as they're missing paperwork and nobody knows what to do with them. Having been stamped out of Pakistan, they're now stuck between two countries; India will not let them in and Pakistan will not have them back as their visas have expired.

A customs officer wanders over and looks relieved as he asks for, and receives, our correct paperwork before merrily stamping everything with multiple brightly coloured marks. The satisfying heavy thumps echo around the deserted hall as rubber smacks down onto paper before we're waved through to the Indian gate. The two Polish riders stand forlornly by their bikes as we pull away. Waiting for officialdom to decide their fate.

Between the two official gates, coaches full of Sikhs head in the opposite direction. Singing and noisy celebrations fill the air as they cavort around the border, dancing and singing, before heading onwards to the birthplace of the founder of Sikhism. When the borders were redrawn with the creation of Pakistan in 1948, his birthplace was suddenly in another country. Thus the annual pilgrimage occurs between their religious centre in India and the founder's birthplace in Pakistan. Lines on maps dividing people, lines through hearts creating division.

Back on the bike, leaving them dancing and swirling around in their excitement, enormous Pakistani Rangers check our paperwork several times within a hundred yards. Crossing the white painted line into India, the same thing checking is done by equally huge Indian Rangers.

Through three-and-a-half hours of paperwork processing we meet a wonderful Sikh at the Immigration counter who makes us feel at home with his sense of humour, his prayers for a happy marriage. He laughs with such infectiousness, we can't help but join in. It feels a relief to laugh again as the welcome is genuine and so different from the sombre crossing into Pakistan under such tight restrictions.

Indian security, meanwhile, involves people walking through airport-style metal detectors screaming loudly. In Pakistan troops would have assumed firing positions as everybody else hit the floor. Here? Nothing. The shrill declaration continues, but no notice is taken. Meanwhile, people walk on by as soldiers continue leaning on their chairs watching the world go past.

In a corner is a large wall map and Bernard photographs it as he has no maps of India. Uploading the photograph onto the GPS, at least now he has some idea of the route to Amritsar. By the bike, bar owners descend from both sides of the road saying, 'You have come from Pakistan, come in for a beer.' Little do they know we found the only legal bar in the whole of Pakistan so our declining leaves them puzzled.

The traffic seems calmer after Lahore, less dense, and it's a relief to ride the 30 km towards Amritsar past open fields where people work in the sun; it's picture-postcard perfect. Entering the city we try to find the guest house located on the internet and quickly find the right road, but cannot fathom the seemingly random numbering of the houses. Twenty minutes later, after driving up and down attracting a large crowd who gather to watch, a car stops. The driver laughs when he hears our predicament of house number 143 following 29, sitting beside number 3 while we look for 47A. The driver shakes our hands while laughing. In perfect English he tell us that, yes, the numbers are random with people free to pick their own. Fortunately he knows 'the 47A house' and leads us straight there. Pulling into Ranjit's guest house across the most enormous speed hump ever constructed, it nearly rips both exhausts off. A check underneath reveals all is well apart from a few bent fins on the bottom of the engine.

The guest house is from colonial times when it was used by visiting UK officials, royalty and famous people. Still existing in the 'maam' and 'madame' language of the past, the grounds are full of little balconies, bushes and trees, in an oasis of calm and tranquillity. It wraps itself around us, calming us like a soothing parent, settling our feelings and emotions after the recent traumas.

It's been a long time since we've sat outside and we pass days sitting on balconies relaxing around the courtyard. After leaving Karachi the security arrangements precluded it, and the air was so thick with dust and pollution it was impossible. Sitting, letting time flow, Bernard tells me how he can see the sun for the first time in weeks, no longer obscured by a permanent yellow haze. Slowly beginning to feel better, sleep takes us through nights without chest-wrenching coughs.

Eventually venturing out towards the beauty of the Golden Temple of

Amritsar, a Sikh guide resplendent in bright pink turban walks with us towards the temple. He tells us of Sikhism and the five Articles of faith by which Sikhs live their lives, the physical reminders of their duties, carried with them each day.

Perhaps the most visible is the turban containing their long, uncut hair, denoting living in harmony with God in dedication, self-respect and courage. In many ways, it is part of the uniform of their faith, showing a commitment to all that Sikhism entails. Their hair has a small comb hidden in it by the layers of cloth, arising as a reaction to the matted hair worn by Hindu 'renouncing the world' holy men. To a Sikh, renouncing the world means renouncing others and so the comb reminds them to act with commitment to people. His wrist is raised for me to feel the steel bracelet (Kara) encircling his arm, telling the wearer to avoid behaviour bringing shame or disgrace on themselves or others. Meanwhile a small religious dagger sits on his body, reminding its owner to always act with courage, to stand ready in defence of the weak and the oppressed. The need to live a moral life is expressed by the wearing of the Kachhehra (long shorts), denoting the need for self-control over human passions and desires. Many problems, he states, begin from this one aspect of life's temptations as, too often, we are led astray by them.

Walking along the causeway into the middle of the man made lake, the 1604 temple sits shining brilliantly in a yellow haze of 24-carat colour. We cross to the small doorway where people drop to their knees, kiss the step, before falling to their knees inside to kiss the floor. So many people prostrate themselves the orange-robed attendants work hard keeping the doorway free of bodies for the lines of still waiting pilgrims.

Physically it all seems very small to me but perhaps I'm comparing them with massive gothic buildings such as the Vatican or Notre Dame Cathedral. Many of the huge classic structures were constructed deliberately to impress and humble the visitor, but the Golden Temple does it in a different way: it is wrapped in 24-carat gold and glistens in the sun.

Standing on the water's edge under the piercing blue sky we are moved by the history of what surrounds us as our guide tells us of the Indian Army siege in 1984, to arrest 'terrorists'. Much like all use of such terms, it seems so relative: one man's terrorist is another man's freedom fighter. His story retraces the path taken by then Indian Prime Minister Indira Gandhi, of her order to the army to fight their way into the temple to arrest those inside. Days later, when the fighting was over, 83 soldiers were dead along with 492 others. Many Sikhs considered the act to be a desecration of their holiest place. Four months later the prime minister was assassinated by two of her Sikh bodyguards. 'It was a fitting end,' he quietly comments.

We feel apologetic as we wander through the Martyrs' Garden where, in 1919, British troops opened fire on a crowd who had gathered. The gathering was not only to celebrate an annual religious festival but also to protest against the silencing of the press, the introduction of arrest without trial, and the British detention of political activists. Somewhere in the region of 10,000 people were inside Jallianwala Bagh, the walled garden, when the troops opened fire. Circling a deep well into which many people leapt to escape the carnage, our guide tells us: 'The British used 1,650 bullets and the dead and wounded were left through the night. They lay as the city was placed under martial curfew and many died in the darkness as they lay injured.'

The officer in charge (General Reginald Dyer) gave the order to open fire. This single act sparked such outrage that it provided the momentum for the Nationalist (Independence) struggle for self-rule, famously set into history by Mahatma Gandhi. So it was that India moved forward while a British general's name was forever cloaked in horror and ignominy.

Standing sombrely outside the garden digesting our own history, Bernard describes a European woman who stands adjusting her hair and designer sunglasses in the mirror of a parked motorbike, before climbing into a rickshaw. Again adjusting her sunglasses, she disappears into the horn-honking melee. The contrast of this amid the squalor and dust of the street strikes us further as holiday groups fly in and out of the guest house for two-day quick-stopover sightseeing tours. No sooner have they arrived than they are gone to catch trains in carefully scheduled visits to the highlights of India. Sitting and watching the comings and goings, we see things they do not notice as they disappear into their rooms, and watch as their drivers retrieve sleeping bags to curl up in cars through the night.

Meandering through the dusty streets, where tourists do not go, we notice little things. Rickshaw drivers shadow us constantly looking for a fare as others stare at our passing. We see cows and dogs scavenging among the piles of rubbish strewn everywhere before sitting on a kerb with a group of rickshaw drivers as one shows his prized possessions: postcards, Christmas cards and letters from an English couple whom he'd pedalled around years earlier. This experience of sitting in the dust is something we treasure.

The local streets fill with parked school buses, excited girls waving at us frantically from the windows as a Sikh driver opens the door to motion others on board. Bernard answers, 'No thanks we're fine, we'll walk,' and his face splits into a wide grin; he gets the joke, turns to the occupants, and translates for the girls. They wave even more frantically at us to get on the bus. Bernard blows them all a kiss and they blow them back as we wave, laugh, and walk on by. Another small event is burnt into our memory as we wander in and out of shops where new clothes replace my bedraggled items destroyed in Karachi by a person who feared for his job if we complained.

Our appearance in the store brings it to a complete standstill. Reappearing from a dressing room in traditional Indian clothes of deep maroon, with a spare golden set for 'best', Bernard stands before me declaring, 'You look very lovely.' Sometimes he just knows when to say the right thing.

Returning to the guest house in the darkness, other guests seem startled by my transformation, admitting they didn't know of the shops nearby. Having never left the compound except by guided car or bus, they miss many simple things.

Returning to the Pakistan–Indian border on Bertha we watch the same 'closing of the border crossing' ceremony from the Indian side as we did from the Pakistani. Security is tight and there is some confusion as men and women must pass through different lines to be searched. With nobody in the female queue understanding my blindness, Bernard cannot leave me and so he becomes the only male in the female line. Shuffling forward all the men wave furiously at him from ten feet away.

Reaching the front, the military staff eventually realise Bernard is there due to my blindness rather than being gender confused. Taking over, they guide me gently forward for the briefest of searches after passing through a metal detector. Bernard meanwhile sets off the men's metal detector with a sonic scream and soldiers tell him to 'empty his pockets'. I settle into a chair that suddenly appears for me and kick myself for not bringing a Braille copy of *War and Piece* as he starts to empty his pockets. This could take some time.

Depositing corkscrews, penknives, multitools, lighters (3), cigarettes (40), baby wipes and compasses (2) I know this is only the beginning. Paracetamol and antimalarial drugs find their way out of his pockets as people stare at the growing pile. Settling deeper into my chair, I wonder if *Lord of the Rings* would have been a better choice as it might keep me awake as he continues to empty the other 35 pockets. He carries so much it often takes 20 minutes to find anything; he denies this of course, declaring, 'I know where everything is,' before going on to ask, 'Are you sure you haven't got it?'

As I sit thinking they must be regretting the simple 'empty your pockets' request, the pile gets bigger and bigger. Every currency so far encountered appears along with spanners, pliers, notebooks, pens, cameras, batteries, wallets, documents, and melted chocolate bars (4). The legs of the table start to creak under the increasing weight when he is not even half way through. Once they discover his suite has protective armour in it as well they give up. Truly, the ceremony would have been over if they had continued.

My cane (or Bernard's pockets) does its trick as a nine-foot-tall soldier leads us to a front-row seat feet away from the stamping, strutting, Indian soldiers. I feel differences between them and their Pakistani counterparts with the Indian Rangers feeling very 'British Military' in their precision. As the show unfolds I nudge Bernard with the thought. He agrees with my comparison and wonders how I picked up on it. It's nice being able to catch him out with my 'observations'. Sometimes it takes a blind person to see something.

Bernard keeps up a running commentary of the closing of the border ceremony until the event finishes with the lowering of the respective flags. His descriptions of the ornate, fan-like, headdresses are a little unclear in my mind and so he guides me towards an officer from whom he asks a simple favour. The officer bellows at a soldier who stamps across to where we stand before bending very low as he towers above Bernard who mutters, 'Christ these guys are big, I need binoculars to look up at him.' My fingers meanwhile feel the peacock-like fan headdress as Bernard tells me of the redness spreading across his face. Everybody else is shoed away by a fierce sergeant major, even bigger than the blushing soldier. Another small act in a faraway land by people who recognise the way I see the world, painting pictures into memory with fingers and people's kindness.

Wandering back to the bike a budding seven-year-old entrepreneur does not understand the words 'No thank you,' as he, and several others set out to sell us postcards, DVDs and anything else they carry. They buzz around constantly offering India flags ('only 10 rupees') and picture postcards ('best offer'), while all the time grabbing at sleeves and anything else to attract our attention. Groups of young girls constantly stop us, wanting to take pictures and each successive request means it takes a long time to walk the short distance to the bike in the fast-approaching darkness.

Two other bikes, one German and one Swiss, are now beside her and their riders appear from the dark before they sadly summarise a whole country by muttering, 'Pakistan was shit.' They round on the gathering people that they can 'Look but don't touch'. In India this is about as possible as Bernard doing without a cigarette without physical restraint.

A throng gathers around us like wide-eyed children, curiosity written all over their faces as they take in every aspect of the bike and of ourselves. The braver ones ask Bernard if they can take a photograph. The clever ones make a small request before making the larger one of sitting on the bike. As the bike is on firm ground, secure on her stand, excited people are allowed to climb on and off Bertha before hands are shaken in thanks as they have a prized picture. Like a politician, Bernard is handed children to clutch while camera lenses are pointed in his direction. Whole families gather as serious-looking men hold handlebars as smiling wives and children stand arrayed in groups behind. Meanwhile, our Swiss biker defends his bike from the foreign invader until all the photographic opportunities are expended.

We offer to lead our two compatriots into town towards the district where guest houses are to be found for the night. Secretly I think Bernard is hoping for some 'like-minded' biker time but they decline his offer.

'Which side of the road does India drive on?'

The days in Amritsar soon pass and Bertha is loaded for the journey to Delhi where we've arranged to meet George Abraham, chief executive of The Score Foundation and the founder of Blind cricket. George had contacted us nearly two years before as we sat in Land's End one evening on a journey from one end of the country to the other to test equipment. Our phone had rung and there, on the other end, was George. He'd read of our proposed route through his country and soon an invite came to visit him if we ever made it.

Winching our way over the speed bump of our home for the last few days, no longer do we cough and splutter our way through the next hour while getting lost in the back streets of Amritsar. People fall out of their doors to look at the 'spaceship' trundling down four-foot-wide alleyways as Bernard stops the bike, points up and down the 'road' and then repeats his 'fluent' Urdu for 'Delhi' (which sounds remarkably like 'Delhi' to my ears). People gather round listening. Then the laughter spreads. Guessing we are not going the right way, we turn around in a fifteen-point turn to bounce back to find the right 'road', a term very loosely defined.

The two-day journey to Delhi is our first real experience of driving in India and it is to shape our experience of the country in many ways as the standard of driving was truly appalling. Actually, 'driving' is another loose term, much like the term road. Pulling in for petrol Bernard asks an attendant 'On which side of the road do you drive in India?' 'On the left,' he innocently answers. It leaves Bernard shaking his head for some time before asking, 'Are you sure?'

As we make slow progress, cars and trucks pass on the inside, the outside, on the gravel verge, often resulting in hundreds of sharp little missiles being launched at us. Bertha sounds like she's being machine-gunned as they clatter against every surface. The air is full of the constant honking of horns. People force the bike across the road as they pass and then immediately pull in, leaving Bernard with little choice but to brake, hard, otherwise they will take the front wheel with them. Trucks and buses come straight at us on the wrong side, expecting Bertha to go off-road into the deep sand lining the edges.

The 'highway' passes through small villages where animals saunter across the road and people step out without looking. Rickshaws and tractors pull across junctions without checking if anything is coming while every vehicle has their wing mirrors folded flat. It is Chaos with a capital C as the carnage of head-on crashes litter the roadside. For the first time ever I experience Bernard and road rage. It is not pretty as I hear a car inches off the left-hand pannier and Bernard's voice through the intercom: 'Are you a fucking idiot! Where did you learn to drive, Lahore?'

Meanwhile I feel the bike tugged hard to the right to avoid the underpassing car and hear the exhausts reverberate against something solid on my right. A few hundred yards later we stop at a rare set of lights and Bertha leans sideways.

'I'll fucking punch you... you fucking idiot, you moron... if you do that again I'll kill you!'

The bike wobbles violently to the sound of a hefty metal thump.

Bernard – 'Me and road rage? I don't think I've ever experienced it before, not really. The car driver looked truly shocked as my boot put a substantial dent in his wing; a gloved fist indicated my displeasure at nearly being shoved into a concrete dividing wall as the only other optional route. Little did I know this was to be the standard for Indian driving all day and every day. I must admit, though, I was immensely proud of the – accidental – wheelie I pulled away from the lights, two-up and fully loaded.'

After our frantic introduction to Indian driving, we're relieved to arrive at Ambala. After showering and eating, Deepak introduces himself, telling how Enfield club members had been ringing each other all day with notifications about 'the spaceship' coming their way; arrangements are made to meet at a town further on the next day.

We cover the 42 km to Kurukshetra City the next morning to find a local rider has been killed in a head-on. We learn how he'd been in India for only a week, having arrived from the United States where he'd lived for many years. His friends had told him not ride in India as it would be too dangerous. Not listening, he'd set off on a friend's bike and within an hour was dead. It is a very sobering experience for us.

Bernard – It's hard to describe what it's like to ride a bike here. I don't think I could have ridden if I'd flown straight in. Naïvely I might have tried, perhaps, with my 'Western' head sifting through non-existent driving rules in an effort to anticipate certain events. It's these rules which fill your head with things that 'will not happen' and in many ways, driving is about anticipating what will, but more importantly, what will not, happen. On your first day in India, you find there are no rules.

It's a country where the mighty shall survive and these are the trucks and 4x4s. You learn very quickly to get out of their way as if you think they will stop, slow down, or move over for you, they will hit you. You can die here. Instantly. Staying alive is a fraction of a second decision, involving things you never think will happen. It goes on all day, constantly, without a break. It leaves you desperately tired as you try to stay alive.

After three months on the road through deteriorating roads and driving standards I thought I'd seen most things. Originally, the Italians were number one in 'The Worst Drivers' league table. After crossing Montenegro, I gave number one spot to the Serbians. After Pakistan I shunted them down to number two. So far, India is turning out to be a hundred times worse than anything encountered in any other country, making the Italians look considerate and sensible.

Fear is a funny thing when you realise you can die very easily and India is a frightening place for a bike rider. When all anticipation is removed, when you understand you cannot predict anything, it reduces you to surviving. Accepting that everybody is out to kill me is the only option I have left and I try to ride accordingly. It is so far above 'normal' Western defensive riding as to be on another dimension.

With their friend's death it's a sombre meeting with the club riders and very, very sad. When they lose a rider, they all feel it. It's true. Meeting other bikers on the road Bernard always says 'Drive safe' on parting, reflecting this bond that seems to exist across the world. After experiencing bikers for some time now I have to say they really are a unique set of people: kind, helpful and sincere when they meet. It really does seem to be universal. Whether in England or India, they stop to help each other. Deepak and his friends place India stickers on the bike before we set off. Leaving them to their mourning, we enter a frantic ride towards Delhi for our meeting with George Abraham.

Over the subsequent miles I can feel Bernard changing, becoming more aggressive, much like he became in Lahore. Now undertaking wagons doing 20 mph, carving his way through traffic, he tries to follow what other drivers seem to be doing. Alien and bizarre for him, he suspends instincts of 'European' rules in order to make progress.

People stop and stare as we pass by until pulling over for a stop at the roadside. Through the intercom comes the sound of Bernard chortling away as he describes a 200 foot long boat sitting in a burnt desolate field. With porthole windows and a ramp leading up to a massive wooden front door cut into the side, washing hangs out on the deck, suspended on lines; sheets and clothes are tugged by the continuous hot breeze. The boat has been immaculately restored and painted sky blue with a long drive leading to the ramp and enormous front door. I fully expect animals to be going in two by two as it sits miles from any water, but, then again, it is India. Perhaps the next Noah is in training and the world will come to know of it through a heavy Urdu accent?

On the Delhi outskirts the traffic ramps up to an unimaginable degree of density, no doubt fuelled by the 14 million inhabitants, with drivers compressing five lanes of traffic into one as everybody wants to move that extra inch forward. I can touch vehicles on either side as they creep forward with our panniers resting on the car beside us. Not an inch is spare around us and conversations can be heard clearly through open car windows. The roads deteriorate as miles of gravel and hardcore greet our eventual entry to Delhi.

Pulling over several times, trying to follow directions of people sending us all over the city, we end up 25 km in the wrong direction. After crossing and criss-crossing Delhi, it dawns on us that distances and time estimates are all meaningless. When somebody tells you 'just straight' it can mean anything and 'five km' can mean 25 in a place where people will not admit they do not know where you are looking for. A lifetime after entering the city and after several phone calls to George, we pull up outside his organisation.

'Why would you want to be with a blind woman?'

To say we are warmly received by George (who has a sight impairment himself) and his staff is no understatement as the office comes to a standstill on our arrival. The Score Foundation is a nationwide trust offering information through its telephone helpline (the first in India) and its website Eyeway. A radio programme is also aired, something akin to BBC Radio 4's In Touch in England and the Foundation handles emails, letters and telephone calls from all over the country, questions relating to employment, education, discrimination and legal matters.

The office sits underground down several flights of dark stairs and, compared to UK organisations, the contrast is stark. Little seems wasted on imposing edifices as every rupee is directed towards services. Settling deeper into chairs for a long interview about the journey, life, the universe and everything around blindness, an hour later we find the interview was not recorded. The sounds of our laughter can be heard through the office on finding out that, perhaps, two sight-impaired people may have needed a little assistance to make sure the correct record button was pressed!

Over the next few days George and Siddarth Sharma put together a schedule of engagements for us. Siddarth lost his sight in a motorcycle accident as he drove into a black-painted barrier at night, which the police had helpfully placed across the road at face height. Hitting it, his vision ended with the impact. Nobody was ever held to account for the stupidity of such an act and compensation is a land of distant dreams for ordinary people caught up in such things in India. Thus Sid (as everybody calls him) was left to salvage what he could from his new life in the dark. Meeting George when the first World Blind Cricket Cup was being organised, he became involved in the promotion of the event and his talent for PR was discovered. The engagements Sid and George arrange for us involve visits to various organisations, and interviews with New Delhi TV, India's major channel, and the largest paper the *Hindustan Times*.

Early the next morning, a car arrives from the TV station for our first live interview to be broadcast at 8am. Listening to the news, I am struck by all the stories of robberies, car crashes and the impact of financial meltdown on India; it feels like home, in an Indian way.

The presenters use our journey as a contrast to all the bad news noting that, occasionally, there are good stories; stories about everyday people doing extraordinary things. It is strange to think of the millions of people watching their TV while our images flicker across the screens as we talk of the wish to show people that, yes, there is so much a blind person can do. It takes faith. Both in yourself and others. I am lucky, having both of these things.

From the TV studios another car takes us the to the Delhi Boys' School where a wonderful morning passes with pupils fascinated by the concept of a Blind woman going around the world on a motorcycle. I was very touched, and humbled, to be asked to present the Achievement awards at the Assembly and it was a very moving experience when you think of the hardships people have in this huge country. Life is hard here for many people, but to be blind is to make it so much harder still. When the children sing at the end of the assembly I listen to a hundred voices accompanied by a young boy playing the harmonium feet away from where I stand, a distinctive, and Indian, sound.

Bernard will forever remember the walk from the headmaster's office to the assembly hall when the headmaster took his hand to lead us both through the building. In the hall itself Bernard takes pictures of the proceedings and later on it is apparent something has been lost in the translation; the headmaster thought Bernard was partially sighted. Bernard, meanwhile, thought the headmaster was just being friendly.

In the afternoon, the celebrity reporter Itee Dewan of *The Times* talks about our thoughts and experiences across the journey before settling onto Pakistan. In all sincerity we answer that the Pakistani people were fantastic (but can't drive) and were very kind during our journey. It was a very good interview and so funny as Bernard recalled managing to pass 'industrial-sized' condom machines without actually seeing them in a German hotel in Kosovo.

The afternoon is very poignant at the Centre for Blind Women where 20 women ask us a huge range of questions. Their curiosity knows no bounds and it was very sad to listen to their stories about what it means to be blind, and a woman, in India. Questions fly at us about relationships and many questions were directed at Bernard, and how a sighted person feels about a blind partner. The centre manager had prepared us for this by talking about the culture in India which frowns on a sighted/non-sighted relationship. The group is totally fascinated by Bernard and our relationship. The single most important question they ask Bernard is: 'Men do not want you if you are blind; why would you want to be with a blind woman?'

I feel Bernard pause as he thinks before responding: 'If you knew Cathy you would not have to ask the question.' The women break into spontaneous applause.

Neena speaks of how her husband promptly divorced her when her eyesight started to fail through the onset of retinitis pigmentosa, as she was now of 'little use to him'. I felt both sad (for her) and grateful (for myself) that my world is so different, despite us having the same condition. As she talks of her painful separation and of being 'cast off', I was mindful that it is only when you meet such differences that you realise how thankful you should be for your own life. When she'd finished telling us of her experiences, Bernard asked if she knew what RP really stood for? She shook her head shyly.

'RP can also stand for Really Pretty.'

Her face lit up and colour spread through her cheeks, blushing furiously as her friends laugh and clap loudly.

Hearing stories of young girls losing their sight through undiagnosed glaucoma, of being confined within family homes with no prospects of a career or of forming relationships, it is so hard to listen. Their lives are summed up, or reduced down, to being a poor match for marriage (still largely arranged) and of all the visits this was the one Bernard was most affected by; how the girls desperately just wanted to know there was somebody out there for them.

As we talk about being blind, my own past, and the fact that Bernard is not my first sighted 'husband', I recount how I ended up alone and unsure about the future. With the loss of my husband, Peter, after 19 years of marriage it was possible for me to reinvent myself through education. Thus I met Bernard and arrived in India riding on the back of his motorcycle. The overriding message I tried to send to them was a simple one: that sometimes life presents you with an opportunity. They may be few and far between, but they are always there at some point and should be grabbed with both hands. Never be frightened of change, as you never know where it will lead or when the next chance will come along.

While our conversations explored many different directions, covering things such as how it is possible to live alone as a blind person, guide dogs and travelling alone, the underlying question always returned: relationships and the need to have someone in their lives. It came across very powerfully throughout our time at the centre and it left us both very sad, and much moved. The extent of 'need' in the room was palpable. We could feel it, encircling us. Powerful, emotional yearning. The centre manager later told us that in India these women 'are doubly disabled for they are both blind and women'.

It is a very powerful statement from a person who knows far more than we do what it means to experience sight loss in this economic engine room of the world. Leaving the centre very subdued, Neena was etched firmly into both our hearts.

Over the following days many different institutions and providers of support, advice and hope for people with sight loss show us how hard life can be and it leads into a very wide-ranging radio interview. George returns to the level of support received from UK organisations for the blind in the preparation for the journey, and while on the road. He shakes his head in puzzlement at our two-year struggle to gain any support at all before leaving the country. 'If it had been here, I would have had you riding with Bollywood stars on National TV, and the papers would have had you everywhere. There is no doubt they would have all been fighting each other to do it,' he announces. His sentiment leaves us, this time, shaking our heads in agreement at the opportunities lost.

Exploring my early life as a young girl growing up with failing eyesight, my experiences in specialist and mainstream schools are trawled along with the time traversing the fourteen countries so far. Finishing the interview, George tells me it will be broadcast as 'a special', in its entirety, as 'it's too good to cut down, too funny'.

As the daylight ends, Sid invites us to visit Rahul, who has recently returned to India after fourteen years in Mozambique, and who later that evening invites us to stay at his home. Thinking about it for at least two seconds before accepting, our belongings are packed from a completely trashed hotel room. Outside, Rahul stands with many others as our spaceship is readied for launch. He explains my blindness to nearby people along with the purpose of our journey as a man comments: 'In India he wouldn't marry her never mind take her round the world on a motorbike.' Sadly, the sentence sums up everything people have told us of what it means to be a blind woman in India.

Moving into Rahul's, we spend our evenings talking with Sid and Rahul, sharing our thoughts and perceptions about everything experienced. It's good to talk to Sid as I sometimes feel Indian blind people are very isolated, having little, if any, opportunity to talk through feelings, barriers and problems they encounter.

In England I have been very fortunate to live a balanced life, having many friends who are blind and also many who have sight. I have never believed that a blind person should exist in either/or because it limits and restricts opportunities to live a full and complete life. Some visually impaired people spend most of their time among the blind and partially sighted, and have little opportunity for personal interaction with sighted people. In India, I'm not sure if it's possible to live such a balanced life, as opportunities for independent movement are so restricted.

Neither Sid nor George use a long cane but rely totally on sighted assistance, largely due to the environment. On talking to Sid, he says if you turn in any direction in India you will find someone to help you. With a population of 1.2 billion this is hardly surprising. Indeed Sid has what Rahul calls 'a man Friday': full-time domestic help. In India this is a way of life for many as labour is so cheap; if you have a reasonable income, everybody seems to have live-in 'servants'.

Sid asks about daily life at home, my gadgets to aid me in daily living, things such as a colour identifier which helps me match clothes. Long conversations take place about using Braille, which he gave up in frustration, never being able to develop the speed to make it really 'useful'. I too understand this frustration as I learnt it much later in life, resulting in a much slower speed, in reading and writing. Even after many years of using Braille, I am a tortoise compared to many of my friends who learned it as a child (when I could still see something).

In many ways I'd rejected Braille as a teenager as 'it was for blind people'. I was not blind. Even when teachers tried to tell me it would be useful, I refused to contemplate learning it. It was for 'blind people'. As a teenage girl staring at the world through misty failing eyes I would have none of it. Failing eyesight makes you run and hide from the truth and it was years before I understood what my teachers had tried to tell me: Braille is a weapon in the armoury of tools. Perhaps the saying 'you cannot put an old head on young shoulders' will always be true.

Over the days Rahul and Sid look after us we come to understand nuances of Indian life, culture and history. As I wander in and out of shops to explore clothes, jewellery and artefacts of Indian culture, I have to buy something even though Bernard witters on about the lack of space. As always, he relents in a small Tibetan shop where a necklace becomes mine for the princely sum of 250 rupees (under £3). Sitting and eating muffins and drinking vanilla smoothies, the hustle and bustle of the roadside passes by.

Visiting the famous Red Fort my fingers trace the long history of the Mughal Empire and the subsequent invasion by the British who stripped many aspects of the fort's ornate and beautifully crafted gold leaf decorations.

Prising them from the walls with bayonets, all that remains are black stains showing the remnants of glue. Many people became very rich when they returned to England to sell off a part of history.

On our final day in Delhi we lunch with George Abraham, his wife Ruper and youngest daughter Tara and talk turns to our onward journey to the Taj Mahal. On hearing of our next destination we set off across Delhi with his wife's car horn blowing her way through the traffic. Telling us how her horn was once broken and she could not drive the car for days, it amuses Bernard. Ending up in a shop, a very lovely marble model of the Taj Mahal is placed in my hands to explore, later bought for me as a gift by George and his wife.

A further package is sent home containing all of the leaflets and booklets accumulated on our travels along with Bernard's leather jacket, given as a gift by the Istanbul agent, Cem, who once hoped to buy a bike himself; years later the jacket still hung in his wardrobe waiting for the arrival of the bike. Then Bernard arrived and the jacket was released from the confines of the darkened space. Carefully folded, a treasured memento, it is packed into the third box sent home so far.

The morning of leaving seems strange as we gather outside Rahul's, sad to leave but knowing it's time to move on. We can feel it. Bertha calls from where she is parked and her voice has been heard for days now. Also, we haven't slept well due to the incessant traffic noise filling the night air with car horns blaring constantly. As a blind person the city is a wall of noise and it can be very startling, tiring and disorienting.

Setting off alone down the road it feels good, and bad, to be on the move again. After several days of rest everything seems harder; the cars seem closer; the horns seem louder; the braking of Bertha heavier; the bike moves far more than I remember.

Meanwhile, people blast past us in a wave of horns inches away from my legs. Crawling through the multiple jams, I hear people talking through car windows, so close are they. Bernard is quiet. I know he is struggling to adapt, to find a way through the frantic chaos. With fingers crossed we struggle out of Delhi unscathed until eventually finding ourselves on the road to Agra, the home of the Taj Mahal.

'Truly, they have to be felt to appreciate the craftsmanship!'

The first few hours of travel are very, very stressful and in each small town we run a gauntlet of animals, cars, pushbikes and rickshaws. The police also have a really annoying habit of putting barriers across parts of roads to funnel everything into a small gap, causing huge logjams, Bertha moving at such a slow pace that bicycles pass us. People aim for the smallest spaces and sometimes the bike moves sideways as cars push past to the sound of panniers being scraped. It startles me.

At one rare traffic light the whole junction grinds to halt while people look at everything on the bike. Getting out of their cars, they come and peer at us. It becomes too much for Bernard as he wills the lights to change; people reach into the cockpit, touch instruments, the Sat Nav, press the horn, the indicators; 20 hands reach to explore.

While this goes on street sellers come and grab at us, trying to sell bunches of brown bananas, trinkets and endless other items. Bernard disables the engine with the 'kill switch' as with all the jostling from so many people he is worried we'll go over. I can hear him saying, 'Please change, come on, change' and when they do, a frantic scuttle occurs as people launch themselves back into cars. We pull off, relieved.

Petrol stops are the same. Everything halts on our arrival and we're instantly surrounded by 50 people poking at everything on the bike and asking a stream of the same questions answered a trillion times before. It's so tiring; the concept of personal space does not exist. The fuel pumps often do not zero – a common scam that sees you paying hundreds of rupees for fresh air. You have to insist on change as attendants go missing when you hand over a 1,000 rupee note for 800 rupees of petrol. Bernard stands while people nod at his request for the change. Everybody smiles constantly and Bernard starts to practise a curious neck movement signifying 'Yes, no, maybe, certainly, I haven't got a clue'.

Sometimes we search for an empty section of road so we can stretch our legs. It can take miles to find. Finding one, we get off and work our muscles.

The clicking sound of Bernard's lighter is often accompanied by him groaning as people appear from nowhere and everywhere, from deserted countryside, from cars that suddenly stop alongside us. Even motorcyclists coming the other way pull over, turn around, and come back to sit feet away, looking at us. Always looking. The cigarette is smoked quickly before we flee up the road to escape. The only personal space is on the road, riding Bertha, but always moving. It makes the days too long, covering far more mileage than we should. Other riders say 200 km is a good day in India while we cover over 400. We're tired, irritated and dispirited.

The roads are full of holes filled with sand, branches or bushes, and we weave around some and a quick 'Hang on' tells me to prepare for a resounding 'bang' followed by severe jolts as Bertha shudders from the impact. I feel the shocks through my body and wonder how it feels through the handlebars. Crossing and re-crossing carriageways with diversion after diversion, the 'road' to the other side is often little more than a ramp of gravel and loose rock hardcore. 'No problem, just a bit of loose stuff,' comes through my helmet and I brace for the shifting and weaving which comes with this sentence. Skipping and sliding through surfaces which, months ago, would have had Bernard stressing and getting off to walk the road is now simply 'a bit of loose stuff'.

The weather is warm and fields stretch all around us as Bernard describes what he sees: canvas shelters or, at best, mud structures with whole generations of families gathered around the small plot they exist on. Women carry enormous bundles of branches and straw and we marvel at the toughness, the strength of people who live under such circumstances. Poverty is all around along the highways and byways off the tourist route.

Entering Agra, Bernard nervously watches the setting sun in his wing mirrors. As bad as daylight driving is, it is ten times worse arriving in a new town and looking for accommodation at dusk or in darkness. Following the signs for the Taj Mahal a rickshaw shoots across the road in front of us with no warning to pick up a fare on our left. The bike skids sideways under heavy braking and I brace myself for what ever is to come. The front of the bike dives and I am thrown to the right but we stop safely as a stream of oaths comes through my helmet. Bernard describes the passenger leaping into the rickshaw without it even stopping and the driver's maniacal grin as he turns and looks at us.

We find a hotel with somewhere for the bike and gratefully climb off, staff running down the steps to welcome us past the wandering cows that live on rubbish piles nearby. Unpacking and settling in, the noise of the evening is compounded because it's the wedding season. Streets reverberate with loud music as elaborate processions make their way up and down the road announcing the happy event. Behind us another celebration is in full swing with enthusiastic and out-of-tune Karaoke singers. Constant horn honking and wild dogs barking add to the cacophony going on unabated throughout the night, with no rest, no stillness.

The visit to Agra is our chance to visit one of the Seven Wonders of the World. Having explored the marble model that George bought in Delhi I hoped it would be easier to appreciate the layout and structure. We employ a rickshaw driver for the whole day, a lovely man who drops us off at the 'quiet' south entrance where we enter through tight security screening.

The Taj Mahal is a tomb built in 1648 by an emperor for his beloved wife who died giving birth to her fourteenth child. Wanting to build something extravagant, something magnificent, he truly succeeded. So far beyond extravagant, it is a testimony to the 20,000 workers who toiled in its construction for 22 years. The story of beauty and love, however, is ever so slightly spoiled by the Emperor having ordered the stonemasons' hands to be cut off when the structure was completed. In this way, people tell us, he wanted to ensure it could never be repeated. Whether true or not, it seems just a little drastic, but regardless, the intricacy of the engraving on the marble surfaces is superb.

Truly, they have to be felt to appreciate the craftsmanship. Using sight alone does not testify to the skill of these men according to Bernard who, closing his eyes and touching, came to appreciate the sheer beauty, the fantastic smoothness of the carvings: incredible, astonishing, ornate patterns swirling over smooth marble surfaces in unbroken delicacy. Words can never suffice to describe their skills. The emperor himself was later imprisoned by his own son during a coup and he sat in the Red Fort 2 km away from where his rooms looked across the river to the Taj Mahal.

Visiting the 1,000 year-old fort itself 35 guides instantly pounce on us, all offering the definitive tour of this walled palace city. Much as with everything concerning India, what follows is a round of extensive negotiations over the price until agreed. Unfortunately, then you have to argue all over again when the tour finishes. It is sad really as our tour was conducted by an elderly man rushing us around as he counted the rupees of his next tour before ours was even finished.

I suppose we can never really understand what it must mean to try to earn a living in this country. Our appearance will signal rupee signs flashing and the colour of our skin makes us rich and, relatively, we always will be but each and every day a little more drips away as everybody sees us in this way. Paying the guide for his rushed tour, we return to the grounds on our own with Bernard reading every board and information sheet available in the grounds. We play like two schoolchildren at the 'telephone exchange', talking between rooms due to the construction of the walls, marvelling at the water supply circulating through channels in walls. It leaves us wondering at the cleverness of the liquid air conditioning; keeping the water cool against the cold marble surfaces.

Again the British presence is commented on in conversations around us as missing gold leaf is pointed out, plundered by the colonial rulers on arrival, leaving their tell-tale dark stains, nothing left but the emptiness of the lost beauty of what once was. We also learn of the ex-Emperor's failing eyesight and of how he resorted to holding a diamond to his eye to focus on the whiteness representing the final resting place of his love. For eight years he was imprisoned in the Red Fort until his eventual death in 1666. Fittingly, he was interred beside his wife within the structure.

Wandering through the Taj Mahal and the final resting place beside his wife, it would have saddened him to hear the level of noise in the Mausoleum. The whole thing feels wrong, but perhaps it merely reflects India as attendants blow shrill whistles to keep people moving with hard marble surfaces bouncing sounds in a cacophony of noise. Painful to the ears, after a short time I have to retreat from the noise.

Arriving back at the hotel after a very long, and mentally tiring day we find there is still, for three days so far, no hot water. Without this it is almost impossible to remove the permanent layer of dust, dirt, and sweat that sticks to you in a permanent oppressive film. Some days it is the only thing that can restore you as, once again, Bernard attempts to resolve the distinct 'lack of hot water' with our constantly smiling manager.

Bernard:	'You remember I told you my wife will kill you today if we still have no hot water?'
Manager:	'Sir?'
Bernard:	'Have you settled your affairs and made your will?'
Manager:	'You want hot shower sir, I turn boiler on!'
Bernard:	'No, no, you can turn boiler on, but no hot water comes.'
Manager:	'Hot in five minutes'
Bernard:	'It might be hot, but not in our room.'
Manager:	'Maybe ten minutes sir, you want me to turn boiler on?'
Bernard:	'You do not understand!'
Manager:	'Understand sir, want shower, I turn boiler on. You have cigarette and water will be hot.'

Bernard:	'it will not be hot!'
Manager:	'yes, yes, very hot.'
Bernard:	Bangs head on desk in true Fawlty Towers fashion much to alarm of manager and staff.
Manager:	'So sir, you are saying water will not be hot?'
Bernard:	(lifting head off desk) 'Praise the Lord, you understand!'
Manager:	'I will turn boiler on for you'

And so it goes on.

In the end, as I wait patiently, the staff deliver a very big bucket of hot water to the room with enormous smiles. In the best 'customer focused evaluation principle', they insist Bernard tests the bucket to check the water is truly hot. When he nearly burns his hand a big 'Problem solved?' grin appear on their faces. Sitting in the room with the staff hovering around the bucket we start laughing. Helplessly. They stand watching, puzzled, before leaving, quietly closing the door behind them as we sit and giggle, finally accepting a simple fact. It is India.

'Which way are the wagons going?'

We leave Agra at dawn. Pulling onto the road at 6.45, there's no need to dodge the hundreds of missiles (sorry, vehicles, cows, rickshaws, pushbikes, dogs and beggars) coming at us from every direction. Even the bad roads do not seem as bad as no competition exists with other users for the 'no pothole' route.

The road from Agra leads us to a much more rural India than experienced so far and troops of monkeys cross the road as we gently slow down, working our way around them as they groom each other in the morning light. Stopping to watch the playful groups, Bernard describes a man on a small motorcycle throwing fruit to them as they scamper across to pick up the offerings before running back to families. Youngsters cling to mothers as they congregate to the excited chatter of dozens of them milling around the road. We sit and listen before breaking the sound with Bertha's engine firing up.

There's a heavy mist or smog which reminds Bernard of a long-ago England as it billows and rolls across the road. It limits our speed, making it hard to avoid the potholes as they appear abruptly with no warning in front of our wheels no matter how Bernard tries to avoid them. As the mist starts to lift semi-deserted roads lead us towards Kanpur, roughly halfway to our destination, Lucknow.

Things start to go very badly wrong on entering the outskirts of Kanpur as the Lucknow signs take us down into traffic hell. Space on the 'road' is at a premium and everybody thinks we are little more than a buzzing local 100cc Honda Hero, i.e. get out of the way. Bertha climbs speed bumps the size of Everest, the bottom of the bike grounding with a loud bang as no quarter is given; if we stop it will be hard to get moving again. Thus junctions are approached with the intention of not stopping and it is a very dangerous, and scary, way of riding but there is no other way in India – it is what everybody does. To ride any other way is more dangerous as nobody expects anyone to stop.

Indian wagons hover inches away as we bounce through exploded road surfaces, feeling like they have been shelled while trying to find the road to Lucknow. Fighting our way through the heaving mass of metal we end up back on the 'highway' with no signs for Lucknow. Three times the return journey involves the same frustrating fight through this hell. In the end we stop short of a chaotic junction while Bernard sits watching the traffic, trying to work out which way to go. Sitting puffing away on his favourite anti-stress stick in front of 50 people who surround us, description of the carnage around us fills my ears while, from somewhere, I hear Gordon's voice (from Athens) in my head. It poses a question. 'Which way are the wagons going?'

Looking around the wall-to-wall traffic he sits waiting, counting wagons and directions. Hopefully, we follow two of them, with their brightly coloured tailboards declaring 'Blow Horn please' in mural displays begging Bernard to blast away for all he is worth. He does not disappoint them as eventually progress is made towards the NH25, indicated by a tiny barely visible sign. Unfortunately, it was not before ending up in a tangled heap as a rickshaw driver comes from our right and Bernard has to choose: hit the rickshaw or lay it down. So it was we end up with our very first – but very gentle – meeting of the ground as he manages to stop the bike sideways before we fall off. Within seconds, hundreds of people surround us as Bernard picks me up, reassuring me that we are perfectly safe.

Two police appear and help Bernard lift the bike as petrol pours from the tank filling my nostrils with the fumes. They want him to clear the junction by pushing the bike away but he refuses, explaining my blindness, how I have to come first. They understand and patiently wait as he reattaches dislodged equipment before I take my place back on the seat. A huge crowd has gathered and the front wheel nudges people out of the way before, several hundred yards up the road, we pull over. The lighter clicks several times as Bernard calms himself with nicotine. At times like this I wish I smoked. It may have helped conquer the shaking in my own hands.

We set off again, into even worse road conditions as diversions take us over unsurfaced roads thick with dust and slow-moving traffic. We go right through the centre of a busy market where gravel and stone chips fly in all directions from wagons all around us. Moving forward with inches of space between vehicles it takes forever to travel several hundred metres. With the driving conditions, it is hard for Bernard to watch for hotels, traffic, bad roads, and keep us alive, all at the same time. Leaving Kanpur, the road goes onwards to the NH25 towards Lucknow. We resign ourselves to travelling further.

Bernard's second real 'road rage' occurs shortly afterwards, approaching the rear of a car following a wagon on a dual carriageway. Bertha moves over to overtake while he watches the driver's eyes in his rear view mirror. Just as we reach the back of the car, accelerating to overtake, the car pulls out. The only thing I know is the feeling of being launched sideways and the feeling of hard acceleration.

> *Bernard – I have a choice, brake hard and probably hit the car or accelerate and aim for the gap between car and barrier. It was just one of those choices. The bike shuddered and wobbled massively as I threw it hard right and then left, accelerating to go for the gap. We missed him, but only just. As I pull past the wagon, the car passes me as I decelerate and the driver scowls. The scowl sent me over the edge to hurl abuse through his open window; furiously punching his mirrors, pointing to them, and using two fingers to indicate use your eyes. Then I close my fist, point to him, and let him know my intent. I would willingly have got off the bike there and then and gone for him. I was furious. Unimaginably out of control.*

Listening to Bernard's tirade of every unprintable word in his description of what he will do to the driver, his family, his descendants, and anybody who vaguely knows him, the car drives off. Bernard, meanwhile, pulls over and ponders what is happening to him as I stand waiting for the adrenaline to work its way out of his system, his hands shaking violently. Setting off, the day continues in the same vein with unremitting pressure and stress as we fight our way further east.

> *Bernard – The road from Agra to Lucknow is my worst experience so far. It had all of the madness of Lahore and Delhi along with shocking roads deteriorating further when you think it can never, never, get any worse. There is no road, nothing but gravel, hardcore, dust and traffic. My heart pounds in my chest. By the time I reach the outskirts of Lucknow I hate everything about India. Absolutely. Completely. Totally. I want out.*

Pulling up into the town exhausted and emotionally drained after 448 km, the hotel staff pay the price of our accumulated experiences as within an hour of arriving Bernard complains with brutal honesty about the standards of the hotel (which charges more than a good hotel in London on a bank holiday). He savages the restaurant staff and when our room is invaded by the noise of an extremely loud wedding celebration he bounds down to reception where he unleashes his frustration at the manager, refusing to pay if he is kept awake all night. Needless to say, they change our room. From that point people walk around him warily. Sitting in Lucknow trying to summon up the courage to go on, we pull apart what is happening to us, trying to make sense of the changes.

Emotionally, it feels like we're falling apart. Now I constantly startle at unexpected sounds or movements, feeling frightened for hours on end in a state of breathlessness verging on panic. I spend my days surrounded by noise, waiting for a sudden catastrophic impact against the bike. I'm tired and stressed far beyond anything I have ever known. Bernard boils over quicker and quicker at each new event, so unlike the person I know him to be. India is pulling us apart psychologically in different ways, reducing us down to little more than two frightened rabbits looking for some bolthole for refuge.

As we talk a small light illuminates a feeling I have. Struggling for coherent words, I search for meaning. Slowly, it dawns on me: Indian drivers use their horns to let everybody know they're there. They don't look before pulling out because they're listening. If they hear no horn, they pull out. The horn is the signal. It's the clarion call, the bugle, the claxon of universal understanding. It shouts, 'I'm here!' I wonder why we've not understood sooner. As it fits together perfectly with our experiences, I wonder how to bring this insight to Bernard who is now so psychologically fragile. On top of all his feelings of fragility, anger, fear and insecurity, how does a blind woman tell him he has missed something fundamental? Something obvious, perhaps. I gently broach it with him. He quietly listens to my thoughts.

For a few moments he sits silent, then admits this makes sense in explaining some of the lunacy he is seeing. My reasoning turns his understanding on its head as he struggles to put into words the shock of what he is becoming, what the driving is doing to him. Emotion pours out of him as his voice recounts his irrational responses to hotel staff, and of how he is now so aggressive. He does not have to put it into words for me. I know. I can readily feel the escalating temper, threatening to rapidly boil over into barely controlled savagery. It's a profound change and frightening to listen to. Each successive occasion brings him closer and closer to some cliff edge of violence.

Like all gradual erosions, I worry he'll reach some critical point where he'll be unable to draw back from physical violence. I worry as he's changing into something barely recognisable at times. India is pulling him apart, boiling him down to core survival. Either he runs, or he fights. So far, he has run.

After we talk our way through feelings, he promises to start practising movement of his left thumb to prepare for furious bouts of 'horn pressing'. His mood slowly lightens as part of his old self reappears. He declares his need to instantly prove his sincerity to me, his willingness to comply with the thoughts of a blind woman on how to drive a motorcycle in India. Convincing me he has actually dropped to the floor in the foyer, of his struggle to perform one-thumbed press-ups, I sit laughing at the likely image.

Lots of exaggerated huffing and puffing occurs from below me while people walk past, no doubt watching the performance of 'the Angry Englishman'. As I sit laughing, his arms encircle me in a hug to try to drive away the insanity of where our mental world has taken us. I return it.

The road to Gorakhpur

Leaving Lucknow early the next morning his first attempts of 'Hello, I'm here' are very 'British', involving small timid 'beep, beeps'. It is a very apologetic sound that, over the day, becomes as loud and boisterous as anything else on the road. He beeeeeped anything and everything. If it moved he blew his horn. If it didn't move he blew his horn. Sheep, cattle, birds, trucks, cars, camels and hobbling grannies felt the wrath of his left thumb. He begins to wonder, with great concern, if his horns are actually loud enough, the BMW ones not being quite masculine enough. Perhaps they need extensions?

Talking the previous night a revelation of such startling clarity had come to us: get out of India. Enough is enough. We need to go before the country kills us. I'm not overstating things. It's a simple truth. The odds of getting through this in one piece worsen each day. Neither do we mind admitting it. After all there's nothing to prove: no illusions about 'credibility' or personal 'challenges' to drive across the country. Many other riders simply avoid India completely. Our challenge is to circle the world on our own and come back in one piece. In India, your mortality is thrown in your face every minute of every day and it's not a good feeling.

These feelings are manifested each morning when Bernard now disappears into the toilets as he prepares the bike. The first time I hear him being sick he confesses it's been this way for several days. No longer does he want to ride Bertha. No longer does he want to plough through the chaos, with every minute involving the wait for an Indian truck to kill us. Thus, we decide to head north for Nepal. Our first run north on the NH28C to the border is blocked by trucks stuck in deep sand, forcing us to take the NH28 towards Gorakhpur, where another road north leads to Nepal.

Bernard is now in ultra-defensive mode, using cars, trucks, bicycles or anything at all to act as a shield in front of him. The concept 'your side of the road' has no meaning as vehicles constantly appear on the wrong side around corners towards us. He now pulls over and waits for something to pass him before he tails them, letting them take the risk of head-on collisions as we pass ten or more twisted wrecks everyday.

Bernard – About 50 km short of Gorakhpur the road stops and we're diverted off the highway to descend into a lunar landscape which looks impossible for a road bike, as if thousands of mortar-bombs have exploded, or an air force has carpet-bombed the surface. The potholes are close together, leaving no path through. The wagons bounce up and down at 10 mph as they chuck up white dust in our faces. It is impossible to ride under these conditions, you bash through them.

It is not possible to ride slowly as the traffic is too dense, the bike too heavy, so we are launched up and down through the holes. The only way to survive is to drive quicker than I think I can, all the time hoping the forward momentum will allow us to go from pothole to pothole. While smashing through this landscape, 4x4s are beeping their horns to pass 2 mph quicker than we are travelling. Wagons doing 12 mph want to pass others doing 10 mph and everybody wants to pass us as we hammer the bike through these conditions.

The shocks and jolts are truly tremendous and it feels impossible to get through this without coming off. My hands go numb from the impacts and every muscle in my body hurts with the shocks and bangs. Physically it's torment, like riding a bucking jackhammer all day while keeping clear – by inches – of vehicles all around us. It is motorcycling hell.

How Bernard feels I can only imagine but I hate it. I absolutely hate it. It is the most frightening thing I have ever encountered as every second, for hours and hours on end, my mind streams crashing pictures of wagons hitting Bertha and then running over us. Every bang means we are coming off. Constantly bracing myself for the next shock or impact, my head, neck, even my ears hurt from the obsessive horn blowing inches away from us. I am truly frightened and willing it to all end.

As bad as I feel I know it has to be truly horrendous to manage the bike under these inch-perfect conditions with wagons bouncing all around us. Bernard cannot speak and all I can do is imagine. I don't like what I am imagining. Wanting to shout 'stop the bike, stop the bike, let me off' I keep quiet. I know if stopping was possible he would do it. Gladly. All we can do is endure.'

Bernard tries to lighten our experiences at one point as we crash through the potholes asking, 'Have you still got the fillings in your teeth?' Retribution is a wonderful thing as a few kilometres down the road a bridge on his teeth falls out; sometimes he really should not tempt fate. Now when he smiles two broken teeth show a gap for the world to see what the road to Gorakhpur did to him as we arrive in the city destroyed; emotionally, physically and psychologically.

Pulling up at the city entrance exhausted, a young man appears alongside on a scooter. Bernard asks him about a hotel and he merrily sets off with us struggling to follow through the traffic. Bernard tells me he is mentally shutting down, having to berate himself for these final miles: swearing at himself, criticising himself, all to maintain his concentration. Talking through what he can see in the same way as an advanced driving test, he keeps his focus.

The young man will never know how much he helped us and how grateful we were; to him, it was a simple act but to us it is a sign of the contradictions of India: tragic driving conditions involving wonderful people. Kind and considerate, but ruthless on the road, it is a land of smiling and intensely curious people who will kill you in a second by their driving. Sometime later the little scooter turns into a drive leading to a hotel where we fall off the bike to shake hands with our young companion who simply smiles happily before setting off into the traffic. Perhaps he will tell his friends and family of acting as the vanguard to the huge foreign motorcycle he led through the city. Stumbling into the hotel, we collapse in all senses.

Bernard – Sitting in the middle of the hotel room I am completely finished. My body feels numb. Worse than that, psychologically I am destroyed while my emotions are beyond anything understandable. I am finished. Staring at a bottle of beer, I hear Cathy calling from the bedroom. She needs something but I cannot move. I really cannot move. Even words are hard to find in the big blank space my brain has become. I feel paralysed. Eventually I put together a sentence, word by word, to call into the next room saying, 'Give me ten minutes, that's all, ten minutes. Just leave me alone. Please. Enough Cathy, leave me alone.'

Eventually Bernard drags himself off the floor and for the next few days the slightest thing causes me to jump like a frightened rabbit. It takes three days for the memory to begin to fade, to become manageable. All through this time I don't want to be left alone. Neither can I face the prospect of getting back on the bike and Bernard is the same. We are both shattered with levels of stress reactions that need more than sleep, which is elusive, to repair.

This last journey seals our agreement: get out of India as fast as possible, by any means, by any route. We are paranoid about road conditions and it results in us checking and rechecking maps and information on the internet: feeding our paranoia with more and more unanswered questions. Little things hit me hard, impacting profoundly, minor things previously shrugged off now clash loudly in the person I have become. I start to react badly to events. To people. To anything.

One evening in the car park we are approached by a group of men and one comments to Bernard: 'You are a great man.' He has heard this before, usually responding with pointing at me and saying: 'She is an even greater woman.' It tickles me when he says this. But not this time. Not now. More than anything I feel annoyed, angry. In my mind people appear to be saying: 'She is blind and a burden, why do you do this?' Bernard, in his naïvety takes the comment to simply mean: 'You've brought a bike all the way from England.'

It's not meant in this way. I've heard it before, in Pakistan, in India. To me, it's building on what was said to Neena, and the other women in Delhi who suffered rejection. Their blindness summed up with the sentences, thoughts expressing 'you are blind and no use to me'. Inevitably people eventually believe it, the inability to contribute to another's life in any way. To be 'meaningless'. Discarded in all senses. It's terrible to be so sensitive, to question your very existence in this way. Feelings of being useless, of little value as a person, with no contribution to make. Worthless. How I hate what I am thinking, what I am feeling right now. The world and Blindness with a capital 'B'. Fear and loneliness for some. Welcome to the adventure. Welcome to a small part of my learning.

It will never be possible to know what is in people's hearts when they say these things, or when they think these things. But, in many ways, this journey was always about challenging those thoughts, those perceptions. The meeting of people on roads, in cafes, hotels, or petrol stations should allow this as it is what we do, every day, away from the newspaper, TV or radio interviews that make little inroads into people's thoughts about blindness. Like everything else in life, it is about starting with the little things and then, perhaps, bigger things can change. It is about shifting entrenched attitudes.

First I have to move my own mental world back to what it once was. It takes several days before, mentally, we feel well enough to leave Gorakhpur, to head back out onto the road to Nepal. We're both very nervous. Neither of us wants to get back onto the bike, or to even think about it, but we have no choice. For us there is no backup team to turn to, no support vehicles, nothing but our own will and determination to get through this.

On the morning of departure Bernard disappears into the toilet once the bike is repacked. All too soon I hear the familiar retching sounds until he has nothing left as his meagre breakfast of cigarettes, toast and coffee disappears with the threat of the day. 'Let's do this thing' has become his saying over our time in India as we embark on another day we want to run away from. He climbs back onto the bike. We have no choice.

We escape from the city at 5am to find our way to the dusty open road. Bouncing down fog-covered landscapes for several hours, mist clears near the border with Nepal and we climb off the bike to hug each other for a long time. Wordlessly. In silence. No doubt, our faces share the same broad grins: we're alive. In many ways it is the most fabulous prize of surviving the game of motorcycle Russian Roulette as played by Indian rules. You automatically sign up for it when you bring a large motorcycle to this country. It is a game we never want to experience again.

'What kind of restaurant is this?'

(NEP) When our grins and tears of relief subside, all the normal border crossing formalities begin. As in India – taught so ably to create paperwork by the British – the Nepalese also employ weighty tomes, leading to much shuffling from office to office as the reams of paperwork are patiently tackled, with the aid of a young Nepali. Three hours later everything has been signed, sealed and delivered.

Outside the visa office ('one month please') talking to backpackers from all over the world, the inevitable questions are asked about travelling by motorbike when you are blind. It seems so hard for sighted people to understand that seeing is only one of the myriad ways that we experience the world. It appears beyond most people's comprehension, so focused are they on those two little squidgy things called eyes. Their processing of information, their understanding of the world, completely filtered and dominated, and even dare I say, constrained by it. Without this sense, like me, people have commented on what we have done with the question 'Why?' In many ways, the same thought was voiced in radio interviews at home as people asked variations around the concept of 'What's the point of doing this when you are blind?'

Sometimes they're even brave enough to phrase the question they really want to: 'What's the point?' Meanwhile, other people all over the world use the word 'scary': 'God it must be so scary.' Perhaps something is scary when you cannot understand it. Perhaps it is when you are not able to function within its limitations but these are not applicable to me. Being blind isn't scary. It just is.

Perhaps you will never understand how you operate like me in so many ways. You see, your world too is constructed from words and it happens every time you open a book. In the reading you create the people, events and landscapes of your imagination. They come about through the interplay of the words and the images you create are real, concrete and absolute for you. It will never matter that they may be different from your friend who reads the same text. They are as they are. To you.

As we travel across so many countries the speakers in my helmet receive a constant stream of words from my narrator sitting before me. Fulfilling his promise of not sparing me verbal information because it might frighten or upset me, his words build images in my mind, pictures of what might be. To him, if I could see, I would know. Therefore it would be wrong to use my blindness 'against me' in this way. Even if it is frightening, it is part of the journey.

Thus, you do not need sight to experience many things and recently we have felt a great deal of fear, emotion and anxiety in crossing some countries. In some ways it is true that no sight leads to greater fear as I tell you now it is not true to say 'you cannot see a cliff, therefore you do not feel the same fear'. The problem is when you are blind every single corner is or can be a cliff.

While crossing India Bernard often went quiet, trying to keep us alive as we battled our way through the country. In this silence my fears threatened to overwhelm me. Drawing pictures based on what I could hear, feel and sense, it nearly engulfed all. India threatened to swallow me.

'Him in front' once told me that you have to try to control the fear otherwise it will control you. 'Try to distract yourself, take yourself somewhere else, to the sounds of waves on the beach,' he offered as a way of explaining how he coped with the riding. Fear itself is a funny thing and I have felt it with life's events. Never though have I felt I was going to die at any minute. Never have I felt it across days, weeks, minute by minute, second by second in an unending wave of 'it's going to happen right now, right this second'. Riding in India made me feel mortal. Intensely so.

And so I repeat again, being blind isn't scary, it doesn't contain fear for me. Neither is being on a motorcycle. After all, Bernard has taken us through Europe, Turkey, Pakistan and India. My fears in India reflect and are forever bound up with the sounds of retching from behind closed doors. It was there that my sighted companion battled his own demons. Being blind isn't that scary. I don't throw up at the prospect of it.

Pulling away from the border Bernard feels his way through the protocols, the driving habits that each nationality adopts. His first impression is good as the traffic is slower and there is a lot less of it. The roads seem better although many Indian trucks are delivering goods to Nepal and the horns remind me of what we have run away from. The Nepali drivers use their horn similarly but there is less traffic and drivers use their indicators and wing mirrors – bliss, sheer bliss, according to Bernard.

Four kilometres down the road is a hotel that has safe parking for the bike. Climbing off, we greet the reception staff with our finely tuned skills of negotiation, extensively honed over our time in India. Settling into the usual 'too high' first-price discussions, the manager reflects on our negotiating, commenting it is obvious we have been in India. Nepal is different he says, 'In India they will cheat you, in Nepal this will not happen.' Shrugging our shoulders once again, we remember the Macedonians speaking similarly about the Greeks, the Greeks of the Turks, the Turks of the Iranians, the Pakistanis of the Indians. It all sounds so familiar. After a little humorous banter, everybody ends up happy with the price and we lie awake to unfamiliar sounds. Silence. After weeks of unremitting noise it is strange to hear the sound of our own breathing, listening to the 'nothingness' of silence for a long, long time before sleep eventually claims me.

In the morning we're on misty mountain roads twisting and turning with such tightness we meet ourselves coming back constantly. Hairpin bends on narrow gravel roads makes it hard, slow work as Bertha growls along in first and second gear for most of the day. The popping of the exhausts with the poor-quality fuel echoes back to me from the hard rock surfaces in several places where the road has disappeared. Crunching and bouncing our way, my nervousness is returning; emotions are still raw. I tense and brace myself as the shuddering begins. Shaking and rattling for miles, sparse traffic helps as there is no competition from wagons and 4x4s for the inches of available room. Still apprehension reigns.

Meanwhile Bernard's cheery voice reassures me the surface presents 'No problem' as the shaking starts again, careering over the broken roads while I console myself it will not go on for hours and hours. The roads are narrow and wagons pass us going to the border with drivers tooting in welcome, waving from their open windows. The same happens on stopping to savour the mountain quietness as overloaded trucks lumber up the hills behind as Bernard describes the big smile appearing on faces as they slow down to take a look. It is the same smile we saw throughout Pakistan and India. Huge and welcoming.

We already like the space of Nepal and the coolness of the mountains after weeks of heat and pollution which left our faces black and our lungs aching from coughing. The people, the air, the room to breathe, the whole scenery has more of 'something'. We can't define it beyond 'something' but we know we like it and feel instantly comfortable.

People come out from their homes to wave at the sound of the exhausts, shouting greetings to us ('Namcste') while we rumble past as Bernard describes the changing scenery and the smiling people working on the terraced fields climbing the sides of the mountains. Even though the day is hard and slow it does us good as our confidence is being slowly restored. Meandering through the mountains allows time to readjust our thoughts, while stopping in silence and isolation soothes us. No longer swamped by people watching our every move, for the first time in many weeks, we feel 'alone'. It is a good feeling.

As the sun sets, Pokhara appears and we settle into the Lake View Hotel with the Annapurna mountains in the background with their snow-lined peaks reaching to the sky like fingers pointing to God. Our own batteries are flat, depleted, completely gone as we unload the bike into our new 'home' with the realisation it's now safe to collapse. And collapse we do.

The room is quiet except for the constant hum of diesel generators due to the constant power cuts. Nepal had no power at all for 48 hours per week (and in our time there it increased to 112 hours per week). As in Pakistan with 'load sharing', people have to supply their own electricity for some hours per week. If this were England there would be riots in the streets as the government came under siege – blind people would be king at night! Meanwhile, in Nepal, they reach for candles or generators and get on with it.

However, you do get used to it and adapt accordingly, doing the things you need power for when it's available, planning your time and consumption accordingly. This is, of course, apart from Bernard who shaves by head torch while wondering about how all the blind men he knows manage this in the dark? They just do. They just get on with it, much like the people of Nepal.

As we sit in the Lake View people turn up on package tours looking for the Nepalese 'spiritual experience'. They tell us of their disappointment on encountering the pollution, noise and congestion of Kathmandu. Their tours leave them feeling herded from place to place with little time to explore anything. They express envy at our way of travelling, allowing decisions about where, what and when each day is to begin. It's true we have that luxury, that freedom. The next morning waves of goodbye come as they climb back on their tour bus to head off, still looking for the special 'something' they had anticipated and not yet found.

For days we struggle with coughs and colds, feeling completely drained – it's as if we've kept going because we had to. Now with complete collapse bone tiredness sets in with massive draughts of sleep. Even though sleep claims us easily, with it come dreams of brightly coloured wagons inches away from me while Bernard's night fills with crashing and flying through the air – he wakes up before hitting the ground. I wake before the wheel runs over my head and the sheets stick to me with the sweat of such dreams.

Spending hours talking of our experiences, reliving many things, we're in a far worse condition than either of us appreciated. I now startle at the slightest noise and cannot bear to be left alone. It strains our relationship as we walk the town while I hold on tightly, trying hard not to jump at the sound of a horn, or a car passing close by. Often I fail. I feel like all the life has been sucked out of me, like a vampire's victim limping along on struggling heartbeats. Both of us go off into long silences, staring into our own troubled thoughts.

Over the days, several real arguments occur in quick succession over trivial things, inconsequential matters previously laughed off. When they start Bernard goes quiet on me. Everything then spirals out of control as the 'silent treatment' shuts me off from everything as the flow of information ceases. After the first time it happens he explains that, for him, 'the least said, the soonest mended'. But this does not help me. Feeling isolated, helpless and alone, it merely amplifies my own anger and emotion. The bickering leaves us both upset and more confused than ever about what I'm feeling.

It is as we suffer these consequences that several blind people approach us as we wander through Pokhara in our silent worlds. There's a 'training centre' for visually impaired masseurs in the town and they are obviously so pleased to meet me. Unfortunately we are at such a low ebb there is little energy, or inclination, to stand in the sun talking. Saying goodbye with promises to visit the centre in a few days, we walk away feeling guilty, with little enthusiasm for anything but breathing.

As we wander the town we meet Ian, a nurse from London, on another BMW, an F800GS, who has been on the road for 6 months. We instantly like him and in one of our 'sharing experiences' exchanges he asks Bernard what he thought of India? For a long time Bernard doesn't answer. Eventually Ian fills the silence, saying, 'he has that India look' and the people around us laugh; it seems we are not alone in our feelings. Ian has been in Nepal for five weeks recuperating and, day after day, he puts off getting back on the bike, finding excuses to stay, to the point of overrunning his visa.

Walking the streets reveals workshops everywhere and it's obvious the young men have tremendous skills and seem to be able to fix anything and everything coming in through the wide gates onto the roads. Like many countries, scarcity is a fact of daily life and with it comes tremendous invention and creativity.

Other travellers turn up as we rest in Pokhara, other 'overlanders' who stop when they see our bike. Soon our little band of weary motorcyclists grows bigger with Ralf and Marianne (from Germany) who have been on the road for two and a half years. Learning that they've been to Russia, Mongolia and a whole host of other countries on their bikes puts our 'little trip' into perspective. Feeling like happy novices, they tell us of selling everything while their treasured possessions have filled friends' lofts, garages and hallways to await their return. Perhaps, this is all we ever really need in our lives, the truly treasured things.

When you travel on the road and live out of two panniers and your pockets, there's a shift in your perception of the 'importance' of objects which once, long ago, you attached value to. After a while, you realise how most things are actually meaningless clutter with which we fill our houses and lives. If I were to be asked, right now, what sits within drawers at home, I would struggle to remember. This now tells me how insignificant such things are.

Sitting one evening, people ask about my experiences while noting our intercom system which, obviously, has been a godsend for me personally. Ralf recounts the story of a friend who ripped one off his bike due to his wife's incessant chatter. After hearing this he gave up the plan to install a bike-to-bike system for himself and Marianne. Bernard asks what he thinks it would be like to listen to his wife's voice constantly for six months in his helmet, as he had with me. Ralf throws his hands up in the air and pronounces one word, 'Divorce'.

Banter aside; they are interested in my perceptions of the journey as a blind person and, as always, what it means to be blind on such a trip. I've got used to such questions and, in many ways, it is nice that people ask such things openly instead of skirting around the question. It usually means they feel comfortable to ask. I tell them of the kindness and consideration of people all over the world, of my descriptions and pictures in my head of everywhere I've been. Ralf intuitively understands how my pictures may be right or they may be wrong but that it doesn't matter. They are right for me. He is one of a very few people I met who 'got it' immediately.

We pass the first seven days shopping, eating, recovering and talking as our emotions settle piece by piece, little by little. Trying cafés and bars along the length of the road, our first Italian pizza house has no cappuccino. I ask the waiter – who instantly locates things on the table for me by placing my hand on drinks etc – 'What kind of Italian restaurant is this?' Quick as a flash he answers: 'A Nepali-Italian restaurant.' We laugh and I tell him that I love Nepal even with its Italian cappuccino-less menus. Old ladies sit outside their shops on wicker stools. Putting fingers to eyes, they shake their heads to ask Bernard 'No sight?' Moving out of the way as we pass, they smile as my hands browse rows of items in embroidery shops. 'Walking' shops selling anything and everything for the intrepid explorer/hiker open late into the night with owners seeking to close one more sale under the dim bare bulb lights hanging outside. Closing up their shops in the darkness, they retire to their single room at the back where whole families live.

People come to recognise us as we walk India out of our systems, out of our minds. Even the cab drivers give up stopping and asking if we need a taxi – so used to us do they become that a simple wave of 'hello' suffices as they pass by looking for their next fare.

Eventually Ian packs his bike and it is sad to see him leave as we have become attached to him. You meet many people on the road and while most leave you glad to have met them, occasionally, you come across somebody with whom you 'connect'. It's hard to explain this but at times you just 'take to' somebody. Ian is one of those people. As he prepares to go back to India, we give him a hug. As he leaves we know what going back into India means.

Bernard meanwhile talks about the possibility of going back and I just say 'No'. My response convinces him to give up thinking of reverting to our original route of driving to Kolcatta (Calcutta) before catching a ship to Thailand. It may well be he just wants to prove something to himself by going back, like some form of masochistic male tendency where certain tribes stab themselves with sharp pointed sticks to demonstrate their masculinity.

I just said no.

I think – secretly – he is glad at my refusal.

But, he will never admit it.

Ants and elephants

A week later we move hotels, to a very quiet guest house further along the road, where our costs are more than halved, and our new third-floor home catches the sun all day. We can now feel the 'Nepal' inertia Ian talked about: the inability to contemplate getting back on a bike after India. It's settling into our bones, making it hard to move, to get back on the bike at all.

I arrange a very important (girlie) hair appointment as I'm starting to feel better. Arriving for the fateful occasion the male hairdresser tells me he's not been able to get the colour I'd chosen days earlier but was able get another one though. We hesitate, which puzzles him. 'Is good colour,' he repeats constantly. 'Will be fine,' he nods as we consider (well Bernard does, as he can see it). I go ahead as my head feels like a bird's nest after weeks of sun bleaching and the twin assaults of Pakistani and Indian pollution. He leaves the colour on so long I end up with a very nice multi-tone shade of hazel blonde. Helpfully he holds a hand mirror up for me as Bernard describes the vaguely reddish/blondish/auburn/brownish colour now adorning my head.

After my hair 'make-over', his daughter performs a very fine example of eyebrow shaping, reducing my gorilla-like eyebrows into something more feminine. A length of twisted cotton thread is wrapped around each individual hair before being ripped out, and Bernard watches fascinated, taking pictures of this medieval torture method. It kept him amused for days afterwards.

Once he stops laughing at female vanity we retire to a boat on the large lake dominating the town. Our first excursion ends with a rather hasty paddle back to the bank as the boat rapidly filled up with water, to the point where snorkels would have been more useful than paddles. Ever pragmatic, for our second foray out in the watery wilderness Bernard chooses a boat with cycle peddles to save his hands from blisters. With our brief 'Titanic' experience, he'd discovered how being female and blind meant that splashing was fine but the concept of paddling was quite beyond me. Keeping a straight face while protesting my innocence, being both blind and female can be very useful. When it suits.

Bobbing up and down in the middle of the lake, Bernard describes ants leaping off the nearby mountain before brightly coloured handkerchiefs open, allowing them to float down to earth. He sees them climbing the mountain paths to the top before they jump off. I take it he means parachutes and base-jumping as only Bernard could describe such things as ants and hankies. Everything feels beautifully serene and I think back over the years I've known him, back to another boat with peddles, in a different lake. A chance encounter on a day trip for visually impaired people, left me thinking of the 'what if' possibilities as I was drawn to him. A stream of questions came as I knew then what I still know now. He was 'the one', the person I wanted: I felt a connection, an overwhelming sense of certainty that is hard to explain. I just knew.

Then came the fear many blind people have, welling up inside about 'the blindness' and all that it could mean, all that it could stop. Would he be able to see past 'it', to the person I was, or would he run from it? Would 'the blindness' drop like a perceptual, impenetrable, barrier forever sealing off possibilities? A hundred 'what if' questions passed through me and all have now been answered so completely. So fully. Each answer sealed the path that has led me to bobbing up and down in a lake in Nepal while he paints silly, funny and simple pictures for me of ants jumping off mountains wearing hankies. He is what he is and I love him for it.

During our stay at the Greenland guest house various people come and go until we're joined by Bruce, Erika, Mack and Hamish from Australia travelling for a year around their homeland, India and Nepal. In one of our many conversations, they mention the National Park at Chitwan and a glimmer of a plan starts to develop. We had already considered staying in Nepal for Christmas because our next destination involves flying to Bangkok from Kathmandu, as the current situation in Myanmar (Burma) does not allow us into the country with Bertha. However mass demonstrations in Thailand mean thousands of tourists are currently stranded at closed airports. Thus we decide to make the two-day journey to spend Christmas at the National Park and once organised we finally sit down to write about our experiences in India.

Even after so much time had passed it still turns out to be hard to talk about. Trying to put our thoughts onto the page, we fight with the words and worry that people will never understand it. Capturing the experience in some meaningful way, what it felt like, makes it all too easy to relive our daily experiences while recognising, perhaps, it will always be true that 'you had to be there'. In many ways, the pages flowing from our recollections bring everything up from where it has been buried. At the same time, perhaps it is true talking can exorcise ghosts. It may also be true however, that some things are best left buried.

During breaks in the writing – to get away from it as I start to relive India too much – we commission T-shirts from a local embroidery shop, along with badges to commemorate the journey. Our sunny veranda soon resounds with many an 'ouch' puncturing the air as Bernard harpoons his fingers while sewing the badges onto our bike jackets. Deciding his fingers need a massage after a bout of man-dying, we keep our promise to visit the Seeing Hands massage centre where we catch up with two of the students we'd met days earlier, Anita and Chiran.

We learn how many people there became blind because of childhood malnutrition. Chiran himself comes from a family where four others suffered blindness due to malnutrition. As we listen to tale after tale of preventable blindness it left us sad as it spoke volumes of how international priorities are at odds with the true concept of need. Billion-pound wars rage all over the planet while people earn fantastical amounts of money for pushing financial buttons on a computer. Meanwhile, others go blind for want of a decent diet. It leaves us disgusted with the concept of priorities. Coming to understand that fairness exists only for the wealthy, which is something we always knew, this is something else entirely when you have your Western face rubbed in it.

Conversations flow under a bright blue sky and, as always, focus on my relationship with Bernard, much like in India. Anita and Chiran married 18 months ago, having met through the centre. Their home is a room in a house an hour's bus ride away and they feel lucky to have it. Questions come thick and fast as they ask if there are many blind people in England and the extent to which relationships exist between blind and sighted people. Their interest stretches far and wide as they go on to ask about the causes of blindness in the UK and whether it was true, as they had heard, that all blind people in England have jobs? Telling them how blind people are marginalised in the UK to such an extent in terms of employment, with three-quarters being unable to find work, it was plainly not what they expected. Still answering question after question we climb onto massage tables where moans and groans come from Bernard as Chiran proceeds to find every sore spot accumulated from riding a motorcycle for 5 months.

Chiran – 'Does this hurt?'

Bernard being a man – 'only a little' (through gritted teeth).

Chiran – 'Is this sore?'

Bernard – 'A little uncomfortable' (squeezes out of his throat).

On finishing the massage Bernard staggers away, limping for a few hundred yards before having to sit down on a wall not far from the clinic. Within seconds a young man approaches and tells us of his unmarried sister, 23 years old, and blind from malnutrition.

'Nobody wants a blind woman, life is very hard in Nepal if you are blind,' he tells us.

We sit and talk about what she does, and does not do, during each of her lonely days before he offers to sell us marijuana.

Bernard: 'No thank you, don't smoke it.'

Him: 'It make you happy!'

Bernard: 'We're always happy, don't need to smoke to be happy.'

Him: 'It make you fly.'

Bernard :   'No thanks, I don't like heights.'

He gives up and moves off to find some other born again Nepali/Western hippie who wants to sample the demon weed before the grim reaper comes to visit. Over our time in the town many such people have appeared on the streets. Bernard says they are easily recognised by their sound if I really listen. Jingling and jangling their way down the streets dragging themselves along under the weight of ethnic jewellery, their uniforms are typical: open-toed sandals, Indian dress and long thinning hair all tied back in a ponytail. The women are the same apart from the thinning hair. Meanwhile Nepali men wear short hair, jeans, branded training shoes and T-shirts declaring rock bands from all over the world.

Our two-day journey to Chitwan starts with a bus journey crammed in among livestock before transferring to inflatable dinghies that need bailing out every ten feet. Moving on to local rickshaws, helpfully pushed uphill by Bernard, we clamber into 4x4s to be bounced down the back of beyond slamming into each other painfully. Eventually deposited on the bank of a wide slow-moving river, stiff and sore from the battering of the jeep ride, another boat takes us across the river into the night darkness. A guide waits on the jetty to lead us through the jungle undergrowth, along rough paths as I wave my white stick for all I am worth to find my footing on the slippery surfaces.

Arriving at our 'lodge', electricity is available from 5pm until 9pm and hot water from 5.30pm until it runs out, pretty quickly we're told, usually due to Westerners having an incessant need to shower. There are no electrical plugs in the room thus no TV, also no mobile signal and no radio network, nothing but a helpful manager offering us a 5.45am call to go on a jungle walk. Bernard declines gracefully as this is far too early for him, unless he is escaping Indian traffic.

On Christmas morning we embark on fulfilling our main reason for coming here: to ride an elephant on Christmas day. The staff at the centre are nonplussed by my arrival, never having come across a blind guest before. Great nervousness spread through them the previous day on presenting ourselves for the jungle walk. So it is that the manager tells me that a special boat has been organised. Just for me. To save me walking.

He is such a nice man I do not have the heart to distinguish between blindness and paralysis. Bernard, in his most tactful mode, tells him how walking is not really an issue but the poor man proceeds to dig the most enormous hole for himself by asking, 'Does she walk?'

I feel the hairs bristle on the back of my neck as I've heard such questions many times before in Pakistan and India. Bernard thinks such queries result from the problems sighted people have with not being able to make 'eye contact' with me. Thus, they always look to him for confirmation. Meanwhile, Bernard's arm circles my shoulder and I feel a comforting squeeze before he says, 'In England we climb mountains and we have crossed the world on a motorbike. Cathy can definitely walk my friend.' The voice turns in my direction. 'You can walk, Cathy? You want to walk?' My bookend and I both reply 'Yes' at the same time.

The two jungle guides with our eight-strong group clutch long bamboo sticks and proceed to tell us of the 'very important safety' instructions for walking in the jungle. 'If you see rhino and they charge, hide behind a big tree. If you cannot find tree then run zig-zag as they have poor eyesight. If we see bears and they attack, climb tree but get high as bears stand on back legs very high (as Bernard mutters 'and don't give them honey'). If tigers appear do not run, stand to look them in the eye. Do not turn back on them.'

Thus briefed we set off armed with nothing more than two bamboo sticks and a white graphite (made in England) cane for defence. Across the first several hundred yards Bernard frets about his nakedness in terms of not having a big enough stick with which to beat off marauding animals. He goes on to consider finding a big enough tree for us both in case of rhino attack. Before solving this dilemma he shifts to getting me 6 feet up a tree while a bear bites his bum and, God help us, if a tiger attacks. After all, how can I look it in the eye? At this point he gives up and decides I am snookered, completely done, dead meat if Mr Tiger comes to visit.

'Just follow my voice,' he laughs. 'And run as fast as you can to keep up with me.' Sometimes it is not good thinking this much, as I keep telling him. I suppose he will never change, but really, he definitely thinks too much.

Setting off we have one guide at the front and one at the back to make sure no rhinos tiptoe up behind us. The parents in our group clutch their video cameras hopefully should Mr Tiger make an appearance while chattering away among themselves as their children run amok in the jungle, the chatter probably driving the animals away. Our families film each other walking through the jungle in a disappointed air as little else shows.

Even the birds stop singing well before we reach them. We see one crocodile with its front legs over its ears, perhaps blocking out the sound of our passing. It gives up the unequal struggle and slides beneath the water, muffling the noise of our progress. After several attempts by the guides to get the six Indians in our group to be quiet they give up. At this point Bernard starts walking slowly until a huge gap opens up between us and the group in front. It was either this, Bernard mutters, or he will have to resort to wearing earplugs.

Our tail-end guide, Saroj, stays with us as the gap opens up enough for the birds to notice and soon the jungle comes alive with sounds of their singing. Saroj names each one heard and he calls to them, encouraging responses. For the next two hours we walk and listen to them, to the insects, to the very backdrop of the jungle itself. Eventually re-joining the group waiting for us by the river, they are probably muttering, 'It's the blind woman, she is very slow.'

A long canoe-like boat waits to take us back to the camp. Clambering onboard it sways gently with the slow current as we pass crocodiles sleeping on the banks under the hot sun. Birds perch on floating debris as a truly overwhelming feeling comes over me. It is hard to think it's Christmas Day. And we are in Nepal. Sometimes it is all too much to take in.

The afternoon arrives and we're feeding bananas to four-ton elephants that take the fruit from my hand leaving me surprised how gentle this enormous animal can be. The one 'finger' of the Asian elephant's trunk carefully wraps itself around the banana before easing it slowly from my grasp and it is special, very special. I think it is at this point I fall in love with elephants.

A demonstration is given of how to mount an elephant: the animal lifts you using its trunk. I'm fascinated but it's so hard to picture it, never having a chance to find out as a Spanish couple dominate the group, both completing the 'climb', before we have to move on. Mulling it over I wonder if it is something I could do. Could I climb an elephant in this way? Bernard describes what happened as we walk towards the elephant safari and it leaves me pondering. Is it 'doable' for a blind person? I want to try. I know I do.

Tourists usually mount an elephant by a platform structure, about 12 feet high and reached by climbing stairs. The staff seem to consider the stairs beyond me ('can she climb stairs?') and so they make a loop with the elephant's tail once it kneels down on all fours like a big dog. Bernard guides my foot onto its hind leg, while the other foot is guided into its looped tail. My hands grasp the ropes hanging down from the cage-like structure far above me where I am to sit. As I start to climb the elephant gives a loud pain-like trumpet and lurches upwards as I hang on tight before getting anywhere near the seating platform – well, think about it, how would you like it if somebody stood on (or should that be stood in) your tail? The staff panic as the animal launches upwards as I continue to hang on for dear life.

Excited voices (including Bernard's) try to calm the animal down before I manage to crawl across its back onto the platform, much to everybody's obvious relief. Bernard decides he will give the 'standing on an elephant's tail' method a miss; climbing the stairs like a true adventure hero to settle in beside me. As two complete novices expecting a gentle meander through well-designated paths, we were not prepared for bashing through trees and bushes which left us looking like scarecrows with Bernard picking branches and leaves from my hair.

Our elephant driver is named 'Pim' and the female elephant is called Tamparkin. Pim tries to take great care of the bushes and trees as they pass me and Bernard explains how he reaches with his 'spittle' (a long curved and spiked fishing-like gaff) to push obstacles away from me as we pass. In the more dense undergrowth, Tamparkin reaches up with her trunk to snap branches off so they do not tear at my face in passing. Bernard's hands, meanwhile, hover around my head to protect my face from the assorted foliage fluttering around me like confetti.

Soon we encounter snuffling rhinos and, unusually, two rhinos have a bit of a disagreement complete with the loud crack of clashing horns. Pim gets excited and exclaims, 'You very, very lucky to see.' Little did we know how 'lucky' we were to be over the next two hours.

Soon Pim excitedly whispers 'Bears'. I was at a loss to know why he is whispering as we crash through the jungle on a four-ton animal. I suppose it is to do with 'natural sounds' of our jumbo friend uprooting trees rather than human whispering. An adult bear with two large offspring are wandering through the undergrowth not too far away from where we sit and by the size of them Bernard cannot call them 'children' unless, of course, several hundred pounds of sharp teeth and claws can be defined as such. Ever closer Pim guides Tamparkin to the family ambling along trying to keep ahead of us. I can hear their footsteps as they rustle through the undergrowth while Bernard describes the unfolding events. Suddenly there's a huge roar, followed by the sound of crashing towards us, coming ever closer before an enormous double trumpet from Tamparkin announces, 'Enough now, back off.' Meanwhile, from Bernard erupts language that is not for the faint hearted.

Bernard – Closer and closer we get to the bears. In the end the mother, I think, got fed up. From a stationary position sitting in the undergrowth she exploded at us, all teeth and claws and I have never seen anything move so fast from a sitting position. As it happened I thought to myself – get six feet up a tree in that time? Not a chance. My camera was focused on her as she sat in the jungle and at the precise second I pressed the shutter on the camera, she launched. My next pictures are of the sky, several of them, one after another. When Tamparkin trumpeted she slid to a defiant growling halt, ten feet away, before turning back to her cubs. They all disappeared into the jungle as I waited for my heart to start beating again.

At the end of our jungle foray I stroked Timparkin's head, to say both hello and thank you to this enormous animal. Apologising for hurting her tail, I think she forgives me as her trunk gently strokes my hand as if to say 'It's OK, I'll let you off... now where's the banana?' She ambles off with a wave and a grin from a still excited Pim as the news of our afternoon spreads through the camp and staff tell us that to see rhinos arguing is rare and to see bears is truly unusual. For a bear to chance its luck with an elephant has never, ever, happened in the 15 years they can remember. Thus, we are 'charmed' according to the staff and all the elephant drivers want to take us out the next day. It's a huge topic of conversation for several days and I'm now thought to be 'special' by the staff. From 'does she walk?' to 'lucky', by a chance encounter with a mum trying to protect her young. Life can be very mysterious sometimes, nicely so, as Christmas day passes in a spectrum of experiences the like of which I could only dream of years ago.

Across the days our awareness of the individual people who work at the centre and their unique culture leads to staff arranging opportunities for me to learn of their background. The story of the Tharu people is of migration to Nepal from India and Saroj (our jungle walk guide) is a member of the Tharu, as is Pim, the elephant driver. Even the elephants understand Tharu rather than Nepali.

The Tharu themselves are renowned as being among the finest elephant workers on the planet and it is with great pride that Saroj talks of many aspects of their life as we eat lunch with his family on Boxing Day. His father sits with us, telling how he started out as a 'lowly' junior 'grass cutter' (responsible for feeding) before moving from junior to senior mahout (driver) before becoming the 'stable' mahout – the most senior 'driver'. For 50 years he worked with the animals before being promoted to work in the breeding centre, where he was now a manager. Between mouthfuls of Dal Bhat, the rice and vegetable-based meal for most of Nepal, I hear of the artefacts and culture of the Tharu as another invite is made to us, to visit the yearly international three-day elephant-racing festival.

This event itself involves teams arriving from all over Nepal and India, and processions representing each geographically separate Tharu grouping. Each has different brightly coloured dress, jewellery and accents and Saroj introduces me to several of his friends who will take part in the procession. It is a gay, colourful and exciting opening to the first day's racing as Saroj leads us to 'his' brilliantly dressed girls. When Saroj explains my sight loss, six excited girls surround me, guiding my hands to various aspects of their costumes as their soft singsong Tharu voices are translated for me. Walking in the procession balancing elaborately decorated jars on their heads, each has such skill any finishing school would be proud of their deportment and posture. One is placed on my head although I need to hold it in place.

The first race sees brightly painted elephants dressed for the occasion as the throngs cheer and shout encouragement. The huge animals are assembled for the 100 metre dash from one end of the field to the other and back down the home straight to cross the finish line. They bear sponsors' signs ranging from local shops (number 6) to trans-global companies such as Honda (number 34) as they delicately sprint the distance. Saroj explains that penalties are incurred if they deviate from within the white painted lines of their individual lanes and Bernard describes how one wanders all over the lanes with gay abandon.

'Must be an Indian elephant,' I declare to the sounds of choking laughter from beside me.

It surprises me how five elephants can run towards me and I hear little beyond the jangling harnesses. In my mind, I have pictures of them tiptoeing along the separate lines of the racetrack. They say an elephant can put its foot on an egg and it will not break, so delicate is its touch. Feeling nothing as 20 tons ran towards me, I can well believe it.

Leaving our ballerina-like elephants, we cross the rickety bridge of bamboo and sandbags stretching across the river to see the 'famous' one-month-old baby twins. After formal introductions, one takes a fancy to my stick, pulling it successfully from my hand before waving it in the air like a prized trophy. They say elephants have poor eyesight but an elephant waving a white stick? Pushing it a little bit don't you think?

The noise of elephants at feeding time is incredible as we learn that each grown animal can eat 300 (1 kg) bundles of food each day, digesting only 40% of the intake. Like naughty children, the youngsters pull the bundles apart to get at the 'tasty bit' in the middle while handlers crack them with bamboo sticks to stop them dismantling the packages in this way. The sounds are harsh as they crack the pony-sized babies but Saroj explains it's essential they eat the whole bundle, which is specially prepared to provide all the vitamins and essentials for a balanced diet. The saying 'cruel to be kind' springs to mind.

The morning sees us sitting on the riverbank under bright sunshine updating our journals, with occasional interruptions from passers by. The manager joins us to talk about Nepal, elephants and motorcycles. As the conversation turns to the possibility of me mounting an elephant by its trunk, he thinks it would be possible with a different elephant that lifts slower.

Rushing off to make the arrangements, a 2pm meeting is called in the briefing circle where I will try without spectators watching me being dropped on my head. Feeling excited and apprehensive at the same time, Bernard merely thinks I am mad, expressing his reasoning with: 'It's a four-ton animal, 12 feet off the ground. If you fall, it will hurt like hell. That's a good enough reason not to do it!' He is not mollified when I point out he's ridden a motorcycle to Nepal. 'That's different,' he observes. Pressing him closely for explanation, he falls silent.

At the allotted time Bernard clutches every camera he has while the manager videos the whole incident as my very nervous companion directs and guides my hands and feet in the way the elephant driver indicates. The driver, sitting high up above me, explains how to grab onto the elephant's ears tightly, my arms spread out wide as they are so far apart.

The skin feels very leathery in my fingers as I wrap them around the lobes while worrying about squeezing the poor thing too hard. Bernard places my foot against the trunk but it keeps slipping off until I realise I have to push my foot INTO the trunk, the signal for the elephant to curl its trunk and lift upwards. Before I know it I am airborne and my hands are on its head with palms feeling the short, spiky, bristly, hairs beneath them. Very unladylike I crawl up its head reaching towards the driver's extended hands.

My heart is pounding, excited as adrenaline floods through me making me shaky, exhilarated in a way never before encountered as Bernard's voice calls, 'Does my bum look big in this?' The driver's hands grasp mine as I sit facing him, the wrong way round, while Bernard translates the hand signals from the driver telling me how to turn to face forwards. A few minutes later, I am sitting forwards with my legs dangling behind the ears, feeling it breathing massively underneath me as the driver's hands rest lightly on my shoulders. Setting off around the enclosure, swaying slowly to the gait of the ambling animal, I hold on tightly with my legs as my hands grasp the ropes behind its ears. I listen to the sounds of 'Namaste' (hello) from the manager, the command for the animal to raise its trunk in a big 'hello' gesture.

All too soon it's time to dismount and my lumbering friend sits down and leans to one side, stretching a back leg out like a slide for me to slip down into

Bernard's arms. I stand shaking with excitement, wondering if this is another 'world's first'? 'Blind woman crosses world on motorcycle, then climbs elephant using trunk before sliding down leg like big kid'.

The Guinness book of records perhaps, who knows? The manager and the driver have even bigger grins than the one plastered across my own face at the fact I have done it as I stand stroking my new big friend called 'Coli', waiting for my pounding heart to settle.

I am led to Pim nearby who takes us tiger hunting well off the beaten track; tiger tracks are found on a riverbed. The trail disappears into the long grass and we follow them while Bernard mutters, 'Is this such a good idea? It could be in the grass,' he whispers. I feel him shuffle, picturing him pulling his legs up out of reach of the rampaging tiger who sits waiting for him in that swaying grass. We trace and retrace the tiger's route through the afternoon without ever seeing it ('Thank God,' according to Bernard) and, secretly, we think Pim hopes the 'lucky' streak will hold. According to Bernard, the fact that it didn't is a good thing. He didn't want to meet a tiger in the long grass anyway.

All too soon our time at the Chitwan National Park ends as we climb into the long boat to cross the river after saying farewell to all the staff who turn up to say goodbye to the first blind person who has ever visited the centre. Hopefully, a little something has been left behind in terms of understanding that blindness means something about a person. But it does not mean everything. Perhaps the next visually impaired person will benefit in some small way. We hope so.

The jeep bounces us over the rough tracks for the first part of the long trip back by road and then by train to Pokhara. It is the first time we have ever returned to the same place and it feels strange coming back to the Greenland guest house, a bit like coming 'back from holiday'. Only halfway up the drive, Bernard drops the bags and goes over to Bertha, starting her up as he listens. Contented rumbles of the bike lead to pronouncements of satisfaction. He did fret so at leaving her alone.

'Nepal you like?'

Our priorities shift to arranging the airlift from Kathmandu to Bangkok as news reports indicate that Thailand is now running smoothly after all the recent political unrest. Over the days spent organising everything we overrun our visas and extensions have to be arranged but the magic of the white stick sweeps away the 'closed for the day' visa office as very kind officers issue a two-week extension.

Leaving the Greenland guest house, our journey to Kathmandu is very difficult as we've not been on the bike for over a month. Nine hours pass covering the 200 km due to poor road conditions and a fatality shutting the only road to Kathmandu. Eventually crawling past miles of traffic to an army barrier, an army officer waves us off towards a tiny mountain path disappearing into the darkness. Bernard can see small motorcycles taking the route but it is obvious Bertha is too large for us to even contemplate it.

'You from?' a voice asks as we sit thinking.

'England,' Bernard replies.

'Nepal you like?'

Minutes into the conversation the officer understands that we would consider applying for citizenship. Importantly he also understands that the mountain goat track is impossible. Rapid exchanges occur between the officer and those around him and the barrier is removed for two soldiers to lead us through the mass of cars and people completely jamming the road. Crawling past the sprawled, unmoving body of a man, a bus sits above him bearing signs of the impact of flesh against metal and a crowd is gathered around the poor soul. It slowly separates, allowing us to pass inches away from where he lies. People look with the morbid fascination that descends with the appearance of death. The suddenness, the brutality, the finality of such an event provokes a similar response all over the world.

Ploughing through miles and miles of jammed roads once the troops wave farewell, the route involves walking-pace riding until we arrive in the pitch-black city as we (again) break Rule 1 (Don't ride in the dark) and Rule 2 (avoid pulling into a strange city under cover of darkness). As always, our tried and trusted 'Plan A' comes into action. And so we stop at a taxi rank and hand over the address of a reasonably priced guest house (the Holy Himalaya).

The taxi driver leads us through the completely blacked-out city where no streetlights brighten the way before arriving at a hotel of vaguely similar name (the Hotel Himalaya). It is four times the price we expected and the colour drains from Bernard's face. Settling into his usual humour and outrageously funny counteroffers ('I'll wash the dishes and clean the floors') he drives it down to a price that would pay to restore half the city's electricity. Since it's been weeks since we've ridden for so long, we cave in at half-price to take the room. At least it offers a base close to the airport and shipping agent.

Arriving in Kathmandu on Saturday night arrangements are made to leave Nepal on Tuesday. Unlike the previous air shipment from Turkey to Pakistan, this time the package is much smaller as I sit listening for hours to the sound of spanners (Bernard) and hammers (the craters) in the Customs shed as Bertha is stripped down. A parcel bound for the UK is crammed in as everything happens so quickly there's no time to post it.

Kathmandu airport welcomes us the next day as Bertha is waved into her cargo hold before we climb the steps for the same flight to Thailand. In many ways it feels symbolic boarding at the same time as a new stage is about to begin in the odyssey of 'A Blind Woman, Two Wheels and 25,000 miles'.

South East Asia is before us with a new set of unknowns, which no longer worries us. As the plane lifts off we settle into seats and reflect about our experiences of Nepal. Leaving the ground way below we reach the conclusion that the place left us with one profound feeling, that of relief.

It will probably never be possible to explain the multilayered fear which led us to stay for five weeks in a country where we never planned to go. Nepal was the balm for our emotions as it gave us time to return to who we were, rather than the two frightened people we had become. In recent days news had reached us of a head-on collision in India of another English motorcyclist. Fortunately he survived and is now in the UK with multiple injuries. While not knowing his name, as is often the case with motorcyclists who scour overland books across the years, if the person ever reads this we said a little prayer for you and wished you well when we heard. You will, more than likely, never be able to explain to people what it is like to ride in India. But you will know. Much as we do.

Nepal is a very beautiful place occupied by beautiful people and it gave us space and time to recover. The roads are not good but the traffic (apart from in Kathmandu) is low in density and probably results from the country being the 12th poorest in the world. Despite their relative poverty, the people themselves are kind and considerate.

Never will I forget the reservations I had when Bernard said of India,

'Enough, we get out of here.' My picture of Nepal and the Himalayas in December, of all months, was of mountains, cold and snow. Nothing could have been further from the truth. In England we would have been very happy with the climate during our own summer. While this is true, even the shine of the sun on my face was never equal to the warmth of the people I encountered over the weeks.

It stretched from Nepali-Italian waiters in cappuccino-less restaurants to the sounds of old ladies creaking upwards from stools outside shops clearing a path for me. It all made Nepal, in many ways, a very special place for us both. Importantly the country will forever be wrapped up in our own intimate emotional and psychological responses to a sustained period of deep pressure and profound stress. Thus, Nepal taught us many things about who we are, including a rare view of our own inadequacies, sifted through to recognise what we had become. Two people trying to rebuild themselves.

The beauty of the country and the people do, however, allow other more dominant memories to drift easily into consciousness as I sway along on Tamparkin and Pim looking for tigers as long grass tugs at my legs. I can still feel being swept high upwards onto an elephant named Coli from where I hear a voice calling from way below me: 'Does my bum look big in this?' As I laugh at the memory I realise that this tiny country taught me how to do this again. Perhaps this is the biggest compliment I can pay to its people.

SOUTH EAST

ASIA

THAILAND AND MALAYSIA

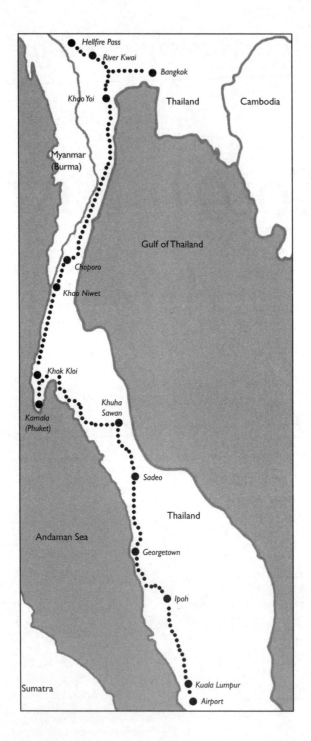

Map of route through Thailand and Malaysia. 6 January - 10 February

How you view things

Three and a half hours after leaving Kathmandu the warmth of a Bangkok evening envelops us and it is lovely to feel the heat again. In Nepal when the temperatures descended into the low 20s, we donned our fleeces and the mere thought of sub-ten degree temperatures in England has us shivering. Here the warmth of the Thai evening is luxurious, a sense of well-being radiating throughout our bodies as it seeps in, easing our tiredness from the flight.

After negotiations, a taxi takes us into downtown Bangkok at 120 kph. Flying through the traffic, Bernard comments that the last time he saw this speed a very nice Turkish police officer was collecting for his retirement fund. Unpaid, the coloured speeding ticket still sits in the journal.

Bernard is mesmerised by the road lights and white lines, carefully regulating the traffic; surely so many highway lights are not needed? Perhaps half would be enough? Multicoloured traffic lights appear, red, amber, green, the likes of which we have not seen for ages. Noticing all these changes he points out drivers staying in lanes, judiciously using indicators, letting people know where they're going. The reverse culture shock continues on checking into a hotel. It seems opulent after Pakistan, India and Nepal.

Constant hot water flows and electricity pours out with not a power cut in sight. The TV displays multiple channels while the radio receives more than static as English pop songs cascade from speakers. It feels strange at first and takes a few days' to adjust as no longer do we have to ask, 'What time is the power on today?' It feels eccentric being able to enjoy simple things like showering under powerful jets nearly punching holes in your skin. Like thousands of little needles, the (hot) water never runs out. No matter how long you stay under it.

We engage in familiar routines dealing with agents and Customs to reclaim Bertha. Three days later she is in the agent's car park where Bernard amuses a large crowd by reassembling her. Many handshakes later we hunt for our hotel hidden away among the towering blocks all around. We're stopped by a Thai police officer who haltingly tells of our heinous crime of going down a bus lane. Asking for Bernard's international driving licence, the princely sum of 400 baht (about £8 or $5) is demanded for its return. Bernard starts to hum 'Stand and Deliver' (by Adam Ant) under his breath while waiting for the paperwork to begin.

It soon becomes obvious there is no paperwork and so we receive our first introduction to Thai Police procedures, involving a lot of smiling; welcome to Thailand. Many people at this point will start to mutter 'I wouldn't pay a bribe, no way, no how' and yes, you are right. It is wrong, bad, awful, shouldn't be done. It should be challenged wherever it happens. By giving him the money it is condoning his behaviour and, no doubt, he will set off to find the next western, rich, passerby who drops a sweet paper. Then again, it is always possible to rant, rave, or quietly insist (while smiling) on a legal route. This will involve a cross-town visit to the local Thai Police Station where numerous forms in Swahili (or Thai but equally indecipherable), will involve several hours of wasted time before culminating in a night time drive through Bangkok.

Mmmmm, let me think... (two seconds later) ...give him the 5 dollars and be done with it. The funny thing is when the 'off-the-record' fine is handed over, he stops six lanes of busy traffic to enable us to turn around. Thus being philosophical certainly helps when you come across situations like this. Now we just shrug our shoulders, leaving the purists to mutter about bribes

Back at the hotel, we turn our attention to Bertha's bruised luggage frame as she displays the scars of passing through Asia. Several breaks and cracks are revealed, needing welding before Bernard can remove the spanners cable-tied across the weaknesses. Currently the frame looks like a child's Meccano set is holding it together. But the building next-door gives off the telltale flashes of welding, and clutching the pieces, we set off with one of the hotel staff to find their source. Clambering over piles of rubble and debris to enter the building, a wooden ladder is climbed two floors up to where several people hunch over girders. The hotel staff explain and within minutes the luggage frame is restored to its original shape without any further need for spanners and cable ties.

Meanwhile Bertha draws crowds to the hotel entrance while we use public transport involving water taxis which ply the canals along with the brightly coloured 'tuk-tuks' (taxis), all sounding like Formula One racing cars despite being powered by small motorcycle engines. Days later we pack up and head north to see the famous River Kwai bridge along with the Australian memorial of the Death Railway at Hellfire Pass. Heading out into the traffic, within 20 minutes another unscheduled appointment occurs with the police.

Things are not looking good. Officer 1 speaks no English and Bernard is convinced he has done nothing wrong. Officer 2 arrives and speaks a version of English learned from Americans on leave during the Vietnam War. Drawing pictures on his hand it seems we were travelling in the wrong lane. Bernard explains he was in the correct lane but the officer jumped out in the middle lane (on a busy three-lane highway) to stop the car in front so he was forced to go around the car. The officer will have none of it. Wanting Bernard's international licence, we know where this is going. He tells us the fine: 'It cost 1,000 baht' (about £20) as he smiles and grins. The broad smiles and lovely nature of the officer does little to stop the huffing and puffing in the intercom. An impasse is reached as Bernard tries the 'I'm a daft Englishman and have no idea what you are talking about.' We quietly ponder whether to force his hand and insist on the paperwork. To go official will take hours as the officer will not be there with it until his shift is over, six hours later. Bernard hands over the 'fine', gets his licence back and puts it down as a toll for using the road. At times like this, it's all about how you view things.

Now, now, stop the huffing and puffing from the back row, you sound like you have asthma. Think positive and be nice. At least he smiled a lot and never reached for the gun on his hip.

Remembering

Three hours later Kanchanburi appears after drifting along at 40 mph, talking, with the lush green vegetation going past as time and distance have both lost all meaning. Our world has slowed down. No longer is there a rush anywhere now as the journey has stopped being a journey in many ways. Now it is merely how we live, day by day, and country by country as before us appears the famous Bridge over the River Kwai.

Slowly trundling past the famous rounded arches of the supports, the search begins for somewhere to sleep for the night before finding a lovely riverside 'resort' for a fraction of the cost of one bent Thai policeman. The restaurant is set on a pontoon in the river itself and the bridge is within striking distance. Sitting here with the feel of the pontoon moving underneath us as the water rustles past, the staff have taken some time to comprehend the fact we have driven here by motorcycle, along with the fact that I cannot see. Their faces display incredulity when they understand both things.

The next day we hop into a riverboat with a huge diesel engine and eight-foot-long prop strapped onto it which churns the water to white foam, such is the power and speed it generates. The boat is like a missile as it moves, hitting the wash of other boats and nearly taking off in a noisy, unstable, scary and exhilarating experience. The boatman is excellent, understanding instantly a little more time is needed for me to get on and off the low-hulled boat; never easy when you are blind as it is like stepping off a cliff without knowing when your feet will land.

Slowing dramatically as we approach the bridge, descriptions and camera clicks fill the air as Bernard explains that the 415 km Thai–Burma railway employed forced labour in its construction with scant regard for human life. It is said that for every railway sleeper set in place along the 415 kilometre length one life was lost and there are approximately 120,000 sleepers.

Visiting the immaculate Chang Kai cemetery filled with Australian, British, and Dutch soldiers who died on the Death Railway proves to be an extremely moving experience. The 6,982 people resting here shows that many of them died in 1943 and 1944 when they were so, so, young; in their early 20s. Walking between the headstones Bernard reads many, many, names from plaques sitting on immaculately maintained graves, each with different plants, flowers, and bushes, sitting between neatly manicured graves. His voice becomes too husky to continue, for reasons not to do with the constant reading. Men from every part of the UK which we know so well lie here in pristine rows, buried in a foreign land under bright blue cloudless skies. Walking in silence for some time, my companion's voice eventually returns with descriptions of the inlayed sword forming the basis of the large white cross at the head of the cemetery.

In the nearby War Museum Bernard ignores all the 'Do Not Touch' signs on exhibits while hundreds of photographs display their nakedness of intent. The level of cruelty and torture revealed is beyond imagining. The walls show the story of the camps and the building of the railway itself. How things like this happen is beyond my comprehension. It is a very sad experience, leaving us moved for days afterwards.

Bernard has always believed history should never be lost due to the danger of repeating the same mistakes again. He has a quote he often uses which states: 'The difference between the fool and the intelligent person is that one only makes a mistake once.'

Perhaps, one day, our politicians will learn this as well as it is seldom the soldiers put their hands up shouting, 'Me, me, me.' Seldom, if ever, is it the military who shout for war as it is they who pay the ultimate price. It is at times like this I realise that my blindness probably protects me from the savagery of such events and images, from the true depravity of what people are capable of doing to each other.

In my own naïve world people are kind and considerate, whether in crossing a road with my guide dog in the UK or with our passage through strange lands. Overwhelmingly I meet with consideration as blindness seems to bring out the best in people. Inevitably it colours my view of the world and its peoples. Many times over the journey this has been true and Bernard has no doubt it has aided us in many ways. He is utterly convinced that he would never have received an entry visa for Pakistan in Athens if he'd been on his own. We know, for example, of several motorcyclists turning up at Pakistani embassies around the world, only to be told to apply for visas back in their home countries. Thus, they had to fly home, get their visa, and then fly back to continue their journeys. Me? I had a conversation with a lovely embassy official (in Athens) about what it means to be blind before he reached for the fax. My local Pakistani embassy in the UK (in Manchester) had then talked among themselves before everybody agreed, 'Ahhhhh, go on then, give her a visa, and one for him as well.'

This 'helping' mentality, probably, is wrapped up in my perceived 'vulnerability' and people's implicit understanding of that vulnerability. Often it's demonstrated by their willingness to, in some small way, 'protect' or 'assist' me in whatever way they can. I've been fortunate to experience this throughout my life, and all through this journey. In some ways, perhaps, it a small recompense for not having sight but it is hard for me to know. My possible naivety reminds me of the case of a person called Sydney Bradford. Sydney had his sight restored after 50 years or so years of vague shifting images bordering on total blindness. When his eyes opened the world turned out to be very different than he'd expected, tragically so in many ways.

Born in 1906, from 1915 he spent his youth in the Birmingham School for the Blind in England, eventually leaving in 1923. In 1959, after 50 or so years of vague shifting images bordering on total blindness, his world was transformed by a corneal operation, resulting in a world full of frightening fast-moving objects and people. From a cheerful and extroverted outgoing person he slipped into a drab and boring world, full of decay, violence and insecurity. Depression soon followed as his daily experiences became full of fear, changing him in hundreds of little ways from the person who confidently crossed roads in his blindness to a frightened, indecisive individual. His confidence deserted him and he lost the sense of 'peace' in himself, ultimately leading him to commit suicide in 1960. His story is sad, in many ways, as prior to his sight being restored, he pursued life with a great deal of confidence and energy and his experience of 'seeing' left him with a huge sense of disappointment.

It may be true that, much like Sydney, the images in my mind are firm and secure in their construction, not open to challenge, having no comparison. Daily I meet with the best in people while history perhaps sits uncomfortably with my internally constructed world. It becomes even more so when viewed against the backdrop of the images portraying violence and thuggery pinned up on walls and boards, faithfully read to me by Bernard. I'm disturbed by the acts of barbarism described to me. As we walk into town subdued and cross the famous bridge by foot Bernard tells me that Japanese tourists are conspicuous by their absence.

Wandering through the local market, I handle and explore all sorts of exquisite objects, from silver jewellery to large wooden elephants. I buy a necklace for myself and a green wrist bracelet of Burmese jade for Bernard to remember our trip to the Kwai. It's funny that while in Nepal Bernard described the ageing hippies festooned with bangles and necklaces shuffling along under the weight of their ethnic clothing. Now he wears three bracelets and the only thing missing is long hair.

Sitting together in the warm evening air, with the pontoon rising and falling from the flowing water, I fall silent, thinking. From somewhere words spill out telling him how I feel, of how he guided me through the dust and fear of India under seemingly impossible conditions. Of how he kept me safe, always watching, of his patience meandering through markets and shops while I explore everything possible, engraining memories into my mind. Words spill out, unexpected, without any forethought. A few seconds pass before he responds.

'I was coming anyway and, besides, I had a spare seat.'

I can do nothing but smile at his response as the conversation drifts through so many events and feelings, of ourselves, the journey so far, and of what is still to come.

During our time here, we take the fifteen-minute rail journey across the bridge and back, passing the tall Japanese bamboo watchtowers complete with red and white Rising Sun flags with the arm-like rays radiating outwards from the sun. It must have inspired such fear for many people when it appeared across this continent. In some ways it feels uncomfortable riding the train, a tourist thing perhaps, a 'must do' activity that is possible only on the backs of the tens of thousands who died in its construction. The descendents of the native people who died during its construction still live and work around the railways, on the stalls and markets that have sprung up near the bridge for the tourists. With all that has gone before, at least somebody benefits from what happened and, importantly, their presence keeps the memory alive. In this, we are all able to learn and remember.

Our bike is parked in the shadow of the bridge and many tourists from around the world are photographing Bertha, seemingly as much as the bridge itself. Conversations flow for a long time before we leave for the Theravada Buddhist Temple or Tiger Temple, as it is widely known, 40 km away along the 323 Highway.

It is in the Saiyok district of Kanchanaburi province and not far from the border of Myanmar, coming into being as a Buddhist temple in 1994. Its fate, however, was changed forever one day in 1999 when local villagers turned up with a tiger cub whose mother had been killed by poachers. Over time many other tigers were brought to the monks as poachers killed the parents or Thai laws became stricter, stopping 'pets' from being chained in gardens and outbuildings as a status symbol. The tigers are cared for by the monks, local staff and international volunteers.

In the beginning the big cats wandered around freely, so used were they to human beings but nowadays, with so many visitors, they are chained during certain periods of the day. It is during the afternoon when the heat is at its height that visitors are able stroll around the grounds, sitting, stroking and being photographed with the big cats. International controversy rages (as we found out later) about the centre but at this time we had no idea there were such strong feelings about the practices here. Allegations of the cats being drugged, mistreated and poorly handled abound across the internet but in our time at the monastery Bernard saw nothing representing such concern.

Waiting to enter, there are no concessionary entrance fees for disabled people in Thailand. It's the first country I've seen this in with every attraction in Bangkok full fee, and the same is true today, even though the attractions are Buddhist in nature. I find it strange that a religion that eschews personal possessions and materialism should be this way.

At the allotted time, clutching our tickets, Bernard guides me to the barrier to cross rugged, uneven ground in the trail of rushing tourists. When we reach a large wooden pagoda everyone else has already taken their pictures and gone in the 'must see everything quick to get back to the bus' frenzy. Signs indicate that entrance to the pagoda is forbidden and we stand listening to the silence. A praying Buddhist monk notices me clutching my white cane and, gesturing to Bernard, indicates that I should come forward (past the large sign saying 'No Ladies') to join him where he is kneeling, praying. Crossing the large wooden expanse, he indicates I should kneel.

His cool hands encircle mine as he lights three incense sticks, placing them one at a time in my fingers, guiding my hands to where they should be pushed into the soil as he asks 'Madame no sight?' Bernard tells me he is shaking his own head in a silent 'No' as he describes the emotions flickering across the monk's face (understanding and sadness seemed to be the best description). His hands encircle mine, folding them, moulding them into prayer fashion before placing my palms on the floor saying 'bow'. Three times this happens before he leads me to a gold-covered Buddha statue (with eyes painted black) holding a large bowl and in it Bernard can see coins and notes. The monk's voice quietly says, 'Make offering' and Bernard places money in the vessel. The orange-robed man seems happy as he guides me back across the floor to our waiting shoes before retreating to his place where he returns to silent prayers.

Slowly wandering through the reserve we pass deer, water buffalo and horses until we catch up with a crowd in a clearing where there are 20 or so tigers, all with handlers. Restrained on long chains, they play happily in the sun with their cubs, or doze under the canopy of small trees protecting them from the heat of the day. Joining the lines of quietly excited tourists to have pictures taken with a large tiger, the handler stops anybody from touching it. When he realises I cannot see, he gently takes my hand and strokes it along the tiger's back, which feels smooth and silky, its fur a little coarser than a domestic cat. My heart is pounding as my fingers trace the tiger's spine, feeling its breathing through its fur as its chest rises up and down, up and down.

The same tiger loses patience several people later and gets up as everybody is urgently ushered back as the handler tries to settle the animal. Trying everything, he eventually starts to stroke the tiger's testicles with his fingers and the muffled laughter of Bernard starts everybody off with his comment, 'No, no, not the testicles!' At this point, the tiger settles down. Other staff appear, asking if anyone would like to feed the cubs. I propel Bernard forward to make sure I am involved as one of only four people allowed.

Bernard – Personally I didn't want to play with the cubs. Actually, I didn't even want to be here at all as tigers are big, sharp-clawed, powerful animals that like meat and I am made of it, plus a lot of water and it is hot here. I can just about cope with domestic cats and even they seem to delight in drawing blood, despite you being nice to them. I thought she was nuts to even want to stroke tigers but I talked to the staff and they realise the uniqueness of the event for Cathy. Leading us to where the youngsters are penned in an indoor area, they retrieve the cubs who play with their handlers, chewing on leads like happy puppies as we walk to the cub's 'gymnasium'.

I am not sure if you will ever realise how powerful and memorable my experiences are as a blind person as I play with the silky smooth-coated animals. Feeding 12 week-old tigers is not something many blind people ever get to contemplate. My arms, however, do end up with long scratches as permanent trophies of the event as one wraps his front paws around my arms as I bottle feed it. The sharp scratching feeling engrains itself into me, along with the noisy sounds of furious and frantic sucking on the milk-filled bottles.

Bernard, meanwhile, stands defending my back from all comers (the other three cubs) who seem determined to play king of the castle on me. 'Get off you bugger' travels through the air from my knight in shining armour. Other sounds come from him denoting pain due to his own experiences of scratching sharpness that appears to be leaving imprints on his soft delicate skin. 'Would you like to feed one of the cubs?' he is asked by one of the volunteers 'No chance, but thank you anyway,' comes his exasperated voice as he continues to fend off the twelve-week-old playful kittens the size of my Labrador guide dog.

Leaving them to gently fall asleep in their post-meal lethargy the staff take multiple pictures of the two of us, eventually happy they have the 'right' one and Bernard assures me it is one of 'those' pictures, describing how it shows him hiding behind me.

Leaving the centre on Bertha for the 40 km ride back to the Kwai bridge, Bernard patiently listens while I talk excitedly about everything experienced until pulling up back at the bridge where a man approaches us with broken

English asking 'Where you come from?' It signals the precursor to all the usual questions about the bike. As the conversation flows, he realises I am blind and disappears for a couple of minutes before reappearing to place two small carved elephants in the palm of my hand – 'a gift for you' he mumbles before retreating to his wares that are spread out on a blanket on the ground.

His act touches me and I walk over to where he sits cross-legged on the ground, carving his wood and small splinters of ivory into ornate animals and images of bridges and temples. Sitting beside him, his hands guide mine as he shows me beautifully carved woodwork and lattice-like work in hide, both of which are enormously elaborate and skilled in their creation. My fingers trace ornate patterns with elephants and temples, the bridge itself and many other aspects of everyday life.

As he talks Bernard describes that, for some reason, he is getting upset talking to me, of his eyes becoming 'man-like and misty' as emotions rise within him. Perhaps there is 'something' in his history triggered by my appearance but we will never know. Perhaps he is just a lovely caring person the likes of which I have met so many times over the years.

Climbing back on Bertha, we ride to a museum 80 km away that opened in 1996 to commemorate the men treated so dreadfully by the Japanese as they rushed to supply their forces in Burma. The site is free and is jointly run by the Australian War Graves Commission and the Thai government. It tells the story of Hellfire Pass and the men who built this section of the Thai–Burma railway. They arrived with few if any possessions and when they left there was nothing but the echoes through history of their deaths through disease and maltreatment.

Hellfire Pass was so named by these men as it described the images of nighttime as they laboured by torchlight. Locally Hellfire Pass is known as K3 or Kenyu in Thailand and it is a cutting through solid rock that was begun in April 1943. Four hundred Australian prisoners originally began working on the cutting before a further 600 Australian and British prisoners were brought in during June to speed up the construction. They worked 12–18 hour days around the clock in shifts, without a rest day, for six weeks until the section was completed in mid-August. The channel cut through the rock is in two sections: one, seven metres deep and 450 metres long, and the other, 25 metres deep and 75 metres long. Using nothing but 8 pound hammers, hand drills, explosives, picks and shovels, the prisoners removed the tons of waste rock by hand. This section alone cost the lives of at least 700 Allied prisoners. Sixty-nine of them were beaten to death by Japanese engineers and Korean guards.

We spend a very sobering afternoon wandering through the cuttings made by the Allied prisoners and 100,000 South East Asians, including whole families who died in the construction of the railway – a fact we did not know. The audioguide consists of the spoken testimony of Australian survivors who made it through this tragic period in history, telling their tale with humility and humour despite their terrible sufferings. Perhaps the experiences of the Australians, and all the other people who struggled, lived and died together at this place, is best summed up by a poem on the audioguide, written by an Australian named Duncan Butler who served with the 2/12th Field Ambulance:

'I've travelled down some lonely roads
Both crooked tracks and straight
An' I've learned life's noblest creed
Summed up in one word 'Mate'.

Someone who'll take you as you are
Regardless of your state
An' stand as firm as Ayers Rock
Because 'e' is your mate.

Me mind goes back to 43
To slavery and 'ate
When one man's chance to stay alive
Depended on 'is mate.

And so to all who ask us why
We keep these special dates
Like Anzac day, I answer: 'Why'
We're thinking of our mates.

An' when I've left the driver's seat
And handed in me plates
I'll tell old Peter at the door:
'I've come to join me MATES.'

I loved this poem very much and that's why we've quoted an extract from it here. Within the poem Duncan includes the lines 'Why… do we keep these special dates?'

History is a teacher of us all. Long may it continue to be so.

'Do you have white wine?'

The days flash past wandering through the north of Thailand and soon it is time to leave Kanchanaburi and head south. Accompanied by constantly rising heat, we pass by kilometres of thick jungle while pickup trucks loaded two-stories high seem to be in danger of falling over on every corner. Covering 350 km is easy with decent road surfaces and relatively little traffic. Stopping for the night, we pay £11 for a room and a Penang curry that would strip paint off doors. Alternating between laughing with tears running down our faces, and gulping water by the bucketful, it still doesn't matter that the staff tell us it will make it worse, pass me the fire hydrant please.

The next day brings petrol stations where attendants blow whistles to direct cars on and off the pumps. Listening to the hilarious sounds of all the whistles, we can identify at least six different ones, all unfathomable to Bernard. Setting off and driving through the gorgeous heat it's 20 minutes before my hands feel the top of the panniers and discover no long cane. Slowing down, Bernard swings Bertha round to head back to retrieve my errant wand.

The road continues straight for miles with few corners as pickup trucks blast pass us constantly as we meander through the dense jungles and smooth surfaces. Virtually everybody drives 3- and 4-litre pickups but with petrol under £6 for 21 litres (our tank range), we can understand how it is affordable compared to the £1 a litre in England. 'I never knew (Thailand) produced its own oil' comes from the front. Sarcasm is the lowest form of wit, I tell him.

Heat and sweat build in passing through small towns and villages on the road from Prachuap Khiri Khan to Ranong. Small hamlets, a few hundred yards long, suddenly appear before quickly re-entering jungle on both sides for mile after mile. Turning right at Chumporn the road turns west towards the border with Burma (now the Union of Myanmar), which does not allow independent road travel for foreigners, even during the aftermath of Cyclone Nargis in 2008 they would allow no access to aid agencies as tens of thousands died.

The road towards the isolated country of Myanmar twists and turns in 30 degree heat that saps our strength. Even sitting still it erodes your mental world into one of complete lethargy. Little 'buzz' bikes (small-capacity motorcycles) hug a narrow lane on the left while road signs indicate bikes (cycling and motorcycles) should stay in this one-metre wide lane; the width of Bertha.

Car drivers toot us constantly to move over, drifting in and out of the lane as necessary to let people past. The car drivers of Thailand aren't used to seeing a 1000cc motorcycle in their mirrors and want Bernard to slow down and pull over rather than overtake them. The cars themselves all have black heavily tinted windows to keep out the ferociously bright sun and drivers appear from behind these black curtains as windows wind down for a better look at Bertha as we pass by.

Stopping at a beautiful pagoda, a panoramic view of the jungle landscape sits far below us, with the road winding ever upwards into the distance. A man sits with his bird in one corner, complete with its bamboo cage. Eating his lunch, the bird chirps happily at the chance to talk to its jungle cousins, until we turn up. It feels like an invasion of his tranquillity as we clump up to the pagoda where Bernard lights a cigarette. The bird stops singing. When it starts making vague coughing-like sounds Bernard comments 'Perhaps I should have lit a Marlboro rather than a Thai cigarette?' It may have been a coincidence but within five minutes our friend is gone; strapping the birdcage into the front seat of his car. It's nice to meet a considerate pet owner.

Continuing, the hills drop us down into the district of Ranong where a hotel welcomes us, dripping with sweat on to its immaculate foyer. The price is very high though and the receptionist justifies it with a 'free' swimming pool and spa as Bernard puts his nose towards his armpits and sniffs loudly before asking the critical question: 'Do you have white wine?' Assuring us they do we agree a price for the night. Although most of the evening menu is unavailable, they do have white wine; the bottle of Australian was so nice I took it to bed.

The next morning a BMW motorcycle is parked outside with local plates and a petrol tank large enough to go to the moon and back without a stop for a cheeseburger. It reminds us of one of the interviews completed before leaving England when Bernard had been asked if he was worried about running out of petrol on the journey? He'd pointed out that there are few places in the world where 200 miles will not find you petrol; even if it is jugged into the tank or siphoned from another vehicle.

Standing by the petrol tanker this bike had become, Bernard thinks having another five stone (as it must weigh) sitting in front of him, high up, cannot be a clever idea considering some of the roads encountered so far. 'Would have been better to buy two five litre cans, strap them on low down, and save the money' he mutters walking away.

It takes three days to reach Phuket, a popular European tourist resort destroyed in the 2004 tsunami. Although (more or less) completely rebuilt now, large blue tsunami evacuation signs point this and that way indicating

'Run like hell' according to my companion's interpretation. Settling into the rebuilt area we write about our experiences in Nepal and work on web updates.

Emails wing their way to us, arriving from blind people in Japan, Russia and virtually everywhere on the globe. Some are so sad in their longing for adventure. The least we can do is to respond to each, writing back throughout our time away. The evenings find us retreating to the beach, eating meals and clearing our heads of words.

European 50+ men stroll arm in arm with stunning 'nearly dressed' young Thai girls. Recent UK news reports an increase of AIDS and the facts seem to firmly locate this increase within the 50+ age group, one possible explanation being what we witness here on the beach. The funny thing is that Bernard does not see any European women with very young Thai men on their arms. Discrimination I shout, unfair to women. But then again, perhaps women are a little more sensible in their holiday practices? I certainly hope so.

On one evening Bernard guides me to where several people are lighting Thai paper lanterns which drift high into the air as a symbol of good luck. Buying one, his hands guide mine while I light the small candle sitting in the base before holding it and feeling the warm air slowly filling the drum-like shape. Like a hot air balloon it expands and I can feel it pulling upwards, wanting to be released on its journey. When I let go it glides up into the sky, glowing brightly, to join the others floating off into the night's darkness. Streams of light come from around the bay as many people assign wishes and dreams to the soaring, flickering lights. Many may well share our own simple wish for the onward journey, that of 'Good Luck'.

Leaving Phuket by the 402 towards the Sarasin Bridge, a thin bridge links the mainland and Highway 4 onwards, which takes us towards the Thai–Malaysian border at Sadao, reached a day later. The Thai border guards helpfully point us towards a narrow bike lane with high raised kerb stones on both sides which Bertha's cylinders just about scrape over. A large queue of 50cc bikes follow us impatiently, nibbling at the back of us like hungry piranhas as Bernard paddles Bertha's girth through this tiny space, panniers overhanging both sides by several feet. Before we know it a huge 'Welcome to Malaysia' sign appears as we come to a dead stop. It seems we have crossed another border without even trying.

Parking the bike past the official border, the next hour is spent chasing back through the various windows on the Thai side in 100+ heat before Bernard (and the Thai paper machine) pronounces everything signed off, finally. Climbing back on Bertha, the no-man's land between Thailand and Malaysia beckons us forwards.

'Is that the sound of a ring pull?'

(MAL) Even though the countries have rolled on by, we never dismiss the excitement of crossing into somewhere new and usually the event is commemorated, or noted, by Bernard saying 'I've brought a bike to.........' It may seem a small thing to many people but to us it is always exciting and if this feeling is ever lost then it will be time to go home. Rolling past the borderline, the 17th border shows a steady confidence in what needs doing, so well versed are we in the nuances and patience required. It used to be so different. However, after 32 in and outs, as we call them, a confidence develops in being able to solve whatever, bureaucratically, comes your way. This is true even if you cannot understand the paperwork.

The exit from the Thai side is not what we expected as stories tell of people being strip searched, or of their bike being dismantled in the great drug search. It is a border where people get nervous due to many things possibly going wrong and while anything could have been in, or on the bike, in our case however, not a pannier was opened, not a question asked. Again, despite all the stories, never has there been a problem on any border so far. It has not mattered whether it involved a black uniformed Serbian guard or a machine gun totting Pakistani. In many ways, we have come to believe people react to how YOU are. Thus a smile can be infectious, and an offered handshake has never been refused. Sometimes even a shared cigarette can solve a problem which seemed insurmountable only minutes earlier. I leave that situation, however, to Bernard!

The Malaysia side takes nearly two hours of walking from window to window and from office to office in the heat. Arranging only a month's insurance for the bike, the local police issue us with a temporary import disc the size of a dinner plate that's consigned to the pannier for if the police ever stop us. While the hours pass getting into Malaysia, it would have been far longer if we were going the other way with queues to get INTO Thailand being enormous! Coach after coach are parked along the road and the form filling itself would probably keep Parker pen refills in business for years.

Passing the long line of traffic going in the opposite direction, we set off towards a recommended hotel which turns out to be more of a hostel than anything. It all starts off well until hordes of children descend as part of a two family set up. Our room sits between the two family rooms and with the number of children they have it is obvious their television must have been broken for most of their early-married life. It quickly becomes budget hell and like something from a wildly exaggerated sitcom. The children would be swinging from the lights if they could move the ladders from the corner of the building to reach them. It is chaos, pure chaos.

Doing our best to be philosophical, we wander around the town staying out of the chaos for as long as possible until the children burn themselves out, searching for a glass of beer in an Islamic state. Despite hunting through every supermarket fridge not a single drink can be found. Heading back to the hotel, sulking, Bernard reaches for his earplugs to block out the Simpson-like families and retires for the night. Falling fast asleep in his artificial quiet, I lay awake hearing every noise in the hard-surfaced building until hours later he sits bolt upright in the bed saying:

'Is there a party going on?'

'I think it's a revolution,' I reply. 'But then again,' I continue, 'It could be a popular uprising with the natives revolting.'

'Is that the sound of a ring-pull on a can?' he mumbles; it's amazing really how, for a sighted person, his hearing can be exceptionally good when required. Even though the kids from hell are still racing up and down the corridor exercising the full extent of their considerable lungs he still manages among this tornado-like activity to hear the sound of a ring-pull.

Getting dressed, he sets off to investigate the sounds of WW3, and finds a dozen men laying around the reception area drinking beer while the helpful headscarf-wearing Islamic receptionist opens tins of Heineken for them. Coming back muttering 'Am I missing something about an Islamic country here?' he tells of the pile of takeaways just delivered. It's obvious they're in for the long haul as the empty tins mount up while the noodles go down with raucous laughter.

After listening for another hour we consider leaving and riding – for the first time – in the night (Rule 1: Don't ride at night). Bernard assures me the roads are fine and the traffic – if any – does have rules and so it will be a gentle trundle through the night before finding somewhere early to stop. Getting up and repacking our few belongings, it takes three trips to the bike to reload it (at 2am) and as the men realise we are leaving they start to engage with us.

Gathering around, they ask about the bike, the journey, where we have been, enthusiastically taking pictures with cameras and mobile phones. Picture after picture is taken as we pose in the darkness with them climbing on and off the bike. It turns out they think we are leaving on an early start towards Singapore. They are so nice we don't have the heart to tell them the real reason we're leaving. Is this a typical British response perhaps? Who knows?

Our decision wasn't – we think – an overreaction as no sleep was ever going to be possible (even with ear plugs) as the festivities were obviously on for the night (by the amount of beer Bernard described). Thus, for the first time, we set off into the night with a dozen happy people waving us off.

Within ten minutes the alternator light (indicating how well the bike is charging) starts to glow red and the voltmeter shows no voltage coming into the battery. Bernard drives for the next two hours trying not to touch the brakes. Eventually he turns the Sat Nav system off to conserve power and all talking through the intercom is banned. Saving the precious battery to run the essentials, i.e. the engine and lights, we manage 130 miles by 4.30am, before the lights run dangerously dim. It's obvious our night is done and we reach a large service station just as the engine dies, with her battery completely and utterly flat.

Drinking coffee, the unfolding of tool rolls and bike dismantling begins. The head torch goes on and – like the usual magician – tools appear from all over the bike as the manual comes out, the petrol tank comes off, and all the leads are checked over as the next few hours to reveal – nothing. The engine cover comes off and myriad parts are described to me as the night air fills with the sounds of both head scratching and pages being turned in the manual. Gradually Bertha is laid bare in the car park as a crowd gathers to watch her dismemberment. Some wander off to get chairs so they can sit comfortably and watch as the process continues into the dawning light of daybreak.

The top engine cover is removed, where a lead runs from the charging system and nothing is apparent. Meanwhile the mound of cigarette butts mounts to the point where it may soon block the road. As he puffs furiously, more and more chairs appear for the gathering crowd. When one person gets bored watching their seat is soon inhabited by another.

Bernard reads and re-reads the same pages of the manual repeatedly to himself until I know it by heart and can recite each paragraph word for word. Still nothing is clear despite the pile of bits in a nice circle around Bertha. Everything seems to point to one part but Bernard is not sure and anyway, it's the one part we don't have with us; sod's law really.

As daylight starts to spread its heat the head torch is switched off. The traffic increases and coaches pull in to disgorge their passengers for rest breaks and they join the chair-bound spectators watching us. In the end the café staff refuse to let people bring their chairs close to the entertainment as there will be nowhere for the actual patrons to sit.

As always, many of the men know more than Bernard about fixing the bike and the suggestions fly in a mixture of Malay and English. Bernard politely listens to everything and agrees with them. 'Yes, it may be that but I've checked and it is not.' One young man – in between mouthfuls of noodles – makes several suggestions to which Bernard thanks him and tells him he's tried those things. The same young man suggests contacting the Malaysian equivalent of the Automobile Association (AA). He helpfully rings them although Bernard is sceptical about how much they'll know about an almost 20 year-old BMW motorcycle. However, nothing ventured, nothing gained, and so he continues head scratching until they turn up.

At this point he discovers the engine won't turn over at all. Not even a click, which leads to thirty minutes of checking leads and starter circuits before he discovers the bike is in gear. With some motorcycles – like this one – there's a safety feature that prevents the bike from firing up if it's in gear. Moral of the story? Don't ever work on a bike when you are dog tired, have been up all night, and your brain has gone to mush.

Eventually the Malay AA turn up to spend 30 minutes marvelling and fondling all the shiny tools while Bernard continues to work on the bike. They jump start her with Bernard's jump leads (off their battery) and then stand back to take the applause of the crowd as they tell everybody they have fixed the bike.

Bertha rattles gently on her stand ticking over after she's been reassembled and tools disappear into compartments and niches around the bike while everybody is thanked for their assistance. Finding out that the small town Kuala Kangsar is not far away we set off to cover the 8 km. Instead it's 28 km and everything unnecessary for life support (brakes, indicators etc) are left alone as Kuala Kangsar appears. With one last sigh Bertha gasps and dies but thankfully on a downhill stretch to a resort hotel where we coast to a halt under a tree and step off. It was to become our home for longer than we thought.

The resort town is surrounded by spacious parklands and bordered by the Perak River which cuts through the town where the Sultan officially resides, being the royal seat since the 18th century. The parking for Bertha has plenty of shade and Suliyati (the head of Housekeeping) turns up and is so nice that Bernard asks her where the Malay shops hide the beer as it is obvious that it does actually exist. Offering to go and find some for him, he thinks – for a few seconds – before asking for six cans (increased to eight when she prompts him whether six will be enough?). Bernard suddenly thinks breaking down in Malaysia will not be quite so bad after all. Unfortunately for me she does not think wine is available and, sadly, this is confirmed when she returns with the dull clunk of cans but no delicate clink of glass. Two hours later, with one can already gone, he admits defeat over Bertha, retiring to plan his next campaign in the morning.

The morning brings the heat and humidity of Malaysia and continued mechanical searching. As Bernard rips out what little remains of his hair he decides he must order parts from England but there is little idea of how long before they'll arrive; between five days and three weeks is the best guestimate.

Cats wander around the resort and startle me when they suddenly rub against my leg while eating. Feeding them chips from our plate, more cats appear from everywhere – it is like a Hitchcock film but with cats instead of birds. Sitting watching from walls, in trees, on cars, in the bushes, they all wait for some indication food is in the offing. A dozen wander around our legs under the table as we sit in the outdoor section of the restaurant eating: waiting, always waiting, a bit like ourselves.

Meanwhile Suliyati is, I think, somewhat taken with Bernard, not being able to do enough for him. I tease him about being her 'Blue-eyed boy' – even with his brown eyes – and I can quite imagine him pulling his big innocent 'little boy look,' as he asks, 'Are there any chairs for the veranda we could have?' Within ten minutes chairs and a small table arrive. 'Do you have a clothes maiden we could borrow to hang some of our clothes on?' Bang, a clothes maiden appears for our washed clothes. After several days I ask him to see if a bottle of wine is to be had. The next day he pops the question into the conversation.

'Suli' (as he started calling her before continuing) 'do you think (I can imagine his eyes, flutter, flutter) it would be possible (flutter, flutter) to track down a bottle of wine (flutter, flutter)?' She laughs, agreeing to go wine hunting for him as we sit messing with the bike (all the instrument lights have died as well). Eventually she reappears with a bottle of Australian and life is complete again.

Finding a lovely little corner café, time passes sitting talking and consuming cold drinks with curries and exotic salads. The Chinese New Year (Year of the Ox) is ushered in with streets filling with dancing dragons and invites from strangers to the festivities. Plates of food are pressed into our hands as people place small red envelopes containing money into dancing dragon's mouths and Bernard introduces me to one cavorting around the square. The two dragon dancers in the costume do not understand I cannot see them but the 'master of ceremonies' does, keeping them still while I explore their costume. My hands trace the elaborate head as the rear paws scratch behind the head's ears. It feels like a big scary blue Father Christmas all covered in fur and full of sharp teeth and fangs.

Walking through the town, people now wave and say 'Hello' and 'How are you?' as they become more familiar with the sight of us passing by. Schoolchildren in Islamic clothes shout greetings as word has gone around in the schools about 'the English couple' or 'the Blind woman'; all the children greet us in their broken sentences. Many times we wonder if all the English teachers are in their classes saying, '... and if you see them in the town say 'Hello, how are you?' or 'What is your name?' Both greetings are common as everybody smiles and waves while car drivers stop to let us cross the road, indicating 'No problem, after you', really helpful as Zebra crossings are scarce or non-existent.

The promenade into town from the resort has signs declaring no bikes, cars or canoodling. The canoodling sign shows two people with their arms around each other with a big red line through the middle. Wandering past, hand in hand, we see teenagers sitting the regulation two feet apart under the watching eyes of passing people.

For two days a vertical wall of water falls from the sky and the whole town stops while waiting for it to pass; nothing moves on the streets and cars pull over to wait for the onslaught to end. Bernard tells me you cannot see 10 feet, such is the volume of water falling from the heavens. Each time it happens it comes in a wave and then, suddenly, it stops. It doesn't fade away, it just stops like some big tap has been turned off. Seconds later the sun blasts out from behind the clouds and everything is turned into steam. You can smell it and taste it as everything is roasted, as the water burns away.

When not walking the streets of Kuala Kangsar, our balcony becomes our home while schoolchildren play in the nearby grounds, chanting their outdoor lessons. They laugh so much, sounding so happy and excited as Bernard tells me of his life in teaching. Years of experience and being told how there was 'too much laughter in the classroom' and of how his pupils 'cannot be learning properly'; of using music and cold drinks during lessons years before it actually became a 'good idea'. It is obvious when listening to him that he still misses it, even if he were stuck 'in one room, all day, everyday'. Sounding wistful in the remembrance of how all the 'fun' disappeared, as 'education' and 'learning' became replaced with 'targets', 'tests' and examination 'results', he gave up the unequal struggle in 2004. Then he'd gone to work for a large national sight charity. Lucky for me that he did.

We listen to children singing into microphones and wonder if one of them will appear on 'Malaysia's Got Talent' (called One In A Million here). One boy seems to dominate the stage and what he lacks in vocal talent is made up for in pure enthusiasm. Meanwhile the sounds of the mosque are frequent and the call to prayer reminds us of Turkey and Pakistan. The sound tugs at you when you listen in silence, waiting for the final notes to fall away before talking again.

We begin planning for the next leap, to Australia, and change our intended destination of Darwin, in the north, as shipping is too expensive, plus it's flooded by the rain and crocodiles are swimming in the streets. So the decision is made to fly to Perth from Kuala Lumpur. Suliyati arrives clutching the precious spares after five days of waiting and Bernard leaps up and down like an excited schoolchild as Bertha will soon again be singing her sweet song of movement. He is so excited he takes the stairs two at a time as I follow him down on my own using my cane. We've been here long enough for me to learn the resort layout and more around freely and independently. By the time I get to the bike spanners are already in his hands.

When I approach him he watches as I make my way across the grounds and his laughter tells me the cats are scattering in all directions as if to say, 'It's that woman with her stick again, mind your tails!' Pressing the starter a little while later Bertha growls into life as my companion hops up and down with happiness; the voltmeter shows full speed ahead for Australia.

During our wait for the parts we took a chance and arranged to attend a Motorcycle Overlander meeting in a small 'off the track' town called Mitta Mitta in Victoria. For many years, Bernard has been visiting an Overland website and has always wanted to go to a meeting while on the road. Now there's a chance to tick off this dream, but only as long as the 2,000 km across Australia is covered by the 12th of March.

Our final day in town seems incredibly noisy and something feels 'different', and not in a good way. Loud chanting fills the air as open-back 4x4s pass by full of people waving flags, driving up and down the streets with slogans pouring out from loud speakers. The crowds part for us on the walk back to the resort while others step aside until two long lines of Malaysian Riot Police in full body armour stand before us, complete with riot shields and long batons drawn. Suddenly realising something, indeed, is very different photographers leap in front of us to take pictures while camera crews turn their attention towards our sudden appearance.

'Ooops' comes from Bernard's mouth on realising things are a tad tense right now, right where we're standing.

Bernard — When we get to the front of the line it is obvious we have stumbled onto something very, very tense. I look at the line of riot police and give them small hand signals to ask, 'Is it OK to go though?' Many on the front line give back little smiles, returning my hand signals to indicate which way to go as a small gap appears in the line. It is quite funny as our appearance seems to take the sting out of the situation; chanting declines as people watch us making our way through with our bags of shopping. Exiting the rear of the police cordon, the chanting regains its volume before receding into the distance as we make our way back to the resort. Somewhere on Malaysian television that evening, there are probably images of us clutching shopping bags, wandering through the police cordon. Little did we know at the time but it was the start of serious political unrest spreading throughout the rest of Malaysia.

After passing through the demonstration the riot police had fired tear gas into the crowds, triggering a series of running battles with the people we had passed through, once Friday prayers had finished I hasten to add. In the evening and long after the sound of the demonstration had faded, lines of police vehicles pull into the resort to park on grass verges and fill every available space disgorging hundreds of police.

Bright sunlight finds the riot police lounging around the resort watching the grass grow along with our multiple trips to and from Bertha the next morning. They are now 'on call' should they be 'needed' so Suliyati tells us as the staff gather for farewells and police wave goodbye as we pull out onto the road. Passing through the town Bernard says 'Farewell' to all the little shops (the Chinese bike shop where bulbs and oil were bought) along with the little cafés we have come to know. The staff return our waves as they serve the little tables on the street as we pass them by.

The main highway towards Kuala Lumpur is quiet as we head for a hotel booked on the internet days earlier. Near Kuala Lumpur International Airport (KLIA) our fingers are crossed as there is only the roughest map of the area on the petrol tank and no Malaysia maps on the Sat Nav system. The signposts to Kuala Lumpur soon change to KLIA and everything is running well with the hotel suddenly appearing like a magical beacon on the side of the road. Following the sign right to the entrance of the hotel, a security guard salutes, lifts the barrier, and we pull into the car park where staff rush to find a big parasol for Bertha — to shade her fevered brow from the truly awesome sun. Climbing off the bike, within seconds I'm dripping with sweat as a wall of heat and humidity drenches me instantly.

The hotel has been converted from the dormitories of the workers who lived here to build the airport but the facilities are fine and it has everything needed, close to the airport and the cargo offices of Malaysian Airlines. The evening passes with a group of Belgians in Malaysia for the Moto GP racing at the Sepang circuit and they ask the smallest details about what it is like to ride a motorcycle this far, this long and alone. They express great envy as it is something each of them has always wanted to do, much like many other people we've met so far.

Morning comes early as Bertha has to be scrupulously clean to enter Australia due to the rigid quarantine restrictions, and negotiations occur with the migrant Bangladeshi staff of a nearby car wash. Four of them descend on the bike, covering her in soap, scrubbing furiously until she shines. Dusty grey trim turns black with the liberal use of elbow grease and polish. The tyres are washed, looking new an hour later and she looks likely to pass muster for the Australian authorities. Everybody is delighted with the outcome as Bernard pays twice the (minimal) asking price and hands are shaken all around.

In the morning heat, the entrance to KLIA arrives and negotiations commence through multiple layers of tight security to the cargo depot. Hours pass and eventually six officers lean over the shoulder of a colleague who resolutely fills out reams of paperwork for a motorcycle now completely wrapped in 'protective' cling-film and waiting to be loaded onto a pallet. Helpful suggestions fly around in many excited voices, calling on Bernard to assist as nobody can read our English documents. Eventually everybody is satisfied that all the 'i's have been dotted and all the 't's crossed and we can wave goodbye to her. Our own five-hour flight passes in the blink of an eye; talking and laughing, not even noticing the passage of time until Perth appeared below us.

Banking hard left towards the runway I voice my thoughts over whether any of the Indian passengers are tempted to bang on the side of the aircraft to let the pilot know it's OK to turn, as they do on the buses to tell the driver it is safe to turn or overtake. Bernard chokes on his drink at this distant memory of so long ago, made real here and now, as the descent begins towards Australian soil. We feel happy to be nearly halfway around the world despite losing nearly six weeks with visa problems and a budget shot to pieces as the pound has plummeted on the foreign exchange market. There is still a feeling of satisfaction: 12,000 miles give or take.

Having crossed Ireland, France, Switzerland, Italy, Croatia, Bosnia, Montenegro, Serbia, Kosovo, Macedonia, Greece, Turkey, Pakistan, India,

Nepal, Thailand and Malaysia we are still laughing despite everything; or should that be, because of everything? Overcoming problems, be they barriers, breakdowns or silly rules, we've done it alone. The funny thing is, living by our wits and ingenuity, it is not hard to do.

Yes, there have been some very, very hard times and arguments when tired, hungry or frightened. They have happened when we've been unsure what to do or when extreme heat has led to sipping water, making it last while looking for our next meal. The hard times have included extreme conditions for a two-up road bike, wondering how far we can cover before falling off, before seriously hurting ourselves. All through this time when squabbles have happened, they've not lasted long. Bernard told me before leaving England: 'We will not be fighting with each other but with the conditions, or with our own fear. It is never personal. Remember that.'

It's this simple thought that I've tried to keep in mind as it allowed us to survive being constantly in each other's company, as few people have ever experienced. Twenty-four hours a day for weeks and months on end. Alone. Setting our timetable, rather than being rigidly tied down to dates and places, has allowed us to meet and spend time with many fantastic people, some of whom took us in and looked after us as we passed through their lives. We've had tremendous experiences along the way, all of which are burned into our minds. We talk about the things that used to bother us, little things that used to seem so big: the unnecessary clutter filling our lives, surrounding ourselves with possessions, signs and symbols of who we are and what we own. Now they're all gone.

There are few things really needed but some are fundamental to your emotional well-being: someone to trust with your life along with the support of your friends and family. These people inhabiting our lives give us time to dream, to think the impossible – as many said this journey would be for me. They said the same for Bernard, given the peculiar difficulties he would face with my very presence and the strain it would place on him. The importance of those people around me, who believed and supported us, is something I knew all along. Now I completely understand and appreciate them more than ever before, being so far away from them. It's something Bernard and I have talked about as the miles built up over the months. We know they are there and we care about them. Nothing much else matters really.

The wheels gently bump onto the runway and the whole of Australia beckons us.

AUSTRALIA

AUSTRALIA

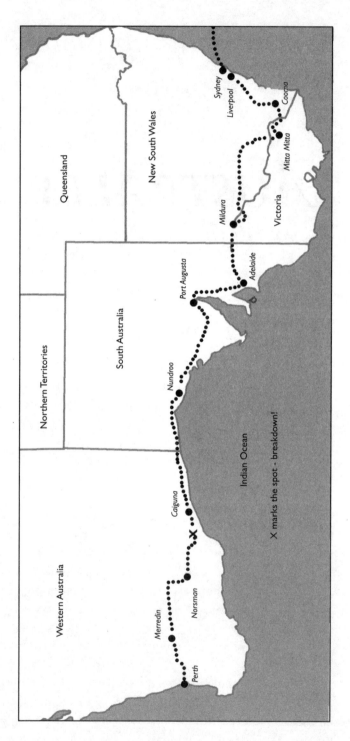

Map of the route through Australia. 10 February - 29 March

'G'day, stinking bloody weather'

(AUS) Australia and halfway around the world. Where is 'halfway around the world'? Is 'halfway' when we land or when we depart? Is it when we've passed 12,500 miles of 25,000 or is it a specific location? We are not sure anymore. In the end, it doesn't really matter. The only thing we know is the sentence 'halfway around the world on a motorcycle' has a certain ring to it. The 'meaning' is added to by the emails reaching us from China to the United States, strangers who are friends we have not yet encountered.

Barely have the wheels touched down before the aisles fill with people leaping up from seats while 'fasten seat belt' signs still burn bright. Cases are dragged from overhead lockers as we sit and wait, recognising there is no rush, no time limits anymore for everyday things. Having waited in Indian post offices for two hours to send postcards home, our world revolves slowly. Everything now runs at a different speed.

Making our way through the airport, the immigration queue seems to stretch for miles as we shuffle two paces forward, put our cases down, pick them up, and then shuffle forward another two paces, for 45 minutes. Reaching the counter, a mighty 'thump' in our passports along with a cheery 'Have a nice visit' indicates we have truly arrived. Two hours after landing we step into the airport terminal of Perth to find, well, very little actually. After Istanbul, Kathmandu and Bangkok, it comes as a shock. No hotel agents can be seen, the shops are closed (it's 5pm after all) and there's no information desk. Wandering around a deserted building we find there are no hotels at the airport and the nearest is in Perth itself so a Russian taxi driver whisks us across the 25 minute drive to the city where we settle into one.

Further recognition of the 'developed' world comes in the evening as drunks weave their way down the street. Several of them stop, aggressively asking for cigarettes as Bernard tells of having only the one he is smoking. Weaving away across the road it's obvious the denial has done one of them fatal injury as he aggressively scowls backwards. The experience hits us hard as we try to remember the last time we've seen somebody, anybody, drunk. Watching him cross the road, Bernard describes others weaving along and we're saddened and a little depressed, as everything here seems so 'loud' and 'frantic' and out of control. People rush everywhere without exchanging pleasantries. When you've lived with complete strangers smiling 'Hello', its absence is apparent and we miss it.

Another taxi takes us back to the airport in the morning, this time with a Turkish driver, to the Freight Office where paperwork begins to reclaim Bertha as an officer complains bitterly about the weather. 'G'day. Stinking bloody weather,' are his first words before a hand extends in greeting while he looks up at the cloudless blue skies. The heat is rapidly building into the 30s as Bernard describes the burnt landscape around the airport. 'Stinking blue skies' – his second gambit to the conversation before he gets on a roll continuing, 'We're even drinking stinking desalinated water.' We're not sure how to respond. Eventually Bernard tries:

'At least you don't have the cold?'

'You English are strange, you like this stinking weather.'

By this time, we know his favourite word is stinking. He walks around the bike.

'Give me clouds and rain anytime, anything but this stinking weather.'

'You wouldn't like it if you had the English weather, you really wouldn't,' I try.

'Cold would be good, you can put a jumper on,' he continues walking around the bike.

'One wouldn't be enough!' Bernard assures him before our friend changes tack:

'What's in the boxes?'

Bernard lists everything in each pannier and points out the two compartments in the fairing where spares are kept, along with the two hidden tool tubes. The officer seems happy with the answers as he records the temporary import document's details (known as a carnet) before leaving, bitterly complaining, once again, about the 'stinking weather'.

The quarantine offices are a short walk away where arrangements are made for an inspection of the bike after paying the $120+ fee. The officer arrives and Bernard tells her of all the precautions taken in cleaning the bike at Kuala Lumpur. She seems satisfied when we even declare our packet of unopened Nescafe coffee, unopened Horlicks Malt drink, and a Nepal bamboo flute (which she wants to see). Inspecting the flute, it too can enter Australia and so avoid being consigned to the quarantine fires of hell inside a plastic yellow 'hazard' bag, the destiny of such 'risky' materials.

Catching us by surprise she asks to see the soles of our motorcycle boots and Bernard holds his breath, steps back, and opens a stuffed pannier and I have visions of everything else passing the strict quarantine rules but of our boots failing, consigned to the fiery hell of the furnace. Examining the soles (without a biohazard mask on) she is satisfied and they too are allowed in. It takes five hours in all before Bertha is freed after we pay a final $136 terminal fee.

Pushing her out of the warehouse – where she cannot be started due to health and safety concerns – we remember the minimal restrictions elsewhere, and it seems strange after watching people hanging off bamboo scaffolding in bare feet. Hundreds of feet up with not a safety harness or hard hat in sight, window cleaners have hung on ropes dressed in shorts and T-shirts on multistory buildings. After swallowing the fumes of buses screaming along belching black diesel smoke while 50 people hang onto the outside of the windows as 20 more sit on the roof it all feels overly cautious.

We ride towards Joondalup (north of Perth) where we'll stay with a friend's daughter who emigrated several years ago from the UK and her family: Jacqui and Jason and their two children, Freddie (6) and William (2).

Over the next few days Bertha's oils are changed, filters inspected, and again she is gone over with loving care as the next roads take us across the Nullarbor, an area we've heard much about, in particular about the kangaroos that can make a mess of the front of cars if you hit them; hitting one on a bike does not bear thinking about.

We go to the registration office in the town and completely confuse the poor woman behind the counter with a request for temporary registration of the bike. After filling out paperwork, she makes calls before telling us we have to drive to a testing centre (called the 'pits') for a road worthiness examination; only then can the documents be issued. Within minutes of setting off, the howl of a police siren stops us. Bernard is roundly trounced by a female officer for 'pulling a UE' which, it turns out, is Australian for U-turn. I smile inside my helmet as he responds:

'I'm awfully sorry, Officer (eyes fluttering no doubt). We have just arrived in Australia and are heading for what, I believe, you call the 'pits'. So sorry (flutter, flutter), there was no sign to say you could not turn around.'

She explains to him slowly and deliberately, as if he has a learning difficulty, that if there are no signs telling you can do a U-turn it means you cannot do it.

'I'm really sorry officer (flutter, flutter) it is SO different and completely the opposite in England where signs tell you not to do something. I can assure you there are a lot of those signs in England and so I am used to looking for them. I am usually ever so careful.'

Passing over his licence she disappears into the squad car where I can hear her giving his details. A voice comes back telling her that he is welcome to stay as there are no outstanding warrants for his arrest (apart from in Turkey, for non-payment of speeding fines, but we won't go into that). Coming back she reinforces the U-turn scenario again before handing his licence back and waving us off. Taking station 100 yards behind us she escorts (or follows) us to the test centre before turning off to Bernard's cheery wave. 'Nice woman' he comments as we pull over.

The pits involve an examination by John, who is very helpful and happy with the condition of the bike. The staff gather round and ponder who will take it out for a test ride. 'Jesus, it looks heavy' seems to be the common thought before John makes the decision and pronounces:

'If you have come this far you must trust her and know her well enough to fix her?' I assume at this point he is talking about Bertha rather than me.

'I do,' Bernard answers, like a groom at the altar pledging his allegiance.

'I don't suppose you would risk her life with bad brakes or steering would you?'

'Not a chance,' Bernard answers. I wonder again is he talking about me, or Bertha? I decide me.

'I guess we'll let the test ride go then.' John signs everything off but tells us the bike cannot be registered there as nobody knows how to do it. To their knowledge only one other foreign bike has ever turned up before, and that was over ten years ago.

Heading back to the main office, the woman seen earlier dives down behind the counter as she spots us and Bernard heads straight for her. Waiting patiently as the queue shrinks and we're at the front, he explains our return. Disappearing into the back office, 20 minutes later she returns with a very nice (white on blue) Western Australian number plate bearing the registration WA123. As she starts to fill out the paperwork, we muse at the chances of ending up with a number plate with the same beginning of our postal address at home (WA).

'That's not for me, is it?'

'Yes, it's your number plate.'

'Sorry, but there seems to be some confusion. All we need is a temporary registration for OUR number, not a NEW number plate.'

He helpfully pulls out a copy of the Australian regulations (which he just happens to have) and points out the paragraph. By now she is huffing and puffing, clearly being out of her depth as she disappears once again into the back office for reinforcements. When they arrive Bernard helpfully guides them through the pages of regulations. Over the next 30 minutes and with several other people now involved, they manage to input the 'foreign' number plate into the computer system, although it doesn't like our H497 AJV number or black on yellow plate colour. Heaving a sigh of relief, we leave clutching two months' insurance and a Western Australia (WA) windshield disc. No doubt they're glad to see our backs as, ever the showman, Bernard insists on taking a bow to the assembled people who have watched the whole scene play itself out for the last hour.

Returning to Jacqui and Jason's an email has arrived from *The Times* in Perth, who want to send a reporter and photographer the next day. Turning up the following morning the talk turns to the journey while the photographer takes picture after picture – even convincing Bernard to take his glasses off for one shot ('Which way is the camera?'). It leaves him less than amused the next day to see the article contains that very picture: 'I look like a mole squinting in the sun,' is his less than amused description of his appearance.

We come to appreciate the space Jacqui and Jason give us, so used have we become to being on our own. It feels strange to be in a home with a family, sharing a living space with other people. In many ways it takes a lot of getting used to not being on our own, or on the move, constantly surrounded by languages we cannot understand.

Our final afternoon with them finds us at an Australian 'barbie' full of ex-pats. There are big cool boxes, with bottles and cans clinking and clanking inside, for people to reach into through the afternoon. Cold drinks are pressed into stubby insulated holders to keep them cool and children leap in and out of the swimming pool. Many people congregate around me, asking questions about what it has been like dealing with life on the road as a blind person.

One couple, on holiday from the UK, are thinking of riding to India on a motorbike as the husband has always wanted to do it and his wife asks what was it really like? Bernard is reluctant to answer as it always seems impossible to explain, and it will be very different for them. Her husband (a police officer) presses for information, listening as we try to describe what it is like to be a Westerner riding a large bike in India. It is apparent he is not happy with what he is hearing, dismissing Bernard's account with:

'But surely if you ride defensively, it can't be that bad?'

Bernard understands his wish to ride a bike through India; he too felt it through most of his life as he tries to point out the difference between 'defensive riding' and riding in India. In the end it proves impossible, much as we thought at the outset. Even telling him of the five UK bikes in the country at the same time, of the three riders who survived unscathed and would never do it again, nothing seems to dent his view. Hearing of how one rider went home in a body bag and another in an air ambulance still does not change his idea of what is involved. Confidently he maintains staying safe will be through 'good defensive riding' and 'good anticipation'.

Bernard lets the comments wash over him, not feeling the need to respond to the implied criticism of his riding style, of his 'weakness' or 'poor anticipatory skills'. I know he has nothing to prove. There is no macho, masculine, bike-riding ego to be defended about surviving each day as whenever anybody asks him about our own survival he reduces it down to pure luck rather than any inherent riding skill on his part.

'We were just lucky, nothing more,' he always answers.

I doubt it myself, I really do. I know. I was there.

In the end it's probably true that riding in such places, under such conditions, is far, far beyond what most motorcyclists think it will be like. Perhaps they think we're exaggerating rather than telling how it was for us. Many people say, 'You'll either love India or hate it,' and this seems to be true. The people of India are fantastic, the culture is colourful, the history is stunning and poignant. It's such a varied experience in many ways it's not to be missed. But get the bus. Get a coach, anything else as when you throw in a motorcycle as a method of transport, it all becomes very different.

At this point we would both say, 'the riding will scare you like you've never been scared before.' Such was our experience and, we admit, it's something we never want to do again. Perhaps it's easy to say this once you've done it. Before that, you cannot ever truly know or understand. It is this we try to impart but to no avail. He wanders off commenting, 'If you ride defensively and be careful, it'll be fine.'

His wife, however, seems a little more pragmatic and she continues to talk to me as her husband stays away from us, never to return. Perhaps a few days of dodging Indian Tata trucks, suicidal rickshaw drivers, and all such things will change his mind. It is also true, sometimes, that the IDEA of doing something is more attractive and achievable than actually doing it. Things become very different when it is for real, rather than a wish, as Bernard will readily testify. Talking to his wife, the afternoon passes by in the sunshine as other people constantly introduce themselves, and talk about life in Australia, their work, their children and everything about what it means to be in the land of down under.

All too soon it's time to move on and we leave Jacqui and Jason with a little sadness as life has settled very quickly into something like normal daily rhythms for us. Exchanging emotional hugs with them we ponder on how attachments to people sometimes happen so quickly. Pulling out of the drive on that final morning the 2,700 km ride across the south of the country to Adelaide stretches before us.

'But you don't look...'

We've heard warnings about crossing the Nullarbor, the inhospitably hot and desolate area between Perth and Adelaide where 100 mile distances between petrol stations are not uncommon. Other warnings about water needs and breaking down in this region have come through loud and clear. Steeling ourselves, we'll carry spare water and stop for petrol at every opportunity; crossing our hearts and hoping to die, we vow not to ride at dawn or dusk in case the 'roos' (kangaroos) 'get us'. It seems they come out at these times to feed close to the road as the water, when it rains, nourishes the plants nearby when it runs off the tarmac.

At a motorcycle shop on the way out of Joondalup, Bernard buys a new pair of gloves as the right hand has worn through with seven months on the road. Soon we're high above Perth in the hills overlooking the city and the bike feels like home with all the familiar sounds: exhausts, engine, all the little rattles joined by the flapping and snapping sound of the Union Jack flag on the right side of the bike. The whistle of the tyres on good roads makes everything feel more predictable and safer. We stop for burgers, French fries and petrol. Couples wander over thinking our route has taken us into Australia direct from the UK but their talk turns to 'bravery' and 'how hard' it must have been across the months when they discover otherwise. Our answers flow, whether about blindness or Bernard fixing the bike.

Our first night's stop is 300 km later in Merriden at a caravan park called 'Av-a-rest', which brings laughter to us in our small rented 'van' with roos wandering around wearing little pink T-shirts. Watching them munching the grass, Bernard describes them as we eat in the failing light.

Early the next morning Bernard is muttering about the roads being boring to ride: straight and stretching for kilometres in front of the bike, with very little traffic. The surrounding landscape has been burned by raging fires, leaving everything blackened and bare apart from where new undergrowth sprouts at ground level. Just where it meets the side of the road are warning signs about the suicidal 'roos' who might appear to 'get you' at any moment.

Forty-metre long wagons (road trains) appear for the first time coming towards us and when they pass, they blast us sideways as a huge wall of 100 kph wind hits. Like huge shiny chrome houses on wheels, they tow two or three enormous trailers and the bike lurches violently each time, startling me badly with the sudden ferocity of the wind, sound and movement. I become tense, waiting for the sudden movement before Bernard realises the impact it's having on me. Soon he warns 'road train' and gives me a countdown '3, 2, 1' before the huge blast hits us with the bike accelerating slightly to cut through the trailing wake of the displaced air. Then the noise returns to normal. Predictability. Knowledge. Sometimes it takes so very little to sooth my anxieties: just two words and a count down.

The heat is profound and our water consumption rockets with temperatures hovering in the 40s as the sun beats down on us, cooking our brains inside our helmets. The smell of heat is overpowering as the bike starts to reflect the temperature – smelling different and much, much, hotter than before. Bernard frets a little at the change and I feel the bike tilting sideways, as he looks down, first at one side of the engine, then the other; looking for something, anything which may signal trouble. Seeing nothing, the bike settles again for a bash through the furnace surrounding us.

After 475 km Bernard calls it a day as riding into the sun along with powerful wind gusts sending the bike tilting crazily is tiring him. Pulling into a 'cabin park', the site is full of roving road repair crews, living away from home for long period. The reception couch becomes a temporary home as we sip cold drinks until enough energy can be summoned to settle in for the night.

On the bike by 7.45 the next morning, the plan is to cover 800 km due to our changing concept of distance, such are the huge gaps between cities. A little while later a petrol stop finds a 750 Triumph sitting alone and Bernard is approached by Greg who asks if he knows anything about bikes.

'Depends,' comes the noncommittal response as Greg goes on to explain the bike will not start while admitting he knows little about mechanical matters.

'Will it turn over?' Bernard's first question.

'No' the answer comes back.

'Shall I have a look?' Bernard offers and I know we may be here for a while – he likes puzzles and a bike not starting is like petrol on a fire to him.

Greg is travelling from Perth to Brisbane (nearly 4,500 km) with his mother, Diane, whose bike it is. She joins us while seats come off, jump leads are extracted, and Bernard convinces a reluctant car driver on the next pump to pop his bonnet. The Triumph is connected to his battery and 'bang' it starts, but dies when the leads are disconnected; no matter how long it runs for. Sounds of a head being scratched indicates Bernard has his teeth into the problem as the 800 km goal recedes for another day and another time.

Both bikes are moved away from the gas pumps for further tests on the battery before again linking the Triumph - this time to Bertha. 'Bang' it starts and it runs for 10 minutes before being disconnected and, promptly, it dies again. The Battery is showing nothing and even life support will not help it. It is pronounced dead at the scene having died and gone to battery heaven. No CPR (cardiopulmonary resuscitation) is possible. It is a 'goner'. I am sorry but we tried everything possible.

Bernard suggests buying the smallest car battery possible and rigging it up inside the side pannier but the petrol station has no batteries and no leads. There is little to be done but wait for the breakdown assistance they've called, taking in the region of five hours to reach them. Wishing them luck we pull out of the station to head towards '90 Mile Straight', which is precisely what it says – the longest straight road in Australia. It runs through the scrubland of nowhere but, thankfully, the sky has turned overcast, bringing the heat down into the 30s.

Seventy kilometres later Bernard asks if I can smell anything ('a burning smell?') as the bike rocks sideways in the now familiar motion as he looks down at the engine. The brakes suddenly come on to the sound of gears changing down as the right side is covered in oil. We coast to a stop surrounded by silence. 'Bugger' is his exclamation as he tries to work out where it's coming from until the source is found behind the right-side exhaust.

Dipping the oil to find it still registers, the good news is there has been no terminal loss of the precious fluid. Explaining to me that he cannot dismantle the bike without losing all the oil, and that it cannot be fixed without its removal it is one of those situations where you go around in circles looking for solutions. As we sit waiting for everything to cool down, a large chrome road train goes past with an empty trailer. The engine decelerates, gears shifting downwards, before parking behind us. Glen pops down from the height of his cab:

'Problem?'

He ponders if the bike could be lifted onto the empty trailer but the option is soon discounted as Bertha is too heavy.

'Do you have anything I could drop the oil into so I can fix the gasket?' Bernard asks hopefully.

'Have a container in the truck,' he grins and comes back with a plastic container which soon loses its top as scissors are deployed from within my crammed wash bag and the oil is drained. Problem one solved.

'Anything else you need?' Glen asks.

'Some cardboard to make a new gasket would be handy,' came Bernard's reply.

'Gotta coco pops box in the cab, had it for months and never opened them, will that do?'

Striding back to the cab he returns with the cardboard carton of breakfast cereal which is soon six inches smaller as the scissors go to work again. Glen settles himself onto a beer crate retrieved from his cab as I sit on a pannier listening as he talks of Australia while Bernard creates a new gasket. I hear of the scrap metal business he runs and of how everything is so slow that the truck helps make ends meet even though it means not seeing home for 6 weeks.

'Is it hard being alone so much?' I ask. He laughs.

'It's good to meet people and break up the day – I thought it would just be another boring day in the truck. Then I saw you and here we are!'

While we talk vehicles fly past as everything is dismantled, the repair completed, the oil poured back in. Bertha fires up with Bernard nervously watching the suspect joint – now resplendent with a homemade gasket and copious amounts of red gasket cement; something else he always carries. The engine ticks over happily with the heat sealing the joint as the back tyre is cleaned with handfuls of baby wipes before the rubber is finally rubbed with handfuls of the fine roadside dust to absorb any final residue of the slippery substance.

Glen returns from his cab with three cold cans of coke and only at this point does he realise the woman he has been talking to for hours cannot see him.

Bernard sees it happen and guides my hand to the cold drink offered in Glen's outstretched fingers as his face falls, understanding; redness spreads across his features as he stands lost for words, misting and moist-eyed as Bernard steps in to cover his discomfort. 'I had no idea.' The words eventually come out 'But you don't look...' His voice trails off. 'Blind, Glen?' I laugh. 'The word is OK to use, really it is.' Sitting in the dust of the passing road trains our conversation turns to blindness and life on the road as Bernard goes back to making final adjustments before packing everything away.

Glen climbs into his cab with promises to follow for awhile to make sure everything is fine as we rejoin the '90 Mile Straight' (now the '45 Mile Straight') with the big chrome truck filling our wing mirrors. The bike tilts as Bernard checks the repair and it holds fast across the kilometres and with one last honk Glen waves farewell and then he is gone.

When things like this happen, I'm often reminded of a saying that the interruptions are the journey and it really is all about the people you meet, such as Glen. It's not about the distance you cover each day. It's not the country you are in. It's not even about the motorcycle. While it's true that a bike can act as a distinctive 'calling card' in its reflection of people's dreams, a journey is, and always will be about the people whose path you cross. They leave indelible marks that never fade away and each one has a name and a voice sprinkled through your memory. Glen now inhabits one of them for me.

Later in the afternoon we reach Caiguna and call it a day. Pulling into a service station, a room is booked just as the sound of Triumph exhausts cut through the air to reveal Greg and Dianne rejoining us having been given a bike battery from a passerby.

A bottle of red wine is soon on the table as talk turns to our separate journeys and of the kindness of people; they with a battery from an unknown car driver towing two motorcycles on a trailer and we with Glen, our road train 'truckie' who provided friendship and our coco-pops gasket. Retiring to our room hours later, sleep comes with hope for a better day tomorrow although, today has been very special in many ways. It's one that will never be forgotten due to the simple act of kindness from a stranger who became Glen.

Leaving early the next morning, we're expected in Adelaide, more than 1,600 km away, the next day to meet Bernard's uncle Pat. He last saw Pat at the family home in County Laois in Ireland at his mother's funeral in 2006 when he immediately flew from Australia to be with his brother, Bernard's father. Having lost his own wife years earlier, he knew – as I do – what it is to suddenly find yourself alone after a lifetime of friendship and marriage with one person. It was at this time of grief that my companion promised Pat that we'd visit him and meet part of his family not seen since childhood.

The day is full of straight roads, road trains, warnings of kangaroos, camels (yes, camels) and flying doctor airstrips and it all reminds us so much of the 1960s TV programme *The Flying Doctor*. Hours pass by in conversation, sparked by a simple road sign, as childhood memories reappear with the kilometres flashing past. In the learning of each other's friends, dreams, fears and triumphs, we talk as perhaps few people ever really do. With occasional breaks for the 'click, click, inhale' when Bernard stretches his legs, the conversation ebbs and flows around such memories as the day passes.

Pulling in for petrol, the clock on the wall says 45 minutes later than both our watches declare while a sign notes, 'Yes, this is the right time!' Bernard is tempted to go over and ask, 'Is that the right time?' but it has probably been done so many times he resists. Finding that we've crossed another time zone from west to south Australia, after 675 km of straightness, we call it a day. Once again, the next stop is too far away to reach before nightfall when the landscape becomes full of 'marauding' kangaroos.

A small garage with cabins for rent has a sign shouting 'NO Vacancies' although one magically becomes free when the owner comes out to talk to us, realising no TVs will be thrown from windows or mattresses cut up, the sign being used as a filtering mechanism. Eating at the garage, an enormous grey and white Irish wolfhound bounds over to say 'HELLO' and 'fuss me', while a waitress complains of not having been paid for several weeks. Perhaps the chef hadn't been paid either as Bernard ends up with food poisoning and morning arrives to find him sore from vomiting through the night. By evening he thinks a beer might do him good and so I know we can move on tomorrow.

The next day there are 942 km to be covered to Adelaide and we pass through Quarantine Borders where customs officers check if you are carrying anything illegal in terms of fruit, vegetables or any other possible 'insect haven'. With a 'Nice one, no worries' on declaring there are no food items in the panniers, they wave us on. Cars, meanwhile, are emptied by the side of the road in the never-ending search for the little blighter called fruit fly, considered to be the world's most damaging pest.

After hours and hours of straight roads Bernard gets excited with the appearance of our first corner in days. Nearly overshooting it to send us straight off the tarmac surface, groups of Aborigines wait to cross and Bernard tells me how their faces light up in genuine Nepal-like smiles as they wave to us. Slowly turning that corner, they stand watching as we wave back in greeting before leaving them to cross in peace.

The traffic gets heavier as we turn north towards Port Augusta with Bertha's exhaust note turning into a cross between a WW2 Messerschmitt fighter plane and a Harley-Davidson (but somewhat quieter than the Harley). Convinced that everybody in Australia can hear us coming he is guilty of somewhat exaggerating; you can hear some of the Harleys much farther away than that.

His uncle's house is too far for one day and with 614 km on the clock he gives up, too sore from vomiting and riding having eaten nothing all day. Pulling up at a motel and shutting the engine off, we shake our heads at the blown exhaust as birds settle back onto overhead wires with the advent of silence. In the corner of our room a TV spills stories of bush fires in the south and east and floods in the north before moving on to how obesity is on the rise in Australia.

Looking at the plates sitting before us in a café later on, it's easy to understand how this would be true as we find space for less than half the meal.

With only 360 km to Adelaide we set out into the constant, heavier flow of traffic and after days of emptiness in the Nullarbor it all seems so busy, so noisy, so congested. Streams of motorbikes pass the other way as we realise it's Sunday and they're out for the universal 'Sunday ride'. A final petrol stop sees us sitting in the shade with lunch and ice-cold drinks as people do a double-take on passing Bertha. Seeing stickers from all over the world they wander over and talk for a while before wishing us 'Good luck' and leaving.

Two loud Harleys pull in ridden by bearded, cut-off-denim-wearing riders sporting German WW2 helmets. Climbing off nonchalantly, all leather and chains, they stand and light cigarettes while trying not to look at Bertha. Bernard cannot resist driving slowly past, waving in greeting, while we wonder if they belong to what the Australians call 'The Bikie Gangs'. It seems the Australian government is having problems with the 'bikies' in their portrayal as criminal gangs who happen to ride bikes, rather than being 'bikers' as we understand the term. Many of the 'everyday' bike clubs fear becoming caught up in the proposed legislation, outlawing membership of 'bike clubs' and, under which, the various bikie gangs operate.

In the outskirts of Adelaide are layer upon layer of traffic lights with an annoying frequency of stop, start, stop, start, every few hundred metres. After months of 'open' roads it takes us forever to get anywhere, although the upside is that people lean out of their car windows calling 'Good on ya' and 'G'day Sport'. Taking in the dust-covered Bertha they probably imagine far-flung places and cheerily wave goodbye as lights change to green.

Passing through the constant stream of junctions and flyovers it all seems so busy towards the south of the city and 'Happy Valley' where Bernard's uncle is expecting us and soon his car can be seen by the side of the main road, lights flashing in hello. Following him for the final stretch, we're soon greeted by a family who sprung from one of the five brothers of the small Irish town of Bagenalstown (Muine Bheag in Gaelic). Only two are still alive, Bernard's father and Pat himself who has lived in Australia for over 40 years. With an accent that changes from Irish to Australian and everywhere in between within the same sentence, he is a lovely man. I like him instantly.

The morning of leaving. Left to right, Elsie whose daughter we would stay with in Australia, Linda the recipient of so many parcels she nearly needed an extension, Cathy, Bernard, Cathy's sister Annie with Guide Dog Quaker and, far right, neighbour Kim.

(Additional photos about this journey can be found at http://worldtour.org.uk)

Right, Bruno using a model to help Cathy understand the layout of the Swiss Guide Dogs centre.

Left, Cathy with a guard at the Greek Parliament

Right, crowds at the Pakistan embassy.

Above, Bertha waiting for tyres in Gebze, Turkey.

Right, part of the Pakistan anti-terrorist team assigned to us.

Below right, Bertha arrives at the hotel in Karachi.

Below, the Wagha border ceremony. The Pakistan Rangers are very theatrical in their baiting of the Indian border guards: the locals love it.

Following lorries in India - the instruction should be followed at every opportunity.

Left, Indian traffic is never ending, noisy and unrelenting.

Right, more ceremonies at the border between Pakistan and India

Above. Cathy painting pictures into her mind at the Taj Mahal and, below, at the Royal Palace at Bangkok.

Left, often Cathy's understanding of physical layouts was aided by using models, as here at the Golden Mount in Bangkok

Right, the first blind woman to mount an elephant from the front.

Below, Cathy stroking a tiger at the Tiger Temple.

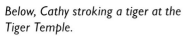

Right, The Bridge over the River Kwai - an emotional experience which left us feeling that history should be the greatest teacher of us all.

A Blind Woman,
Two Wheels and
25,000 Miles

Cathy with Suli and another member of staff at Kuala Kangsa in Malaysia on the day we left.

Below, Australia and we meet Al at Mitta Mitta.

Right, Bernard's distant family who went from being on the other side of the world to just down the road.

Below, the hero of the hour: Glen and his truck rescue us in the Australian outback.

A Blind Wom n,
Two Wheels a d
25,000 Miles

Top left, two little children count their
'soles' in Peru.

Top right, the weaver by the roadside
in Peru whose work Cathy explored by
touch.

Centre left, Cathy senses the local flora.

Centre right, a little girl called Samikai.

Opposite, Cathy climbing Wayna
Picchu in Peru where every step was an
achievement.

Above, on top of Wayna Picchu. A picture that can never truly show the effort it took to get there. It was a truly hard climb for a blind person and the journey down was incredibly frightening as every step was a leap of faith in the person with me. Machu Picchu itself sits in the background.

Left, Hector who will forever be remembered by his voice saying 'Meester Smith'.

Sitting in the rain at the US border. Our smiles say it all.

'Meeting a koala bear named Peter rather than Fred, or John'

Apart from meeting distant relatives who now live 'down the road' instead of 'on the other side of the world', we discover Australia truly is the land of the car. Even the local 'bottle bank' (alcohol store/off-licence) is a drive-in. You pull up, wind down your window, order your beer, pop your boot and pay the attendant who helpfully puts it into the car to save you even getting out. It is a land where everything is recycled and four-litre cars fill up with gas for half the cost in England while everybody complains at the expense.

Whole roads are completely deserted as we walk the streets, devoid of anything other than air-conditioned cars as 'it's too hot to walk'. Pat offers us his own car but we're happy to wander off and explore, even locating a hairdresser where a little TLC is lavished on my Nepali bedraggled (vaguely blondish) head. Outside the hairdressers I get to stroke my first ever kangaroo in a shopping centre where tickets are being sold to help the rescued 'Roos'; only eight months old and wrapped in blankets like babies with gorgeous soft fur coats and big ears.

Water is on everybody's lips as bush fires rage and people die in the infernos that are constantly on the news. 'Black Saturday' (7 February 2009) cost 208 lives and donations and collections spring up everywhere to rebuild shattered lives. The flames engulf every treasured photograph, every childhood item, all gone forever, leaving behind only memories. The collections had started as we crossed the Nullarbor with signs on garages and motels asking, 'Are you heading for Victoria? Can you carry supplies and donations?' The whole country mobilises to assist Victoria while Darwin drowns in water, Queensland submerges, and crocodiles swim in the streets; people lose everything in the same way but, thankfully, retain their lives to rebuild.

At the same time radio stations are full of debate over water shortages and drought, of the need to install rainwater tanks in homes rather than watching what little rain does fall swill down open drains. There is endless talk of the 'dying Murray River', which feeds Australia, and of the cost of domestic water spiralling ever upwards, along with the water companies' profits, which incrementally match each price hike.

Settling into our new surroundings, Guide Dogs of South Australia track us down through our interviews in Perth and arrange a live outside broadcast with ABC Radio for the following morning at Pat's house. The breakfast news leads into the broadcast from beside a dismantled Bertha, needing new piston rings and exhausts.

The reporter asks about our experiences across Pakistan and India as the airwaves have been full of regular updates about attacks in Mumbai. He engages us with humour and questions about blindness, our experiences of Australia, the size of meals, and everything in between. People who heard the interview asked us if we carried any weapons for self-defence due to the broadcaster's fascination with our route through Asia. Bernard merely answers 'Just a big smile' before going on to describe the sticker in our windshield: 'What you see depends mainly on what you look for.'

Even in countries people define as dangerous, most people are only going about their everyday lives, trying to make a living, looking after families. In England, the United States or Pakistan, whether from China or Australia, children grow up all over the world with parents wanting them to have more than they did. It's the same everywhere and if you look for the similarities, you will soon find them. If you set out looking for differences then they will shout out at you. Perhaps, in the end, we were just fortunate in our encounters. Perhaps our roads led us past people like ourselves who happened to speak a different language.

Over the following weeks Bertha is fitted with shiny new exhausts sent from the UK and various other new engine parts (like piston rings and gaskets) to stave off further breakdowns. The mechanical problems are wearing us out as Bertha is breaking down in more and more severe ways while Bernard admits his knees are starting to feel their age with all the kneeling down. Pat, meanwhile, watches patiently as his drive becomes a workshop. Engine parts sit everywhere until the whole thing is sealed into oil-tightness and pronounced fit for the next leg of the journey. Only then can Pat reclaim his drive from under tools and sheets of cardboard.

We keep a promise to my eye surgeon who had operated on both my eyes before leaving England and pronounced me 'fit to travel'. The story had featured on BBC Radio 4's In Touch: the importance of regular eye tests. My diagnosis of glaucoma came quite by accident after experiencing severe headaches for several days. Bernard had taken me to an optician to have the internal eye pressures checked and the resulting readings indicated dangerously high levels; normal range readings are below 20. My readings were 58. Rapid treatment reduced the pressure, followed by laser surgery and cataract operations. Fortunately everything eventually settled down.

It was through this experience that we came to understand that even for blind people it's still important for them to having their pressures checked. In many ways being unable to see makes the checking of eye pressures even more important as you do not get any of the visual warning signals. If left unchecked, the internal pressures build, becoming so severe that the physical structure of the eye itself is threatened. Like many blind people who have lived with sight loss for so long, my days of regular check-ups had stopped years ago. Thus it was never discovered. Wandering into a local opticians, the receptionist is puzzled by a blind woman wanting an eye test but the kindly optician understands the simple test I need, revealing internal pressures of 18 and 19 and so everything is fine.

With Bertha now in one piece, and my eyes having been checked, I get a chance to get up close and personal with a three-year-old koala named Peter at the Cleland Wildlife park in another one of the mysterious, touching coincidences – like the Australian number plate designated WA. Peter was my late husband's name and Bernard considers the probability of meeting a koala bear named Peter rather than Fred or John, or anything else. This Peter munches contentedly on eucalyptus leaves for the five (or so) hours he is awake each day. After standing in line for a child-like experience in a queue of adults, with not a single child in sight, I find my arms are around him feeling his really soft fur with very long sharp claws digging into my shoulder. He is so cuddly and gorgeous I do not want to let him go. As pictures are taken I can hear all the people going 'Ahhhhhh'.

Overlanders and deep-sea divers

The time passes surrounded by an extended family that we grow attached to very quickly but all too soon two weeks have gone by and it is time to leave. In an air of subdued quietness the bike is loaded for departure with 1184 kms to cover getting to an overland motorcycle meeting in order to fulfil one of Bernard's other dreams; attending an Overlander meeting while on the road. Forcing ourselves to move, eventually, the bike is ready at 11am - two hours later than planned. Embracing Pat in a quiet emotional way, it leaves us wondering if we will ever get to see this dear man again as he will soon have his 80th birthday. We hope so.

Travelling slowly in order to allow the new piston rings to settle in, speed is limited to 80 kph for 400 km before increasing it to 90 kph for another 400 km. Meanwhile cars blast past us all day at 100+ and we think perhaps there should be a 'Running In' sign on the back of the bike. Throughout the day Bernard tilts the bike, checking for any signs of problems but it is obvious everything is running fine as the new – throatier - exhausts become my 'normal' backdrop of sound as I get used to them.

Arriving at Mildura, another time zone is crossed, losing a half-hour as the clocks go forward in a small motel where staff are very aware, putting knives, forks and condiments down onto the table; describing where they are for me. The meal is delivered and descriptions occur concerning the meat (12 o'clock), veg (3 o'clock) and potatoes (8 o'clock) are located and it is all so helpful to have this without even asking. It is so very rare for people to appreciate the difficulties of eating when you cannot see what is on the plate, or where it is. The morning brings the sound of rain.

Malaysian torrents pour from the sky and the manager wanders over to thank us profusely for bringing our English weather with us. It hasn't rained here for four months as the rest of Australia bakes in the sun and forest fires rage. Water runs down the road with no sign of abatement. An hour later we don our waterproofs and splash towards the exit with the strange sound of rain bouncing off my helmet. The whole world sounds different sloshing through wet roads with the bike slowing down as running water grabs the tyres, quickly turning to a smell and taste of steam as it dries on the hot engine and exhausts. We make steady progress before stopping in glorious sunshine to remove our rain gear but within ten minutes we're drowning again. So the journey continues, steaming as the sun dries us out before being soaked again. While feeling wet, it's not uncomfortable as the sun and warm breeze soon dries us out after each, short, ferocious downpour.

One stretch of the highway has been dug up by a roving road crew to leave behind only red rain-soaked mud. The bike fishtails alarmingly for several miles, slithering and sliding down the road as trucks going the other way spray us in sticky redness with their passing. The tarmac eventually returns and, pulling over, Bernard tells me that we look like we've been immersed in a bath of red mud.

Heading along the Sturt Highway towards Albury, our destination is Mitta Mitta, a small place south of Albury itself, just past Tallangatta. Soon the twists and turns of bends appear unlike anything we have experienced so far in Australia. Tilting and dropping into corners, Bernard's happiness is clear through the intercom. Lining the bike up for corners, dropping a gear, he rides through before setting up for the next corner with a repeat of the whole process. Arriving outside the Laurel Hotel in Mitta Mitta, bikes are already there and Bernard describes each new arrival to me: bikes, riding gear, luggage set-up. Happily, the organiser Dave has been to work and found us a small caravan in the grounds of a lovely lady (Margaret, 79 years young) who helps us unpack before settling in at the bottom of her garden. We fall asleep in the absolute quiet.

At 4am we find that the caravan backs onto a chicken house and, you've guessed it, cockerels only too glad to announce that it's time to get up. Shuffling around the caravan looking for his earplugs, Bernard manages to bounce off every piece of furniture in the unfamiliar environment. Hearing me laughing from under the covers, he mumbles:

'What's so funny?'

'You,' I reply, 'You don't do the darkness thing too well do you!'

He grunts that I've had much more practice at it before settling back under the sheets, only to be woken three hours later by the Hound of the Baskervilles, who lives at the same house as our – still crowing – cockerels. It starts howling ten seconds after a car leaves – presumably the owners – and continues for the next hour and a half before we give up and get dressed.

The day passes talking with bikers from all over Australia, about trips, bikes and equipment as we sit on the grass at the rear of the small pub. Exhaust sounds signal the arrival of bikes and voices constantly change, coming and going from our group. Following the arrivals and departures is relatively easy as Bernard lets me know as people drift in and out of conversations. This was to be our first encounter with 'Al', who turned out to be 'one of those people', like Ian in Nepal, whom we 'take to'.

Sitting and talking, with the 'stubby' pile getting bigger around the site, Al asks many questions about blindness – with no discomfort, no hesitations about the 'right wording'. I like conversations like this, so refreshing after the constrictions of England where political correctness often stifles conversations, leaving people frightened of using the wrong words.

He's a deep-sea diver, and it's interesting to hear him talk about the comparisons of the ocean blackness at depth while trying to orient himself, to work in the darkness – something blind people do throughout their lives. Comparing the skills of blind people he thinks we would make excellent deep-sea divers and so perhaps this is a new career opportunity for blind people? Could you imagine the application form with the question 'Do you have any disabilities?' to which the answer could then be written;

'Well actually yes, I'm blind. But then again, I believe you can't see a damn thing at the bottom of the ocean anyway so it won't be a problem will it?'

Among the gargantuan BMWs pulling in, little red 'postie' bikes start to appear. Used by the Postal services of Australia to deliver mail, they have a 'cult' following with people re-boring the 110cc engines to larger capacities and fitting bigger fuel tanks before going 'walk-about' around Australia. It appeals to Bernard and he looks at the little red machines, talking to the riders about the challenges they undertake through the outback. I know that, given half a chance, he too would be on one of these little overloaded bikes.

Back at Margaret's house a BMW GS650 is parked on the drive, belonging to Bonnie from Sydney who has travelled for her first meeting. Bernard says she has the 'Gleam of the Faithful' look in her eyes. Over the days she throws herself into learning about what it takes, and means, to ride around the world on a motorcycle. The fact that she turned up alone, knowing nobody, convinces Bernard she is already halfway there; psychologically this is what is involved in riding around the world. There are evening presentations on equipment, roads ridden and people met in far-off lands and Bernard hears of Mongolia, and a landscape with few roads but many tracks make me picture the 'gleam' in his own eyes and it wouldn't surprise me at all if at some future date...

The next day 80 bikes set off for Dartmouth, the largest dam in Australia, which is currently only 20% full due to chronic water shortages. The air is full of motorcycle testosterone as Mitta Mitta buckles under the weight of it with people charging up the road while we putter off following a small postie bike. Hitting the hills, Bernard's own testosterone kicks in with a vengeance as my world becomes full of the sound of scraping metal as he fires a – still loaded – Bertha into corners, catching a large group of 1200cc BMWs before he settles down.

Sitting on the edge of the dam people talk about shipping, breakdowns and carnets. Conversations ebb and flow around living on the road, other countries and people as small groups drift off to the sound of bikes firing up to disappear back down the hill. A single bike follows behind on our downward journey, but this time without all the frantic cornering and metal scraping of the climb up.

The heavens open in a deluge leading people to scamper to the pub yards away from the stand before the 'Secret women's business' meeting starts. Men are barred, although Bernard does try to convince people he'll be needed. He is propelled to the door. 'Secret women's business' is an Aboriginal term, meaning strictly NO MEN. Limping away after my cane left a bruise on his leg in 'Goodbye', 'be gone' and 'get lost', I hear him harrumphing as he shuts the door with a final (loud) 'women'. We laugh.

The meeting concerns the same things the men talk about: shipping bikes, riding distances and the use of Skype to stay in touch with people. It's difficult at times to keep track of what's said, due to both the heavy rain on the roof and a table full of people making conversation difficult; much like it always is for blind people in a large gathering. When the large group splits into smaller groups, it's far easier as I can share my observations and experiences of the journey so far.

There are enormous lightning flashes and rumbling thunderstorms raging in the distance as we sit in the hall after presentations by people who have crossed China, Bolivia and other exotic places. Some of these we'll soon experience as we cross into South America, the next stage of our own journey.

A new day sees tents disappear as bikes are loaded and people wave goodbye to new friends. We sit and talk to Al and Mick, who are feeling somewhat delicate after a drunken 4am attempt to weave their way back to waiting sleeping bags. Mick has ridden in five Paris–Dakar rallies and he arrived with a tent and sleeping bag strapped on his trail bike. 'It's enough,' he comments as he laughs and looks around the campsite at a mountain of gear for a weekend away. Bernard is intrigued as to why he did not give a talk. Mick is nicely understated and dismissive as, like many others who have done so much, he is happy to sit listening to everybody else. As he pulls out for his own journey home, Al's tent sits alone in the corner of the field until the evening welcomes us back to the now empty pub.

Wandering over to Al's lonely semi-dismantled tent the next morning, we find we're travelling in the same direction and he's genuinely pleased when Bernard asks him if he'd like to stick with us for a while. It will be nice to have some company as both Al and Bernard usually ride alone, having done so for years. An affinity has been struck between these two loners as we set off towards the 'Alpine Way' and 'Snowy Mountains' with Al taking station behind us. Swooping through the mountains it feels like being back in Montenegro, or the Swiss Alps, as the road twists and turns in ever tighter corners; so much so that I feel I could reach down and touch the floor as we career around them.

The engine howls as we descend the steepness and I hear the constantly changing gears, feeling the engine slow us down with the little 'tipping' of Bertha's nose indicating front brakes being used. The smell of garlic pervades the air, brought alive by the recent rain releasing a thousand smells from the surrounding forests; it's so pungent my eyes water. Continuing on a roller-coaster ride to climb the 1,565 metre heights, Bernard describes the ski lifts and lodges, the shops with signs declaring 'Snow Board Hire' or 'Snow Chains for Sale'. It's so unlike anything we expected in our naïvety about the vastness of this land.

Stopping for the evening in two cabins Al tells of his time in Mogadishu during the American operation 'Restore Hope' or 'The Invasion', as the Somali people called it; of the 'wet kitchens' set up by a local woman around the city to distribute food in an effort to stop it being stolen by the warlords. As the evening passes he tells how many of the bikers had felt humbled by the two of us, the way we deal with each other. It seems there were conversations concerning our battered dust-covered bike sitting among the 'bling, bling' of new machinery, of our 'lived in' dashboard which needs only a set of net curtains to add a finishing touch. We laugh at the image and understand the sentiment. It truly is our home now.

The next morning our roads are set for different directions and Bernard tells me of Al becoming 'misty', the look men get sometimes and, after a hug, he is quickly gone. Pulling out of the site we wave to one of those special people whose lives we cross briefly, a stranger who feels like a friend despite knowing so little about them.

'Armadillos and sea shells standing on end'

Before we'd arrived in Mitta Mitta, Vision Australia (The Australian National Charity) had picked up on the story of the British Blind Woman on a motorcycle and invited us to visit them in Sydney. Making steady progress at 100 kph, soon only 40 kms remain to Sydney as we stop for the night in Liverpool. It feels strange to arrive here, halfway around the world, in a place name where it all started. But then again, perhaps it is just another one of those coincidences.

Our first attempt at a hotel involves twice the (advertised) cost of the one across the road and the receptionist's words of 'Ask to see the room' ring in our ears. Dodging the busy traffic to enter under a sign stating, 'Half-day price of 65 dollars', it leaves us puzzled, but nothing more. Mohammed from Hyderabad in India is genuinely pleased we know of his hometown and is happy for us to look at the rooms.

Opening the door a smell of stale beer and cigarettes washes outwards before Bernard describes walls decorated with holes where fists have left their mark. The beds are circular and the landing is full of laundry at 4.30pm. Girls on the floor above wave to Bernard with big smiles. 'It's another Kosovo isn't it?' he mutters. I have to agree. Mohammed does not even attempt to negotiate as we leave. He knows we know. Back across the road we stump up the extra cost as I ask, 'What is it about you and brothels?'

Parking Bertha under our room's veranda, wash bags are thrown up into my open arms, warnings of 'incoming' shouted as I try to catch each item ten feet above. Eating and talking through our meal we realise that in about a week, we'll be in South America: another milestone, another continent.

Vision Australia have arranged for the media to be present on our arrival and the press officer, Megan, 'gongs' out reporters after allotted time slots as the bike is ridden endlessly up and down. Photographers take streams of pictures as amused and curious onlookers watch as we are 'arranged' like exhibits. Lying on the grass with Bertha in the background, voices say 'Can you just move...' an arm or a leg, in this or that direction. The words come quickly now in answer to their questions, before the afternoon is spent talking to staff and clients in a seminar room for 'about a 15 minute' talk. One-and-a-half hours later people are still asking questions as the business day ends, without much business going on.

Pauline (one of the staff) offers us accommodation while arrangements are made for our departure from Australia. We also need to source tyres for the final leg up through the Americas as we're not sure where the next replacements can be found in South America. Chanting 'safety first' they are replaced in a country where language is not a problem (as neither of us speak Spanish). A good set of rubber on the wheels will also keep punctures at bay according to Bernard, as our third set to date are installed with not a single one experienced so far.

Days pass tracking down a shipping company until Bertha is eventually booked onto a flight with Qantas departing Sydney while our own flights are with Aerolineas Argentinas to Santiago. Both bike and ourselves should arrive at the same time so it should be possible to clear the city in about two days; saving time and money. Slowly, after six weeks on this huge island, both factors are becoming shorter in supply; never-ending days are suddenly becoming finite as reality intrudes. It does not feel good.

With logistical matters dealt with, we climb Sydney Harbour Bridge and our guide, Seamus, gives Bernard the day off, guiding me himself while describing the history of the bridge as my shadow walks behind. The only thing nearly spoiling the day was Bertha breaking down a kilometre from the bridge, causing her to be left (in disgrace) for Bernard to contemplate later. Standing at the very pinnacle of the massive metal structure Seamus asks me what I sense. How does it feel? I have to admit it seems 'eerie'. It's the only word that comes to describe the sound of the wind high up, the silence.

At the very apex of the bridge a seaplane flies close by and Seamus tells us to wave and if we are lucky the plane will waggle its wings. We are lucky. Nearby, meanwhile, three storms are moving in from different directions and the order comes to evacuate the bridge as lightning flashes to the west. Beginning the 1,437 step descent of the widest-most load-bearing bridge in the world, no doubt our legs will later remember each and every step.

After the climb a planned radio programme has to be cancelled as Bernard searches for the fault which has again stopped Bertha's battery from charging. Offering to do the interview 'in the heat of battle' they don't think the sound quality will be good enough on a mobile. After a jump-start from a taxi we head back to base, conserving voltage as we did in Malaysia.

Hours pass with Bernard wearing a head torch as the rain starts to fall.

Replacing this and that he curses, 'Next time, a new bike, I'm too old for this shit!' His frustration is obvious, understandable. Midnight comes and our legs are stiffening from the bridge climb as fingers are crossed for the morning when we'll start her, successfully as it turns out with the fault cured until the next time. The feeling in our legs is quite another matter, however, evidenced by the loud groaning companion beside me as he eases out of bed, very slowly.

Bertha is driven to the Qantas freight terminal showing a healthy 13.5 volts with the fault fixed and we are met by many helpful staff who magically shed 40 kg (or $360) worth of weight from Bertha before pushing her into the warehouse. Leaving everything with the bike to take only a few overnight items, unlike our previous shipments in Istanbul, Kathmandu and Kuala Lumpur, no case is bought this time to give away upon landing. Bertha is duly covered with Dangerous Goods stickers and the only thing missing is an armed guard with a sign saying, 'Stay clear. This bike is truly dangerous, it can injure you health.'

After a short taxi ride back to Pauline's there's time enough to prepare for our evening visit to the Sydney Opera house, our way of repaying her kindness for giving us a roof over our heads, meals, and even running us around to organise the leap of countries.

Arriving at the opera house Bernard struggles to find a good description of the building; 'armadillos' and 'sea shells standing on end' are used with no great success. In the end he convinces the reception staff to open the closed souvenir shop from where a model of the building can be retrieved. When it's in my hand it all comes together. Now I can appreciate what everybody marvels at as it feels more like a work of art than a building. It must look truly magnificent.

The Sydney Symphony Orchestra plays Beethoven and Bartók in an environment where the rustle of a programme can be heard rows away. The sound of Beethoven is enchanting although the music by Bartók is, dare I say, like the sound track for a horror movie, so full of clashing dissonance is it. Perhaps he is one of the great composers of the 20th century but I had nightmares for days afterwards.

Arriving at the airport clutching our two small bags we start to dread the length of flights involved under cramped conditions: across the date line gaining a day, with a 15 hour time difference at the other end, arriving four hours after we leave Australia. Bernard is as ready as he can ever be. He clutches his packet of Nicorettes to stave off the dreaded nicotine withdrawal symptoms due to the barbaric (his word) 'no smoking unless you are on fire' conditions of all the airports. Telling me the last time he was 20 hours without a cigarette he was asleep after a long motorcycle ride up through Spain and France. In fact, he goes on, 20 hours is longer than he's ever given up smoking.

We hug and wave goodbye to our hosts as layers of security envelop us, involving the removal of my lethal shampoo, conditioner and toothpaste as I try to explain that the pump action toothpaste makes my life easier; have you ever tried to squeeze a toothpaste tube when you cannot see it? My pleas fall on deaf ears. The same is true of my containers of shampoo and conditioner, with different tops to enable me to distinguish between them. Stony hearts and regulations win the day as they are consigned to a bin while my white stick is X-rayed. It is funny that while relieving me of my hair care items and toothpaste, I am left with a metal penknife and corkscrew. Perhaps I'm missing something here about 'dangerous items'?

Climbing onto the plane Bernard sucks on his Nicorette before the wheels even leave the ground as the first part of the journey takes us to Auckland, New Zealand. Waiting in the lounge at Auckland, I hear our names over the public address system and nudge my already dozing partner into motion. Aerolineas Argentinas has upgraded us to business class for the fourteen-hour flight to Buenos Aires at no extra cost. Sitting in the lushness of reclining seats bigger than many single beds, I listen to a TV which folds into the armrest. Blankets, newspapers, food and drinks are delivered to the half-full cabin as the hours are wiled away, alternating between talking and sleeping 35,000 feet above ground. When the staff bring anything for me they give descriptions, even gently guiding my hand to drinks on trays sitting on foldaway tables. Drifting in and out of sleep, the date line and time zones are crossed as Bernard wakes in his 'night'. Already feeling the confusion of jetlag, his body is saying 'night' as he tells me of bright sun streaming in through the windows.

Australia and everything that has happened consumes most of our thinking and talking during the long, long incarceration as the plane takes us towards our fourth continent. In between bouts of sleeping, our minds turn towards the future and it feels uncertain in many ways. Bernard has always been able to 'see' Australia in his head. Now, for some reason, all he experiences are rolling mists full of shifting, indistinct, shapes flitting just out of reach when he tries to bring them into focus. After 12,000 miles or so of clarity in his thinking, he is falling into a world of uncertainty as his confidence slides in a downward spiral.

'Perhaps you've just had enough?' I tentatively suggest.

Thinking for a few minutes, he admits that Australia had felt like 'the end' to him for some reason he cannot fathom. Right now something is missing from his mental world, leaving him unable to see past it and I've noticed for several days how his mood has been shifting, changing in ways I've never noticed before.

Promising to tell me if he starts to think of murder and mayhem, he admits it may be just the cumulative effects of tiredness after months on the road, with the constant straining to keep us safe over days, weeks and months of riding for thousands of miles. Tackling everything from fixing Bertha by head torch light in the dark as his knees grind with every movement, to sifting through and editing photographs, or video clips, he gets little respite. Even when we stop moving for a few days, he sits with me in the search of words for web pages, fighting blank thoughts when they will not come. Thus he's had no real down time. It's a part of the journey people do not see, nor could ever appreciate unless they live with a blind person.

Hours later we land in Buenos Aires and shuffle towards the smallest plane Bernard (or I, by the description) have ever flown in. 'We are going over the Andes in this?' he asks as we climb steps to enter a cabin where he stares enviously at the empty business class seats just in front of us. Flying over a landscape of snow-covered peaks and red-coloured mountains that slips into long shadows, our final flight, to Santiago, is mercifully short (two hours). Our bodies are now sending urgent signals to shut down and descend into peaceful and complete sleep, despite the bright sunshine streaming in through the windows. The wheels ground on our 19th country with a screech, signalling our arrival on a continent full of history, political problems, instability, strife, wars and difficulties. While this is all true, I turn to my sleepy companion and nudge him into wakefulness before asking: 'What's the Spanish for red wine?'

Let the Latino adventure begin.

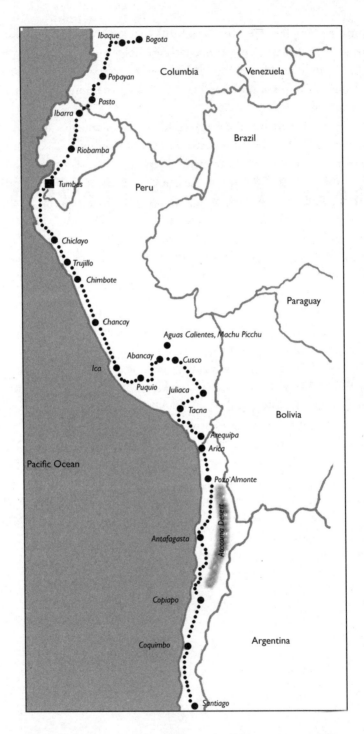

Map of the route up South America. 30 March - 2 June

SOUTH AMERICA

CHILE, PERU, ECUADOR AND COLOMBIA

'With a life time of work'

(RCH) Stumbling off the plane with my left leg not talking to my right, tiredness leaves my brain wrapped in cotton wool. Every sound and sensation seems removed, filtered through a mush, with a flattening of all sensations. Fortunately the anaesthetic effect of jetlag enables us to sit like zombies as the evening landscape flies past for 25 minutes of Chilean warp speed taxi driving. On reaching the hotel in downtown Santiago, thankfully unscathed, a room is booked for three nights with a plan for Day 1 (arrival), Day 2 (retrieve Bertha) and Day 3 (repack and prepare to leave). The terms confusion, disorientation and dog-tired do not describe our feelings in falling into the room to pass out at 11pm. Waking every two hours, 5.30am arrives with sore eyes and aching bodies but happiness as Day 2 is about to begin.

After breakfast another Chilean Lewis Hamilton takes us back to the airport where Bertha is nowhere to be seen. We're told she's not due until Wednesday at the earliest. Confused, we show documents, booking slips and confirmation of cargo space, much shaking of Chilean heads occurs as the same sentence is repeated: not before Wednesday, at the earliest. We have nothing but the clothes we stand in.

In another office our English-speaking taxi driver helps us through the labyrinth of Chilean motor insurance before a nice young woman struggles with the computer system which does not like our foreign number plate or our British passport numbers. She concedes defeat and no insurance is gained. Trudging out of the office, Bernard ruminates how it was easier to get things done in Pakistan than in Chile and this amuses our driver Jorge no end, who chuckles all the way back to the hotel as he repeats, 'It's easier to get things done in Pakistan than Chile.' Projecting the car through the traffic like a missile, slinging the two us against each other on the back seat, we are too depressed and worn out to care.

Jorge rings the local police station after our safe arrival from the descent into the city. Explaining our predicament, the answer is surprisingly simple as they suggest, 'Just show the UK insurance if anybody stops you as it is unlikely they will be able to read it anyway.' We laugh as Jorge innocently suggests, 'Problem solved and much cheaper this way.' Perhaps the Chilean police are different than expected? After all the tales of baton-wielding toenail-rippers using sharp-pointed sticks on unsuspecting naïve tourists, we did not expect this.

Jetlagged, my legs feel like a deep-sea diver's in lead boots as the world passes me by in a fog of indecision. Falling back into bed hours pass with us muddled in time and space as our body clocks have lost all normal rhythms. Bernard suffers more than I do as I have no signals of sun and dark to reset the internal wheel. It's probably the same for many blind people all over the world as they wake in the middle of the night to reach for speaking clocks as we try to locate ourselves in the artificially constructed world of time. Many blind people are often inevitably tired because of this inability to adjust our body clocks using light and dark. Meanwhile Bernard struggles to adjust while sunshine streams in, or he wakes in the pitch black of night.

Watching movies to pass the time, it's suddenly 6am and in a flash the cleaners wake us at 1pm to service the room. Bernard now includes the term 'jetlag' in his Spanish vocabulary to explain his tardiness and shuffling geriatric gait. Frustration sets in as emails wing back and forth to Australia. It's clear that Bertha has left Sydney and we cross our fingers she will not be offloaded at Auckland, a euphemism for 'taken off the plane because somebody else's goods are more important than yours'. It happens a lot and was the initial explanation for our predicament. The term is dropped like a stone when Bernard pointed out to Customer Services in Australia:

'It wasn't offloaded. If you never put it on, you can hardly have offloaded it can you!'

Ever Mr Direct.

I badger him to write the postcards originally bought in Malaysia, still in our journal after 4,000 km across Australia. We walk miles in the heat to find a post office and join the queue. Shuffling forward, Bernard flicks through Spanish phrases needed before reaching the front of the queue and reverts to English as the whole queue watches amused. The man behind the counter pulls out a book of stamps the size of dinner plates that will cover half of our writing. Interest in the queue rises as he roots through folders before disappearing to find smaller ones, eventually returning with Christmas 2007 stamps – all 54 for 1,350 pesos (about £1.60).

Giving us a bucket of water we thump our way through all 54 under the baleful glares of the Chilean office intelligencia on their now destroyed lunch break, their wait quickly turning them from interested and amused bystanders to foot tappers, huffing and puffing with impatience. A hefty thump signals the postcards landing in the box before we quickly exit the building with heads held high at another job achieved, wondering if people realise the effort involved in the sending of a simple postcard.

Retiring to a café I'm sure the sigh of relief could be heard halfway across Chile when a phone call reveals Bertha is now in Santiago. Girding ourselves for battle with Chilean bureaucracy, our mood lifts once Bernard has fired off an email about the delay to Qantas.

We set off in the morning with a new taxi driver, Raimundo, who we call Ray. As attentive and helpful as Jorge, he is though without the fluency in English. Bernard bounces like a Labrador at a reunion with a long lost friend when we leave the hotel. At the airport he is so eager to see his 'beloved' that he nearly leaves me behind, shooting out of the door of the taxi before the wheels have even stopped. As he stands hopping from foot to foot waiting for me, he can see the bike through the open doors of the warehouse.

Then follows the inevitable paperwork trawl, going from here to there, and back again, with the staff still laughing at the big hug Bernard gave the back box on being reunited with Bertha. We hand over dollars at each new desk, with little real clue of what each payment is for but with no doubt of their legitimacy. Hefty thumps fill the air as receipts flutter like confetti while Ray does his best to explain. Disappearing to find us some petrol, Ray comes back puffing with five litres of Gasolina after walking three petrol stations further than anticipated before finding one with a container he could have. Meanwhile the staff are patient and helpful, offering chairs for me, as paperwork is completed and signed off. Eventually Bertha is pushed out of the warehouse as the temperature gauge shows 35 degrees.

People gather to watch as she is brought back to life before she sits rocking on her centre stand on firing up. The voltage shows 13.5 and we heave a sigh of relief as the charging system is working perfectly. Bike gear is retrieved and boots unloaded from panniers and we dress to an appreciative crowd that grows to block the warehouse entrance.

Setting off with a full tank of petrol and the whole of South America before us, the tyres sing a song of freedom on the tarmac following Ray back to the hotel. Under the warm sun Bertha sounds fantastic and our mood lifts at the reunion, even forgiving her all the recent troubles – so much has she been missed. Bernard has been irritable, short-tempered and moody, and if it were caused by anything other than a bike I would worry.

Three-and-a-half hours after leaving the hotel our return draws a crowd as cars stop at the lights to take in the details as Ray helps carry our belongings up to the room. Reflecting on our morning we feel nothing but gratitude for all the people we've met; all in their own way helped us along the process. From the disentangling of language differences to the reams of baffling paperwork before us, all were overcome through people's help and patience.

Bernard now has a smattering of phrases and words in Spanish and, as always, so confidently are they used that people return a volley of language at him, leaving him (in my head) shrugging his shoulders before admitting, 'I do not understand' or like poor Manuel in Fawlty Towers with 'Que?' We are struggling here more than anywhere else so far as English Imperialism was not big in this part of the globe; the Spanish got here first. Not only did they set down their roots in terms of horses, cannons and swords, but also in terms of buildings, architecture and terracotta roof tiles. And their language.

On TV the evening news is full of the new USA president, Obama, declaring Pakistan the most dangerous place in the world. Really? The story rapidly switches to a man in America shooting and killing elderly people in a care home as we sit shaking our heads at the comparison. Bang, the story moves on to Mexico where 1,400 drug-related shootings have occurred in three months. Like a child with a short attention span, the sound-bite stories switch to the worldwide financial meltdown as financial storms rage through the world. It's the same storm we nervously watch as the value of the pound bobs up and down like a ship with a broken mast.

Filling time, we watch internet clips of Miles Hilton-Barber (another blind 'adventurer') and are reminded of the people who asked 'Why?' before we left England. Miles himself has flown micro-lights around the world, trekked to the South Pole, along with a whole host of other amazing experiences. People ask, 'Why is he bothering when he's blind?' Interestingly, it is always sighted people who ask that question. Never once have either of us heard a blind person ask this.

Perhaps you have to be blind to understand why. When you can see and are able to do things (like drive a car) it may be a puzzle to you why a blind person would want to do the same. Laughing at his definitive line, 'Life is too short to drink bad wine', we also love the concept, 'If your boat does not come in then swim out to it'.

Which is what I did: I swam to my own little boat of reinvention when I ended up alone, passing the years following the ebbs and flows of the current before arriving here, in Chile. Through the memories of the long and torturous years of struggling to 'be', I sit and listen to his words. I like them. They sit well with me in the preparation to move onwards.

Sleep comes fitfully until 6.30am and we give up, get dressed and prepare to leave. Old routines re-establish themselves as Bertha is brought up from the underground car park to stop the traffic as she sits outside the hotel.

People appear to talk to us the instant the side-stand drops. Car drivers stop to look only to be disturbed by the urgent honking of horns behind them as they fail to realise the traffic lights have changed, so deep in their reverie are they at the sight of the bike. It is only when paying our bill that the hotel staff realise how far we've travelled on the bike. It seems many thought we'd come straight from the UK. At the reception I hear the best answer so far to the question, 'How have you afforded it?'

'With a life-time of work,' answers the young receptionist before we have a chance to respond.

The words stick in my head and I know the sentence will never leave either of us. It's true you, and we, spend a lifetime in the track of daily life deviating little, if at all, from the routines of existence. Then in one definitive moment you have, perhaps, the only opportunity to 'swim out to your boat'. You don't know where that boat will take you but you know it will be somewhere different and perhaps this is the problem. Many, at that point, will choose to keep their feet on dry land when 'their' boat appears. The 'unknown' to that person involves insecurity and so they merely wave at the boat as it passes them by. Preferring to swim in the gentler waters of life they watch as others plunge in and hope for the best. After all these months on the road, we now swim quite well. No longer is there fear of what we have done, or might do, in the future.

Saying goodbye to our wise receptionist, the Chilean traffic soon draws us into its wake as Bernard keeps his new arrow stuck in the windshield (pointing right) to remind him of the side of the road to stay on. It has been months since driving on the 'wrong' side (not since Turkey). In Pakistan, India, Nepal, Thailand, Malaysia and Australia, all drive on the 'left' so now he has to mentally switch back to keeping us alive on the right.

The maze of Santiago ring roads leads us through on-ramps, off-ramps and side streets as we set off with nothing more than a compass due to road maps of Chile being rarer than snow. Entering slip roads in the hunt for a road marked number 5, eventually we join the famous Pan-American Highway.

'Some things never change'

Stretching somewhere in the region of 47,000 km in length, the Pan-American Highway is the longest defined single road in the world, starting in Alaska before reaching down into South America. It runs continuously through the length of the continent except for a 99 mile stretch between Colombia and Panama that separates South America from Central America, called the Darién Gap. It's an inhospitable terrain of swampland and forest, which would make it ferociously expensive to construct the final link. And there is much resistance to destroying the eco-system, which has remained intact due to the isolation of the forests and people of the area. Many have crossed the region by vehicle – pushbike, motorcycle, 4x4 – even though there are no roads through. But it's not for the faint-hearted. Many of the spectacular stories of crossings talk of running the gauntlet between horrible jungle conditions, drug traffickers and guerrillas wanting to kidnap you for your boots.

Happily both of us agree within a few seconds (was it that long?) to give this a miss. Deciding to leave the real 'out there' stuff to people 20-30 years younger than ourselves, the limitations of age soon leads to a graceful - unconditional - acceptance of not being really 'hard-core' bikers. The people who have made their way through the Gap probably did not struggle to un-kink their poor old arthritic bones every morning as they hauled motorcycles up the side of a mountain with a block and tackle. Meanwhile I would be standing asking, in a puzzled tone, 'Why?' Perhaps in this question I become as guilty as those who have asked the same thing of me.

Apart from short sections of chopped-up tarmac, Bertha's wheels romp along this famous road, singing happily with all her gauges showing 'normal'. Regular updates pour in from the laughing voice coming through my helmet and all is well with the world as the first day passes gently on Routa 5; stretching 1,600 km in front of us towards Peru. While knowing the distance, it does not really register anymore. 'A long way' has become 'not a long way'. Bernard recalls the receptionist's eyes widening when she realised where we were going and where we have been. For her, both existed on another planet far, far, away.

As we ride along, ever careful and meticulous with the nearly 20 year-old bike, Bernard looks and listens over the early hours for anything 'different' or 'not right'. Down in the underground garage of the hotel in Santiago he had, once again, gone over every nut and bolt of the bike in preparation. Finding nothing wrong with either his ears or his eyes, he settles back into his seat for the first day of mileage.

Navigating largely by road signs and compass, we head north, following the highway stretching along the western spine of the country. The sum total of our 'mapping' consists of keeping the sea on the left, the mountains on the right and the compass saying north. Simple. The landscape is much like the Nullarbor, apart from the backdrop of big hills and mountains, with the same bleached colours of beige and gold dominating all around us.

Traffic is light and our thoughts turn to how we'll cope again with the density of people and traffic at home in the UK, where 200 miles can take all day, instead of all morning. After travelling in such wide, open spaces for so long, where stillness and openness can be sensed without being seen, we both think it will be hard, very hard.

Calculating the town of Coquimbo as our confirmed destination for the end of day one, it leaves us with 300 miles to cover before dark with the light fading about 6.30pm and Rule 1: Do not drive at night - comes back into our thinking in our aim to be there early so we leave Santiago at 10am. Stopping for petrol, John Lennon is on the cafe radio 'Imagining' and it all seems so true after eight months on the road; it is always about people. From Bruno in Switzerland, to Gordon in Athens, from a truck driver in Australia, to Neena in India, it always involves people. Long may it continue.

Occasional stops to pay road tolls interrupt our thoughts as I place money in Bernard's gloved hand before we accelerate away again through deserted roads stretching before us. Under a canopy of cloudless blue skies the roller-coaster highway causes exhaust notes to change, quickening and growling in the progress towards Coquimbo. Exhausts pop on the overrun in the descent of steep mountains to valley floors full of beigeness.

As we ride Bernard tells me of the history of Chile and South America, of the Mayans and Incas of Peru in the old world, of the secret police and the days of Pinochet in the new; of the sadness of the 'disappeared' in countries such as Argentina. Talking of Argentina, of not being able to travel through it now due to time constraints, it leaves a creeping, uncomfortable, realisation: there is less in front than has passed behind.

Coquimbo soon appears and Bertha slithers and slides down red clay roads to a 'Cabaña'; a wooden self-contained cabin like a big triangle sitting on the ground. The walls inside are steep and it takes a little getting used to in order to avoid scalping myself on the steeply sloped roof. But I adapt quickly as no longer are my routines, my needs, so rigidly organised due to the months of constant change. Now I am able to relax, flowing easily with the differences each day brings.

A black Labrador dog bounds over, reminding me of my own dog so far away. Bernard helpfully looks up the Spanish for 'sit', 'stay' and 'down' while his front paws end up on my thighs, searching for my hands, begging me to keep up their attention.

At a tiny local café Bernard frantically searches phrase books to translate the menu but fails miserably as so many words are missing. Muddling through, we end up with huge steak and cheese sandwiches, and the most enormous bottle of beer Bernard has ever held. As I listen to him struggling to work out the menu I suddenly realise that I no longer feel frustrated by his inability to translate and give me choices. I've grown beyond it and now recognise how it only increases his own frustration. Becoming more like him, I now eat whatever is on the plate as I've become something, someone, different after so many experiences. Forever out of my comfort zone of predictability, which needed precision and organised experiences, I now settle into whatever comes my way, without fuss, without the flashes of irritability which so marred the earlier times. I am better for it, of this I have no doubt.

The next morning Bernard is feeling irritable as we set off, with lethargy and tiredness coming through his voice and I wonder, again, if the antimalarial drugs are affecting him. Riding in complete silence for a long time, his mood lifts little by little, no doubt aided by the copious amounts of caffeine and nicotine he ingests at our first petrol stop, kick-starting him in a way previously lacking.

Everywhere the Chilean people try hard to help in our continued struggle with communication; nowhere this been truer than at petrol stops. Often a small crowd gathers as we sit and munch 'something' before people appear to start conversations. Sitting eating 'tostada' and drinking coffee in the morning sun of a foreign country surrounded by interested people who are eager to talk to you - it can never be better than this.

The road winds upwards to 1,200 metres (4,000 feet) as the sun blasts down to where Bernard wears two pairs of sunglasses, so powerful is the glare. Covering himself in factor 50 sun cream against the power of it, he insists on doing the same for me at each and every cigarette stop, despite my protests. Thumping along through vast empty spaces makes the Australian Nullarbor look like an overpopulated city as we roll along at 80 kph, climbing and then dropping down hills throughout the day. Occasionally local motorcyclists on small bikes come towards us, returning waves as we pass through this 'nowhere' land to the sound of their 'beeping' of hello fading behind us.

Two motorcycles complete with metal panniers bearing the words 'Alemania' (Germany) pass us at over 100 kph as Bernard describes the outfits and the happy waves at meeting another bike on this road. Each aspect of their luggage is described before he pronounces them 'too light' to be travelling the world as they disappear at high velocity over the horizon. Discussing the speed and the overall layout of their bikes, he reaches the conclusion they are 'time-limited'. My suggestion that, perhaps, they just ride faster and do not carry as much rubbish as we do leads to a loud grunt through the intercom.

After hours of passing through miles of scorched sand, we stop for petrol and meet Peter and Bernard (would you believe) sitting under a covered veranda as we hear of their six-week ride around South America. Flying into Santiago, they are taking in Peru and Bolivia before returning to the capital to fly out for Germany. Sitting in the shade drinking coffee it is quickly clear they are two nice men and Peter has obviously been around bikes for a long time as he and Bernard trade talk about fixing bikes and all things bodging.

Peter rode India 25 years ago and he still bears the scars showing us the long ugly rip dissecting the palm of his hand. It reaches upwards into his arm and is a memento of an Indian truck. It must have been a truly ugly break to have left such a scar and he goes on to tell us of the doctors saying 'simple break' while they wrenched the bones back into place before he flew home to recuperate.

Bernard (mine!) comments that the world must have been a very different place in the 'before' times of mobile phones, laptops and credit cards. Peter readily agrees, going on to tell us how the Indians thought he was a very clever man as his (twin cylinder) bike 'had a spare engine'. We laugh as 25 years later we heard the same thing. 'Some things never change in India,' he agrees.

It is obvious 'there is something' about Peter which my companion recognises straight away; like Mick in Australia who had done five Paris–Dakars. Simple statements about extraordinary things, neither exaggerated nor 'ramped up', but merely what happened.

Peter and Bernard are not fazed by my blindness as we sit and talk while my companion heads for the petrol pumps. To the sound of Bertha firing up the conversation continues as they strip off their bike gear leaving two scantily clad men standing before me on the veranda; both overheating in the extensive body armour they wear. They were kind enough to tell me they were undressing as the rustle of heavy clothes and Velcro fasteners reached my ears. The rumble of Bertha announcing her arrival back leads to handshakes while Peter takes photographs, mementos of people and machines forever engraved onto paper and memory. Waving behind, we pull away towards Copiapo.

From Copiapo we move ever northwards towards Antofagasta and the

568 km of sand before us as we enter the Atacama Desert. Bernard carefully plots distances, along with fuel consumption, before doubling the water we carry and adding a bit more 'just in case'. His descriptive capacity is tested to its maximum as every word to describe 'sand' is used. The Eskimos have over 100 words for snow but Bernard reaches nowhere near 100 for sand while blasting through this barren landscape.

Huge plumes of dust are visible for miles on the road towards Antofagasta, an area where 35% of the world's copper comes from. Small-gauge narrow railways cross and re-cross the road near the mines and everything slows down to walking pace, hazard flashers on, before traffic bounces over the little tracks. More trucks than cars use the road and it is a flat world with little to interrupt the whirling dust.

At the seaside town of Antofagasta, the hotel receptionist starts to talk to us before immediately breaking off to answer the phone. It happens a lot in Chile, exasperating Bernard who stands in mid-sentence as the phone gets priority while our boots fill up with the sweat running down our legs. Eventually Bernard asks the English-speaking receptionist:

'Could I have the phone number of the hotel, please? We'll go sit over there on the couch and ring you. It will be quicker than standing here.'

We are booked in instantly when his call finishes and the phone continues its dance across the desk until our check-in is completed. We leave the next morning to a day full of petrol stops and long stretches of nothing. And I mean nothing. When asked about the landscape Bernard struggles to describe the flat, barren land, 'devoid of a blade of grass', 'not a tree, a bush, anywhere on the horizon' as the straight road stretches off towards the sky.

I think he's actually pleased when he sees a car with its bonnet up as it will break the monotony as we come to a halt and dismount. It seems the Atacama has claimed a victim as the driver walks over and words like 'agua' (water) can be heard as Bernard tries to find out what has happened. The car has lost the water from the radiator and Bernard discovers it's not so much a water problem as a radiator problem – a big hole where it once sat now fills the bonnet with emptiness. Through smatterings of language and a great deal of play-acting, the missing item from the beaten up old car has gone 'somewhere' with 'somebody' to be fixed. Its failure had left him sleeping in the car all night and it must have been a cold, lonely, night out here in the middle of 'nowhere land'. The poor man has had nothing to eat or drink since the previous day and we give him a bottle of water and an unopened packet of biscuits. Thanking us constantly, there is little else that can be done for him and we wave goodbye as he returns to his wait.

As the tarmac continues winding through the hills shrines appear beside it, varying from simple crosses with flowers to enormously elaborate structures complete with flags fluttering in the stiff breeze. Suddenly appearing by the roadside, statues of the Madonna or Jesus stare outwards towards the passing traffic from the doorways of these white chapels. In the open barrenness they appear beautifully maintained and whitewashed to perfection, gleaming against the backdrop of sand and desert in the brightness of the sun. Like small oases of the spirit sitting in the desolate surroundings where life must be so hard, tracks lead off into the hills towards the people who come to commemorate a loved one.

The Chilean flag flies everywhere above these shrines and it is noticeable as the Pan-American Highway drives straight through the middle of small towns how the flag adorns everything: lampposts, buildings, cars, wheelbarrows and anything else it can be attached to. We've seen the same thing in other countries where national flags fly everywhere: from Turkey to Thailand, from Nepal to Malaysia. Everywhere. It leaves us wondering why in our own homeland there is such a general resistance to 'flying the flag' without the trigger of an international football match.

The miles pass as we contemplate such things along a road of nothing but sand taking us ever northwards towards the next petrol pump. Eventually an oasis appears where food, water and, more importantly, petrol can be found. Coasting off the highway we find drinks and relief in the shade as two Harley-Davidsons and a BMW sit loaded as their owner's smile at our approach.

Two Brazilian couples and a friend are completing a loop of Chile, Paraguay, Uruguay, Peru and Bolivia before returning home. Muddling through our language problems, they speak in halting English, all the time apologising for it while our Spanish is atrocious and primitive, leading us to squirm with embarrassment at our inability. Talking to us in accented but relatively fluent English, I wonder at our island mentality and poor grasp of languages, wishing I were something more.

Bernard wolfs down a stew and I sip cold Fanta before we leave the shade of the café and each reaches for my hand to wish me a 'good journey'. Leaving the petrol station, people and bikes at Oficiana Victoria, we head towards Pozo Almonte. It turns out to be a small town where the Pan-American Highway heads straight up its main street and children play beside the road while dogs chase vehicles, particularly motorcycles, in a snarling frenzy of noise. Church bells peal above us as the side-stand drops outside the only recognisable motel.

In the Hotel Estancias Bernard ties the window latch to a chair with a chord to stop it banging in the stiffening evening breeze. Buses and coaches compete for noise with our TV as Manchester United play Porto at Old Trafford in the Champions league. Bernard describes Sir Alex Ferguson chewing furiously on his gum as it ends up 2–2 on the night; he is not a happy bunny by all accounts as the intricacies of the 'away goals' rule is explained to me.

The chair grates noisily on the floor as it moves with the stiffening wind catching the window and not to be beaten by this, the chair is tied to the table before that too is loaded with all our clutter. Standing semi-satisfied, he considers tying it to the TV stand but decides against it, not wanting to pay for a new TV should the wind get any stronger. Whatever the shortcomings, the staff are lovely and we eat pizzas against the backdrop of church bells rattling the windows. I listen to the diminishing sounds of people heading home as the town settles for the night until sleep soon claims me, despite the occasional scraping of chair legs on the tiled floor.

The morning sees staff fussing around us and we talk about how much we like small, local motels rather than the big chains, which we find impersonal. So it is we wash our clothes in the sinks of small motels, hotels and guest houses. Hanging our wet clothes to dry on balconies, or even on Bertha at times, the world seems more personal, more memorable than within 'bigger' hotels that just do not imprint on us in the same way. In India Bernard would disappear for a smoke, often coming back an hour later apologising before telling me of sitting on grass, pavement, or a wall, talking to a gardener or a driver whose accommodation was the front seat of a car as he waited for their affluent passengers. At a small hotel in Delhi staff sat outside on the steps as Bernard puffed away while watching the Indian police stopping vehicles yards away. Small places staffed by people who left big imprints on our minds. The Hotel Estancias is one such place and my hand is taken by women who kiss my cheek many times, as if I have been known them for far longer.

Leaving the next morning, we accelerate and outrun the dogs before settling back into the rhythms of the day. Bernard is worried about petrol, hoping that the information he has is not accurate. The only place he can find a mention of is Arica, a much greater distance than Bertha's tank will take us, considering the big climbs to come. He tries to conserve our resources by easing up on the throttle and free-wheels where possible. Pulling into a zoned crossing at Punta Camarones, the Carabineros (police) flag us down to check our documents.

'Gasolina?' Bernard asks the officers hopefully.

'Arica,' they respond (100 km away).

'Cuyo?' he asks, naming the local town.

'No, Arica,' they come back, again shattering his hopes.

We stand by the bike, pondering the distance as it will take us to the extremes of our fuel range. Meanwhile the police continue to stop cars for document checks while we calculate distances and fuel consumption figures. Bernard wanders over to one car, trying to find an additional 2–3 litres of fuel, but to no avail. He looks at the police car hopefully, but it's obvious the police will not help as they stop car after car without asking if anybody can spare 2 or 3 litres. It's all it would take to see us safely through to Arica.

Pushing on at a constant 60 kpm, coasting down hills and riding gently up, after a very nervous 100 km Arica appears below us with 328 miles on the clock, 40 miles past our reserve capacity. Breathing a huge sigh of relief we freewheel down into another Chilean coastal town, our final port of call before Peru and pull into the first petrol station, dispensing their finest into the tank.

We drive around Arica until finding a hotel, having covered 2,200 km in the four days since leaving Santiago, all within the hottest landscape ever encountered. The next leg sees Cusco in Peru and the magical land of the Incas (Machu Picchu) before us. With the altitudes of over 15,000 feet (4,500 metres) there will, no doubt, be some physical problems for us so rest and recuperation seems called for in order to catch up with the writing as the days, and kilometres, are now passing so quickly.

Much has been said and written about the road through the Atacama Desert, often describing how hard and dangerous it is to ride, how it can kill you. We did not find it so. It's stiflingly hot – unbelievably so at times. It's also true that water consumption skyrockets upwards and Bernard tells me that if I could see, I'd need three pairs of sunglasses to cut out the harsh brightness which nearly left his eyes bleeding each night. You can feel the moisture being ripped out of your skin with each passing kilometre and Bernard's insistence of factor 50 cream every hour was something I should have thanked him for, rather than resisted.

However when all is said and done, the road was mostly good-quality tarmac. Bernard told me it was hypnotic in much the same way as riding in parts of Australia were. Bright, glaring sunshine and straight roads stretching off into the blue sky have led to many poor souls now inhabiting the numerous shrines. Allowing their concentration to wander, it cost them their lives according to what people tell us as they ploughed off the road at the high speeds at which most Chilean drivers travel. The hourly stops at which I was smeared with sun cream was Bernard's way of refreshing his focus, using the time to stop himself from 'drifting off' into the comatose, unthinking, way of riding which could have cost us dear.

After reading so much doom and gloom about riding this 900 km strip of desert it all passed off uneventfully. Perhaps we were just lucky as in so many other countries. Perhaps it depends on how much luck is really involved under such circumstances and conditions. At times like this, ultimately, I believe the person who sits in front of me recognises his own limitations, abilities and weaknesses. Are we lucky, compared to other riders who have travelled this way?

Perhaps being lucky is about knowing when to stop or when to think things through. If being lucky equates with these aspects then Bernard is probably a very lucky rider.

Settling in for our rest, two motorcycles ridden by Jaime and Conti appear bearing Chilean number plates. A husband and wife team from Salamanca in Spain they've hired bikes in Chile for a month-long tour. As we stand reading their card they ask us to do an interview for their internet TV site in Spain.

That evening Jaime's first question is about Bertha having so few commercial sponsorship stickers as Bernard tells me of their bikes sitting 20 feet away with panniers festooned in company logos. We spend a long time discussing financial backing and it's clear that it didn't take Jaime long to attract the support. Ruefully we recount the two years spent trying to engage with people, only to give up six months before leaving. The softly spoken husband and wife team thought a trip such as ours would have attracted enormous interest in Spain. Convincing us to consider moving to their country, they think the life-style, sponsorship, people and weather would make it a much better place to live. Having sampled the UK once, and seen constant cold and rain for two weeks, they quickly sought refuge back across the channel within warmer climes.

Discussing rebuilding cylinders in Australia and charging problems in Malaysia, Jaime doesn't understand how anyone could undertake such a journey without knowing something about engines. Conversations meander around the 'trade-off' of using easier-to-fix technology (read older motorcycle) versus the likelihood of breakdown (read newer) before he thinks:

'Perhaps if you know nothing, then nothing will go wrong?'

It sounds a very pragmatic way of looking at it as we sit with the evening drawing in before turning in for the night, having arranged a filmed interview for tomorrow.

In the morning, Bernard describes the horseshoe-shaped pool he is soon patiently walking along as I swim up and down. The occasional 'left a bit' or 'right a bit' comes from the side to redirect me before walking for hours around Arica searching for a map of Peru without success. Neither do we find appropriate spare fuel containers for our limited space. It plays on our minds every time we pass Jaime's bike with its five-litre can strapped onto his seat, a constant reminder of things not getting better in Peru – from where they have just returned – regarding distances and petrol.

Daylight fades while completing the video interview before retiring to sit and talk into the approaching darkness. They're leaving early in the morning and we'll miss their company.

'You will need to always remember it is only you who have changed and people will never understand this. It will cause you problems,' Jaime adds, summarising his thoughts.

In our absence, they go on to explain, everybody else will have gone on with their daily lives in the same way as when we were there but no longer will it be possible to share the same reference points, the same ideas over what is important. Everything is altered by what has been experienced and, perhaps, it's never really possible to return to what you were. Fundamentally changed, altered, and honed into something different, your priorities are different, and that difference will be forever out of reach to the people around you so they can never truly understand it. Thus, in many ways, we both gain and lose by travelling the world. The gain involves everything experienced while the loss is the tranquillity of normality within which everybody we know will still be operating.

'It is you who will stand apart,' Jaime quietly states.

We lie awake mulling over their comments of how we (and they) become 'separated from everyday life', how we'll discover this separation on returning to the 'real world', finding it changed and different in so many ways. They've told us of experiencing this feeling in a way that's hard to explain as the struggle to 'fit back in' takes place. Both talked of how the normality of life seems altered regarding the patterns and worries which everybody else seems to live by.

I drift into asleep wondering if these thoughts are prophetic. Perhaps as two people addicted to an experience, it will never again be possible to 'settle' into normality. Waking in the morning to find an empty space where two other motorcycles once sat unsettles us, as it always does. When you meet and then have to say goodbye to people who understand and share your own reference points, it is always so.

The day passes in relaxing and catching up on our journal entries before repacking the bike as tomorrow involves crossing into Peru. We are no longer jetlagged and enjoy the normal cycles of day and night, re-established, enabling sound sleep in continuous streams. Wandering around the room in the dark and silence of the night waiting for sleep is consigned to the past.

We leave the next morning to criss-cross Arica and it takes us a long time before the distinctive small shield bearing the number 5 appears. The road leads us all the way to the border with little traffic in either direction. Scorching brightness floods the landscape, quickly returning to sand, sand and more sand, while in the far distance Bernard tells me of the Peruvian mountains shining white with the heat.

The border crossing can be seen from some distance away with its queue of cars, coaches, wagons and people milling around. We edge forward past other vehicles before the side-stand drops, helmets are tugged off and the heat crashes down on us instantly. Within a short time the inside of my bike gear is awash with sweat. Ten feet away gleam two bikes bearing Chilean number plates, an immaculate 750cc Honda Africa Twin and a 900cc KTM Adventure.

Police officers hiding from the fierceness of the sun under a canopy beckon us to where they stand in the shade. They realise within seconds we have absolutely no idea what they are saying before one of them smiles broadly and indicates my companion should follow him while leaving me safely in the shade. Bernard does the whole 'so sorry but no can do as she cannot see a thing'. He nods in understanding, gesturing for us to follow him to several flights of stairs where he stops, looking up the long set of steps. Quizzically he points at them as if to say 'Will she be ok?'

'Si Senhor, no problema' my fluent Spanish-speaking companion confidently replies. We ascend to the first floor and are handed over to a woman who gives us numerous forms to fill out – all in Spanish. Bernard reaches for his trusty Spanish-English book only to find half the words are missing but the woman helpfully reappears from behind the counter after seeing the frantic flicking in the vain search for translations. Either that or she was worried the draft from those frantic turning pages threatened to blow all her leaflets off the counter as my hair feels their turning. Struggling to fill out the forms, eventually there are congratulations all around and 'our' policeman takes us under his wing the instant we reappear. Shunting us past huge queues of form-clutching people, uniformed customs officers disappear with our passports before returning them with the 'Departed from Chile' stamp. There are more forms and a policeman fills out half for us and waits patiently as we work our way through the lines of questions; then all the papers are piled together for everything to be stamped. Handing them over he points to a building on the Peruvian side saying, 'Pasaporte'.

In the cool of the Peruvian building a 90 day stamp is bashed into our passports and a security guard leads us across the building, out the door, down the steps, around the back, then across the road to another customs hut. Here our Chilean bikers bake in the fierce noonday sun. Waiting for the wheels of bureaucracy to pound their ever-turning circles while sweltering with no shade, Bernard considers retrieving our large golfing umbrella from the back of our bike. Deciding against it, we remain mad dogs and Englishmen and all that out in the noonday sun.

The other bikers smile but silence descends on the queue as Bernard leans forward to look at the sheaves of paper everybody else seems to be filling out for their bikes. The officer at the front is meticulous in the details and only when, and if, papers match his approval does he go to inspect the bike, parked on the other side of the main building. Shuffling from foot to foot to stop our feet melting on the concrete, the Chilean bikers continue to fill out paper threatening to explode into flames with the sun. The customs officer eventually gestures us forwards and, hopefully, the carnet is passed through the small opening.

Within seconds, details are completed and the officer is out of the cabin and across the car park with us struggling to keep up. Looking over Bertha, he points to the engine and chassis number on the paperwork and Bernard locates them on the bike and, bingo, we are done. Meanwhile, arriving back at his cabin the Chilean riders have nearly run out of ink as they still fill out paper. With one more stamp, our entrance to Peru is completed and envious stares follow us as we walk away clutching the 'not needed carnet'.

It may well be true that a carnet (import/export) document is not necessary for South America but it certainly makes things a hundred times easier and quicker. Time and again this has been true and it's probably the most thumbed document at our disposal. Jaime and Conti told us when they arrived at the same border the customs staff nearly stripped their bikes as they examined every bag, every canister. Our own experiences, here and now, cause us to wonder if it is something to do with the number plate or, perhaps, something else?

People have subsequently told us that the history of Peru has left many with a 'not very fond' genetic memory of the Spanish conquerors who destroyed their civilisation. We saw this in India when dealing with indigenous people, in relation to wounds from English rule and the mistakes made long ago.

Perhaps Jaime and Conti paid a small price for the arrival so long ago of Francisco Pizarro in 1526 who, coming back two years later, found the Incas already decimated by the diseases they left behind.

Landing for the second time with only 102 men on foot and 62 mounted soldiers, he clutched the Spanish King's permission to conquer the country we now call Peru. In less than fifty years an empire was eradicated to the sound of horses hooves, cannons, guns, and the clash of steel, leaving behind only the echoing whispers of what once was.

We will never know what the truth is and whether a number plate or an accent has such an impact, although Jaime and Conti thought it did. Being Spanish in Peru was to be 'different' in a way that being 'English', they told us, we would never encounter. Perhaps they were right. People could not have been more helpful to us at the crossing from Chile into Peru, whether Chilean or Peruvian. Talking about such things, it dawns on us we are free to go as Bernard looks across the border towards the heights of over 15,000 feet to be crossed. Walking back to Bertha I listen to the contented sighs of a happy man with his cigarette filling the air. As I wait in our shared comfortable silence my mind floods with images.

Backdrops of mountain heights covered in clouds leading to mystical places create kaleidoscopes inside my head as I reflect on everything so far and everything still to come. Never had I dreamed of setting foot in such far distant places, or of experiencing so many things. Coming so far in this beautiful world, now I find new place names before me that previously only ever existed in books, on TV or radio. Places such as Machu Picchu, nestling on its lonely heights, hidden valleys and a hundred other places are now nearby and through them we shall soon pass. Sounds of Peruvian pipes, cannons and horses intermingle with the images and thoughts swirling through my mind in rapidly changing patterns of sound and light. My reverie is disturbed with a sudden movement beside me as the click of the ignition switch indicates new adventures awaiting us.

Climbing back on the bike we pull slowly across the border into Peru with Bertha gently burbling away beneath us. The Land of the Incas stretches out before her wheels.

'A simple thing like ice cream'

(PE) Passing beneath a sign above the road declaring, 'Bienvenidos Al Peru' (Welcome to Peru), the road stretches before us as Bernard repeats his traditional greeting on entering each new land:

'I've brought Bertha to Peru!'

Sometimes it comes through with such amazement, like a child in many ways, the rising and falling cadence demonstrating the enormity of his achievement. Despite passing through so many borders, overcoming so many problems, truly, he still cannot believe another line has passed; some other far distant place on the other side of the world in the dream he has longed for his whole life.

'I can't believe I'm actually riding a bike in Peru!', he laughs.

Always cautious on the first day in a new country, experience has taught us never to underestimate how long it will take to cross borders, shuffling from line to line, from form to form: anything from an hour to a day. Long ago a pattern fell into place of early finishes when in a new country. It's part of our way of adapting to the newness and it's largely for Bernard as he observes the new ways of driving with the different nuances in how things are done. So it is he watches and tries to figure out how things work, the priorities, the 'danger signals' to be rapidly tuned into. Forty kilometres later we see the Gran Hotel at Tacna and despite it only being lunchtime Bertha turns into the car park without any hesitation from either of us.

Filling out all the immigration documents, we wait as the receptionist hunts for elusive bellboys before summoning the manager who finds them all out in the car park pouring over every detail of Bertha. Even the kitchen staff have evacuated to the car park as the manager gently scolds them, ushering them back while 'our' bellboy laughs sheepishly climbing the stairs discussing 'la Moto' (the bike): how big it is, how far we have come and myriad similar questions. Coming out of the hotel to hunt for a bank machine, people step out of the way while taxi drivers stop their cars – and other traffic – to enable us to cross the busy roads and beggars approach us in droves as we try to find the elusive 'hole in the wall'.

Walking under the Alto de la Alianza (the Arch of the Heroes), which stands like a giant commemorative wishbone to a battle in 1880, it commemorates the regional uprising against Chile during the battle for independence. It talks of the region wanting to be part of Peru once again, achieved successfully in 1929. As we walk Bernard ponders about the Chilean riders at the border who seemed to be there for so long as, perhaps like people of Spanish descent, the Peruvians have long memories which look backwards.

The roads are noisy and busy as we continue our search and people stare at us, mildly inquisitive. Bernard meets their eyes with a smile, readily given back in this border city. Eventually finding a bank machine, we cross back under the careful tutelage of two laughing female police officers while local people play 'chicken' in their death-defying leaps of faith between the streams of cars.

The next morning two sets of directions back to the main highway leaves us completely lost due to the absence of any road signs towards Arequipa. Driving round and round Tacna trying to lock onto a GPS compass setting, a police roadblock stops any further progress. However, all talk of documents is soon forgotten with the awareness of my blindness and a wave of helpful directions to the north descend upon us.

The long climb out of Tacna takes us into a burnt wasteland where the ground has been deep-fried to gold and yellow. Not a blade of grass exists; no bushes, nothing for as far as Bernard can see, only yellow shifting sand on a road turning steeply through the hills like a huge snake. Hairpins bends come thick and fast as the world tilts crazily from one corner to the next. Seeing five cars in two hours sets us laughing at the 'rush hour' when several pass at the same time while talk turns to home across the miles, increasingly coming to the forefront of our thinking of how different it will all feel from this land which is twice as long as Britain. The engine continues to growl through our reflections, taking the strain as Bertha hauls us up and down 370 km of heat and glaring sun.

Coasting to a halt at a Customs post, two Chilean-plated Harley-Davidsons sit and Bernard wonders how the riders can stand the temperature in full leathers while we feel hot in our vented suits. One of the riders wanders over to shake hands saying words like 'Buenos' (Good) – pointing to the bike – and 'Muy Buenos' (very good) pointing to all the stickers testifying where we have been.

A customs officer joins us after leaving his shaded area as my blindness and white stick alter the dynamics of our interactions with officialdom. Collecting all our papers he motions us to 'wait here' as there are several banks of stairs up to his shaded position on a balcony where he needs to record our details in his voluminous ledger, the thump of which I hear from many feet away as it opens. Our Harley riders meanwhile start their engines in a wall of noise frightening everything for miles around as they wave farewell to disappear up the road with exhausts emitting throaty bellows. The officer soon returns and documents are locked safely back into the pannier as a local ice-cream vendor turns up on his 100cc Honda. The bike has been heavily modified with front forks replaced by a handcart within which sit polystyrene containers full of ice cream.

Bernard – It is really funny to watch all the armed riot-stick-toting police and soldiers lining up like well-behaved school children. Borrowing money off each other, shifting machine guns, it all looks so incongruous as they root in pockets for money. Banter fills the air amid laughter as a simple thing like an ice cream suddenly turns them into something very different for me: people, not uniforms.

As Bernard describes what is happening I deem it impolite not to support local business, and we join the queue. Reaching the front there is a choice of Peruvian Melon ice cream or Peruvian Melon ice cream as one of the soldiers helpfully sorts out our money to hand over the cost. After one last crunch on the cornet I climb back on the bike to ride slowly past the soldiers, police and customs agents who all wave from their shaded positions – some of them clutching second ice creams, so enjoyable was the first.

The road winds in ever-tighter circles until we reach a plateau at 2,133 metres (7,000 feet) where 90 kph cuts us through reasonable road surfaces straight across the flattened top of the mountain where nothing grows. Dropping down, we're soon on the valley floor with lush green vegetation and trees everywhere, like little oases, before once again climbing to leave the greenness behind.

A large army outpost appears in the middle of nowhere with its high concrete walls painted in desert camouflage colours. Large signs declare 'Live Firing' and 'Live Missiles in Use' and a Peruvian Air Force complex appears further down the road with other signs indicating you cannot stop, take pictures, or do anything else that the multiple signs say you cannot do. More signs refer to the possibility that loud, sudden, explosions may occur to startle the unwary but the only sound is Bertha's engine and her tyres on the road surface. Not a single explosion can be heard.

Soon the 470 year-old city of Arequipa nestles 2,377 metres (7,800 feet) up the Andes under the snow-capped shadow of El Misti (the eighth-largest volcano in the world) towering 5,790 metres (19,000 feet) up into the sky. The white stone of the volcano, from which many of the city's buildings are constructed, led to 'The White City' label by which it is widely known in Peru.

Rolling into the outskirts the road instantly deteriorates to leave us bouncing down pitted and potholed side roads left ruined by the earthquake in 2001. Obviously repaired hastily, they quickly fell back into complete ruin. After driving around for 20 minutes trying to avoid the wheel-swallowing holes looking for an elusive hotel, we resort to Plan A, which involves following a taxi.

Leading us through the streets of gleaming white buildings, he deposits us at a lovely little hostel where the staff insist that Bertha is brought through the marble-floored foyer into the covered garden 'in case it rains'. Convincing them Bertha could do with a wash anyway, she stays parked outside.

The next morning the smell of smog hangs in the air, reminding me of Kathmandu, as it grabs my throat in a vice and my eyes water under the assault. Driving round and round Arequipa looking for the road to Juliaca, we climb out of the city to 4,527 metres (14,854 feet) – a new Bertha height record – on a road that twists and turns throughout the 280 km. Ascending the steepness, road signs warn of marauding alpacas.

The other animal that constantly appears is dogs. Lots and lots of them. Everywhere. Even in the middle of the emptiest landscape, around a corner a dog will be lying in the middle of the road. Type one simply watches the world go by with a lazy, heat-dulled expression while type two engages in the great Peruvian Doggie past-time of 'Chase the Bertha' whenever we appear. Snarling, growling, barking, and snapping, they race alongside us, pitting their legs against Bertha's fifty horsepower; an unequal battle but one they never understand as we blast up the road away from them.

Stopping to let air out of our inflatable seats, we imagine them exploding from pressure due to the altitude, hurling us up into space like two ejector seats. Bernard also lets the tyres down a little as the altitude is making them harder, causing the bike to slide on corners with little warning. Even our tubes of sun cream have expanded under the pressure and the cream shoots out when the lids are popped.

Passing snow-capped mountains on plateaus lush with green vegetation full of plants and pools of water, alpacas graze while farmers and children wave as we pass. Wagons and cars beep in greeting as strangers meet on deserted roads stretching off to the horizon.

Bertha struggles with the altitude and she wheezes under the effort. Newer bikes have onboard computers that constantly monitor and adjust the fuel/air mix without you ever realising there's a problem. Bertha has carburettors and Bernard is up and down the gearbox several times per minute in the ever upwards climb wondering if he should stop and adjust them. Pushing on, we wait to see what happens. Even though Bertha is feeling the 4,000+ metres, she continues to puff her way up and down the Andes with gentle coaxing through the gearbox.

It's cold up here, very cold. The wind blows from the snow-capped peaks and it's not since eastern Turkey that we've felt this cold as our mesh suits allow a thousand freezing needles to pass through and our breath comes in short puffs, the air is so thin. You breathe in and you wonder if you missed it. So you breathe in again. Still you feel breathless when you exhale, so you breathe in again but it offers little relief. But it didn't stop Bernard lighting cigarettes whenever we stopped, swearing it would be worse for him if he did not smoke. Somehow, I don't believe him.

The whole day is spent climbing upwards before freewheeling down hills to conserve fuel while in the midst of this barren isolation. Tollbooths (peaje) appear and seem so out of place in the mountains, but motorbikes are free and we're waved through, our feet never touching the ground; the police, present due to mountain bandits, wave to us as we pass them. Dropping down towards the town of Juliaca with only 30 km to go, serious roadwork is going on. Actually, soil works is more apt as there is no road, only dirt, which the road crew busily packs down.

Nowadays, Bernard is a completely different rider when he comes across things like this. In the early days he would stress over mud – then he drove in Turkey. He stressed over sand – then he drove in Pakistan. His gravel fears were overcome in India. He pulls up and looks at the surface, considering routes while talking aloud so that I'm aware of what's happening. I don't join in as he's not talking to me, but to himself, articulating options while letting me in on his thoughts and decisions. The big question to answer is, 'Is it safe?' The click of his lighter tells me it's serious as he continues to describe what's in front of him as he watches wagons going through, measuring the surface, the depth of the soil, the slipping of the wheels – calculating, always calculating.

Bernard – When you come to conditions like this there are so many things to consider. First and foremost, is it safe? Then 'is it doable' with the two of us on the bike? Would it be better if I walked the surface first? Should I walk Cathy up the route and then come back for the bike alone? Should I take the heavy side panniers off and carry them past the worst sections? There are so many questions and options to make sure of getting through in one piece. Some of the options will take far longer but they're always worth considering as an accident here could be catastrophic.

I can tell he is pensive as he lights a second cigarette. Through his one-sided conversation, I know he's waiting for the wagons to flatten the road surface down, compressing it into something more manageable. The road crew watches while Bernard waves off their signals telling him to go through. Wagons come the other way as the stream of traffic alternates on the single track just laid with big earthmovers flattening the surface with their weight in between the alternating flows of traffic. However, their huge wheels – with massive treads – chop up the hardened soil into enormous ridges a foot high that run sideways across the ten-foot wide strip – not a problem for cars or wagons but for us? After two cigarettes, Bernard is ready. As the bike nudges into gear his voice leaves me laughing as he comments, 'Brace yourself, Sheila'; he has never been the same since Australia.

The road crew understand our vulnerability as they hold the traffic to give us a free run. All work stops and 50 people stand watching. I feel Bernard stand up on the foot pegs to aid the bike's balance as my hands grip the top of the panniers. The bike starts to slip and slide immediately when it drops off the tarmac onto the corrugated surface with the back wiggling and slipping. The growl of the engine fills my senses and I feel each twitch we plough through, bouncing over the ridges with Bertha skipping, sliding across the surface like an ice skater. As his voice comes through my helmet repeating over and over 'Keep the power on', I know he is searching for harder sections to aim for, anything to give our wheels extra purchase in the chopped-up layers of soil and dirt. Several hundred yards later we slide up the steep gravel ramp to applause from the road crew who downed tools for the up and coming show. In a theatrical gesture Bernard takes a bow to the sound of applause as we cross back onto the tarmac, which recedes into the distance behind us as we pass the workmen.

Within a few hundred yards, the road is nothing more than a cavernous cracked surface interspersed with potholes filled in with sand and gravel. Bouncing though this lunar landscape nearly loosens every nut on the bike, and any dental fillings. Descending into Juliaca after 30 km of these bad, bad, surfaces we enter the chaos of taxis and rickshaws all competing for spare inches on the town's dusty roads. Not since Asia have we experienced such traffic. Far off the tourist trail in a world of dust and impermanent transient populations, we'd been told the town had little appeal to visitors, which was why little work had ever been done on the road infrastructure. Despite being in central Juliaca, we dodge or drop into cavernous potholes before a taxi driver leads us to a hotel where we're greeted with 150 soles per night. I prepare for a long wait as £33 for the night is very steep and it's only the starting point.

Bernard: 'No, no, really, so much? A hundred would be better. It must be lower than that.'

Staff: '120 with American breakfast.'

Bernard: '100 would be better, we don't like Americans.'

Staff: '110 without breakfast.'

Bernard: 'We like the Americans more than that. 110 with breakfast?'

So with humour and much laughter, the price is agreed and the bike is led into the courtyard behind high steel gates. Throwing Bernard out of our room so I can find my way around without my protective mother hen hovering in case I bump into anything, he sets off in a mildly spurious huff to restock with cigarettes, his last one smoked when pondering the roadworks 30 km earlier. Returning later he's just in time to receive a knock on the door as a tray of tea appears.

The waiter explains the tea is coca and will help us cope with the 3,825 metre (12,549 foot) altitude. Consumption of it increases energy levels during pain, hunger and thirst and the hot drink is prepared from the coca leaf itself. Due to the presence of cocaine as an extract from the leaves, it also relieves the headaches some people (including us) experience as a side-effect of altitude. Two cups each are downed while laughing about the possibility we'll be flying tonight and it wasn't long before it began.

Sitting downstairs I can hear my steak being beaten into submission for at least 20 minutes by kitchen staff as the coca tea kicks in, leaving us giggling like two naughty schoolchildren, dissolving into fits of laughter at the least thing. At one point, while trying to cut my steak a twanging sound can plainly be heard as Bernard innocently asks:

'Do you want me to go and get that piece of steak for you?'

He kindly explains that my steak now sits ten feet away having been catapulted across the room with my tugging between knife and fork. Retrieving it we descend into further laughter which continues until we fall into bed. The last thing I recall is deciding that Britain should definitely import this tea as it provides instant cures for most woes – or at least the perception of those woes. 'Let's have a cup of tea' would bring on a whole set of new connotations; people would certainly feel better afterwards. The problems would still be there but, perhaps, they would feel slightly smaller. At least until it wears off.

But then again, you could always have another cup?

'Hey Gringo!'

In the morning we set out to cover the 344 km to Cusco, the last seat of the Inca Empire. For once we find the S3 right away heading north back into the mountains and it starts well, winding through the streets of the town, until we approach a roundabout where burning tyres block our route and thick black acrid smoke fills the air. The road to Cusco has been blocked and barricades have been thrown across all routes forward and each is manned by very determined-looking people clutching lumps of wood and machetes. Bernard sits watching events unfold. Cars, buses or trucks approaching the barricades are all stopped before being forced to turn around.

'No way through it seems,' Bernard explains, watching, looking for options.

Patience.

Soon several vehicles simply drive up the wrong side of the centrally divided route and cross the gravel divide hundreds of metres further up the empty road. Bertha is nudged into gear to follow the next truck through. The oncoming traffic beeps furiously and then we nip across the gravel divide onto another appalling road. The bike bounces like a jackhammer and it's 50 miles before anything remotely like tarmac appears. Bertha shudders and vibrates the whole way, sending shock waves through the panniers where I hold on with tight fingers.

Climbing higher, the landscape changes from brown to green as rivers appear beside us and sheep and cattle graze peacefully as we ascend over 14,000 feet to find Peruvian women tending flocks. In contrast to the men, the women never return our waves while boys and girls happily wave back. We pass through small villages on narrow roads, with houses of mud brick with thatched or corrugated roofs, where adults stare and children wave furiously back to our greeting.

The road continues to hammer at Bertha and coming around a corner we find huge boulders across the road surface. Slowly rounding them, the next miles show the same debris everywhere. Initially we think it's the result of a landslide but the obstacles become progressively denser as tree trunks and huge boulders appear on the road when we come around corners. Our speed drops considerably and Bertha is virtually walking through the obstacles.

With 344 km to go, across high-altitude roads, we wonder if we'll make Cusco by nightfall. We ride into a small town full of military in riot gear and then it dawns on us: something is not right.

The debris gets worse and worse, soon including glass-strewn corners glinting in the sun. No traffic moves on the road and we've seen no other vehicle for over an hour. It's impossible for anything much larger than us to navigate through the boulders, rocks and glass barring the way. It is such slow work at little more than walking pace as Bernard picks his way through carefully. We're both feeling increasingly nervous.

Coming across cars stranded whenever this strange situation developed, they sit surrounded by boulders blocking progress either backward or forward. Their drivers sit in the sun, ruefully watching our wending route around them. Several drivers try to shift some of the debris to allow six feet further to be driven before getting out to clear another section, only to be confronted by boulders half the size of their vehicle. There is nothing else but to sit and wait.

In two hours we travel 30 km before a line of traffic appears and armed police stand on the road watching our progress past the long line of parked cars, wagons and coaches on the road to Cusco. Making our way to the front of the line, tree trunks block all access. Bernard stops and drops the side-stand by a group of Germans who tell us how the road has been shut for three hours by farmers protesting over prices. The good news is that it is due to open again in ten minutes (at 3pm).

The protest is region-wide and getting to Cusco before nightfall will be a struggle; Peruvian mountain roads, at night, and under these conditions? The idea does not fill us with enthusiasm. Meanwhile the barricade watchers clutch machetes and pitchforks in their hands as Bernard puffs away while drunks approach asking for money in thickened, slurred voices. The word 'Gringo' becomes interspersed with requests for other items and it's constant. As movement begins around the barricade, Bernard stamps out his cigarette and Bertha comes to life.

People mill all around us, their voices a cacophony of chanting and shouting, as we slowly wind through the parked cars, trucks and people on the other side of the barricade. Several voices shout 'Hey Gringo' at our passing, either using it derogatorily or in greeting assuming we're American. We interpret it as the latter, as a form of 'Hello'. It is our way.

The road is a mess with miles of broken glass and tree trunks cynically placed on sharp corners, or on humps, forcing you onto the wrong side. Sympathy runs out for the protestors after hours of such riding as we pass an old woman trying to shift rocks from outside her house. A car stops and the driver and passenger get out, helping her move the stones and this is repeated many times as the great clear-up gets underway. Some sections are so bad we're not sure how it will be possible to clear up without heavy machinery as there are boulders standing taller than a human being, weighing several tons at least.

Slowly it's obvious that people are clearing 'their section' as, little by little, the roads improve. At times, the 'protest' is nothing more than a few small stones spread across the road in a line. Other sections, however, look like there's been an explosion with debris and burning tyres scattered everywhere and dense black smoke drifting across the road to obscure our way ahead, slowing us down even further.

At one point the bike brakes hard and Bernard tells me of a rope lying across the road, of the two young boys hiding in trees on either side, sitting waiting for us to approach. He explains the concept of 'clothes-lining' to me where the rope is pulled tight to take you off the bike as you run into it. He laughs as they let go of the rope and run off as we approach.

Bernard — If it had been me I would have wrapped the rope around a tree both sides. At least then it would have saved their palms from being shredded when 500 kg of weight travelling at 40 mph took it from their hands. It's all about physics.

He laughs again about their attempt but I have no doubt it would have been dangerous enough if he had not been so tuned into the environment. Descending into Cusco after seven and a half hours of riding under these conditions, exhaustion makes us flag down a taxi whose mad driver leads us across chaotic junctions in the way of Moses expecting the waters to part for him.

Dropping the side-stand outside the only hotel in town with parking, the driver wants three soles and is very happy with the five pressed into his hand as staff rush out to greet us and Bertha works her magic. Many of them become very animated at our arrival as the bike takes up residence in the underground car park where she draws her usual crowd of admirers.

'It doesn't mean they cannot hear you'

Over the following days we consume gallons of coca tea even though the altitude (3,500 metres or 11,500 feet) does not bother us greatly due to having acclimatised on the higher roads already ridden. People come and go from the hotel obviously having flown straight in from the USA and they struggle with the altitude, huffing and puffing around the tea urn in the lobby. Sometimes, however, waking in the middle of the night breath does come hard as I breathe in but gain little relief, still needing several attempts before I feel enough oxygen getting through.

The Peruvian people are so friendly they reminded us of Nepal. Even the street hawkers are not particularly insistent or aggressive if you say 'No thank you' but merely smile and move on. The evenings are cool enough to require alpaca tops, acquired at a local shop, as we arrange to visit Machu Picchu, 50 miles away and reachable only by train and bus.

The famous landmark, the most visited site in Peru, is near the town of Aguas Calientes (the local name for Machu Picchu), although the 'Lost city of the Incas' is a further 3.5 miles away standing at a height of over 2,286 metres (7,500 feet). It is overlooked by a mountain called Wayna Picchu (2,700 metres or 8,860 feet) and when Bernard reads of the background to the city and the overlooking mountain, I know I want to climb it. Trying to talk me out of it, he acquiesces in the end but warns me it will be hard to do.

Leaving everything but a few essentials with Bertha, one backpack is filled for the two-day trip while Bernard fusses as the staff assure him the bike will be safe. Setting off through the Sacred Valley towards the waiting train at Ollantaytambo, a tour guide entertains us with a stream of facts and anecdotal stories of the Inca Empire until our first stop sees Bernard guiding me through a market to stroke my first alpaca. Feeling soft and furry, with long pointed ears, the scene is ruined somewhat when two males decide to start mating in front of the video-toting people who pour off tour buses. Comments such as 'Peruvian Porno' fill the air as Bernard, in his most serious BBC audio description voice, feels obliged to give a running commentary of the events, even stretching to supposed facial expressions of an alpaca during carnal relations.

Leaving our alpaca friends, an elderly woman weaves the animal's wool into the rainbow colours of Cusco on a wooden frame nearby. She shouts at tourists when they take her picture without handing over the 1 sole gratuity (about 20 pence) but is quiet in understanding I cannot see when we approach with Bernard indicating 'Would it be OK to look?'

Gently her hands guide mine towards her weaving loom, placing her wooden tools into my fingers as Bernard describes the woven garment and her own bright red tunic and bonnet. My hands explore the soft fibres while my mind pictures the colours and combinations in exploring her bonnet as she sits perfectly still while my fingers trace memories in my mind. Thanking her for her time and patience two soles are placed in her hand as thanks. She smiles back. Nearby a little boy sits on the plinth of a statue wearing traditional dress of poncho, woollen hat and blue cloth trousers as people happily snap away at him before departing looking for their next picture. He looks sad at our approach, sitting with not a sole in his hand but his face breaks into smiles as Bernard places five in his palm.

Further along the valley we stop at Inca burial holes to learn how the spine of the body was removed to enable the remains to fit into the tiny circle cut into the hillside. Two children sit on a nearby wall talking, deep in conversation with each other, while their mothers try to earn a living selling belts or hair bands to the stream of tourists marching up and down the hill to the burial site. Trying to sell Bernard a hair band, they laugh when he whips off his hat to prove he does not need one.

After travelling half the world, and using every toilet arrangement imaginable, I find myself in one full of the English language yet struggling to find my way without help. Given this problem, Bernard usually marches into women's toilets to orient me – apart from in Turkey where a nice female Turkish Muslim attendant threw him out. In Malaysia women would gesture to him before guiding me into the inner sanctum where they would care for me in gentle ways. This has happened all over the world and yet here I'm surrounded by North American and European voices with no guidance at all. It's a strange experience and it stands out in a very marked way but I manage to muddle my way around to emerge unscathed to an annoyed Bernard. 'Probably too busy doing their hair or adjusting their sunglasses,' he retorts.

Arriving at Ollantaytambo, we climb steps to the waiting train before setting off for the one-and-a-half-hour journey through the mountains as Japanese men, each with three cameras, leap from seats to take pictures of everything as the guide tells how there used to be snow from 9,000 feet. Now it is nearer to 13,000 he states; sadly global warming reaches everywhere, even to the heart of Peru.

Pulling into a darkened Aguas Calientes a man stands waiting bearing a large placard with the name 'Bernard Sniff' scrawled in huge letters and we laugh, following him through the labyrinthine market which greets us on disembarkation. Down the hill a hotel nestles as roaring water rushes past leaving rooms smelling musty, but this smell is everywhere due to the raging water crashing down the mountains less than 30 feet away. Falling into bed with alarms set for 4am, we steel ourselves for the mad rush of the morning, with only 400 people allowed to climb Wayna Picchu. We must be on the first buses (5.30am) to stand any chance so everything is packed to enable a quick exit for the bus stop in the morning. By the time sleep claims us only five hours are possible before 3.55am comes and the sounds of 'Ohh God'.

'God won't help you,' I respond helpfully, listening to his shuffling footsteps followed by tooth brushing complete with sighs and moans. Getting ready quickly, Bernard returns from his morning constitutional (a smoke on the veranda) to tell me of people streaming past the hotel to begin the one and a half hour trek to Machu Picchu. It already looks like there's a danger of being gazumped as many others are also heading up the hill towards the bus stop and about a hundred people are there when we arrive at 5am.

People helpfully part to let us through to sit on stone steps about 20 from the front as a street vendor wanders up and down with flasks of coffee and sandwiches, conducting a roaring trade under the streetlights glowing dim orange. As the queue gets longer and longer, more and more people arrive to see the queue before turning back to their still warm beds; a wasted journey for many. All the time the line stretches steadily up the hill for hundreds of yards. At 5.25am lines of sitting people stand, seemingly in unison, to gather their belongings as officials arrive and Bernard nudges us into the queue as all social niceties start to disappear with people jostling for bus space. A stream of 25 vehicles appear as an official spots the white stick and rescues us from the crush by placing us on Bus number 2 after people had bashed past us for the first one, knocking us out of the way in their haste.

The pale light of morning starts to appear in the wind upwards along the unsurfaced road upon which only buses are allowed to drive. Thirty minutes later the bus depot appears and people launch themselves towards the doors, bashing us unmercifully and I worry of Bernard retaliating against this madness. Restraining his physical inclinations, verbal lines are drawn for people in a deadly serious voice as several are told to cross them at their own peril.

People run past us over the rough ground as the competition for places involves reaching the first gate as loud voices try to 'save places' for their 'friends' on later buses. All around me people respond badly to each other and the whole experience starts to feel 'wrong'. Even the compressed, frantic, chaotic places in India did not descend into such an air of 'me, me, me' with all forms of consideration swept away in self-pursuit.

The staff on the barrier notice the white stick and Bernard's defence of our space, waving him forward but the movement starts a stampede with people rushing past us, pushing us out the way as they think a second turnstile has opened. Reaching the front after dashing forward, they are turned back by staff as we alone are allowed through to head for the entrance of the 'Young Mountain', Wayna Picchu.

The ground is rough with multiple banks of uneven stone steps as behind us the floodgates open, allowing people to stream past in a rushing stampede for the distant entrance. Running, tripping and even falling in front of us, Bernard's voice loudly warns them and they look sheepish on seeing the stick they have fallen over as it tries to find steps in front. Picking themselves up, looking apologetic, they rush on regardless.

I start to get angry as I realise my disability may prevent me from getting to the entrance within the 400 allowed, walking as fast as I can with Bernard coaxing and encouraging me with his words, his presence. More and more people pass but I will not give up. Not yet. I simply cannot walk fast enough to keep up with them on the rough ground. Arriving at the tail end of the queue it is not as long as anticipated; perhaps a hundred people are in front of us? Did only 75 people run past us – three busloads? It felt far more. Staff approach asking, '7am or 10am?' Assuming the question concerns start times for the climb I respond '7am' and they wander away. It is now 6.30, daylight has arrived, and it has taken us half an hour to get to this point. Eventually, after much shuffling, our tickets receive stamps with the numbers 62 and 63 and with them comes the realisation we have made it.

Slowly edging closer to the small-gated entrance, 7.30am comes and our names are entered into the register to log a start time as my walking stick replaces its white counterpart. I do not hold onto Bernard from this point onwards but slip into our tried and trusted method of 'independent walking'. Listening to his instructions about the next step, section or obstacle appearing, my stick then finds them and I move on my own. It has taken a long time to develop this way of working together and we call it 'Free walking' but the level of trust involved is considerable as it takes complete and utter confidence in what he is telling me.

Bernard – When walking or climbing I usually stay behind Cathy while watching

*and giving information about what lies before her. When descending I'm usually
in front of her. Both ways mean if she does slip or fall (very rare) I have a chance of
catching her. It's a very labour-intensive way of working with a blind person and
the concentration is considerable and very tiring for us both but in different ways.
For the blind person it takes a great deal of courage to give this trust while for the
sighted guide you have to be able to 'step back' and let go. It's something you learn
to do with confidence as the blind person gives you that certainty by the way they
deal with the information you give them.*

Several people had fallen on the previous day and it is easy to see how as
you can seriously hurt yourself on the centuries' old paths before you even get
to the base of the 1,000 foot vertical climb up Wayna Picchu itself. The steps
are uneven, offset, slippery, narrow, the likes of which trekking people usually
come across in only small doses. But these go on forever.

As the ascent begins, I start to realise why Bernard had urged caution
about wanting to complete 1,000–1,200 feet of winding path going straight
up in the air. Grab rails are few and far between and the worn slippery steps
go ever upwards. In many ways it is something akin to climbing a 100 story
building, but with far steeper steps than normal, with the distance between
any two never being the same. Eroded and cracked due to the rocks they are
constructed from, the surface is slippery and smooth from centuries of use and
the morning dew. Imagine knowing there are sheer drops of hundreds, and
eventually, thousands of feet just a step away at times. Now imagine doing the
climb with your eyes closed.

As we climb small knots of people pass us. They come across Bernard first as
he takes station behind, carrying my white cane as a symbol to indicate the need
for a little patience. Sometimes he leads as it is so hard to move upwards that
my hand holds onto his backpack as we haul ourselves up the steep gradients.
For other sections it is simply a matter of grabbing each other's wrists and
heaving. Stopping for breaks, my face is plastered with sweat dripping into
my eyes, making them sting and 20 minutes in sees my clothes stuck to me
and breathing difficult. While true, we take comfort from the – half our
age – people huffing and puffing as they pass us by. The fastest ascent of this
mountain was by an unknown Olympian God (as they must have been) at 26
minutes whereas mere mortals take 40–60. After an hour we are nowhere
near halfway up and I start to have doubts.

Can I do this?

It is so, so, hard.

People pass by and offer encouragement but I start to worry as, if it is this
hard going up, how bad will it be coming down when all steps are a leap of faith

when you cannot see them? Stopping for a break, I start to ponder whether this is achievable. Voicing my doubts, Bernard tells me it is OK to retrace our steps and go back if I want to. He tells me I have nothing to prove, to myself, to him, to anyone. Then he waits, giving me time to think.

After a few moments of silence, he speaks again:

'It would be a shame to stop now, however, as it's not so much further, really.'

I want to do it. He knows I do. I do not want to turn back. But the descent worries me. Then the little girl in me, hesitatingly, asks:

'Is it possible?'

A cheery voice responds.

'Common girl, you can do this if you want to. Come. We're going to the top. You and me. Together. You can do this. Believe it. Let's go.'

We set off.

Sometimes the steps are two-feet high and Bernard passes by me to reach back and grab my wrist, hauling me up before stopping to let my hand once again find his backpack. Then off we go again. Within seconds the same thing occurs as he stops to reach back as we lock onto each other's wrist to gain purchase. Then he pulls again. The amount of physical strength required is considerable and his breathing is as hoarse as mine and he carries a backpack. Muscles ache in every part of my body as my whole mental world becomes wrapped up in taking each step.

I will not give up.

Words of encouragement flow from my companion, sometimes a little cajoling is required as slowly a dent is made in the distance to be climbed. Stopping for short breaks – he will allow only short breaks as momentum is lost and muscles seize he tells me – never again though did I question I would reach the top.

'Not far now.'

'Just around the corner.'

'Just over the next bit.'

Bernard sprinkles such sentences liberally as other voices join in, encouraging me up the mountain, people who saw us at the bus queue or had passed us earlier in their ascent, are now descending as we continue our struggle upwards. They push me on with their words as they wait for us to climb past them and two hours later the first plateau is reached. It is here people often take the famous 'overlooking Machu Picchu' picture. Struggling up the steep gradient, people above encourage us through the final effort before congratulating us as we step onto the flatness. Many ask if they can take pictures of the two dishevelled people before them as we sit dangling legs over the edge of a drop several thousand feet below us, sweat dripping freely. Bernard is gasping for a smoke in self-congratulation and everywhere there are no-smoking signs due to it being a World Heritage Site. In the end, turning to anybody within earshot he declares:

'If anybody wants to shout at me for smoking then please feel free, do it now and then don't interrupt my smoke. I am going to light up and I will even take my butt with me when I am finished. Anybody want to complain?'

Sounds of laughter and good-natured comments from a group of Americans follow about the use of the word 'butt' but these are lost to me as the distinctive click of his lighter fills my ears. A sharp contented inhale follows from the person who enabled me to believe, who got me here. I think everybody on the plateau knows this more than he does, having watched us fight our way up. Seeing the effort involved, nobody begrudges him his quiet reflection and many even encourage him. Even the solitary staff member smiled, leaving him be.

A deep American voice from not far away comments, 'Man, after what you two have done you both deserve a medal never mind a cigarette. You smoke away.' I have just been guided up the most difficult terrain imaginable under lung-wrenching, muscle-burning conditions, all the time with patience, humour and encouragement. It would have taken a hard person to begrudge him his cigarette. There was not a hard person around us.

Resting for fifteen minutes with the view being described through a second cigarette, the panorama of the Lost City is outlined in my mind. Way below us sit the grassed terraces which thrived to feed three times the number of people who lived here for about 100 years when its inhabitants were wiped out (one theory states) by the Spanish advance guard of smallpox. Bernard tells me that the conquerors were only 50 miles away executing the last Inca Emperor at Cusco without ever realising it was here, so remote and inaccessible was the location. By the time the last emperor was meeting his end it had been long abandoned and overgrown before cannon thunder was ever heard. Descriptions follow of the clouds that drift pass the mountain peaks around us and through which a piercing blue sky can be seen. Far, far, below us people wander like ants around the ancient ruins, standing here for nearly 600 hundred years.

My muscles protest when asked to stand as Bernard comments how I cannot come this far without going right to the very top, which is 'not far'. In fairness it is not far, although it involves a crawl through a slightly flooded 'grotto', scaling a few more rocks, and climbing a log ladder along the way. Then we stand on the summit rock, the highest reachable point you can go and it truly feels like I am on top of the world. Bernard punches his arms into the air among the clouds, proclaiming loudly:

'Look at me Ma, I'm on top of the world!'

He stands silent.

I leave him to his thoughts, knowing he is shouting 'Hello' to his mother who died in 2006. Last night he'd said he would do this if we reached the top, using this line from his father's favourite film (James Cagney's *White Heat*). Once he told me, sitting in the clouds of the French Pyrenees, how some people believe the higher you are, the closer to God you are. This is why, he continued, high places are often sacred in so many cultures as if we are physically closer to God then, logically, we must also be closer to our departed ones. Perhaps, he had told me, they really can hear us across time and space. If this were true he said my late husband Peter would hear everything. Forestalling my next question he went on with:

'Because you don't get an answer, it doesn't mean they cannot hear you.'

Leaving me sitting, alone, on a monolith built high in the Pyrenees, he took station a 100 feet away with Bertha; no doubt, puffing away on a cigarette as he waited. Sitting alone deep in my thoughts, he had taken a picture of me and it is still, he believes, the finest picture he has ever taken in his life. Encapsulating my view on blindness as we set out to cross the world, it came to answer people who thought, or were brave enough to ask the question:

'What's the point when you are blind?'

So it is that I have always responded since then that, 'Being blind means you see the world in a different way.'

Finding ourselves sitting on another high place thousands of miles away, we sit and reflect for a long time as the summit staff leave us alone while constantly moving other people along. The workers had left us sitting and reflecting but only later did we find out the reason why; no such ascent had ever been done before as far as they could recall. A blind woman climbing Wayna Picchu? Who would have thought it possible?

Then the time of the descent came and it was as bad as I'd feared.

Anybody who understands blindness will know that going down stairs is more difficult than going up. Now amplify the problem with near vertical steps varying in depth. Every time your foot descends, you have no idea how far down it's going to go. A small shock wave goes through your leg as you cannot judge how far you are stepping down. Truly, it is a matter of stepping into space, into thin air, and then hoping. There are few hand rails and sheer drops are all around as the pathway is very narrow. Complete trust in what you are being told is the only way to get down; your life is in the hands of your guide.

Bernard spends most of the descent climbing down backwards so he can describe each step to me. I do not know if it is possible to imagine coming down the mountain backwards, giving directions while talking, encouraging and sometimes cajoling another person. Carrying a backpack, my bag and fleece, everything is taken from me that could interfere with my ability to move freely, to move safely. A couple we met on the summit (Sandra and Phil) stay behind me virtually all the way, taking many items off Bernard to allow him to move more freely. People pass us saying 'Good Job' and 'Well done' and other words of encouragement and one group of teenagers from America stop to tell me:

'In all our time travelling through South America, seeing a blind woman climb Wayna Picchu is the most amazing thing any of us have ever seen.'

It is very humbling to hear this when you consider the spectacular surroundings, the beautiful environment, and I treasure the comment. I always will. Other people video and photograph our struggle all the way down as a group of Japanese set up their tripods, filming us until we're out of sight. Fighting our way down, others are engaged in their own battle coming upwards, huffing and puffing, constantly asking, 'Is it far?' much as we had earlier. Offering our own words of encouragement to keep them going, the kind comments continue to flow at us as, stone-by-stone, step-by-step, the descent is tackled with Sandra and Phil behind, and Bernard in front. All three keep me going.

Over four hours pass and physically I am weakening but perhaps more importantly, mentally things are becoming so much harder. Every joint and muscle is in pain as my hips start to protest; every step brings pain as my foot slams down. It goes on forever, wave after wave, step after step, until all the pains merge together into a constant stream of throbbing. As I weaken Bernard's humour increases and people laugh as they pass with his comments to me: 'Come on, it's a bit of a stroll down, stop buggering about and get a move on, it's not that hard.'

A group of Australians laugh out loud with his: 'Will you stop messing about, the pubs will be closed by the time we get down.'

The Australians respond with a 'Good on ya'.

With one bottle of water left, Bernard insists I swill it around my mouth before taking small sips as he knows I am nearing my physical end. It leads to breaks becoming more frequent but shorter in duration as to do otherwise will hurt more when I have to move, 'It's all about will power now, Cath, nothing more,' he says.

When we eventually reach the bottom it is so hard to begin climbing up the end of Machu Picchu to get to the exit leading back into the city itself. Everything is hurting and I am so, so tired. Meanwhile, constant assurances come that the end is not far away. We grab each other's wrists as I am hauled up enormous mountain-like steps, as each one now seems to me, all to the sound of happy whistling as Bernard makes jolly sounds and jokes to which I can barely respond.

'Don't talk, don't answer, just breathe,' he commands, while talking constantly – streams of instructions interspersed with humour.

And then, it's all over.

We reach the cabin at the entrance five hours after setting off, duly recorded in the log book to mark our official exit from the 'Young Mountain'. We may not have been the quickest up or down (!) but neither of us care as the big ledger is turned back several pages to find our entry time. Bernard tells me how people have come, climbed and are now long gone as he registers our exit. We do not care. We are too tired to care.

Bernard – I was immensely proud of what we achieved. To enter a signout time of 12.30pm was one of the best things I have written in my whole life. To watch Cathy engage in such a monumental struggle was awesome, seeing her overcome both the physical and mental worlds involved was phenomenal. It was a privilege to be with her on the mountain and there have been few times in my life when I have been as proud of anyone.

Like two shambling wrecks, we virtually stumble through the gate where a young man approaches us with a question everybody seems to ask when you get back down; how long did it take?

'Five hours,' came our proud, breathless, reply.

'Five hours!' he snorts with derision all too easy to hear.

'We went slowly to admire the view,' Bernard responded.

So it was that this hint of humour is lost on our young friend as he walks away laughing. To be fair to the young climber no white cane is visible and my eyes are blue and open. Still clutching a walking stick in my own numb fingers, Bernard has long since buried the white cane in his pack, needing both hands on the descent. If the young man had looked a little closer it would have been possible to see how my walking stick was actually holding me up and I would have fallen over without it. Thus, he could not know I was blind, nor could he know of Bernard's monumental feat of guiding. Instead all he saw was two 'old' people, completely worn out and barely standing.

Setting off onto the mountain in all his youthful vigour we hope he enjoyed the climb, and set a time to be happy with as, at the end of the day, everything is relative. If you ever get to climb that young mountain, turn the ledger backwards to the page dated Friday 17th April 2009 and look for numbers 62 and 63. There you will find us.

In many ways we like to think a small impact was made on that day in our fight up and down that mountain. Not a nuclear explosion, not even a small earthquake perhaps, but it was an impact nonetheless. Bernard could see the question in people's faces on that mountain, that of, 'How can she do this being blind?' Their faces gave it away and in many ways this journey is all about challenging these perceptions; about what is achievable as a blind person. In many ways as a blind person, often it is not that things CANNOT be done but rather the question revolves around HOW they can be done. Sometimes people have to see something happening before they realise that many things are achievable.

Maybe, in a small way, the people on the mountain who watched our struggle will return home and one day in the future meet a struggling blind person before saying:

'You can do it if you want to. Here, let me help you. Did I tell you about once seeing a blind woman...?'

Bernard is fond of saying, 'It is the hundred small things people see us doing each day which shows what can be achieved.'

Leaving our eager young climber, our shambling frames weave through the ruins with many people giving us the thumbs up as we pass them by, while others wave to us in acknowledgement. Both of us are destroyed. I suddenly realise how tired my companion is when he nearly falls into the café chair, lights a cigarette, drinks two beers in rapid succession before he manages to speak again. Two huge slices of apple pie, along with an enormous bottle of water are all soon gone as we congratulate each other.

Bernard – I suppose like a lot of people given this situation, you stave off the
tiredness and focus on what needs to be done: getting Cathy up and down safely.
Nothing else entered my mind. It really is that simple. Once you have done what
you set out to do, only then can you allow yourself to collapse.

At 51 and 53 years of age we can hardly get up out of the chairs half an hour later to catch the bus down to Aguas Calientes and the four-hour train ride back to Cusco. Lying in bed after our tired journey through the darkness I once again stand on top of the world savouring the feel of the air across my face, tasting it in my lungs. The memories of whispering breezes lull me to sleep where I dream of heights, clouds and people who said wonderful things to keep me going.

The mountain was full of them today.

'A little girl called Samikai'

After a deep night's sleep I wake with some trepidation, waiting for screaming muscles to announce themselves. Nothing. I flex my thighs and await shouts concerning the baseball bat that has beaten them into bruised masses. Nothing. Tensing my calves, I wait for the pain. Nothing comes. There's some soreness in the tendons, some joints are tender, but not the screaming fires from hell. I lay awake puzzling while recalling Bernard's insistence I drink several cups of coca tea the night before as ibuprofen tablets were placed into my hand. Perhaps the combination has staved off the worst? When he awakes a little while later he mumbles, 'a good wander around the shops will do your legs good'. He hits my weak spot straight away. Shopping. Climbing out of bed gingerly no muscles rage in protest and over the morning the tenderness appears wherever steps are concerned. Hobbling slightly, other sore points begin to show but we feel rather better than anticipated.

After buying postcards of Machu Picchu, showing where we stood among the clouds, a ten-year-old boy called George approaches us as we sit on steps; worming his way into Bernard's heart as they talk of Peru and Britain, five hand-painted cards are bought before the boy wanders off waving back to us. Despite my companion resisting anything taking up space on the bike, he weakens to buy a 10 inch high traditional knitted doll from a young girl who looks no older than eight; sometimes he can be such a big softy. Buying coca chocolate to aid our recovery, more tea is drunk to increase the absorption of oxygen into the blood and to combat the encroaching muscle fatigue. Back at the hotel more tea is drunk while sucking chocolate as well as taking more ibuprofen along with copious amounts of water to replenish our depleted physical resources. Sleep claims us quickly.

Cusco and Peru have seeped into our consciousness as we slowly recover; the people of Peru have wormed their way into our hearts. In the same way as when leaving Nepal we repack Bertha the following day with sadness as we could quite happily stay in Cusco, rent somewhere, and sink into everyday life. Bernard even talks of finding a job in the area 'doing something'. After watching various guides doing their work with the predominantly English-speaking tourists, he thinks this could be a career change for him. It is certainly true that he can bring the often dull guidebooks to life by injecting ad lib comments around themes and characters; however, it is not to be. Instead, everything is repacked and two new one-litre fuel containers are installed, acting as a 'fail-safe' in terms of distance. Every staff member of the hotel gathers to wave us off and they even flag down a taxi, pay the fare, and instruct the driver to see us safely onto the S3 and back towards the Pan-American Highway, two days' ride away through the mountains. Waving to everybody 15 minutes later, Cusco recedes below us on the long climb out of the city.

The road is heavily chopped up and we rattle along at a much-reduced pace, both settling back into the bike for the 125 miles planned for an easy day as our legs are tender. Entering the mountains, the roads make the Swiss Alps look straight in comparison despite the covering of fine gravel, like grey cat litter several inches deep. Constant switchbacks bend upwards for mile after mile before dropping in a downward spiral when the whole process repeats again.

Passing through small hamlets, tall poles bearing fluttering red flags indicate where home-brewed corn whisky can be bought. Swooping and diving on the roads with the loud crunching of the road surface coming from the wheels, the miles mount slowly. Torturous bends twist and turn constantly until we stop and Bernard tells that there is no road ahead, just soil and gravel. Somebody obviously sneaked up here in the middle of the night and stole the tarmac to leave us sitting with Bertha ticking over underneath us, rocking from side to side. By now, I know he is waiting for a vehicle to cross the surface to watch what happens, looking at the wheels of the vehicle to gauge the depth of the surface, how slippery it might be, which track to put our wheels on.

'We've done worse,' he comments as he watches a car pass.

'Hang on.'

We bounce and slide over the loose surface with the rear wheel sending loud cracks as it compresses the gravel. Occasionally it skips sideways but the bike keeps moving forward to climb back onto tarmac after several straights and bends. During the day other sections of road have disappeared under the force of raging waters that have hurled the surface down the mountain below, leaving nothing but deep channels through which water flows deeply. Steam hisses as the engine submerges sending warmth up my legs as we power through. The sound of loud crunching fills my ears constantly as miles of gravel and hardcore fill our time while huge clouds of dust thrown up from passing oncoming vehicles obscure the road ahead. Waiting for the clouds to settle before driving on, 2,000 feet quickly fall away through snake-like roads, leaving my ears popping. Swallowing hard to unblock them, the roller-coaster and helter-skelter highway continues through the mountains in the drop down into Abancay where, despite all the effort, Bernard claims today has been his favourite ride as it 'had everything'.

Bernard – It's strange really. I worry about our safety more than anything else. Despite this, I think it was the challenge. I do not claim to be a 'great' rider, far from it. I have no real ego about riding a bike although I am undoubtedly better after riding under so many different conditions. However, I also know there are far, far, better riders than me. While I believe this, for me, and based on what I think my riding level is, it felt like a major achievement to get through today without coming off!

The next morning heavy rain is falling, pattering on the roof, against the windows, dripping noisily and heavily onto the small balcony outside our room. Bernard is pulled into wakefulness by a bout of stomach cramps leaving him doubled over. Multiple trips to 'The Little Boy's room' leave me in no doubt all is not well, as Diafix tablets are swallowed after each visit. Telling me of the ten feet visibility due to rain and heavy mist over this 2400 metre (7800 feet) high city, the feeling is of the God's being against us this day. Both signs of bad weather and stomach are a hint to sit still and spend the day writing our journals.

Clear skies greet us on the next morning on the climb out of Abancay as drivers wash their cars in streams racing across the road surface. Passing through the first, we understand why as our wheels cut through hot water naturally pumped up from underground thermals as the roads above the city turn white with soapsuds.

Climbing and descending on near-deserted roads, Bertha pulls us up to 14,963 feet gasping under the strain while Bernard searches for another 37 feet to go past 15,000. Pulling over to the side of the road he ponders whether one of the side-tracks can be taken up the mountains just to claim this (to him) magical figure. He forgoes this, leaving the barrier unbreached, much to his disappointment.

The rain starts to fall hard before turning into a barrage of hailstones thumping into us painfully as we quickly pull over to haul on our waterproofs, last used in Australia. Fumbling and rushing to pull them on as torrents drop from the sky, this simple act of dressing causes profound breathlessness. And it is cold. Shiveringly cold. Bernard's hands shake as he passes me layers to put on while the hailstones start to crash noisily down onto our helmets. The sky is black and threatening as the road takes us onwards splashing through torrents of water rushing across the tarmac ribbon.

Goats, asses, cows, horses, sheep and alpacas all consider the road a good place to lie down upon during the inclement weather. Wild pigs scurry out of our way with farmers returning wet waves as the rain and hail pounds down. At 14,800 feet, a corner reveals a stationary set of vehicles with the road closed for at least two hours while road crews rip the surface off in preparation for the new. To make matters even worse Bernard discovers he has no cigarettes. It's 2pm as we pull up with 89 km to the next town; the sky is completely and utterly black.

Two hill women sit on the edge of the road with their babies slung across their backs wrapped in blankets with a wheelbarrow before them. To Bernard's delight it's full of biscuits, drinks, and Eureka, two already opened packets of cigarettes. Buying two cartons of orange juice, several packets of biscuits, and all ten cigarettes, he puffs away now unconcerned at the delay while watching several wagons divert onto the old road 100 yards away from us. He disappears to investigate.

Bernard – It was obviously hard going for the vehicles as I walk over and watch several wagons negotiate the surface. It's knee deep in water and extremely muddy and it takes me five seconds to realise it would be beyond me to ride it. Bertha's engine would be virtually under water and mud. Even a couple of 4x4s make hard going of it as I watch twelve vehicles go through before I discount it completely.

Sitting by the roadside the laughing starts: about the weather, the roads, and the image people have of the two English people, huddled under an umbrella at 14,000 feet wrapped in four layers of clothing. Hail and snow starts to pummel us, feeling just like home as the countryside disappears under the weight of descending hail. The hill women run across the road to shelter in the side of the wagons, seeking comfort from the wind, rain, sleet and snow sweeping across the plateau, turning everything into a mushy white colour. Bernard asks them, in his Spangalese and sign language, if he can take their picture but they indicate no and so he puts the camera away.

The weather eases a little and people appear, including two female members of the road crew who direct the traffic with Stop/Go paddles like big table tennis bats. They stand looking at the bike, asking questions, and this prompts the young daughter of the hill women to shyly wander over to look at the bike. One of the paddle bearers (Gwen) translates Bernard's question to the little girl, asking if she would like to sit on Bertha? Looking to her mother for affirmation it is given. So it is that a little 9 year-old Peruvian girl called Samikai sits on a bike made 11 years before she was born, in a country on the other side of the world. Life can be wonderfully magical sometimes as her mum relents about a photograph of the event and then views it with delight. It is a shame we cannot give her a copy.

In many ways, it's a different world despite many Western people claiming 'There is only one world'. There is not one world at all. There are many. It's divided up by so many factors including disability, religion, caste, class, language, culture, and a whole host of other factors. Each shouts uniqueness and, for me, long live the differences between its peoples.

The hail and snow starts again and everybody retreats to whatever shelter they have while we hide, once again, under our Malaysian umbrella. A police officer suddenly appears, gesturing us towards a bus as thunder and lightning crash around us as the sky rages and hailstones fall like bullets to hit us painfully. Retreating to the bus with its leaking roof, it's full of Peruvian policemen, two traffic attendants, two hill women, the young girl Samikai, two babies and ourselves. The thunder and lightning is crashing and blasting around the sky as if Thor, the Norse God, is striking his hammer in the sky while riding a Harley-Davidson with open exhausts.

Hail drops like small stones onto the roof as Eduardo, one of the policemen, reads Bernard's English/Spanish, Spanish/English Dictionary while paddle-bearing Gwen admires our rubberised waterproofs while she bemoans the broken zip on her own. The landscape turns white as time drifts past in the way now long used to when waiting for something to happen. Two hours later the road reopens and farewells are said to everybody as the bus disgorges its visitors.

Climbing back on the bike Bernard waits for the trucks to go through, watching as always, before edging Bertha forward with a clear run in front of her. Slithering and sliding through the mud and hailstones, we judder down onto the new hardcore surface just laid while the road crew wave encouragement at the other end when Gwen tells them to hold the traffic until we are safely through. The surface improves a few miles later allowing us to blast along as quickly as possible as the prospect of being caught on these roads at night is not something we wish to contemplate. It really is just too unpredictable: one minute good tarmac, the next no road, then good tarmac, then huge potholes. A massive black storm hovers over to our right and we do not need more water to complicate the road as water and soil equals mud. Rain also hides the depth of potholes as Bernard hustles Bertha as quickly as he can safely go. Road crews appear sporadically and all wave as we pass seeking mileage above all else.

Entering Puquio the light starts to fall as the 2,500 foot drop begins down into the town where the tarmac suddenly finishes, leaving nothing but hard-packed dirt and narrow streets before we climb the street from hell. Ramp-like, it stretches up into the air except, unlike a launch ramp, this one is full of voluminous potholes. Bertha's front wheel paws the air like a stallion as we explode up its length onto the Plaza, startling everybody with our violent appearance.

> *Bernard — I couldn't believe the street. I really couldn't. The gradient is so steep and I sat looking at it for a long time before even attempting it. It is the steepest thing I have ever, ever, encountered. Single-car width with holes running across, it was incredibly bad and I thought we would certainly come off as we crashed up it. It was truly fortunate there was nothing at the top as we exited, at high velocity.*

The town is so far off the tourist radar people stop to look at us as we search for, and find, an 'authentic' Peruvian one-and-a-half star hostel (−5 star European-rated) where we eat chicken (pollo) and chips and dogs wander around our legs looking for scraps. Showering with lukewarm water trickling over our heads, we collapse into bed where we eventually warm up before drifting asleep at 12,000 feet.

Waking tired and irritable due to the Hound of the Baskervilles barking every hour throughout the night like a finely tuned Swiss watch with its alarm set, the first vehicle fires up at 3.40am in the garage just outside our door, the diesel engine revving constantly for fifteen minutes before leaving.

Like a true gothic horror film, the garage doors swing open with enormous loud creaks for the driver to depart. Drifting back to sleep, an hour later the same process occurs with vehicle number two and eventually we struggle out of bed. The whole town seems to be up with children shouting in the street as cars fly up and down and dogs bark everywhere. It is 5am.

'You complained in Kosovo
when I didn't tell you'

The day is spent riding shattered roads passing orange-jacketed roadcrews working for mile after mile as they whistle and cheer at our passing, giving us V for victory signs. The constant hammering of the surfaces breaks a pannier frame, leaving everything wobbling dangerously. We stop to brace the crack with cable-ties and spanners. Even this simple job leaves Bernard puffing with the effort at altitude as alpacas roll in the roads, kicking their legs in the air like playful dogs. Horses wander across our path and a dog plays with six piglets on a bend as we gently coast to a halt to watch. Hundreds of goats appear around one corner, completely covering the road surface as the farmer ushers them on with his two dogs, one at the front and one at the rear. The tail-end dog limps heavily and seems much older than his more youthful companion as he struggles to keep up.

'A bit like me sometimes,' Bernard confides tiredly through the intercom.

After hours of being shaken to bits across 80 miles, we drop rapidly down the mountains and know that our time in the heights of Peru is ending. The Pan-American beckons us on in the fall through the clouds onto pristine new black tarmac, complete with freshly painted bright yellow lines. Bertha starts to stretch her legs as she's freed from the constraints of hours of first and second gear. Dropping down 12,000 feet quickly, our ears popping, calculations reveal it's taken us five hours to cover the 160 km, but there is a mixture of relief and sadness at reaching the highway. Relief as the days have involved hard roads but also sadness as there is something very special about riding among the clouds and the people of the high places of Peru. We'll miss the silence, solitude and peacefulness of where we've been.

Like a greyhound unleashed, we hurtle along at 100 kph towards Ica where our hearts sink as Bernard describes the mounds of rubbish on entering the town, giving off acrid, eye-stinging smoke drifting across the road. A police motorcyclist pulls up, realises our need for somewhere to sleep for the night, and sets off, complete with flashing lights, to lead us through the city. Taking us to the only guest house with somewhere for the bike, we arrive completely worn out and drag ourselves through the motions of eating before falling sound asleep to the beeping of horns at 8pm.

The 1S (Pan-Am) out of Ica is a hot, straight road full of traffic, neither of which we've seen for some time. The landscape is sun-blasted, flat, sandy, and so unlike the lush mountains. Already I miss the clean air along with the quietness as the air here is full of the sounds of people rushing and loud diesel engines thundering along spilling their fumes everywhere. There are police roadblocks and constant checks of documents but when my blindness is recognised we're waved off.

Entering the capital Lima, horns blare everywhere, drivers cut each other up and buses pass by before suddenly cutting in. They stop for a fare so quickly it leaves Bertha pinging up and down on her front forks, like a yo-yo with the sudden massive braking to avoid the sideways-facing buses now blocking our way. Relief floods us in the climb out of the city before pulling over as Bernard tells me that the pollution hangs over the city like a great dome. It smells like Lahore, with dense black smoke pouring out from all the ancient ruined engines. Reaching the town of Chancay after a very mixed day, everything feels hemmed in, noisy and busy. We don't like it.

The fetid smell of fish drives us out of the town to a hostel on the outskirts where the smell is more tolerable. It's so strong you can taste it long after you smell it and I want to retreat to the shower to wash away both which seem to stick to clothes and face. According to the whimpering sounds coming from Bernard, the shower is stone cold and after living in the same clothes for four days I'm not impressed with the lack of hot water. Our feet have even eaten the 'odour eaters' recently installed and we are ragged, worn out, tired and listless. No longer do we even get changed on overnight stops; it's not worth the effort. Now we simply fall into bed, too tired to be bothered with anything.

The TV has nothing understandable on it and trucks from the wagon park next door rattle the windows deep into the night with their coming and going. They do not, however, disturb my sleeping companion as he still seems able to sleep on a cliff edge while I lay awake deep into the night. Morning comes with me feeling listless and irritable.

Bernard tries to cheer me up, describing everything and anything in his attempt to bridge the gap between us, but to no avail. Eventually he falls silent and we ride through the day under this dark cloud, a mood that will not shift. Meanwhile the day is hot and the sand blows across the road despite the sandbags placed along its length to hold back the fine grains. Nearing Chambote, still in silence, the right pannier moves more than it should and a check shows a lock which attaches it to the frame has broken. Pulling into the town, we're directed to a hotel with rooms decorated in 70s retro style with large round beds and a colour scheme of bright orange and purple. Deciding to stay for two nights, we hope both of us will return to an even psychological keel. Meanwhile, a broken-legged man on reception tells us of his recent motorcycle crash before Bernard sets off to dismantle the broken carrier frame while I have my first hot shower in days.

Bernard – As I dismantle the rear frame I can see workmen inside the compound building a set of steel gates and, presto, they have a welder. As I make this discovery, our broken-legged friend hobbles across the courtyard and I explain my predicament to him. After a rapid exchange in Spanish the frame is welded back together and being installed back onto the bike in under half an hour. That is what I call 'a result'!

Setting off to find something to eat, the lingering effects of my mood cause us to clash before, again, falling into our separate worlds. We talk little throughout the evening as a cloud hangs over me. I wake several times in the night from noise and, after the third time, I listen and realise that, once again, he has brought me to a brothel. Putting together all the information, as in Kosovo, it now all makes perfect sense. The round bed containing only sheets. The 70s retro colour scheme. The stainless steel pole in the corner running from floor to ceiling which Bernard had described as something seen in some clubs. I also recall the receptionist laughing when he had asked if all the rooms had 'Matrimonial' (double) beds. Then there were the pornographic channels found while flicking through looking for something to fill the awkward silence of the previous evening.

Footsteps on the stairs announce constant streams of arrivals before nocturnal activities of the sexual kind can be heard through thin walls. An hour or so later the door opens, footsteps descend, and the sound of mop buckets announce cleaners going about their business. Then the next customer arrives as TV channels are again carefully selected to aid the experience. Either this is true or the people in Peru book into hotels to power nap, for an hour, while watching channels showing people with Kosovo-like respiratory problems. Highly unlikely on both counts I would think.

Bernard is blissfully unaware although there was fastidious cleaning going on in the room next door at least six times through the night. And he slept on. I wake him at 2.30am to report my observations.

'You woke me to tell me that?' comes the incredulous sleepy voice.

'You complained in Kosovo when I didn't tell you.'

'No I didn't.'

'Yes, you did, you said you wanted to listen.'

'No I did not.'

'Yes, you did.'

'If it bothers you use ear plugs,' is his helpful reply before turning over and going back to sleep. Needless to say the two nights became one as we packed the next morning with Bernard grumbling he really liked it here, they welded his frame, the girls were all really nice (I'm sure they were), the bike was safe in the car park etc, etc. Pulling out past all the expensive 4x4s – at least it seemed to be an expensive brothel – we ride towards Trujillo and the road onwards to Chiclayo. Here a very nice rickshaw driver takes us to the Gran Hotel and it is everything we recognise, quiet and spacious, with menus in English.

The last few days have left us so tired our harmony is shattered, and it takes four nights in the end to come back to each other from the place we'd both withdrawn to as the bike is checked, oil and filters are changed, and everything else tightened down. Bertha has taken a real beating crossing Peru so far, much as we had but without ever realising it. After resting over the days, Hector (the receptionist) seems genuinely surprised at our eventual departure.

'Why?' he asks.

'Because it's time to move on,' Bernard says while handing over 15 cards for posting showing Machu Picchu, which arrived home over three months later.

'We have loved your real English accents,' he proclaims. 'Not like American accents at all,' he continued in his vaguely American accent.

Riding out of Chiclayo into the heat of the desert and sand dunes, workmen with shovels try, in King Canute like ways, to hold back the dunes threatening to engulf the road surface. The temperature increases drastically with our gauge showing 45 degrees and Bernard finds the scenery hypnotic. The town of Sullana soon appears and another hostel where the shower is cool, but I make no complaint. There's little that can be done about it and, after the heat of the day, it's actually pleasant. Eating tuna steaks and salad, the football on the TV blares in the background as 20 truck drivers shout at their local teams while watching the two of us in the corner. The same drivers wake us at 6am with their convoy firing up, one at a time, the sound of revving engines threatening to collapse the building.

Back on the road passing through small towns, we cross the biggest speed humps in the world to the sound of Bertha's sump and exhausts smacking onto them. Trying different speeds of attack makes no difference. Ride over them slowly, 'Bang'; hit them faster 'Bang'.

The border with Ecuador is now not far as each speed hump is climbed and we should be there by 1pm. Forty kilometres away we stretch our legs while Bernard lights up after 224 km of brightness. Fifteen minutes later the starter button is pressed and nothing happens. He presses it again. Nothing. Dead. The panel lights are on. The horn is pressed to blare loudly in the silence as the voltmeter shows 13.5 and good on all instruments.

'Damn' accompanies the loud clicking as the starter button is pressed repeatedly; all to no avail. A heavy sigh comes through the intercom.

'We have a problem Cath, climb off.'

A truckload of Peruvian police pull up as Bernard is descending deep into wiring world. Suggesting a bump start to allow us to get to the next town (Tumbes) where a mechanic can look at it, all five take station at the back and run down the road pushing Bertha until she fires up and comes back towards me. More handshakes all around and off we go again until we find a hotel where Bertha is taken to bits to get at her innards.

Bernard – About 10 minutes into the process, a van turns up and the next-door neighbour turns out to be a mechanic. Rapidly the whole starter motor is in bits on the grass and the problem located; the motor is jammed. Over the next two hours, this is fixed but another problem is created as he manages to snap the hard plastic casing which holds everything in place. With judicious amounts of glue it's stuck back together as night falls and clouds of mosquitoes arrive. Beating a hasty retreat, everything is left to set overnight before reinstalling it in the morning.'

Both of us gratefully fall into bed only to be woken half-an-hour later by the loudest Latin American music ever heard, emanating from next door. Bernard is dispatched to investigate and he returns with the comment:

'It's pretty good, sounds much better outside.'

I would have hit him with a pillow if my head was not buried under it.

'It's a stage full of musicians and loads of people milling about. Looks like some form of concert.'

At this, he climbs back into bed, pushes earplugs in and falls asleep leading me to conclude that, sometimes, I do hate him, very much, as each and every drumbeat and shrill 'Arriva' goes through me until the drummer's arms give out at 3.30. Silence falls.

Morning comes with Bernard lamenting the dartboard painted on his back, so covered in lumps is he as we find out, the hard way, that Tumbes is renowned for the density of its mosquito population. Last night they fed well on white meat. As the sun rises, our room soon turns into an oven and the overhead fan circulates the hot air lazily as the sun burns fiercely bright.

Bernard readies himself to work under its glare with tubes of (now) depressurised sun cream being brought out. I sit under our umbrella as the clink of metal on metal signifies Bertha's restoration back into one piece. Some time later the starter is pressed; sounds of clicking and whizzing precede a huge sigh, telling me it has to be taken apart again. The motor is not turning the engine over and there is little else to be done but dismantle the whole thing again. Each part is methodically tested before deciding a new starter motor is needed, meaning more delays in the wait for it to arrive from England. The news leaves us completely deflated and fed up, this being the fifth breakdown.

Checking the internet in our sweltering room, another hotel is located as next door is being prepared for another night of 'Arrivas'; we just cannot face it. Packing overnight cases, a taxi is called before telling the staff we'll be back tomorrow. A short ride takes us to the Costa del Sol, which has everything we need: quiet, air conditioning, English menus, internet, chips and tomato sauce. Peace is restored sitting under palm trees with the rustling sounds calming us before we fall into deep, undisturbed sleep by 9pm, the only sound being the hum of the air conditioner.

The next morning, after reading a menu we can understand, Bernard confirms there is also somewhere for Bertha and so the manager (Franco) is called, who speaks excellent English with a vaguely American accent. Explaining our open-ended request for a room until parts arrive, he shows us around and gives us an 'executive room' for half the normal cost. Promising to return in the morning, another taxi takes us back to Bertha where Bernard swelters under the sun putting her back together while I pack to leave. The heat is unbearable in the room and continues unabated even when an additional fan is called into play. Sweat drips down my face, threatening to drip on the computer as I write emails home under the constant bombardment of the disco which pumps out all afternoon until, suddenly at 7.30, I realise it's stopped as we sit eating our curried pasta – the only understandable thing on the menu.

'Meester Smith'

Daylight arrives and we're out of bed in a flash, the bike is bump started, and everything is bundled into a taxi as Bernard bounces down the rutted road for the short journey. Fifteen minutes later Franco is fussing around us at our new location, where all work comes to a stop on our arrival. He shoos his staff back to work before delivering cold drinks to where we sit by the pool. Life is suddenly so much better as the local area has supermarkets supplying essential provisions that 'clink' their way back to the hotel.

Multiple alarms are set for the 3am call home (6 hours ahead) for a new starter motor to be ordered while Bernard finds out he is big in Japan, with pictures lifted from our website as a new video of us appears on YouTube where a company offers $250 prints of us sitting on the bike. It leaves us chortling.

As we wait for the starter motor to arrive we wander around Tumbes, which lives in a land of 'perpetual summer', so people tell us. It is certainly very hot. Most visitors usually stay a few kilometres away at the beach resorts where they lay on deck chairs all day, but neither of us are 'beach' people. We think our views are probably related to age, and understanding that there is little time left to spend 'doing nothing'; as lying on a beach all day would be to both Bernard and I. We take in the sights of Tumbes to fill our time and run out of things to see in a single day. Searching the internet for more information it tells that the town is dangerous for travellers; that guards accompany tourists to ATMs and from hotel to bus. Other stories recount how taxi drivers all belong to criminal gangs and that they'll rob you.

By contrast we see children laughing, shops full of people counting their pennies and families sitting in the shade of trees talking. It is a town where people step out of our way with a smile and a nod, while others eat ice cream boats full of fruit. Children shout 'Hello' and 'How are you?' as they did in Malaysia when we pass them, this greeting being the only English they know. Smiling back we reply as best we can in Spanish.

I swim each morning, fascinating the staff as I go round and round the circular pool, completing circle after circle for 40 laps, over a mile as Bernard measures the diameter. He insists on covering me in sun cream as it is brutally hot before he retreats to the shade where he sits reading or watching me. The staff shake their heads at Bernard as if to say 'How does she do this?'

What they do not realise is that swimming gives me freedom. It is under my control. I am on my own with 'just me'. There is no white stick, no guide dog, nobody physically guiding me. It is just me, and the water; I am allowed just to be. The sounds of the pool orient me to where I am. The water inlet shaped like two large buffalo horns churns the water into froth as I swim through the bubbles. Ten strokes later and I pass the ladder. The pool gets shallower at this point. I can hear the sounds of another – smaller – inlet in a further ten strokes' time. Ten more sees me past the small pool where the central fountain splashes water gently onto its surface as I swim past towards the sound of the buffalo horns. So it goes on for 40 laps. My body changes colour under the brightness of the sun and Bernard suggests I change to backstroke to even out my tan, laughing as I comment:

'I won't be able to see where I'm going if I do that!'

Bernard sits in the shade as he 'swims like a brick'. I am sure this is an exaggeration and more to do with him nearly drowning in a school swimming session as a child. It has left him with a life-long aversion to swimming although he can swim, reluctantly admitted, but he just does not 'do' swimming. My own sessions are cruelly cut short one day on finding the pool emptied for maintenance, fortunately noticed before I dived in!

From then on men hack away at the painted edges with hand chisels all day, every day, baking in the sun while making little progress on the hard stone surface. The nature of their work tells us a great deal about the brutal cheapness of labour in Peru as they stab downwards with the chisels onto the hard stone surface for 10 hours a day, every day, for over a week. After this, Franco invests in a power sander with a large circular wire brush and only then is any meaningful progress made as great clouds of blue concrete dust fly into the air. Franco frets at the slow progress and other guests complain over the pool's closure and the noise of the sander. Meanwhile the workers are turning deep blue with concrete dust and paint as they breathe in both for 10 hours a day. They wave their thanks to Bernard after bottles of coke and water are sent over from the bar.

Carrying piles of chairs when functions are being set up, helping to carry mattresses upstairs, Bernard joins in the daily operations of the hotel and, shortly after moving in, he can do no wrong; whatever is asked for, arrives. It is in complete contrast to other guests who will not walk ten feet to the self-service breakfast layout but instead call staff to bring them a slice of toast. Bernard calls it 'paralysis of the pocket', or 'I'm paying so I expect you to move for me'.

Soon 'Hello Meester Smith', can be heard all around the grounds as we pass, and no matter how he tries to get them to call him Bernard, 'Meester Smith' is still his name.

I learn the main areas of the hotel and am often halfway down the corridors or stairs before Bernard is out the room while the staff laugh good naturedly at my progress. As I approach they now say 'Good morning' or 'Good evening' rather than Buenos diaz or Buenos tardes and their smiles are genuine smiles at the blind English woman with her 'shadow'.

They give the thumbs up sign as I do 'my thing', learning the layout of the hotel, as the 'staff' become Hector, Pablo or Marco. We too change from being guests to residents, and it allows me to distinguish between their voices, to come to know one from another. Meanwhile my stick learns of the glass wall dividers of the restaurant, the sound of the panelled frames of reception, the legs of the coffee table or the planters in the foyer, of the grass edges leading down the concrete path to the swimming pool where I turn right at the end. All the sounds and surfaces act as markers or 'signs' of location for me.

My solo world expands as I start to be able to 'picture' the hotel as the staff teach me 'Peruvian Origami' (as Bernard calls it), the folding and refolding of place napkins to create elaborate shapes. They take great delight as I create roses, bishop's hats, and fans of various shapes and sizes while the evenings pass watching movies, either ones never seen or never before 'audio described'.

Movies are a constant source of puzzlement to many people when applied to blind people. You may well read this and ask: 'What's the point in watching movies if you cannot see?'

Then I have to respond with, 'Why does a blind person cry over a sad movie or book?'

You see, as we have travelled my understanding of this wonderful world has increased and the images are engraved in my mind from what I hear, sense and experience. Like a movie with 'audio description' skilfully done, it aids and completes my understanding. Picture the film 'Titanic'.

Leonardo Di Caprio rests his chin on the large wooden panel where, above him, Kate Winslett lies. Over time he succumbs to the freezing water until she prises his hand from her own; he sinks down through the depths while reaching upwards towards her. I cried as Bernard described it to me, never before realising the images on the screen. It's true I'd watched the film before, but the additional description now gave me a more complete understanding.

Thus, audio description paints pictures onto the canvas of my mind, imprinting images, much in the same way as when meeting people, or passing through countries when Bernard puts images into words, merging with everything else I perceive. It's like reading a book where you, yourself, create a world from the words. So it is with me.

As our world slows down to reveal new things about this garrison town not far from the Ecuadorian border, we fill our time sending parcels and postcards home and both take several hours at the main post office where no parcel tape, brown paper or envelopes are available. On returning to the hotel to gather packaging, staff rush off to find everything Meester Smith needs before returning to the post office triumphant with a bombproof package, which has to be opened again to enable inspection of the contents. It leaves Bernard less than impressed, to put it mildly, after using a full roll of parcel tape in his paranoia after one had been opened in India. There items had been stolen while others had been deliberately broken, including the small marble Taj Mahal bought for me as a gift and his precious leather jacket – a gift from Cem, our agent – was conspicuous by its absence.

An hour later, after being fingerprinted and providing copies of his passport, the parcel is processed before sitting on the scales to reveal it is too heavy and so has to be split into two separate consignments. Two sets of Bernard's fingerprints later – one for each parcel – along with two more photocopies of his passport and the job is done. One of the parcels contains our priceless journal stretching from Turkey to Malaysia which took over two hours to photograph, one page at a time. Only when every one of the 300 pages had been photographed will he consent to it being posted. It alone weighs 1.2 kg.

Tumbes itself is a land of music. It blasts from everywhere in the town in a loud, infectious, Latin way. Joyfully thumping out all around, from speakers outside the shops, on the pavements and everywhere else, the 'Latino' exists in a mad mixture of sounds. Snatches of songs which make you want to dance float in the air as Bernard leads me to cafés.

The evenings pass in the company of two owls, our little friends Eenie and Meenie, that sit in the palm tree outside our balcony and appear just as day shifts to night. During the day the palm tree is empty and I listen to the breeze as it rustles each stem to create a different sound, becoming familiar with the different tones and whispers. Then the whole symphony changes as a barefooted gardener shimmies up, cutting and pruning, while lowering coconuts to the ground. As the days change into weeks, our concern mounts with the time it is taking for the new starter motor to arrive. In the background Bernard grumbles of being able to rebuild the whole bike in the same period it is taking. Time is slipping away from us and we feel it keenly. Consoling ourselves that Bertha will be like a brush with ten new handles and four new heads, we continue to bake in the heat while dodging the evening's mosquitoes.

Two weeks pass and the delay impacts on the eight weeks we have left to cover the final leg, now cut drastically while people start to follow the 'Tale of the Spinning Thing' on the internet. Americans write such things as 'Chin up' and 'Hang on in there', while others email friends seeking a spare 'spinning thing' to get us back on our way. Bernard's fingernails get shorter with the stress as he frets constantly, nervously watching time dripping away while we sit still. After nearly three weeks his frustrations eventually boil over one day as he kicks the balcony wall several times, venting his feelings outwards after ringing the carrier in England for answers which never come. Calming down, he lights several cigarettes and I know better than to interfere with his thoughts. The shorter time left equals higher daily distances; it is this he is worrying about.

The problem is the road conditions preclude anything involving 'big' mileages. I feel the whole thing is unravelling but there is nothing that can be done. Eventually after three weeks of inactivity, Franco appears smiling hugely, clutching a parcel festooned with stickers. We laugh uproariously at the 'DHL Express' label adorning it as 21 days have gone by and Bernard mutters 'Pony' when he stops laughing.

Everybody in the hotel knows it has arrived as people start to congregate to watch the reassembly. An hour later Bernard nervously presses the starter button and Bertha rumbles into life, first time, while he leaps up and down with glee in true Monty Python fashion. Delight would be an understatement of our feelings after sitting still for so long as everything is repacked to enable departure.

Going backwards and forwards to the room, the staff stop us to ask:

'Mañana (tomorrow)?'

'Si, mañana (Yes, tomorrow),' we respond.

The swimming pool shines luminous green as it fills up with new/old water and the stagnant smell is powerful as we walk past on our many trips to the bike. It feels strange to be moving on and uncomfortably sad as we've settled: each night sleeping in the same surroundings, familiar and happy with the people and the town around us. Feeling both wary and excited, it is a curious combination of emotions.

On the morning of leaving, 26 days have passed since breaking down, involving frustration, irritation and annoyance. However, it was also 26 days of meeting people, of reading, writing and exploring a 'dangerous' town off the tourist route. It's a town where people live their daily lives under the 'perpetual summer' amid Latino music filling the air. It also involved days where a waiter became Pablo or a bellboy became Hector as we learned to sit still and listen to the world around us.

'Have you ever been to Ecuador before?'

EC   The departure, the big farewell, the Hasta la vista or 'until we meet again' arrives and Hector takes station guarding Bertha, leaning on his broom pole before urgently talking to the manager who translates concerns about Ecuador being 'dangerous'. Insisting attention is paid to certain parts of the route as 'there are bandits who will rob you' we promise caution as Bertha rattles into life. With waves over our shoulders the square in which the Costa del Sol resides is left behind, our home for so long. Within an hour it doesn't feel like it has been over three weeks but merely a day since riding as signs appear for La Frontera 40 km away on the road towards Aguas Verdes. Everything runs perfectly, at first, as signs lead us down a (curiously deserted) highway towards the frontier with Bernard questioning:

'There's doesn't seem much traffic between Peru and Ecuador?' Road workers confirm it's the right road to Ecuador as we continue onwards until the road stops dead in front of a 100-foot trench cut deep into the earth with an unfinished bridge to span the gorge.

Bernard – It was a complete mystery to me. There's an earthen ramp down to our right with occasional cars using it but I am convinced wagons or buses could not do it. It seems impossible that this is the border highway. Another dusty ramp crosses the other side to climb out of the trench but I cannot believe this leads to the border crossing. Asking several people about 'Ecuador', fingers all point across the gap but I am puzzled. However, there have been some weird roads in this part of the world so it should not surprise me but it still feels wrong. Easing the bike into gear, using the back brake and second gear, we set off down the ramp kicking up a cloud of dust. Bouncing across the rutted ground, road workers watch in fascination as I gun the engine and hammer up the incline.

Several miles later I can feel the bike slowing down and a puzzled voice comes through the intercom: 'Ecuador E50? Bloody hell, I think we're already in Ecuador.' We stop at a truck with its bonnet up. 'Excuse me, is this Ecuador?' comes Bernard's voice in his halting Spanish.

'Si Senhor, Ecuador,' comes the unwanted reply.

A mile further on a petrol station appears where 30 troops in camouflage gear lounge around with automatic weapons. They look up curiously as we stop. Several of them stand, shifting their weapons, as Bernard asks the young attendant for 'La Frontera?' She points back the way we have come. 'Peru frontera?' Bernard asks and again she indicates the direction backwards as it dawns on us.

Suddenly we realise, somehow, we've crossed the border and are now in Ecuador illegally on a foreign motorcycle with no documentation whatsoever. All the while, the Ecuadorian troops watch us from the shade. Before anybody has a chance to ask anything more the bike turns around to blast back down the highway at warp speed. Down the earthen ramp we fly and up the other side, rapidly making our way back down the road to a sign declaring 'Welcome to Peru'.

Retracing our steps we find the loosely managed crossing down a small dusty side road, nearly invisible to the naked eye. Everything stops as we pull up and soon a small crowd gathers. Hernando attaches himself to us as our fixer and this time we agree as the sum is small for his help and with it comes a border guard to watch the bike. The sweat pores down on entering the immigration building where police stamp us out of the country.

Signs everywhere declare how the elderly or people with disabilities will be given preferential treatment as we are shepherded to the 'exit' queue; where a man is roundly scolded for trying to push past us. The border guards leap from their station and thump the sign about disability while gesticulating furiously at the man, fists inches away from his face as they point at me. He returns sheepishly back into the line as we are stamped out of Peru and led outside.

The Ecuador border is a strange one and turns out to be not one line to cross over officially, but several. First, the Customs office has to be found for Bertha to be stamped into the country, hidden down a side street that would never have been found without Hernando. Directions from our 'fixer' are then carefully followed for the next four-km drive further on to have our passports stamped.

When you are used to rigid 'lines' on a map, it all seems bizarre. But then again, this rigidity will soon join them as we discover that the new road travelled earlier, leading to the 'not finished bridge', will be the new integrated border crossing, finished in about a year's time. Now we understand why the road was so very quiet.

Arriving at the Immigration window we do the inevitable shuffle forward to the counter before being asked: 'Have you ever been in Ecuador before?' We resist the temptation.

The road stretches northwards towards Colombia and we have to travel quickly now, being weeks behind schedule. Our timing is shot to pieces but the only sound to be heard is laughter, this time without the aid of coca tea. It still feels good despite everything that could have gone wrong today. Accidents could have happened descending, or coming up the ramps of the unfinished 'new' border abyss. Being arrested for illegal entry was also a distinct possibility. So many serious things could happen and yet they do not.

If all the things that could go wrong on this journey were analysed it would leave many people too frightened to leave home. Inevitably you'd end up scared of the world and its people. More importantly, if we thought this way it would make us insecure in ourselves, in our ability to cope, to think on the move. Now, however, each day is simply taken as it comes, and we solve each problem as it appears.

Above all, standing in the dust of Ecuador, it is easy to think how incredibly lucky we are to be physically and mentally intact after some of our recent experiences. Appreciating the truth of this, we now understand something fundamental about ourselves; Peru has made us into something else. The country has changed our own perception of ourselves as people, shifting it further away from the two individuals who left England so long ago. I feel it. The climbing of Wayna Picchu, the difficult roads travelled, the people met have all left indelible stamps in our mind. Putting everything together, we are different.

People say a long road journey can change you in fundamental, irreversible ways and we now know that it does. Things are never quite the same again as superfluous layers of reality are lost somewhere, somehow, along the way. It sneaks up on you from the shadows without you ever realising it. Standing here, only now do we feel it fully in the way of a creeping, dawning realisation. It leaves us feeling like the panniers on Bertha which carry so little but which hold everything needed. In many ways we have become those panniers, with the loss of layers containing 'things', now replaced with 'experiences'. The people we once were have gone forever and neither of us want them back. Standing wondering what is in store for us in a new country this truth is mulled over, sifted through in terms of what it will mean across our lives. Time will tell.

Eventually climbing on the bike, Bernard presses the starter and Bertha's engine rumbles into life, moving forward slightly as he clunks her into gear in a now familiar and comfortable feeling. Pulling away, we surge forward into Ecuador, thinking long and hard about the new broom the bike has become across the journey - much like the two people she now carries.

'Ourselves'

Riding into Ecuador the laughter fades as 'time' focuses our thinking. There are 1,000 km (626 miles) to the Colombian border and the same to the capital, Bogotá. From there we must now fly to Panama before covering about 6,000 km (3,750 miles) to the United States, translating into 187 miles every day to get home by July, no matter what the conditions. After riding a motorcycle for 300 days, it is such a foreign feeling to think so rigidly of time and distance as we appreciate that the roads are not infinite and must soon end. It feels 'wrong' to even contemplate.

The pull of reality, the return home, is something resisted as it flits in the recesses of our minds, leaving us wondering where each of the 432,000 minutes of our journey have gone so far. Some countries feel like distant memories, as if different people travelled the roads of Greece, Nepal or Thailand as the journey has became something else to us, something 'different'. We struggle to put the 'something else' into a nice neat bundle, a term, a phrase, a concept, something to describe our feelings. The only word settled upon is 'normal'. It has become normal to ride in the barren empty places. It is now what we do, what we have become. It is what we are.

The words 'normal' and 'alien' have changed places for me when I recall the beginning where I struggled to adapt to days, weeks and months on a motorcycle. Never knowing where I was going to sleep each night or what, with any certainty, was going to happen each day, I often felt vulnerable, insecure and, I will admit, frightened. Now it is effortless. The accumulated miles have made the two of us gypsies, constantly moving on and looking for the new. How others see us also makes everything different; we now view ourselves in the mirror they represent.

A completely new set of values have emerged where I now wear the same clothes for days on end until I can find a place to wash them. Importantly, it does not concern me to be this way and it is so unlike the person I once was. Putting on fresh clothes every single day, and sometimes even twice, that person would open wardrobes where racks of 'things' hung in neat rows, ironed and pristine. I cannot even remember the last time I used an iron and Bernard laughs at this random thought when I tell him. Now it is my previous ways which seem so alien. Transition. Change. It is as if we, and the journey, have become something else. It has become a 'life-style'. The term is settled on to replace 'normal' as it expresses everything in a nice neat hyphenated word. It feels 'right'. It is a 'life-style' and we feel well within it.

Under clear blue skies we enter a land where earthquakes, landslides, volcanoes and floods are common; where people tell us it is dangerous to travel alone, much as the Peruvian bellboy called Hector had told us on leaving Tumbes. We know Ecuador is a major transit zone for cocaine originating in Peru and Colombia as drug traffickers use the dollar economy to launder their booty under weak banking laws and legislation.

Heading towards the northern boundaries where drug trafficking and Colombian insurgents both exist, the news tells us how both have fought and shot it out with the government for 38 years. Riding into the area, we hold onto the thought that everywhere is 'dangerous' according to people in the previous country. It is the way it is when people view their neighbours with suspicion without ever having met them.

Soon we enter the world of black smoke belching into the air from ancient buses as a swath is cut through far more cars than we are used to. The road surfaces hold good and by 4pm Riobamba is only 100 km away, our destination for the night. Thirty kilometres away from our destination is the highest peak in Ecuador, Chimborazo, rising to an elevation of 6,268 metres and able to be seen from 140 km away. Bernard can locate its snow-covered peaks even at this distance as we travel onwards while thinking about distances and time. The light fades about 6.30pm but we decide to push on to reach Riobamba. It will be our first major mistake on the journey.

At El Triunfo the road heads up into the mountains and it soon deteriorates as the tarmac disappears. According to our maps the '60' is a major highway but the surface soon looks like a lunar landscape. Like swathes of India and Nepal, or parts of Peru, the potholes are so deep, so packed together, that there is little choice but to bash through them. Huge channels appear in the road surface where water has ripped out weakened surfaces to leave nothing but infilled loose gravel and sand. Bertha shudders as our average speed drops to 20 kph: even this feels too fast. Pulling up with the road closed for repairs, nails are chewed at the delay as the sun sinks with Bernard watching the sky nervously, telling how time and daylight are both slipping away. Then the road reopens.

Setting off a little quicker, the ride lasts 20 minutes before the road closes again for more road work. The light is virtually gone as the sun drops lower and lower. We recall people warning us of 'bandits' on these very roads and by the time it eventually reopens we are 12,500 feet up in the dark. The voices of people echo in our heads with the warning 'Don't drive at night'. Ruefully chanting Rule 1: 'Don't drive at night', we fret our way through the gathering darkness with Bertha's lights feebly lighting the way.

With 50 km to go utter darkness surrounds us and the road falls into 'nothingness' on our route through the clouds. I can tell Bernard is 'feeling' his way forward with the bike moving at little more than walking pace with only the sound of the engine growling along in low gear to keep my anxieties company. The silence tells me everything I need to know before Bertha pulls over and his voice comes through the intercom. Heavy with a concern last heard a lifetime ago, in Pakistan, it is the same voice as before when his confidence in his ability to keep us both safe in the darkness was nearly shattered. Worry and tiredness flow from him and they are feelings he cannot mask.

Bernard – I can see maybe two feet in front of the bike Cath. The potholes just appear out of the mist and cloud and I cannot miss them – I don't even know they are there until we hit them. I could be riding straight at a rock or the edge and I wouldn't know. It is too dangerous but I cannot see any alternative, we cannot stay here. I need to think this through. Give me a minute.

The click of his lighter and inhale comes through the speakers in my helmet as he ponders. I leave him to think before suggesting: 'Wait for something to pass you and then follow them.'

He laughs quietly. 'I was just thinking the same thing, India driving; use them as a shield in front to protect us. We've been together too long with all these same thoughts!'

So we sit and wait. Eventually a wagon grinds up the mountain, allowing us to take station 20 feet off its lights. Bernard feels better now as descriptions come through my helmet and no longer does he ride in silence; having warning of what is in front. Our progress is slow but it no longer matters as the huge truck floodlights light the way and we have our barrier, our safety shield. Over the next 50 km we traverse tremendous bangs that shake the bike as the weight hits holes and surfaces for which she was never designed. Coldness sets in with us wearing only thin suits that allow air to pass through the fabric while my hands hold tightly onto the panniers until my fingers go numb with cold and tension. The time passes slowly, painfully, until we arrive at Riobamba at 9pm to sit at the first street corner realising how five hours have passed in covering 100 km. It has been five hours of stress. We've been concerned before or worried when events start to, somehow, go wrong but this was different.

Bernard – I think it felt like 'more' of everything was being thrown at me all in one go. The blackness of the night, sheer drops feet away from our wheels, no barriers, dense mist and cloud, atrocious road conditions, fear, the possibility of mountain bandits, all these things combined to rattle me. It felt like every kilometre had to

be fought for, one at a time. Every bone in my body is hurting with the pounding.
My hands, wrists and elbows are sore from the jolts coming through the handlebars:
shock waves reaching from hand to shoulder, from foot to knee. I am aching from
head to foot. It would not be an exaggeration to say total relief floods me dropping
down the mountain into the lights of Riobamba. I feel we have been given an
overwhelming reprieve by coming through it unscathed.

Lying in bed later in a small gated guest house we spend time going over
the day, talking through how something so fundamentally against THE RULES
occurred; the same rules that have allowed us to cross the world, alone,
unscathed. Examining each decision we try to answer the question 'Why?'

Yes, misleading information on the roads could be blamed as 'major'
highways dissolved into goat tracks with no warning. Yes, it is also true the
roads had been 'good' for most of the way and this misled us. The closing of the
road on three separate occasions also seriously delayed us. It is even possible to
lay a finger on our own ineptitude at, for once, not checking the altitude of the
route (12,500 feet). All these factors are true but somehow, they are all wide
of the truth as a fundamental component of the sequence, or mix, has been left
out. Ourselves.

The truth is that losing three weeks waiting for parts in Peru made us
dangerously time conscious, which manifested its full power on this day. We
could have stopped at 4pm. This was the 'break' point, the natural stop in the
safety of a small town. Instead we had 'pushed on' to cover the 'extra' 100 km
and it was this decision, alone, that caused our problem.

For if a stop had been called earlier then the mountain roads could have
been coped with the next day in daylight, without fog or clouds, or searching
for a 'shield' to protect us in the blackness. It would have precluded our worries
about the 'bandits' who are said to roam the darkness. Thus, it was an error of
judgment to have gone on and it is the most serious one among the 25,000 km
or so to date. Perhaps it is understandable when you put everything together.
We both know it is an error we cannot afford to repeat. Not now. Not with us
being so 'close' to getting home in one piece. Falling asleep, we are determined
not to wake up as fools.

Bernard's night is disturbed with nightmares, as I lie awake wondering
where he is in the deepest shadows of his mind as he tosses and turns restlessly.
Usually he sleeps so peacefully. But not tonight. I lay wondering at the
contradiction he represents, one minute so sure and the next so vulnerable.
Huge contradictions within a person who rides goat tracks in the dark and who
has taken me safely through countless shattered landscapes so far. I calm him
several times in his sleep.

'¿Dónde está la moto?'

The light appears with all the time 'saved' yesterday lost as the morning finds us 'fragile', with little inclination to rise early. Hours later than planned, we stand trying to motivate ourselves by Bertha, sitting covered in a layer of mud, sand and dust from the night before. A fine drizzle starts to fall as we summon the energy for another day.

The morning passes as the capital (Quito) flies by before the Equatorial line suddenly appears, leading to a visit with the solitary female attendant standing forlornly looking around the empty landmark. She welcomes our distraction as we walk onto the huge circular stone sundial dissected with lines. Standing with one foot north and one foot south of the line, our talk turns to the country becoming a blur, such is the speed of our passing. It is the first time such thoughts impinge and it is not a good feeling. Bernard's voice displays his frustration and I too share it as Ecuador leaves little impression, unlike so many other countries as it slips between our fingers, beneath our wheels.

Leaving the attendant to her empty site we move on. Always onwards.

Ibarra appears 331 km later and Bertha sits resplendent on an immaculately polished wooden floor after the hotel staff open the doors for her entrance. Slipping a little, wheels move from tarmac to coated wood as the grins of staff light up the room, fussing, as they do, over the first foreign motorcycle to arrive at their door. Animation increases when they realise I cannot see, with many hands tenderly guiding me off the bike. Car park attendants, waiters, reception staff, and other guests gather, all asking questions like so many times across the miles.

Feeling stiff and sore from our time in the mountains, we rise early and head towards Tulcan at the Colombian border, only 160 km away. Three hours of roads that twist and turn upwards, slogging along behind wagons covering us in black smoke that sticks to our clothes while my mouth dries from the taste of diesel. The bike bobs and weaves as Bernard looks for an overtaking opportunities, a twist of the accelerator and we are past. Long before the borderline wagons stretches for miles. Driving slowly along, drivers leap out of cabs to stand and talk in the middle of the road, staring at our passing. The cars move quicker, allowing us to filter between the lines of stationary wagons.

A huge building appears called the Ecuadorian Narcotics Agency and it is a

VERY large building and, mischievously, we laugh, wondering why it is so big?

Ecuadorian police stop every vehicle. At our turn they merely smile and ask 'Colombia?' before waving us on towards a bridge spanning the gorge between these two neighbours. Crossing the structure searching for some sign of where the Ecuador 'exit' procedures occur the bike stops suddenly in front of a large sign saying 'Welcome to Colombia' while a single 'Damn' comes through my helmet as Bernard realises we have crossed a border – again – without any warning. The bike comes to a halt past the bridge before climbing off; trying to work out what to do. Leaving Bertha on the Colombian side, we walk back clutching sheaves of documents while hoping for the best.

Finding the immigration department, we join a long queue for exit stamps on our passports before finding a fixer rather than wait for the end of the, inevitable, two-hour lunch break which has only just started. He leads us to a group of heavily armed soldiers checking vehicles coming into Ecuador and exchanges in Spanish occur before they ask the critical question:

'¿Dónde está la moto?' or 'Where is the motorbike?'

Bernard – I vaguely wave a direction and their eyes widen as they ask if the bike is in COLOMBIA? My second wave is much more towards 'our' side of the border as I tell them it will take 'two minutes' to get the bike, without mentioning 'from Colombia'. To deflect any awkward questions I ask if Cathy can sit while I get the bike. At this guns are shouldered, the traffic stopped, and we are chaperoned across the road to their shelter where a chair is rapidly found. The traffic backs up and guards move sideways to allow Cathy to sit. Everyone smiles at us.

I look around and one of the soldiers assures me Cathy will be safe, indicating the six armed guards who sit near her. It would not be an exaggeration to say I ran across the bridge to Bertha. Pulling around in a tight circle I stop the whole bridge as I wrestle her around – thankfully out of sight of where Cathy and her 'companions' sit. Creeping back over the bridge and around the back of the building, I pull up behind the guards waiting for my return.

Within minutes the documentation is completed, our fixer gains $10 and we pull back across the bridge to Colombia, this time officially. Immigration stamp our passports for 60 days, Bertha's carnet is completed without them ever looking at her and Colombian soldiers wearing American equipment and uniforms step out of our way when they see the white cane.

'Never drive faster than your guardian angel can fly'

CO Pulling into the first Colombian service station Bernard, as usual, can find no road maps. Three stations later it's the same thing. Road maps are scarce or non-existent and we cannot find out why. Having crossed whole swathes of South America with little more than a compass and good luck I can still feel Bernard's irritation growing at this 'unnecessary' problem.

'It's not England,' I chide gently as he mutters under his breath. He goes quiet.

At the fourth petrol station they mention a shop in Ipiales where big sheets of paper showing roads can be found and a fruitless hour is spent trying to find a map. A fifth petrol station has Bernard gnashing his teeth in frustration as the Sat Nav system plays up before dying completely. After much muttering, an old hand compass navigates us further north into Colombia.

The road from Ipiales towards Pasto is full of maniacal Colombian drivers who hurtle around corners on the wrong side while we absorb more diesel fumes, eating them for lunch and dinner as the hours go by. The traffic irritates Bernard as we are pushed over by car drivers constantly harassing him as everybody wants to go faster than the person in front. Some cars are so close I can hear the engine just off our left pannier, hanging there constantly, looking for a way past us on the snake-like roads.

As we wait for somewhere to pass the large trucks blocking our way, cars overtake before shooting into the small space in front causing Bernard to brake heavily. Either we give way or they will take our front wheel; there's only one winner in the car versus bike challenge. Constantly shunted down the pack behind slow-moving wagons, car after car does the same trick and it's not long before colourful Anglo-Saxon terms flow freely through the speakers in my helmet.

Bernard – I honestly don't know why I'm responding so badly. All the time I try to calm myself down and then, bang, some fool nearly has us off as they pull across my front wheel. The thing is I know the Latin temperament precludes me from demonstrating my displeasure fully. It is not unheard of for people to be shot in this part of the world in 'road rage' situations, so I boil away inside my helmet and fume impotently as Colombian drivers climb up the bad drivers' top ten. Soon the Colombians are placed at Number 2, ahead of the Pakistani, Italian and Serbian drivers. Number 1 remains unchanged: Indian.

Pulling into Pasto the entrance to a motel with streamers reaching to the floor appears and a smiling attendant waves us towards an individually numbered garage. 'Looks good, Cath,' Bernard comments before pulling straight into the garage through large double doors that close behind us. Waxing lyrically about how our 'flat' is upstairs above the bike, 'totally private', he goes on 'our own space and private parking for the bike. Perfect,' he concludes.

Climbing off, we make our way up the stairs from the garage to our secluded front door where Bernard stops dead.

'Oooops.'

'What do you mean, Oooops?' I ask.

'Well...' he hesitates before going on.

'The ceiling is mirrored.'

'OK, tell me everything you can see,' I ask him.

'You don't want to know!' he replies.

'Yes I do, go on.'

'There's a poster on the wall underneath the TV,' he pauses for a few seconds as he gathers his thoughts.

'It's a price list... of sex toys... but at least everything is priced in pesos and dollars,' he goes on helpfully.

I stand still and wonder, once again, at his ability to pull into a country and immediately end up in somewhere catering for the sex industry. My fears are confirmed when the first ten TV channels are full of asthmatic performers puffing and panting their way through their 'exercises'. 'My God, that looks painful!' he exclaims as I cut short his description and decide we cannot stay here. As always, he thinks the advantages outweigh the disadvantages: seclusion and privacy, the personal garage, the whole self-contained space. I send him off down the stairs muttering, insisting he find out more information.

The sounds of banging come up the open stairs as his voice shouts:

'Hello, anybody there?'

Calling up to me, he tells me how the garage door is locked and his banging is met with silence. More furious thumping of the metal doors follows as it transpires there is only one way in and it is through the door, now locked from the outside. The banging gets louder and eventually the door opens to reveal two Colombian women and I listen as Bernard starts in English, then Spanish, before switching to French before eventually ending up with Spangalese.

It transpires the price is $22, which he thinks is entirely reasonable for the facilities. I point out that it will be by the hour, not the day. 'OK,' he concedes, 'Let's work on the price,' as he launches into negotiating for all he is worth with the two giggling women. His charm offensive is evident as he explains the 'misunderstanding', as the girls laugh when they realise our mistake. I pick out his explanation that $22 an hour is far too much no matter how he would like to be able to claim to need the whole night. They laugh. I step in.

'Never mind negotiating, let's go.'

'But Cath, it's fine here. The bike is safe, we are off the road after a frustrating day, the girls are nice and seem helpful. We will be fine here. It's only one night and it's all very clean.'

I start to point out a few home truths to persuade him.

'Number one, it's a brothel or something like. That's enough in itself to move on but then number two, the girls may be nice but there is nowhere to eat here (confirmed in the conversation). Number three, there is no bar for you to get a beer.' I'm getting sneaky now and leave the coup de gras until the end as I point out, 'you cannot even get in and out for a cigarette.' I leave the thought hanging. Not to be outdone he ponders:

'Perhaps I can get them to leave the door unlocked so I can get in and out for a smoke?'

I decide to terminate all negotiations with my final:

'Never mind negotiating, we're going now.'

The sentence ends the matter and pulling out of the 'motel', he sits outside looking at the entrance through the big rubber streamers. 'Motel Eros,' he mutters, 'The Greek God of Love' he adds for my benefit before pulling away. 'I actually quite liked it though,' he goes on but my gentle kidney punch convinces him to drop the conversation. The road onwards reveals several such motels as the penny continues to drop with my roving partner noticing their names ('Cupid' and 'Venus' being two such). Many are painted bright pink and have huge hearts adorning the walls leading to the gated entrances. There are so many on the hill down to Pasto we know they must indeed be popular with the local people, or passing naïve English motorcyclists with working eyes.

Waking up in the Hotel Morasurco the next morning (20 minutes down the hill from the land of love), all I can hear is 'just another five minutes' coming from under the covers. My alarm states it is 6.30am and helpfully I remind him, 'You said we need daylight, we don't know what the roads are like, and weeks have been lost in Tumbes etc, etc.'

Like a petulant child he gets up sluggishly through a wall of sighing and groaning as I wonder if his old frame might be reacting to the constant mountain roads and the pace being travelled? Slowly coming alive, he struggles through breakfast before the heavily made-up receptionist glares at him when he comments, 'I could pay off the Colombian National Debt with the prices you charge for a night. Are you sure this is correct? Perhaps there are too many zeros in it?'

We've always carefully checked and confirmed the price before booking, but the night before, dog-tired, we made assumptions that it didn't look expensive. Now, standing in the foyer Bernard reflects that neither the facilities nor the surroundings reflect the level of the bill. And he tells them. Several times. Loudly.

'Should have stayed in the Motel Eros,' he mutters handing over our precious dollars before setting off with fresh air blowing through our wallets, leaving Pasto with 7,000 pesos in our pocket and a destination of either Cali (400 km) or Popayán (269 km), depending on the roads encountered.

The road starts to climb immediately and it becomes obvious our 8.30 start is not early enough to reach Cali as the mountains are full of wagons struggling up and down these small corridors. Their smell comes in waves of burnt brakes which fill our nostrils. Our speed drops as no sooner is the bike upright than another sharp corner comes while all the time homicidal drivers career around the bends at Mach 2 speeds on the wrong side.

We wonder if Colombian drivers are all fatalists in believing when their time is up then so be it? Perhaps many will someday meet their end buried in a pile of twisted metal, reduced to one of the small crosses dotting the corners where fatalities are marked, permanent reminders of a life needlessly ended. There are a lot of such crosses but we no longer wonder why as the road surface disintegrates further.

Bernard describes the terrain, from the gorges with mountains folded like pleats in a cloth surface, to the overwhelming greenness of the surroundings. We soon discover why as intermittent monsoon-like rain descends leaving water dripping off everything, including ourselves. It runs across the road surface as our progress becomes noisy, splashing through the traffic as our final 7,000 pesos is eaten by two gallons dispensed into Bertha's tank as they will not take the mighty US dollar. Now we have little local currency and cannot even afford a drink, much less food. Keeping our fingers crossed we move on and hope.

The road winds through small towns and villages where people sit in the shade watching us go by as Bertha's distinctive engine noise turns heads hundreds of feet before arriving. People wave and whistle, giving thumbs up or V signs as we pass. This is supposed to be the Pan-American Highway but it's hard to believe as the road seems little more than a two-lane mountain road with permanent double-yellow (no overtaking) lines, which everyone ignores anyway.

As the kilometres mount, more and more checkpoints appear manned by the Colombian army. Young soldiers sit behind sandbagged posts from where they watch every vehicle as the military presence is even heavier and more pronounced at bridges. Heavily armed and seeming nervous, they peer out from behind their fortifications, waving us through without us ever stopping. As always, Bernard takes to waving to all and sundry as he mutters:

'You never know, we might need them at some point.' I agree and wave enthusiastically when he tells me to. Everybody waves back.

Tollbooths (peaje) appear and staff wave us towards a tiny little lane by which mopeds go around the station, as bikes do not pay. We pull up to the barrier and the attendant demands we use the tiny lane although it's obvious Bertha is too big. He insists. We block the whole station turning Bertha ('Like trying to turn a small battleship in a duck pond') and lining up for the lane, he proceeds to jam her panniers between two wooden posts, threatening to rip them out of the soft ground. Furious and frantic waving comes from the attendant. They finally understand that a three-foot wide bike will never fit through a two-foot gap, even in Colombia and, lifting the barrier, they allow us through.

After hours of thumping up and down hills at the lightning speed of 20 kph a corner reveals Andy and Maya passing the time of day with their Triumph sidecar combination with a Canadian cyclist (Kurt). Andy and Maya are in the Americas for 18 months and for an hour we swap information and maps as we gain a Costa Rican one while they take our Peruvian one. So, in the middle of nowhere, a map starting life in Spain with Jaime and Conti, given to us in Chile, is transferred to its new Scottish owners in Colombia. Setting off in opposite directions, a shoulder-wrenching 256 km later we reach Popayán along with the gates of a gorgeous hotel called 'The Monastery'.

Built in 1570 as a Franciscan Monastery, it was converted to a hotel 350 years later. It sits at the back of the imposing church in an oasis of calm in the city (founded in 1537). We settle into a converted monk's quarters. The staff tell of the city's destruction by the earthquakes of 1983 and that it has taken over 20 years to restore many of the gleaming white buildings. It's a truly beautiful city and we would have happily stayed in Popayán for a few days but no longer is time the luxury it once was. As the light fades into darkness with each of us lost in our own comfortable silence, sleep claims us both utterly and completely.

The next morning we take a small detour to a motorcycle shop where some elusive 90-grade gearbox oil Bernard has been searching for is located and produced with a triumphant flourish. As in the previous evening every motorcycle, pushbike, taxi, pedestrian and dog stop to look at Bertha, sitting in the street among the stones and gravel. The previous evening little Honda mopeds and small-capacity motorbikes had buzzed around us like flies, not quite believing Bertha's size as she rumbled along. Meanwhile the traffic continues to grind to a halt as dozens of small bikes stop and look as a home is found for the oil before pulling off, waving to everybody.

Our destination is Ibagué but, as always, it is unclear whether it will be achievable before nightfall as the continuous line of HGVs slows everything down so much. Meanwhile manic car drivers maintain their impression of lemmings, launching themselves around bends on the wrong side. 'Never drive faster than your guardian angel can fly,' Bernard mutters into the microphone at one point.

An hour outside Popayán the first decent roads since Chile appear and we blast along at 90–100 kph while everything else passes us at 140. Most of the morning disappears sitting on the '25' happily watching the miles mount up, with hopes rising that the worst is behind us and the road to Bogotá will be easier. As always when you start thinking this way something is bound to happen. Soon it does.

Covering the 137 km to Cali, little convoys slowly grind up anything remotely hill-like until we reach the outskirts of the town where hundreds of cyclists appear, all dressed in brightly coloured very tight Lycra suits. They're everywhere and are of all ages and sizes. Before long, many groups wearing the same contour-hugging Day-Glo colours zip along on roller-blades instead of pedalling furiously on two wheels. Bright yellow and Day-Glo orange colours abound everywhere.

Turning off the '25', heading on to the '40', the surface starts well before, little by little, it descends into rougher and rougher surfaces, the likes of which we had hoped were left behind. While rough, it is nothing we have not done before. Then, in the distance, a mountain appears and it is not just any old mountain but the renowned (read 'dreaded') La Linea, known as the place where there are more accidents than anywhere else in the whole country.

'Burning Wellies'

We start going slowly at the base of the mountain and then go even slower as the climb begins, becoming steeper and steeper. Passing statues of the Holy Mary complete with people kneeling to light candles, prayers are said for a safe passage on this corridor before drivers climb into their vehicles, take a deep breath, and begin their journey.

The road is narrow and so tight wagons can go around the bends only one at a time while local people earn a living standing on the apex of each corner waving to drivers, letting them know it is safe to come around, so restricted is visibility. Standing with their hats out for change to be thrown into in way of thanks for their help, overheating trucks grind ever upwards with water pouring across the road from shattered pipes and radiators. Many drivers sit by the side of the road watching mechanics repairing damage and it seems a good place for a mechanic to earn a living. The plan, however, is to bore a hole through the mountain for a new tunnel – if it ever gets built I'm sure the mechanics will weep.

Climbing the 3,200 metre vertical helter-skelter, barely 6 km is covered in an hour as Bertha moves at little more than walking pace in first and second gear. The camber of the road is difficult, tilting alarmingly. Wagons coming down give off their overpowering smell of burning brakes; four hours pass travelling this way. Through 180-degree, steep, steep corners ever upwards we make our way to the sound of our own engine growling with a slipping clutch to keep us moving forward.

During the climb the sky turns black as we ride ever upwards with coldness descending to the smell of burning clutches and brakes, which permeates everything around us. Even Bertha struggles, with first gear too low, and second too high, so her clutch slips in second to compensate. To stop forward motion is to slide backwards as the front wheel slips several times when she is forced to stop. It leaves Bernard straining to find a foothold to support the bike as the road cants crazily sideways leaving one leg in the air. Time after time Bertha's front wheel slips backwards and reaching the top is a joy but not even a prized photograph is taken of the spectacular view as the road is just too narrow, too dangerous to stop on. Happily, we settle for the feelings attached with reaching it unscathed. Unfortunately, this realisation of vulnerability and mortality is not matched by other drivers.

Cresting the top of La Linea starts an ensuing chaotic, dangerous, missile-like scramble down the other side of the mountain as cars and wagons hurtle like Kamikaze pilots slamming around corners on the wrong side. It is pure, uncontrolled aggressive driving as everybody vents their frustration of the climb up on the road down. It is astonishing from the descriptions of the mayhem around us there are no accidents.

Trying to stay out of trouble on the descent, Bernard tells me of being passed by a man on a small cycle, wearing bright yellow Wellington boots. I think he is joking but in all seriousness, he says not. The man drags his boots on the ground as brakes while passing wagons, cars and ourselves at 40 mph. We start laughing as Bernard tells me this must be what the smell was earlier; not burnt clutches, and fried brakes, but burning Wellies.

Miles later the rider stands adjusting his coat against the cold with Bernard chortling as we go by, explaining the braking technique of our Colombian friend; one foot on the floor for minor braking, two for more serious. Perhaps he stands there waiting for his feet to cool down before setting off again.

A few kilometres further on Bernard cannot stop laughing as the Colombian worker wearing bright yellow Wellies, riding a bike too small for him, passes us again, dragging both feet on the ground. Again, he wishes he could photograph or video the event but it's impossible to contemplate. People die on this road in horrific accidents and neither of us want to be one (or two) of them, thus the event has to be let go unrecorded in anything but our own laughing memories.

Bernard – It is so, so, funny and just what we needed as it released all the pressures we both felt. The laughter does us good as the day has been long and hard, involving walking-pace biking on bad cambers up horrendous slopes called 'a road' with dizzying drops all around. The day has everything thrown in, including a bit of rain for good measure. It was scary, exhilarating and fantastic all at the same time. To say it was 'challenging' from a biking perspective is to understate how it felt. It is a climb I will never forget. By the time we get to Ibagué, it had taken seven and a half hours to cover 400 km, with 140 of them covered in the first 90 minutes.

Pulling into the town and despite stressing we are looking for a 'buenos hotel' (good hotel), a taxi driver takes us to another suspect place with a serving hatch in the door which, we believe, is a sure sign of a 'love shack'. The hatch itself is to place food, drinks or 'condiments' through so the staff do not have to enter the room. For the heady cost of 30,000 pesos (about £10), the room has sheets, but no blankets and piping hot water in the shower. Bernard is mildly amused as he describes the two female staff outside who wear nurse-like uniforms. 'Must be in case anybody gets hurt?' he innocently states before collapsing laughing.

I am not amused. Well maybe I am, just a little.

The road outside the hotel threatens us with industrial deafness due to the traffic and, in the end, I'm convinced to follow Bernard's lead who, by now, is fast asleep with ear plugs firmly in place. The noise recedes into the distance as I slip my own into place and fall into dreams before being ripped awake at 5am.

Is that a group of men talking? Fighting? Arguing? From the din going on I cannot be sure what's happening although it's loud enough to penetrate even Bernard's ears and he sets off to investigate. Coming back minutes later, he tells of people merely sitting on a step outside, talking. With all the racket it's obvious our sleep is over so, at 6.30, the surprisingly busy Sunday traffic greets us on the road towards Bogotá (190 km away) while we search for breakfast.

An hour later we eat the best spicy scrambled eggs known on the planet. Forget the hotels with fancy tables and liveried staff. All you need is a grass-covered roof, plastic chairs, fantastic people and a good cook. Eating rice, vegetables and meat all steamed in vine leaves, the cook beams from the kitchen at our obvious delight and Bernard's thumbs up directed his way. The staff carefully place food in front of me when they realise I cannot see and we get through four cups of aromatic coffee before Bernard buys three packs of cigarettes, still getting change for everything from £10. Contentment reigns as we wave and set off back onto the road.

Ibagué becomes Gualanday which changes to Chicoral, then Espinal, before Flandes follows with a wrong turn at Giradot, sending us on the 'scenic' route. Bernard wonders if it's possible to become an adrenaline junkie without every realising it? Perhaps a need to have fixes of seriously bad roads has invaded his psyche as things start to go from bad to worse over the following miles until, eventually, we turn back. After five days of mountain roads, it is agreed no more fixes of bad roads are needed, but merely calm easy ones, if they can be found. Retracing our route, the 'highway' appears just past the petrol station down a pot-holed side road.

Melgar, Boqueron, Chimanta, Fusagasuga, Silvania and Granada all roll by in a relaxed gentle pace with no traumas or no heart-stopping moments as the sun shines and we feel good. Stopping for a few minutes to stretch our legs people appear and our rest is lost answering questions while Bernard's cigarette burns away. The road takes us onwards to Bogotá. Here the location of the airport is such a highly guarded and well-kept secret that we drive up and down dual carriageways for two hours. Eventually a banner flutters in the breeze proudly proclaiming the mythical area does indeed exist, and so the hunt begins for somewhere to stay close to, but not 'in', the airport as only cocaine exporters or politicians on expense accounts can afford such things.

Plan A is employed, but the taxi leads us to one where Bertha will have to go down a ramp best described as 'vertically inclined'. Evel Knievel would have happily used the slope to launch himself across the Grand Canyon so steep is it and Bernard tells me of the nosebleed he feels coming on just looking at it.

Another taxi leads us to a well-known hotel chain where well-liveried reception staff look down at the pile of dust where we stand as the receptionist finishes a stream of phone calls. By the fifth my trusty companion kneels down at the desk and politely asks, 'Shall I pull up some chairs?' This seems to work as the phone rings unanswered.

The next morning we set off to the airport cargo offices after a round of applause from the assembled hotel staff who gather at the top of the ramp to watch our high-velocity missile-like exit from the underground car park; they certainly do build them steep in Bogotá. Over the next five hours, numerous pieces of paper related to Bertha are completed at the cargo office before she ends up strapped down onto a wooden pallet, which creaks ominously as the forklift hoists her up into the warehouse.

The forklift driver proudly shows us pictures of his wife and four-year-old daughter in a voice full of pride, beaming with happiness at my companion when he hears how his wife is very beautiful and his daughter has the face of an angel. Learning English from MP3 files as he drives twelve hours a day, he hopes it will help him get a promotion and more money. Only then, he says earnestly, will he be able to give his family everything he wants to provide. It leaves me feeling, not for the first time, that such is the way of people all over the world.

Leaving the building, ominous tales and warnings ring in our ears over the Colombian Customs inspection scheduled for the morning as everybody assures us it will be tough in its search for drugs. Leaving Bertha, we have few concerns, however, as she now resides within the sealed warehouse.

Walking to the airport, we buy tickets for tomorrow's flight to Panama before allowing ourselves to be guided to a waiting minibus for 'The Park Way' hotel, a quarter of the price of last night and four times nicer in atmosphere as copious coffee appears for Bernard while we sit in the garden savouring our achievements of the day.

Sitting in bed later with our laptop, trawling the internet for information on Panama, we find our way through distance charts, roads and routes for the next leg across this new country, the start of central America. We even book a reasonable hotel near Panama airport on the internet and it reminds me how technology is a wonderful thing. So many streams of information which, for blind people, have been shut off in the past, closed for so many years now explode open with the advent of new technologies. Falling asleep in the quietness, the day's achievements leave us satisfied and excited about our next leap into the unknown. It no longer concerns or worries us to land in a strange environment where little makes sense at the outset. We know it always does by the end.

The next morning our taxi launches us into the Colombian Grand Prix rush hour, reminding Bernard of the famous chariot race in Ben Hur. The only thing missing are the spikes on the wheels to chop off the legs of any peasant daring to step out in front of the mighty automobile. Arriving at the cargo office for 8.55am, our check-in time for our own flight is 3pm so there's plenty of time, or so we think. An hour and a half later, after several cups of coffee, Bernard spits his dummy out to summon a besuited female executive from the deep recesses of the Cargo Company as he sets about her.

Within minutes Franklin (our assigned agent) leads us from the building to the Customs house where a lot of head-scratching goes on over exporting a foreign-registered motorcycle. Despite having all the correct paperwork, nobody knows what to do with us. Eventually a very dusty file is brought down from a shelf and copies of forms of previous exiting travellers are used to fill out new forms while merely changing the registration details.

Bernard – At one point nobody wants to complete Bertha's carnet. I point out that the bike has been stamped into the country and needs to be signed out. Our 'agent' (Franklin) translates their response, indicating we do not need it. He seems happy, but I am not. I repeat numerous times the bike has been stamped into the country, pointing to the big official Colombian stamps and signatures. The bike has to be stamped out of the country, otherwise we will have problems surrendering the document back to the RAC in the UK. Four people gather around the person thoughtfully filling out numerous forms in non-carboned paper. Eventually they relent, my documents are stamped and signed, although the signature is a little suspicious with the name 'pp Manuel' scrawled on it.

More paperwork is completed at the police station across the road. As Bernard lights a cigarette near a huge aviation fuel tank the police wave furiously at him from behind their glass screens, letting him know they are not happy. 'Should have no smoking signs then, shouldn't they,' he casually responds as everybody glares at him. Three hours pass before we walk back across the dual carriageway to where Bertha waits for her narcotics inspection. Franklin takes another call from his wife, the third so far in an hour, and it's obvious all is not well in the Franklin household as the call terminates in a quietly furious row.

Finding everything is now shut until 2pm for the two-hour lunch, Bernard splutters with impotence telling Franklin this could all have been done yesterday. Franklin's apology has a falseness about it.

Franklin excuses himself; disappearing, he leaves us to sit on a loading bay as people come and go before lunchtime ends with still no sign of the police inspection. While we wait, a car pulls up nearby with a large mesh bag tied onto the roof which Bernard tells me is frantically moving. It takes him a while to realise that a large white duck has been tied onto the roof rack, and it's not very happy. When the driver unties the poor thing it mutters loudly and seeks revenge by biting the owner for now being crammed into a cardboard box. The duck spots its chance to escape as the driver turns his back and it starts hopping away, making ten feet before the driver notices. The tears run down my face at Bernard's description, complete with voices for both duck and driver as the owner runs over and places a brick on top of the box to hold it down. Twenty minutes later we are no longer laughing.

There's no sign of Franklin or the police as Bernard urges the office staff 'Tiempo. Tiempo. Aeropuerto' (Time, time, airport) prompting them to get onto the phone and within ten minutes the police arrive and ask Bernard to unpack the bike. When I say unpack I mean with a capital U. Everything. The whole lot. The back box is dispossessed of our carefully compressed clothes, unceremoniously emptied onto the warehouse floor. Each and every item is gone through, knickers, socks, bras, trousers, absolutely everything. The tank bag is tipped out and before Bernard has a chance to put anything back, the right pannier empties onto the floor. The warehouse becomes littered with everything we possess, scattered everywhere as they move on to sniff the air in the tyres which they insist Bernard deflates, to prove they are not stuffed with drugs. I frantically repack the clothes as Bernard tells me where things are as he continues to empty what ever pointed at. A torch is shone inside the petrol tank, underneath the bike, up the exhaust, as every nook and cranny is examined. Under normal circumstances we wouldn't be bothered at all but we have only 40 minutes left to get to the airport and it's obvious this is going to take some time to get through.

Anybody who has ever packed a bike for a long journey will know it is like putting a jigsaw together, to be done in a certain way, in a sequence, to make sure everything fits back in. It is very hard to repack when every little container is pulled apart and its contents spread all over the floor. In the end Bernard tells me the police take pity on us as the assembled cargo staff tell them that we have a plane to catch and have been waiting for nearly two days by now.

Bernard — The officers point to the left pannier while Cathy frantically tries to repack clothes into compression sacks. Unlocking the pannier I start to get everything out quickly while talking to Cathy about where her hands can find items. One of the officers puts his hand on top of mine, stopping me. He points to the bright red medical kit, which unzips to show assorted bandages and medicines. Pointing to another bag it reveals shoes. He puts his hand on mine, saying 'is OK'.

I think it must have been obvious we would have happily taken everything out for examination. Perhaps it's true that it's possible to tell when looking at people that there's a time to think 'OK enough, we've done our job'. They were not being nasty or intimidating, but merely doing what they have to do in the world they work in. Fortunately the 'OK, enough' came with sufficient time for us to run from the warehouse to the airport which we reach half an hour late.

The staff at the airport are fantastic when we arrive, breathless, in front of their desk to be treated like Very Important People (VIPs) or should that be Visually Impaired People? Either way, the white cane leads to an express check-in through the first-class channel as a constant chaperone takes us through the layers of airport procedures and security, all with kindness, willingness and patience. It makes me feel secure and comfortable with the world that is South America as we sit waiting for the short flight to Panama.

Remembering sitting in Buenos Aires before catching the flight to Santiago, people had told us that disability is treated with respect in Latin America. This regard, consideration, call it what you will, has been shown on numerous occasions on our travels through South America. I met it at this airport and at 14,000 feet in Peru while sitting in the rain and snow waiting for a road to open. Little kindnesses among different peoples spread across vast mileages.

While waiting to board the plane our thoughts turn to the next stop, the start of Central America and the drive through lands with a long and troubled past. Even when you mention countries such as El Salvador, Guatemala or Honduras, many people conjure up images of strife and conflict, bloodshed and wars. The blind woman and her sighted companion, however, have no such images in their heads. After seeing and experiencing so much, it's no longer possible for us to draw this picture of countries and their peoples before we even meet them. While we may well be two different individuals who experience different things across the kilometres, in many ways, we both fundamentally understand and experience the same facts.

To appreciate it all you have to do is look in the windshield of Bertha and the card stuck there that states; 'What you see depends on what you look for.'

It is the way it is. No longer do we ever doubt it.

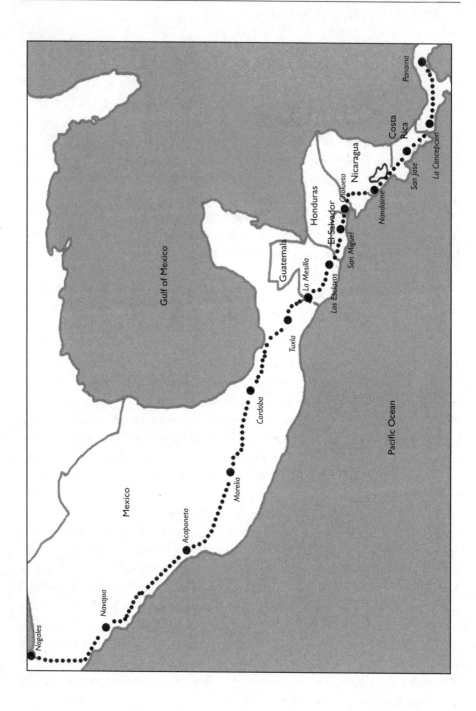

Map of the route through Central America. 2 June - 19 June

CENTRAL

AMERICA

PANAMA, COSTA RICA, NICARAGUA, HONDURAS,
EL SALVADOR, GUATEMALA AND MEXICO

'My white stick is back at the hotel'

(PA) Inspirational is a funny word if you think about it, as to inspire is to motivate people to seek change. Across the world motivational speakers stride platforms seeking to instil a message of change into people's behaviours, attitudes or beliefs. With the prospect of doing 'something different' with your life, they proclaim how it is always possible to become something different. Sometimes you just need that opening, a crack in a doorway calling you through the entryway to another place. In many ways, this was one of the purposes of our journey, to show how many things truly are possible.

When we try to write about such things people may think it pompous or self-important to talk of the journey in this way, but it's not who we are or what we think. You see, we know we're lucky. It's easy to say this when you understand that many times in life an opportunity rests purely on a situation when all the planets line up. In our own case, it became possible to set off despite the hundreds of barriers sitting in our way.

We set out wanting people to know there are possibilities if you believe and have the courage to step through the doorway. Sometimes it's the will to take action that people lack. After all, opportunities mean nothing without the courage to grab them. This view is confirmed as whispering traces reach across to where we sit on the other side of the world as we hear of an Australian talking to a fellow passenger on a train to Liverpool. Mike tells his fellow passenger how he was sitting in Australia reading about a blind woman going around the world on a motorcycle. The next day he went to his bank, withdrew $3,000, bought a backpack and a plane ticket while thinking, 'If a blind woman can do it...'. He used the word inspirational as the carriage rattled its way onwards and he soon learned he was sitting next to Bernard's dad. The world can be a very small place.

Against this backdrop of stories reaching across the world, Panama is gripped in the paranoia of swine flu sweeping the world as we land. Facemasks issue muffled voices, like dentists trying to hold a conversation with a patient. Making our way through the airport, we present ourselves to the immigration department where a voice asks:

'How long do you stay in Panama?'

'About a week,' comes Bernard's reply.

'I will give you three months,' the smiling Immigration Officer says. 'You may like Panama for longer than one week!'

The thump of the stamp signals our official entry in Central America.

Twenty-eight minutes later we walk into our hotel after a short bus ride and on reaching our room Bernard is asleep in seconds while I listen to the final chapters of the *Da Vinci Code* by Dan Browne. I'm asleep soon afterwards.

It's good to wake up on a new day knowing that there is no packing and repacking the bike. This can wait for another day or so. After leaving Tumbes in Peru, and crossing Ecuador and Colombia in six days, it's a relief to lie still and listen to the hum of the air conditioning. The previous frantic days have taken their toll and we're both tired from the continuous mountain passes and pock-marked roads with holes big enough to swallow Bertha. With a leisurely day ahead we relax until Bernard can contain himself no longer, about 39 heartbeats after waking. Reaching for the phone, he discovers Bertha has arrived and can be picked up tomorrow.

The next morning arrives and despite two alarms being set, a brass band playing, and WW3 breaking out in the room next door, we oversleep. It's not that we are tired, you understand. It is worse than that. Much worse. Somebody has stolen our will. They snuck up during the night, making off with it as we find that 'lethargy' is the new name for 'energy'. While both words have a somewhat similar ending we are content to wallow in the former rather than the latter.

Gradually rousing ourselves into action we find our way to the cargo office where Carmen takes us under her wing. She's been telling everybody, when she stops laughing and smiling, of the imminent arrival of 'The Blind English Woman on the big motorbike'. Her English is excellent and she loves our authentic voices, calling colleagues over so they too can come and listen to a 'real English accent'. It's always hard to be sure what people make of our Lancashire (me) and vaguely Liverpool (Bernard) accents, but they seem to enjoy everything we say immensely, if they understand us at all. Waving cheerily to us, Carmen gives us instructions on where to go to get the various bits of paper stamped that she hands over in a thick sheaf.

Walking back to the front gate in the tropical heat for stamp number one to be achieved, we practice our very finest English 'The rain in Spain falls mainly on the British Isles' until it sounds somewhat convincing. On reaching the gate, an officer notices my blindness and issues orders in staccato, machine-gun-like Spanish and seconds later we're bundled like sardines into a 4x4 with Bernard straddling the gear lever. Nervously twitching every time a gear change is required, he manfully refuses to admit it but still cannot help emphasising his masculinity by sounding several octaves lower whenever he speaks.

Arriving at the police hut, officers wear their shields on lanyards around their neck like the best American exported movie characters. One tries to engage us in Spanish before shifting to halting English, which Bernard compliments while apologising in terrible Spangalese about his own poor Spanish. The officer is obviously pleased with the compliment and he already knows of the arrival of 'The English Moto'. Even on arriving at the first gate on the way in the guard had welcomed us with 'Ahhh, la moto Englaise'. Bertha's fame precedes us as always.

The two police officers come to a rapid realisation that my blindness involves a connection with my legs as orders are shouted, and another 4x4 is summoned to chauffeur us back to the cargo offices due to my sudden inability to walk. This time Bernard is not required to perform the splits across the centre consol and his voice remains normal. Carmen is stunned at our speedy return with everything signed, until Bernard explains the help of the lovely customs and police officers before he finishes off with a rousing chorus of 'We love Panama'. The office staff smile at his antics. Flatterer.

People hold doors and step out of the way as we walk the short distance to the warehouse and there she is, 'Bertha the Boxer', 'Bertha the (semi) Invincible' – resplendent in Ecuadorian and Colombian dust and muck. Due to the mad exit from Colombia, and our ineffectual agent (Franklin-the-probably-wifeless), the battery wasn't even disconnected nor the petrol completely drained. With a few swift pumps the tyres inflate and she fires up first time to exit the warehouse where all work has stopped as people appear from all over the compound to watch events.

The Colombian drug search has left our gear all over the place – a bit like Bernard being let loose in a hotel room for several days – so most of it is bunged into a taxi whose driver asks for $15 dollars before one of the cargo managers pounces on him with rapid Spanish. 'Pay him no more than $10, even this is too much for the journey.' It confirmed our view that the $15 to get here from the hotel was indeed excessive. However, it demonstrates one of the problems you will always have travelling overland in this way.

Whenever a new country appears on the horizon it would be very helpful, at least for the locals, to reach into the left pannier and rummage around until you find the big rubber stamp marked 'mug'. Gripping it firmly in your hand you then apply it to your forehead as it avoids any confusion for the locals who may not recognise the huge red motorcycle bearing gifts. Many times over our journey so far we've talked about the hunt locals engage in as they run around searching the undergrowth for Rudolph as, obviously, Santa has ridden into town. There's always an inevitable struggle to understand relative values for a few days while the sound of silent sleigh bells echo all around us, until we catch up. Then we feel foolish when coming to understand how much things really are. It's wonderful thing, hindsight, and it teaches us all. Thus the early days always seems to involve being stung, numerous times, until we acclimatise.

Arriving back at the hotel and parking Bertha in a disabled bay (she has the sticker) everything changes as no longer are we simply two anonymous guests. Suddenly, as always, we become something different, something exotic, something unique. The same attendants who had merely watched us come and go before now come over to talk to us. Bellboys who had simply smiled as we'd wandered through the hotel now stand looking at Bertha as our cloak of invisibility drops away with the bike.

In and out of the hotel we wander under this scrutiny all through the afternoon with fluids being checked and bits of this and that tightened down. A massive crack in the windshield suffered during the recent shipment is glued together after Bernard convinces a very nervous hotel caretaker to drill two holes through the plastic, one at each end of the crack. This, he assures me, should stop the crack from continuing its inevitable route, like a snail's meandering trail. The drill is consigned back into the hotel along with the 100 foot-lead snaking from the reception desk, through the foyer, out the door, and across the road to Bertha. Meanwhile Colombian, Ecuadorean and Panamanian stickers find homes on the luggage boxes while tyre pressures are checked with the afternoon disappearing before Bernard pronounces himself satisfied. All the time people wander over to snap pictures as we work throughout the afternoon.

Relaxing and washing clothes we reflect on how different everything now feels compared to the night before when nobody connected with us. At this instant, with Bertha outside, Americans approach us saying, 'Good to see you two people having a good time,' while other sentences, other thoughts, often involve the word inspirational. Many times they go on to tell us of their own motorcycles sitting at home, how they would love to do such a journey. After such conversations, our own thoughts turn to the opening doorways of opportunity, how turning a dream into reality must still involve taking a final critical decision. It's at this point that dreams either change into something concrete, something tangible, or forever remain fleeting images in our heads of what might have been.

At breakfast the next morning, hands are placed gently on my shoulder and American accents wish me 'Good morning' as Bernard loads up a tray from the self-service array of offerings while I sit listening to the welcoming voices appearing. It's so nice and the whole experience of Panama seems one of being very, very, aware of Visual Impairment.

Hours later we wave to the assembled staff collected at the front door before pulling away to find our first petrol station in Panama. A gallon costs $2 (£1.30) and again it reminds us of the £1 per litre in England where draconian taxes are levied making UK petrol 400% dearer than anywhere else so far.

Tollbooths come and go as we wind our way across the long causeway cutting across the muddy bay towards the city itself, revealing a land of skyscrapers. It's hot, sweaty stuff and the road is missing huge drain covers big enough to swallow the front wheel without even a burp. Cars dive left and right to miss the subterranean entrances to the Panamanian underworld and we weave around in the same manner involving frighteningly late changes of direction as huge holes suddenly appear from underneath the car in front.

Driving round and round looking for the Pan-American we eventually blast across the Panama Canal itself over a bridge full of huge signs declaring dire consequences if you stop to take photographs.

The roads outside the city are good compared to our recent experiences in South America and the suspension easily absorbs the rough surface. We make progress along the C1 as towns drift past and the mileage clocks up towards the Costa Rica border 560 km away. Penonomé (150 km), changes to Santiago (at 248 km), before Tole appears at 348 km. Our speed climbs as good stretches allow Bertha to stretch her legs as the landscape changes from flat fields full of cattle, horses and goats, to jungle closing in on the single lane road.

Bertha's 'leg-stretching' rises to such a point that a very nice Panamanian police officer introduces himself – along with his very shiny new radar gun – on a particularly beautiful sweeping downhill left hand corner. In the ensuing conversation he maintains our speed was 120 kph in a 100 zone. Bernard punches buttons on the dashboard and shows the recorded 107 top speed on the Sat Nav system (which now works intermittently). The policeman laughs and agrees with the speed – recorded on his own offending item – before licence and tickets are both discussed.

Needless to say there is no paperwork for the $20 'fine' as a single crisp note is passed over for the return of the international driving licence as he reinforces the speed limit. Helpfully, he then gives us the rundown on the road ahead, the speed traps, the Drug Enforcement Agency roadblocks, bad bends, dangerous places, petrol stations and where the Martians abduct locals along the route. In many ways it's money well spent as we find out there's no petrol for 100 km after a town called David. Philosophically it is now possible to accept that if people are not paid enough money they will supplement their income somehow.

We can imagine him talking to his wife that night; yes he was married with two children as we found out.

'I met an English couple today'

'Did you love?' she responds, preparing dinner.

'Yes, she was blind, and they were on a big motorcycle. They were very happy people and even thanked me after I fined them. Shook hands with them and it was all laughing and joking. I do like the English, they are always so polite. By-the-way, here's twenty dollars towards the kids new school uniforms.'

So Bernard has now fallen foul of various police forces including the Turkish (twice), the Thai (twice), the Australian (once) and now the Panamanians, all in the name of charity, if you catch my double-edged drift.

Waving to our new-found – and slightly richer – friend, we set off again discussing how Bernard prefers this rather than the silly system in England where marginal infractions can lead to three points on a licence; when these rack up they remove the offending item from you.

It starts to rain on entering David, leading us to take shelter under trees to wait for the torrent to pass with the gauge showing 30+ degrees. It's too hot to climb into 'boil in the bag' waterproofs and so we merely wait it out. Eventually pushing on to Concepcion, a small hotel appears where, just as we arrive, the heavens open and turn the roads into rivers. Pyrotechnic patterns are traced in the sky as water noisily cascades down roofs, trees and everything else as we unfold our umbrella to splash our way to the café where we consume enormous mountainous meals, wines, beer and coffee for the price of one gallon of petrol in England.

All the time the rain beats a staccato pounding rhythm on the roof, causing raised voices as water rushes down in gushing streams outside the windows with loud whooshing sounds. It rains like this for four hours while we sit, watch, talk and listen. All the beautiful green landscapes now make sense as the waitress explains it will rain like this for three to four hours and then stop, like a tap turned off. One minute buckets of water falling from the sky and the next nothing.

Walking back up to our room it's rained so heavily that a family of large frogs have taken shelter on our porch. They hop out of our way as we cautiously navigate our way past them while they wait for the torrent to stop sweeping down the path. Bernard offers to retrieve one of them for me as he swears they are as big as his foot, but I thank him for his kind offer before declining. I can imagine them talking to each other while staring up disconsolately at the sky:

'God it's lashing down' the wife comments in a Northern Panamanian accent.

'Ai lass' her dutiful husband responds.

'Not fit to be out in' she goes on hoping for a conversation with her snoozing partner.

'Ai lass' he mumbles from beneath heavy eyelids.

'Is that all you're going to say?' she prompts

'Ai lass'

Her eyes scan the horizon as she wanders where it all went wrong. Perhaps.

Falling asleep with heavy eyes I can hear them talking to each other outside our door and the last thing I heard was 'Ai lass.' At least that is what it sounded like to me.

The morning brings the border between Panama and Costa Rica and the discovery of a missing 'vital' Panamanian document for Bertha to be allowed out of the country. Various people make that dreaded 'sucking in air' noise which represents an insurmountable problem as huge gales of air are displaced due to this missing piece of paper. We vaguely recall something about a post office when being chauffeured around the cargo compound but cannot quite pin it down. Meanwhile, there is much huffing and puffing about its lack until, eventually, $2 magically makes the problem go away. Thus, the dilemma is solved, everybody is happy, and the gales of sucking noises disappear like the Panamanian rain, instantly.

(CR) On the Costa Rica side three hours of paper shuffling begins involving photocopies and even more photocopies of documents. They even throw in the obligatory charge for soaking the bike in disinfectant in an attempt to bring death and destruction to our recently acquired insectoid – much splattered and already dead – companions.

Standing in a puddle of sweat – with my white stick not working its customary magic – queues of people move forward wearing shorts and T-shirts, fanning themselves constantly with handfuls of paper while we slowly dissolve inside our bike gear. Shuffling forward leaving a soggy trail, it takes 25 minutes to reach the first window where a credit card proves you are solvent and have enough money (or debt) to be allowed to enter the country. 'Ahhh, American Express, that'll do nicely!' Thump goes the stamp. Part one done. A sheaf of Spanish forms appear under the opening.

It is obvious several more photocopies are needed as I walk, while Bernard stamps, back to the photocopy office (again). Twenty minutes later – and several kilograms lighter with the heat – we take station back at the window with Bernard still muttering. I point out he should try being a Costa Rican getting into England, of their probable need of a letter from a divine authority to get in. He relents and agrees I am right.

The forms go under the glass panel before coming back at us again for even more information. Backwards and forwards they go, like a perpetual game of ping-pong until the young woman is very nearly happy. This we know to be true when she starts entering data as a dot matrix printer clatters with the sound of 20 year-old machinery. Three offices later the very nice customs officer proclaims herself satisfied with the bike – without even looking at it; definitely not Colombian-trained we guess.

Outside in the sun we cross the road to a café and a waitress asks, 'Donde?' (where are you from and going?). She looks wistful at the answers and Bernard says her face is full of longing and regret as she, perhaps, dreams of such a journey while serving tables in the dust bowl of the border. Leaving her behind with thoughts of other lives, of other possibilities, we manage a whole 300 yards before being waved down at a checkpoint. Off we climb to retrieve all the papers from the pannier before they're minutely examined. After seeing so little of the police, we trundle through police checkpoints every few miles on our way from the border but, happily, they mainly just wave us through.

The roads are a patchwork of tarmac, gravel, sand and soil as we bash our way across the surfaces like true professionals. Coming to a junction we discuss dropping off the Pan-American as it seems to go a long way around. In front of us there are serious heights and after so much experience we know streams of wagons will be dragging themselves up them like inebriated broken-legged insects. Bernard laughs as he asks me which route to take after explaining what he sees. To me the 34 'felt' right rather than the Pan-Am.

'Here I am in Costa Rica taking directions from a blind woman about which road to take!' His laughter comes through my helmet speakers as he turns off the Pan-American to head down the 34 with the blind navigator as a new first; next stop professional rallies shouting 'left 60'. Miraculously the road is far, far, better than the main highway and it soon becomes obvious why.

The coastal area is full of newly built tourist destinations, hotels and houses built where the Pacific Ocean crashes onto the Coast of Riches (Costa Rica), so named after the fertility the red soil represented to the Spanish when they first arrived. Interestingly it is also one of the few countries in the world (one of only 14) that no longer has any form of military or standing army. The army was abolished a few years after WW2, after suffering a brutal 44 day civil war. It was at that time some bright spark, probably sitting at the back of the Government class, whispered to the President how, perhaps, all the money could probably be better spent on education and universal healthcare for its people? Now there's a novel thought.

Hours later we rejoin the Pan-Am and begin the climb into the cloud forest where mist, drizzle and the occasional deluge brings cold and wet for hours on end. The road through the cloud twists and turns so much, is so narrow, that not even a cigarette stop is called for as it is too dangerous to pull over. Trudging miserably through the cold and wet we know people come from all over the world to see the forest but Bernard tells me there is little to see in the big scale of things. Unless of course you have a liking for grey cloud and sheet rain.

To pass the time he amuses me with his observations that people are probably rushing through the forest at that very moment, clutching butterfly nets, as we splash past going, 'Please God, let this end soon.' Give us both the warmth any time. We have not been this cold since Erzerum, or in Peru at 15,000 feet with a closed road. Not since the M5 in England closed in 2007 due to the 'Great Flood' have we felt this wet. At that time, sleeping on a roundabout wrapped up in survival bags, England had become one big lake. Eventually dropping down into Cartago, the lower altitude leaves the cloud forest (rain and cold) behind us as we potter into the outskirts of the town and the El Guarco hotel appears. Gratefully we climb off the bike after 10 hours with an average speed of 30 kph.

The next morning Bernard is tired, responding like the proverbial 'grumpy old man' and his mood is not helped 25 miles later when I quietly tell him that my white stick is back at the hotel. We pull over and after several seconds of silence travel 25 miles back to find it behind the front door of our room where it had been left for the night. Twenty-five miles later finds us back at the same point but this time Bernard finds the right road instead of repeating the tour of San José taken earlier. Sometimes things just happen for a reason as I try to convince him leaving my stick was a preordained event to save him from getting lost. He is not impressed.

Catching up with a large group of motorcycles following a mural-covered pickup truck, they shatter the silence with their open-bore exhausts and handlebars that reach upwards to the sky like the bike that Henry Fonda rode in *Easy Rider*. Harley-Davidsons predominate with chrome glistening in the sunshine along with cut-off denim jackets covered in badges and chapter colours. Carving our way through the Hells Angels cavalcade, Bernard picks them off a few at a time until we leave them behind at their sedate 50 mph. Perhaps they're out to cause terror and mayhem in the Costa Rican countryside although, by all the friendly waves, horn blowing, flashing headlights and big thumbs ups coming at us, they could simply be out for a ride and a cup of tea. Eventually returning home, they will probably climb into business suites, pick up briefcases, kiss their wives and children goodbye before taking the train to work. Who knows? What you see depends on what you look for.

The roads narrow into single lanes as trees close in on both sides while overhead a canopy forms bringing welcome shade and coolness after the heat as we blast along towards the Nicaraguan border. Black tarmac stretches in front of us and good surfaces abound with another large group of motorcycles soon appearing in our mirrors. They pass us in ones and twos – mixtures of street machines and semi-chopped bikes all chrome and polish, making us look like two tramps in comparison. They dip and dive past the Sunday drivers in the hills and soon we tuck in behind them. Bertha is soon diving into corners, up and down gears, passing everything as we hurtle into the distance. Bernard's brain pulses and becomes infused with adrenaline and testosterone as I begin to wonder if we've stumbled, accidentally, onto the starting grid of a Grand Prix race. After several miles of roaring down leafy lanes with Bertha about to explode every gasket my errant friend's blood pressure returns to normal. His brain stops pulsing and satisfaction is pronounced – on a nearly 20 year-old heavily laden bike as I point out to him at the resulting lunch break.

Within seconds, surrounded by people from the café, fifteen-year-old Ian translates backwards and forwards and we become firm friends seconds after Bernard tells him Ian is an English name. Leaving our young friend to dream of road trips and large motorcycles we ride on to the border a few miles later where hordes of helpers appear. By the nature of their insistent voices it seems we will be stuck here for at least a week without their help. Sadly, they forgot to tell the very nice fully gold-toothed Customs officer who stamped and signed everything off without a Colombian strip search of either Bertha or ourselves.

(NIC) Slowly crossing the border into Nicaragua time reverses as decades turn back with a road that suddenly stops, being replaced by gravel and hardcore. Shoddiness radiates all around in the dirty, once white, grey buildings as Costa helpers are replaced by their Nicaraguan brothers who proclaim it is harder to get into Nicaragua than for an Afghan refugee to get into England. Handing over $3, Bertha is again drowned in disinfectant (and so is everything we possess) as a very nice certificate is passed to us from a very bored-looking young lady in a booth. Meanwhile word has gone round of the two naïve gringos arriving as 'helpers' dive into every bush looking for Rudolph as, after all, he must be somewhere as Santa has arrived. Having seen this so many times before we are better prepared as a horde of them trail our every move. We must look like pied pipers (or in the heat, 'fried pipers') with so many following us until we quite take to one of them and accept his offer, after first checking the price.

Anado is about 40 years old and speaks English very well and gently leads us from pillar to post, from office to window. Health check forms are duly signed declaring that, no, we do not have sore throats, coughs, colds or any other rabid-like or death-dealing symptoms of the pandemic flu. Bernard indicates the only sore throats experienced is from talking; actually, he indicates me much to the amusement of the staff sitting behind their white facemasks.

Anado then leads us past lines of American bus tourists visiting Nicaragua openly, unlike some of their military in the past. Handing over more dollars for the cost of passport stamps, bike insurance, and a stamp from a customs officer, we wonder how much he pays for having his shoes shined by the barefooted boy kneeling in the dust. Nearby American tourists are busily snapping away at Bertha while proclaiming 'Oh my God, you've come all the way from England' just as the heavens open. The sudden deluge turns the dust into white mud as we stand under the porch of the health check area sheltering from the sudden onslaught.

Soon all the local wise boys join us, appearing from bushes and buildings looking for the 'free money' represented by our presence as we move from porch to tree and tree to porch as they follow us. It seems Nicaragua abounds with free money from Santa who now rides a large red motorcycle. Being English, Bernard merely snorts when they demand one dollar for their help when they'd earlier pointed towards the Pasaporte building. Becoming more insistent as Bernard's snorts get louder and louder, eventually they give up.

After guzzling several cold drinks, and packing half a tree of Nicaraguan paperwork into the panniers, we set off only to be pulled over within five heartbeats for a document check. Perhaps it was ten beats but the outcome is the same; off we climb, unlocking panniers before retrieving everything. Personally we both think they just want to look at the bike as most of the documents are in English anyway. With Bernard resolutely practising his Spangalese, it is obvious English is not their fifth, never mind second, language but they are happy with everything. Who are we to deny officials their bit of excitement in livening up the boredom of watching the dust blowing all day?

Heading for Rivas 30 or so kilometres away, we pull into a 'lake resort' nestling under the shadows of a massive, thankfully dormant, volcano with everything covered under a blue haze of heat. The armed guards on the gate carry the weapon of preference (pump-action shotguns) but they happily wave us through to bounce down the pitted entrance road. The resort seems empty with the only visible signs of life being on the floor of the reception area, which is a midge graveyard, as the bored receptionist shows us to a $70 room. Every step taken is met with the sounds of Bernard blowing loudly to save ingesting the clouds of midges turning up to welcome us. Despite questioning if the $70 was a mistranslation of $7, the receptionist does not take the hint. Since we have left our jungle nets at home ('we won't need them') along with our thermostatically controlled survival suits, her offer of accommodation is declined as neither of us fancy being a meal for the black cloud which follows us constantly.

Further down the road Rivas itself soon appears, a town where poverty shouts from all around as people stare at our passing. The level of destitution makes Bernard nervous just riding through it as many men sit around sharpening long machetes. Standing on street corners with the light glinting off the razor sharpness of their jungle cleavers darkness is beckoning and we need to get off the road, but it's another 40 miles before arriving at a blacked out power-poor Jinotepe guest house.

Two parrots declare control of their kingdom to all and sundry in the café next door as they freely wander around the floor while we sit in the (midge-free) dark munching on rice, pancakes and other things only vaguely recognisable. Bernard recognises the beer, happily quaffing several cans of Heineken would you believe while noting, with some justification, 'Well it has been really, really hot today. It'll help me sleep properly.' Funnily enough, sleep never seems to be one of the things he has any problem with.

A young boy sneaks up behind as we eat, being careful to keep out of the sight of staff. Asking for free (gringo) money, 'For my hunger,' he sits on the floor and repeats the same thing over and over until one of our plates of untouched food is offered. Suddenly his hunger seems cured.

It's true that, compared to many unfortunate people, we are indeed Father

Christmas, the tooth fairy, and the leprechaun at the end of the rainbow with a pot of gold all rolled into one, represented by the shiny red metallic parcel Bertha represents to many people. It's also true it's hard to say no when you're sitting up close and personal with need in this way. While this is true, before even leaving England Bernard had told me this is the way it has to be. Once you start giving there is no end. In some countries every day is the same with the level of need only changing by the face before you. You also have to wonder what distinguishes one person's poverty from another.

It's true you can talk about poverty in terms of 'absolute' and 'relative' to the end of the world but it can never help you when a ten-year-old boy sits two feet away chanting 'dollar for my hunger' constantly. Is poverty worse among the one billion people in India? Is it worse in a Nicaragua ravaged by decades of conflict, leaving a country with few natural resources but many shiny machetes? Why give to one person and not another? How do you decide? Eventually the young boy wanders off looking back reproachfully, leaving the plate of food untouched.

The morning brings a 6.30am exit when we find breakfast is as scarce as free equipment from transglobal bike manufacturers. We ride round and round in the capital, Managua, until dizzy and sweating profusely. Hopelessly lost in the dust and potholes of the city, Bertha trundles through shantytowns of cardboard and black plastic covering the sides of the road in the same way as in India. It is a world away in distance and time but not in appearance or sentiment. People sit amid the squalor with empty eyes staring ahead. Lost in thought, they focus on the sound of Bertha before locating us and then a brightness enters their eyes for a few seconds. They smile. Then we are gone. It leaves Bernard wondering if they return back to the same vacant look prior to our passing.

Without a map or working Sat Nav system Bernard uses the compass to find our way forward. Eventually working our way through the rubbish-strewn streets we climb out of the obstacle course our route has taken us through. Stopping for petrol when we do find the CA1, $3 per gallon is handed over for fuel in a country where people earn $1 a day in an economy grinding along in desperation.

Butterflies with broken wings

(HN) Exiting from Nicaragua is quick and (financially) painless, quite unlike our entry to Honduras where an hour passes being officially mugged for this and that. It all has to be retrieved for roadblocks every few hundred yards as each and every piece is meticulously examined for the dotted 'i's and crossed letter 't's. Smiling and trying to make conversation we know often the people merely want to stare at everything we represent, everything we carry.

Soon the Villa Margarita appears, luring us into its bosom by its modern appearance, looking like an oasis in a sea of psychological hopelessness pictured by the dead expressions of the people passed along the way. Somebody obviously thought it would be a good idea to build the complex close to the border, as 'there will be lots of passing trade and tourists'. Obviously. The swimming pool is meticulously clean. The five-a-side pristine football pitch is silky smooth. The fourteen three-roomed apartments sit immaculately painted in sky blue and white façades. Meanwhile, the whole site rattles with the quietness of the three guests, two of whom are us.

Our progress through Central America is now so quick we are running out of information about where we are. Sometimes it's even hard to remember which country we are in, or even where we should be, as there is only the vaguest idea without maps.

The next morning the empty site fades behind us and we ride through six police checkpoints within 45 km, each with smiling people asking for everything and anything about the bike. Pulling over for petrol a few miles down the road Bernard hands over $20 for the 236 lempira at an exchange rate of about 20 to the dollar. Forty lempira appears in change. We wait. The attendant smiles. We still wait. He smiles again and waves us off the pump as cars pull up behind us and Bertha blocks their way. Eventually another 100 lempira appears into Bernard's outstretched hand. It's close enough.

The attendant smiles as if to say, 'Well if you don't try?'

Setting off, our conversation turns to how tiring it is when everybody seems willing to exploit us. It wears us down, makes us distrustful. It's a bad feeling and is happening more in Central America than anywhere else. Mainly, however, it leaves us feeling tired. Every transaction is fraught with the feeling of being eaten by piranhas that nibble away a fraction at a time. Nibble, nibble. Munch, munch. Pulling up on a deserted road several miles later Bernard lights a cigarette but within seconds a one-legged man on crutches comes out of the jungle.

Homing in on us, he asks for money by holding his hand out. Nibble, Nibble. A fatigue settles over us during the length of the cigarette. It is obvious Bernard's Spanish cuts no ice as he stands and stares at us, repeating over and over again, 'dollars'. Becoming more and more insistent, he eventually demands money. Aggressively. Plain and simple. With no more pleasantness, no more smiles, no more soft-voiced tones, just aggressive demands. Weariness settles like a pall on our hearts as we listen to the mounting aggression in his voice. It unsettles me as the voice changes and echoes in my head, becoming Indian voices saying 'Rupees, rupees'. It feels suffocating and painful. Pulling off, leaving him with our 'Buena Suerte' (good luck) echoing emptily, our mood flattens.

The exit from Honduras is chaotic as we're instantly surrounded by money changers and fixers of every size and age and I cannot shake the feeling of India now that it has reappeared. There is no space for me to climb off the bike, to breathe, so close do people press in on us. Everybody wants to 'help' Mr and Mrs Santa Claus. Expectations abound of how the distribution of goodies will soon commence although Bernard refuses to be drawn, discounting the legions of helpers instantly. 'I've done 26 borders so far, thank you,' his voice declares.

I know he is merely exerting control and biding his time, seeing how things pan out before CHOOSING somebody, rather than being catapulted along by others. The whole place is complete chaos as we wander up to the border control until some semblance of 'assistance' is forthcoming at the white stick's appearance. 'Runners' are sent to photocopy relevant documents at the most expensive photocopying machine in the world (nibble) and a passport stamp (nibble, nibble) is issued for the bike while a Honduran flag appears (nibble, nibble, nibble). Meanwhile it is hot, unbelievably so, as we shuffle from place to place while people gather around the bike which Bernard watches warily – for the first time in many months.

(ES)Oozing sweat from every pore we stand in the midday turmoil of sounds and activity all around. After being consumed by all the Honduran nibbling possible we are spat over the bridge onto the El Salvadorian side where a cursory view of our passports leads to directions to the Customs post a few kilometres away. Relieved we set off.

Sometimes life has a wonderful sense of humour as, just when you think it cannot get any worse, three kilometres later it does. It comes in the form of a moustached, sunglasses-wearing Hitler who presses Spanish forms into Bernard's hands. 'Houston, I think we have a problem,' comes the muttered voice beside me as the customs officer rattles on in fast-paced Spanish. Now we know what the English must make people feel like as he starts to shout instructions at us as if we are both hard of hearing and also complete imbeciles.

The penny drops he is going to have some fun with us when Bernard replies:

'There is no point in you shouting at me, repeating the same thing over and over again, I haven't a clue what you are saying.'

At this he snaps and goes ballistic.

People all around us begin laughing and it feels like he's having a lot of fun at our expense but it doesn't feel funny at all, far from it. I wonder why it is that you can never find a fixer when you need one; a bit like a bus, a policeman, or a starter motor in Peru?

Sitting on a plastic seat, with the help of Louis, a truck driver, numerous forms are filled out in English only for all the answers to be crossed out by Mr Hitler (we thought if we called him Mister it might help) as he replaces all the English with Spanish equivalents – after an hour of waiting.

Bernard – I knew he could speak English. Something told me he knew precisely what I was saying at our first encounter. He is making a point and it is very, very, uncomfortable being around him. The temperature is in the high 30s and the sweat drips onto the forms while he finds every excuse to avoid dealing with me. He is a real bugger and exercising every bit of authority and power he has over us as we slowly dissolve in the still airless heat.

As we wait, numerous trucks pull up towing huge cavernous trailers that are soon inspected and searched as various forms are filled out before they leave. Meanwhile we sit waiting with a motorcycle and three boxes as the puddle of sweat gets larger underneath our two plastic chairs. Bernard is despatched up the road several times to gather more photocopies before coming back clutching sheaves of paper which he eventually deems to scan. After two hours we heave a sigh of relief on departing, only to be told at the first police checkpoint that we have the wrong papers. The police take pity on us as Bernard tells me they've seen us, and him, going up and down the road for over two hours to get photocopies. They wave us through the barrier but Bernard refuses to cross, not knowing what will happen when we come to exit El Salvador, without correct paperwork. There seems to be no choice but to go back and face the mirrored sunglasses again.

At our reappearance Mr H is very clearly having a whale of a time as his face lights up with a big smile when he sees us but he is also clearly aggravated by phone calls from the police. Probably they have told him to get his (wrong) form 39-PTFY sorted out from his (correct) 68-HYT. He descends on us purposively for Act 2 but this time we have outsmarted him as Paolo our fixer is in tow. With assurances of how 30 minutes and $10 will fix the problem, his voice is as sincere as a politician's word. We feel confident. Nearly.

Settling back onto our seats, a great battle commences between the forces of good and evil. Empires rise and fall on the strength of these battles and a whole universe of meaning is constructed on the intellectual merits of those engaged. In the meantime, Bernard pulls his baseball cap over his eyes and says, 'Wake me if anything happens.'

Three hours later I wake him to note the 30 minutes Paolo had promised have long since passed. One hour to exit Honduras and five to enter El Salvador makes it appear tourism is not big on the El Salvadorian political agenda – at least not civilian tourism. Feeling as welcome as leprosy, swine flu, or George Bush in Baghdad, at least it's possible to be consoled by the fact we do not need a bulletproof car to go everywhere. Sometimes being philosophical helps as Bernard comments:

'He probably drives a very big car.'

'What makes you say that?' I ask in all innocence.

'Well you know what they say about people who drive big cars don't you? It is a compensatory action for inadequacies in other more physical departments. He must feel the need to drive something really, really big.'

Then he starts laughing.

Actually, a paraphrased sentence is as close as I can get to what he actually did say; it would be impossible for me to record the precise words.

Five and a half hours after arriving Bernard searches Mr Hitler out after waiting until he is beside a very, very, senior officer who speaks English. Marching over to him, Bernard shakes hands with our tormentor saying:

'You are a very, very, naughty man for playing such a long joke on two guests.'

Mr Hitler smiles clearly understanding and as we turn to leave the last words come from Bernard, 'By the way, the name is not gringo as you've called me all day. To you, as a public servant, it is always MR Gringo.'

Reappearing back at the border, the police applaud our reappearance hours after leaving them and with a flourish, the barrier is raised for the road to San Miguel where we find a home for the night surrounded by American voices. The sun falls from the sky as Bertha sits outside in one of the two disabled bays the staff insist we use.

All the frustrations of the day – and previous days – eventually boil over in the evening as tiredness and waves of aggravation sweep through Bernard. He lashes his written journal across the room in a rare show of temper at trying to recount the days through tired brains when all we want to do is go to sleep. Ever meticulous in recording details, it boils over when neither of us seem able to recall very much through the fog that has descended on our brains.

I see the book in my mind as it flutters to the floor like a broken butterfly, waiting for him to retrieve it, to fix the wings before the story can go on, of two people doing impossible things within an impossible journey. The simple image of a broken butterfly reflects the image I have of us at this point: ragged versions worn away with constant rushing and the tension of multiple border crossings within a short space of time. Bernard and borders equals stress and there is no getting away from it; he is what he is.

He had spent the whole day not letting it get to him, keeping things bottled up, feigning sleep, trying to send the message, 'You cannot get to me.' The act of lashing a book across the room is a form of release of all that pent-up pressure I know he feels. Careful to hide the pressure when it is important to do so, like today, it explodes outwards in the safety of our room. I wait for the storm to pass as he can be no different than the person I fell in love with. It is impossible for him to be anything else.

Silence falls as tiredness, irritation and anger flash across our peaceful world like a hurricane. We wait for it to subside, as it surely will. After listening to the tick of the clock he climbs out of bed muttering 'The damn book has split.' There it is, the small opening, the start of normality.

'Probably the wall that did it,' I respond.

'Could be,' he laughs quietly.

'We've got tape haven't we?' I ask.

'Yep,' he climbs back into bed and retrieves his pen.

'It'll be fine then,' my voice assures him as he settles back down.

The words eventually spill out about people with big cars and of butterflies with broken wings as words pile up on the page and the dark cloud fades from our small room. Our world is recognisable and comfortable because we are both together again. The butterfly no longer has broken wings and I know we are ready for another day.

Following the CA-1 signs for the Pan-American we head for San Salvador and the traffic eventually settles, if that's the right word, into something like rush-hour London traffic except it keeps moving at more than 6 mph. Actually if you put several zeros after the six then you have the approximate speeds involved. Perhaps it's wrapped up in their history of everybody driving fast enough so that the snipers will miss them. Who knows? As we hurtle along trucks and buses push out dense clouds of black smoke as I shout helpful thoughts to pass the time like, 'Are we having breakfast yet?' or 'Can I breathe now?' This comes after holding my breath for ten minutes as we carve our way through the volcanic eruptions coming from every vehicle.

Inexplicably the CA-1 sign is lost, becoming as invisible as maps of this country and a petrol attendant gives directions. After putting on his sunglasses to protect his eyes from the fully gold-toothed smile, Bernard heads off and ten minutes later stops again while people wave their arms like windmills in numerous directions. Reverting to our 'follow the wagons' rule, we're hopelessly lost in San Salvador with not a sign for Santa Ana on the horizon. After the customary cigarette in times of severe stress, or not, the compass is called into play and an hour later the mythical CA-1 appears.

The traffic thins out as Bernard starts to describe the small open pickup trucks acting as taxis/buses/purveyors of the people. Leaping onto the still-moving vehicles, hands reach down to grab new passengers to forestall them being swept under vehicles following in the ever-onward motion. On passing through small villages the Pan-American, or Inter-Americana as many call it, narrows and threads its way past market stalls. Selling everything from fruit to T-shirts, buses stop suddenly with no warning while people leap out of the doors (front, side and rear), or fall from windows. Meanwhile others perform perfect leaps off the roof in gymnastic displays that would have judges reaching for their perfect ten score boards.

Children wave as we slowly meander past. People turn a 100 yards in front as Bertha announces her presence with the distinctive rumble of her engine – 'Probably the gear box,' according to Bernard, 'Something's getting noisier.' It is a problem for another day so we simply talk louder to overcome the noise of her grumbling innards.

The road holds good and soon the hills take us into the emptiness towards San Cristobal, further cutting down the mileage towards Guatemala. We hope Mr Gestapo has not been transferred across the country to this border crossing as if he has, a vow is taken to turn around and take to the jungle. There we will happily winch the bike up mountains and down ravines in order to avoid him.

Pulling down towards the border Bernard scans the post for anybody goose-stepping or for any other indication of mirrored sunglasses; all he can see are smiling faces. It makes him nervous. The border guards all smile as we pull up and park Bertha. Are they lulling us into a false sense of security? Finding nothing but firm handshakes all around, there is not a sign of a single goose-stepping guard. They even walk us down the hill towards a hut where all the paperwork is completed within ten minutes. Bernard sniffs suspiciously (or is developing man-flu), but it seems true, El Salvadorian border guards do not all chew on broken glass.

Walking down to the Guatemalan border, the female officer there examines each and every one of our passport stamps; all 27 ins and 27 outs to date. We pull up chairs for the wait as she makes several cups of tea while examining each and every page. Fifty-four stamps later a new thump indicates Guatemala is winking at us saying, 'Come on in, the jungle's fine'.

Felipe is a young man who stands out among all the border touts with his thinness and smiling easygoing manner; he seems very gentle and we take to him straightaway. The feeling develops even more over the next hour and a half as he smoothes the ripples in the Guatemalan paper pond. Leading us from Office 1 (Guatemala Customs) to Office 2 (El Salvador Customs) to Office 3 (photocopy everything) to Office 1 then Office 2 and then Office 4, we hand over the $5 administration fee. Heading back to Office 2 more paper is collected and so it goes as the paper carousel continues in its endless circle.

People may wonder why Bernard gets so stressed with borders but I think he just gets dizzy more than anything as the 'swirling dance of the forest' is performed— most of the greenness of Brazil has probably disappeared into our panniers at one point or another. Then again, we can be thankful we are not Guatemalan motorcyclists trying to enter the UK. Old age would probably strike us down as we waited.

Rock music blasts from a café nearby as Bernard gives a running 'I'll name that artist in one' game of The Red Hot Chili Peppers or Led Zeppelin. He sighs loudly when I ask where is the Mariah Carey or Celine Dion?

'In lifts all over world,' he answers.

'May as well ask where the birdie song is,' he dismisses.

'I like the birdie song,' I tease him, 'It always fills the dance floors.'

He puffs on his cigarette in silence and does not even deem to answer.

'By the way,' I add naughtily, 'Didn't Led Zeppelin make a balloon?'

Ninja studies and black smoke

GCA We're 166 km from the capital, Guatemala City, as Felipe waves goodbye. The roads onwards consist of suicidal cows lying lazily in wait for passing motorcycles before ambling up onto their feet to wander across the road playing chicken. The undulating and bumpy road takes us through many places with little more than cafés, garages and waving children, until we fly past the Turicentro Los Esclavos. Turning around to have a second look, it nestles on the side of a ravine where the river rushes past several hundred feet below. Three large parrots shout 'Ola' (Hello) from their open-air cages while lightning flashes in the sky. Soon followed by rumbles of thunder, we sit by the empty pool sending text messages to people who worry about us passing through places like El Salvador and Guatemala.

At times like this fears can be relatively calmed through the wonder of technology as it sees messages winging their way up into the sky. Around the globe they fly before landing with a thump, or a blast of song, to burrow into circuits of mobiles. Even though our words say we are having a whale of a time, they continue to worry. While most days are spent laughing through most of the world, people at home fret over our safety. The funny thing is if we nipped to France for a bit of a wander they would probably say, 'Enjoy and bring back a few bottles of the red stuff.' It's the name of the country that triggers fear beyond our own, very real, experiences.

Having read motorcycle books for his whole life, Bernard tells me how riders often report on 'the dangers' of riding in countries such as Ecuador and Colombia, along with our old friend Pakistan. Books have been filled with Foreign and Commonwealth Office (FCO) Advisory notices supporting the view that the road they are about to take from X to Y 'is dangerous and *under no circumstances* should foreign nationals drive between X and Z'. The FCO notice then goes on to say if (a) you have several truckloads of local militia with you, (b) at least two local fixers, and (c) your own helicopter doctor then it may downgrade the danger from terminal to only critically life threatening.

In order to further reduce the risk we would suggest some further advice:

1. Contact Harry Potter to arrange to borrow his invisibility cloak.

2. Go to Japan and spend two years doing a crash course in Ninja studies. Included in this should be the compulsory option of advanced meditation. In

this option you can learn to stop breathing for several months so that even the local wildlife cannot hear as you pass them by. It would also be useful in saving your lungs from extreme dieselitus. This disease occurs from weeks of swallowing black smoke from defunct engines that do not know they have died and gone to diesel heaven.

Often the writers then go on to describe the shootings, kidnappings and barely conceived mayhem they may experience. Needless to say, the road is ridden and nothing happens.

Danger sells stories, whether real or imaginary, and we suppose it is understandable. For ourselves, the only time fear truly impinged was in India. Even then it was not the people, the crushing crowds, the (frighteningly) hot curries or even the head nodding which can mean yes/no/maybe or I have not got a clue what you just asked me. The fear centred on the chaotic and seemingly lawless driving culture such that if there were any rules they were so well guarded that even a psychic would have struggled to understand them.

Sometimes it's true that you can read too much. It's also true you can plan too much.

If we'd read about La Linea in Colombia Bernard would have stressed about it, instead of just doing it. The only time notice was taken of people's advice it led to hours of panicking, as in the darkened mountains of Ecuador about snipers and bandits. Sometimes information overload, accurate or not, hides the truth of the people, the road, or the experience it purports to inform about. Sometimes being naïve and open is to be innocent in a guilty sort of way.

'Will the two defendants please rise. How do you plead?'

'Guilty as charged your honour. There are mitigating circumstances however, as we are both technically insane your worshipfulness. Me more than him though your Lordship as I'm supposed to be the sensible one while he's always been completely loony tunes. He was just good at hiding it until he paid off the mortgage.'

So it is that our messages are sent, our calls home made when possible and we hope people do not worry too much. It's not really worth worrying about two people who are often in bed at 7.30 and asleep by 8. You see, our witching hour has had its clock turned back four hours due to advanced decrepitness along with terminal tiredness. Isn't age a wonderful thing?

Sitting bleary-eyed eating breakfast the next morning, a gaggle of bikes pull into the courtyard and fifteen bikers stomp into the large open area. It's obvious they're buzzing like excited bees by the increasing swell of noise signalling their arrival on immaculate Yamahas, Ducatis, Kawasakis and GS

BMWs all adorning the frontage, surrounding Bertha. Clumping in to where we sit, several of them head over and a barrage of questions come our way, translated by friends. Eyes widen and soft whistles come in harmonies as they talk among themselves at the distances the two 'oldies' have covered. The level of noise increases even more as the group of 'growing old disgracefully' bikers order huge breakfasts with boisterous good humour.

They pull off shortly before we wave farewell and head in the opposite direction towards the Mexican border at La Mesilla 400 km away. An hour later Guatemala City appears but long before we ever see the signposts the stench of petro-pollution wafts over the horizon. It leaves the city under a hazy dome as buses and every other vehicle belches out black smoke. Reaching for our oxygen masks we plunge into smoke that should carry government health warnings saying, 'Do not enter'. It's a good job the advanced Ninja course on meditation and (the compulsory) breath-holding techniques exist as without them it would be impossible to make it through. Where are those Foreign Office warnings when you need one?

Holding our breath for at least three bus lengths every 100 yards, the road signs hold good, guiding us through, and the traffic is more orderly than the usual jungle survival of the fittest. The three-laned CA-1 leads us out the other side and up into the hills through intermittent roadworks, slowing our progress dramatically as the tarmac disappears to become hard-packed dirt, loose soil or gravel.

Road teams are everywhere flattening the soil, laying concrete or even, heaven forbid, spreading tarmac. Slithering and sliding, the back of the bike skews sideways as forward progress is made with revs and slipping clutch to keep the bike moving. Sharp twitches of the back remind us how the distance between our soft delicate bodies and the hard surface may be shortened at any second. Coming through several such sets of thoughts we emerge unscathed to start breathing again.

Continuing to climb, the temperature starts to drop after crossing 3,000 metres (10,000 feet) up through the clouds before hurling down the other side with Bertha's side-stand scraping loudly on left hand corners. The recent rise in side-stand scraping seems to have occurred after I promise Bernard a day off riding once we reach Mexico. Since then the same sound can often be heard, and felt – scrape. Scrape, scrape.

It feels like several years (or should that be days?) ago we puttered through Panama on a Friday. Saturday involved Costa Rica, Sunday saw a brief visit to Nicaragua, on Monday Honduras beckoned while on Tuesday El Salvador was battled with (well, one person was, while everyone else was lovely).

Wednesday Guatemala was galloped through and we're pretty sure that's where we are now. Who knows, in five seconds' time we'll probably be confused over which country we're in is as the scenery is turning into a blur – at least to me but Bernard seems no better. And this worries me, as after all, he's the one with working eyes.

Speed humps the size of mountains threaten to leave Bertha's oil spread all over the road amid shattered aluminium shiny bits of her engine. Cows munching, chickens crossing, a lamppost, or poster of a politician nailed to a wall, all seem to trigger their appearance and the traffic virtually stops when they do. Even the regulation 4x4s crawl slug-like over them on huge mountain-busting tyres. With the road conditions (or lack of them) and 30 speed humps per member of the population, it takes eight hours to roll into La Mesilla's main street. We trundle along, weaving slowly with families walking beside us.

Bernard tells me of a small girl who shyly waves to us from feet away and I waggle my hand back at her in greeting. A huge excited smile breaks out on her face as she tugs excitedly at her mother's arm. Then she is left to her excitement as we duck and dodge beneath the low-hanging T-shirts, jeans and buckets.

The (not so) Gran Hotel appears, complete with peeling paint and air conditioning which is turned off at 7.30pm as, according to the receptionist, 'it is cool now'; leaving us to slowly descend into liquid pools. After several attempts to explain how there will be nothing left of us without something passing as oxygen, an electric fan is delivered to our windowless room. The satisfying whoosh of the blades moves the hot air around as the fan oscillates in time to the fading power supply before the morning light appears. Rise and shine, go to work on a groan (at least from beside me). After decanting the contents of our room back to the bike, Bertha is retrieved from the barricade of vehicles erected around her as we slept.

Pulling out at 7.30am without breakfast the street is already packed with people. T-shirts are again hung in anticipation of our arrival so that Bertha's windshield can be cleaned as we pass underneath them, along with our helmets. Within minutes of arriving at the designated concrete hut signifying the border, several hefty thumps signal Guatemala is no more. Puttering on what we think is the road, several stall holders may well disagree with us as our tyres run over jumpers and posters held down with bricks, along with 'everything else on the ground one peso'.

Four kilometres later an oasis of calm appears at the Mexican La Frontera Norte (Northern Frontier), along with a zillion stamps as another section of forest is destroyed on the photocopier. This time it's in the shop on the road, over the hill and up the steps on the left and we are there for so long Bernard develops an even swarthier tan from the passing white light of the copier. One and a half hours later Mexico welcomes us into its bosom with a warning:

'Don't put the registration/insurance sticker in the windshield of the bike as it will get stolen, keep it safe for La Policia.'

Fair enough we think as Bertha's suspension settles under the weight of the newest Mexican paperwork, completed by copying the very helpful El Salvadorian (all in Spanish) versions. Thank you Mr Gestapo, we salute you with a sharp stick in the eye.

Eating cornflakes with cold leche (milk) and bananas, we lose 30% between the official and unofficial roadside exchange rates with the US Dollar. Meanwhile the staff engage in a spot of domestic cleaning nearby by using a high pressure hosepipe to wash the toilets. Don't you just love cultural differences?

'When Jesus changed water into wine he wasn't in the Holy Land'

(MEX) Towns come and go as La Trinitaria becomes Comitán and Amatenango is left behind for San Cristobal. Along the route the heat changes dramatically, feeling pleasant above 2,000 metres where, at 90 kph, everything feels cool. Meanwhile, lower down it feels hotter than the Atacama Desert in Chile, hot enough to fry an egg on Bernard's glasses.

If we thought Guatemala had a predilection for speed humps then all of our previous comments are retracted here and now. This retraction is necessary as in reality they were really tiny ripples, only thin pieces of rope lying on the road, mere child's play compared to Mexico. Here, you need spiked tyres, grappling hooks, or a winch to climb them. What makes them more surprising is that we're on the 190 – the Pan-American Highway, and it's littered with them. Numerous times we hit them at the speed limit. The really sneaky ones lurk in the darkness by the trees and several heartbeats after Bernard is still adjusting to that gloom we smash into them. 'Houston, we have lift off' becomes the new warning through my helmet – when he can see them (often too late) as they appear by anything and everything. On many other sections we resort to our advanced Ninja training of 'holding the breath' as huge white dust clouds envelop us, where road surfaces have been removed but not replaced.

Entering Tuxtla a taxi leads us to the Maria Eugenia, where the underground parking soon fills with curious hotel staff as the familiar 'La Moto' story circulates through the local grapevine and, not for the first time we wonder if admission could be charged. It would certainly offset some the costs of the journey.

During the evening, a very nice red wine appears on our evening bill at 750 pesos for the bottle. Hang on a minute. 750 pesos? That's 60 dollars; quick mental note along with converting it, that's about £40? Surely that's not right, is it? After all, it is not even a Chateau Walmart, or Tesco Merlot.

The manager is summoned.

Bernard: 'This cannot be correct.'

Manager: 'Yes it is sir, 750 pesos.'

Bernard: 'We have bought wine in countries where it is illegal and it was half this price!'

Manager: 'Yes Sir.'

Bernard: 'Is it illegal to sell wine in Mexico?'

Manager: 'No Sir.'

Bernard: 'Is it illegal to drink wine in Mexico?'

Manager: 'No Sir.'

Bernard: 'You know, when Jesus changed water into wine he wasn't in the Holy Land at all. I think he was in Mexico and he couldn't afford to buy it!'

The whole restaurant comes to a grinding halt as he insists his precise words are translated. Several loud laughs echo from the other patrons when it is faithfully translated. Jesus is discussed, at some length I might add, while I sit suppressing my own laughter. He marches forward now (Bernard not Jesus) in full flow and the manager capitulates under the twin onslaught of both him and God's favourite son until the price is more than halved.

Over the days my promise is kept to call a halt to our headlong rush as we take time to wander the city which turns out to be one of chemists, opticians, shoe shops and (since 1994) the base of the Zapatista Army of National Liberation (ZANL). At that time, in effect, they declared war on the Mexican government as the group believed ordinary people's interests were no longer represented by the government. Now there's a novel thought.

We discovered this quite by accident one evening walking along like the two inconspicuous people we are with Bernard wearing his Australian bought Crocodile Dundee hat complete with razor sharp croc teeth set into the rim, and me with my long white cane. All the traffic stopped to watch us. Slowly starting to think something was amiss, it became more apparent when we discovered that our Spangalese also seemed particularly unhelpful here as most of the population speak Mayan. Did I also forget to tell you they tend to kidnap Europeans for a bit of a hobby? Mmm, thought not. This hobby is aided and abetted, we are told, by the Mexican Army avoiding the area as if there'd been an outbreak of the bubonic plague. Mass desertions occur when they are posted to the region: Medical Officer lists suddenly fill up with soldiers ill with the 'Zapatista flu' or something suchlike. Meanwhile we merrily wander through the town learning Mayan so at least it will be possible to talk about the weather (me) and football (Bernard) with our, soon to be, kidnappers. Not.

Actually, the only kidnapping during our three-day stay in Tuxtla was of our dirty washing which was held in the underground bunker beneath the hotel by the Zapatista Auxiliary National Laundry Scheme. Shortly after our arrival most of the staff started wearing facemasks and, in our innocence, we assumed this was due to swine flu sweeping the country. Little did we know our dishevelled, well-lived-in clothes had caused it. So it was they had demanded an upfront payment for their return, at which point I immediately capitulated. After all, the thought of Bernard wearing the same socks for further days was beyond me after all this time on the road. His boots, meanwhile, have been banished onto the balcony for the full term of our incarceration where passing birds fall from the sky if they come too close to them.

Soon the promised stop is at an end with Bertha being mollycoddled with a change of all her vital fluids along with nuts being tightened down (again). Leaving Tuxtla, the following days are a blur of white lines and petrol stops as we bash through a land twice as long as the UK. Each day the heat builds until it feels as if you are riding into a furnace with its door wide open, and there is nothing on the road but emptiness stretching far away into the long distance. Soon we are crossing a gorgeous set of lakes at Pres Netzahualcoyotl. The road weaves between the small islands of red soil sticking out of the water as descriptions fill my helmet of the sun bouncing off the lakes, and pictures drawn for me of small islands being lit up from underneath as if with giant floodlights.

Ever north the 180D takes us, until our wheels turn westwards and place names readily spring off the tongue such as Coatzacoalcos and the easier El Colorado. Taking shelter under bridges or trees the umbrella is often unfurled to provide shade. During the ride ever onwards, bottles of water get so hot I drop a teabag in them and we have a nice brew at the next stop. Without these teabags the water tastes disgusting: hot and arid.

We label the D road system 'Disgustingly' expensive as the tolls mount. We stop wondering why the highways are empty as we hand over money at tollbooths virtually every hour, our only consolation being the saving on hotel costs. Sometimes other roads appear alongside with trucks and handcarts fighting for space as they crawl along while we disappear like a missile towards the horizon. In one day here we pay ten tolls amounting to nearly $60 and the nibble, nibble becomes a massively loud crunching noise.

We stop for the night at Córdoba and the hotel has an underground car park accessed by a concrete take-off ramp so steep Bernard suffers vertigo looking down it. In the morning he removes the panniers before even attempting to bring the bike up, so steep is the incline out onto the main road. The staff stop the traffic to allow Bertha to explode into the daylight and everybody laughs when Bernard points to the Pizza Hut sitting across the road, explaining how he thought this was to be his ultimate destination.

Dropping down into Mexico City with its pollution, smog and spaghetti-like system of roads eating Bertha's gear lever, it brings us to a halt. Tools are spread out as traffic thunders past while repairs are made before riding single roads that explode into 35 directions like fireworks going off. Sometimes we even get to the right road and it is a relief to eventually cross the 60 km of the city, to climb the hills on the other side.

Morelia appears and a halt is called due to being dog-tired, and we pass out early. It's here, at this point that we realise we are finished, mentally. We want to go home. No matter how many times I backhand the thought it will not go away; the final miles to the USA border cannot come quickly enough.

Jointly we understand there seems little point in being here anymore; we're experiencing nothing apart from white lines and petrol stations. Fantastic archaeological ruins from people long gone flit by just out of reach, down side roads we can no longer take. Our clocks now run on a faster time than we're used to; we no longer have the luxury of being calm and sitting still. Each day is now merely a succession of 600–700 km dashes before reaching places we cannot recall, or even name anymore. Arriving at these nameless places we drop into maze-like towns to drive through the middle of a market place.

The same thing happened in India and it took us a long time to realise a lot of countries are not big on bypasses, underpasses, overpasses, or any other form thereof. Many times steps were retraced only to end up in exactly the same place again and Mexico is like this. Suddenly, after hammering along at 100 kph we're surrounded by people pushing handcarts as stallholders shout in passing while pedestrians outstrip Bertha for speed.

The roads remain empty and it's not surprising when two good meals, several beers and many cold drinks set us back a quarter of what we shell out on tolls. All moaning about tolls stops, however, after a wrong turn takes us onto the 'Libre' (free) route 15 instead of the 15D. Grinding along this lunar road surface, jammed with trucks and buses, our speed drops from 110 to 60. After 12 km we find our way back to the 15D before gleefully handing over the toll with a wide grin on our faces after this short detour into metal carnage just waiting to happen.

By late afternoon Bernard has a piercing headache with the sun and brightness in his face all day and we have little water left and it tastes foul – even with teabags – so we detour to Acaponeta, paying another toll for the privilege of coming off when we have only just paid to come on. Finding a small hotel with a central courtyard for Bertha, we eat Mexicana (spicy meat, rice and salad) and laugh with heavily armed police outside the nearby police station. Rows of police bikes going back generations show the development of the mighty 150cc engine as they slowly fall into dust sitting neglected in the sun. Nobody knows what to do with them since they've been officially retired and thus they sit unhappily on flat tyres providing homes for the local wildlife.

Everyone gets excited at our crossing of the road as several police officers leap up from the wall to stop the traffic of three donkey riders and a local bus. We perform this extraordinary feat before following long lines of children and their guitar-carrying priest. Reaching the white church dominating the square, they all disappear inside as the tolling of bells indicates something, but we know not what as we end up alone on the pavement. The square grinds to a halt to watch us as people smile and nod at us wandering through small-town Mexico, the only 'Martians' on the street. Across the road teenagers tease each other, promenading under the watchful gaze of adults sitting under trees that provide shade from the heat and glare. The square is alive with people of all ages and as the sun starts to set the bandstand is occupied by noisy teenagers who exchange loud banter and listen to their music, amid gales of laughter. Hoping they'll be happy we turn away to head 'home' for the night.

Here the ceiling fan gently turns the air in our room as the night passes in sweat and humidity while listening to its gentle propeller-like progress. The air is unbelievably hot, the bottle of cold water on my bedside table is so hot I reach for another teabag ('Earl Grey, Madame?) before 5am comes and the sound of starting cars welcomes us to another new day. We rise to set off before the heat reaches magma proportions.

Stopping to pay tolls every five feet over the hours we get lost and it takes two cigarettes, unrolling the prayer mat, and finding the compass, before eventually the 15D reappears. We rename the 'D' to 'Deserted', which at about $20 per hundred miles is not surprising.

We consume water at every opportunity in the day-long 90–130 kph blast of white lines and three petrol stops, when two other bikes show up. New BMWs, they shine beside a very battered Bertha, covered with the accumulated gunge of her miles. The riders tell us excitedly how they've read about us in 'Motorcyclists of America (MOA)' and it just goes to show how you think you are invisible, anonymous, just a speck on a road while people are reading about you somewhere. It cheered us up as we'd left England to a deafening wall of disinterest from everybody apart from our friends. Wishing us luck, they record the web address on Bertha's side and pull off in the opposite direction.

Every few miles barriers are slung across the road with armed people looking for something to do and at one checkpoint we are asked where we have come from and Bernard happily replies 'Inglaterra' only to be met with 'Este

Mañana?' (This morning?) 'Where have we come from Cath?' he asks me. 'No idea,' is my reply as officers wait for our answer as cars form a queue behind us.

Taking out a recently acquired map Bernard's finger traces where he thinks we are and where we have come from and the name 'Acaponeta' springs to life. The police seem happy with it and wave us off while setting to dismantling other cars in the bright sunshine. The event leaves us feeling our world is a blur of sadness with our inability to even name the town we have just spent the night in.

Consoling ourselves with our new phrase 'Next Time', we use this now whenever realisation dawns of a world being lost within warp speed travel involving ride, petrol, eat, shower, sleep, before the whole thing is repeated day after day.

The wind blows from the west (left) in the ride further north and Bernard has to lean the bike crazily to compensate; it reminds us of the Nullarbor in Australia. Our helmets are battered by it and the noise thrums loudly while my neck is constantly under pressure from the force and eardrums hum loudly for hours after stopping.

All the romance (?) of what is being done is further added to by the aching which starts in your derrière (bum to mortals) before spreading to your back, up your spine, and into your shoulders. It is as if a dotted line becomes joined after 10–12 hours. 'Good afternoon, Mrs Headache,' let me introduce you to Mr Neckache. How are you, my name is Mrs Everything else is hurting as well. Move over please, this body is big enough for us all to exist.'

At this point, we're feeling every one of our 50+ years. Loud groans are heard at every stop with seized knees being flexed back into something like normal movement. Loud cracks threaten to cause an earthquake in the local area with people in seismology labs nervously watching their gauges. As the needle twitches across several pages of paper a colleague comes over to look, only to pronounce, 'It's OK, it's just those two English lunatics on the old bike.' Settling back down into their seats, they reach for the latest issue of 'Shake, rattle and roll'.

At points like this my ever faithful companion, my Amigo, pronounces, 'I'm getting too old for this.' In order to protect those of you reading this who suffer from a milder disposition, I have missed out several other 'colourful' words he actually uses.

Considering we left Tumbes in Peru only 3 weeks ago things have not gone too badly. Despite crossing several mountains and distant planets, arranging an air freight, doing some serious hill climbing in Colombia, we are still in one piece; not bad for two oldies. Actually make this three oldies as Bertha has to be counted as well, although she loudly resists that fact (is that the gearbox again?) with all she has done so far. In my own head she goes on to proclaim: 'Actually these roads are what I was built for you know. I was made to sit sedately doing 100–120 kph, all day and every day. I am a mileage eater. Never did I think you would take me through Pakistan and India (I nearly ate my air filters in them). As I bounced through Nepal, Peru, Ecuador or El Salvador I kept reminding myself that you were both just daft. I was made to destroy German autobahns Mein Fuhrer, to conquer British motorways - when they are not closed for roadworks.'

So she mutters along, reminding us she is as stable as a rock only much, much prettier and even sounding better than ever as it has taken 50,000 miles to run her in properly, as the speedometer now shows. Road crews give her the V sign, which she now understands to be for 'Victory' and she rears up proudly, carrying us to Navahoa where a hotel costs 60% less than we paid in India, although it is ten times better. Pulling into the car park, we feel beaten up and tired after covering 753 km in 40 degree heat, drinking eight litres of water and four bottles of juice. If you could listen carefully not even a slosh can be heard from either of us as everything has been sweated out. The only sound heard is a slight squelching but Bernard confirms it's just coming from his boots and he promises to leave them outside the door of our room. Reaching for the lobby's chilled drinks machine, we top up before collapsing onto our beds.

The impact of America is clearly visible all around now with wide streets littered with billboards advertising this and that 'must have' commodity and American cars fill the roads as we pass 'glitzy' hotels so unlike small-town Mexico. Tomorrow we'll reach the American border and it feels very strange to know it's almost finished. 'Finished.' It's a word that fills us with mixed emotions of joy, happiness, sadness, relief among others. The more we think about it now that it's actually here, the more the feeling settles into the overarching feeling of sadness. Our mood has swung so drastically between wanting it to be over that now it's here we feel guilty at those earlier thoughts.

Tiredness greets us the next morning and a quietness as the 3,000 or so kilometres of the last five days suddenly overwhelms us. A psychological barrier seems to have descended on our normally happy disposition with each new kilometre seeming to take forever and there are 600 'forevers' to cross the border to the USA 'finish line'. Our mood swings around, out of control, with little stability in what we are feeling. It seems to change from kilometre to kilometre, from stop to stop.

Bottles of water are consumed every hour with the next ten minutes spent resisting the urge to urinate as we know the feeling will soon pass as we become dried-out husks within an hour; signalling another drinks stop. Bernard smokes more cigarettes than normal as he wrestles with his feelings while I grapple with my own. The heat is as oppressive as our mood, although both have to be fought through. In this mental helter-skelter, a new expression comes into play at every stop where Bernard now asks:

'Are you ready?'

In as broad a Lancashire accent as I can muster, I respond:

'I was born ready!'

Laughing, we pull off and the world starts to feel just that little bit better.

With the final miles mounting, talk turns to our return to work, of how the trip has wrought changes in us beyond even our own understanding at times. Things have changed us to such an extent it is possible people will be taken aback at our directness and to pass the miles, we construct scenarios to cheer ourselves up, to keep us talking. It really does not bode well for our future and we begin to wonder how much social security pays in England these days?

The border crossing at Nogales appears and with it comes the rain as Bertha is stamped out of Mexico and pesos are exchanged for the dollar. Slowly pulling towards the USA line bristling with surveillance equipment, there is so much of it on show our entire biological and physiological profile has probably already been recorded. The rain falls. And oh boy, does it fall. The last time it rained this heavy Noah did a good line in carpentry as we wonder about the sky blue boat sitting on the road to Delhi.

Within seconds our laughter starts, real, genuine, heart-warming sounds as the water rushes past our feet while birds are knocked out of the sky. They say the Americans do everything bigger and we sit wondering if this also includes the rain? As our boots fill up and Bernard unfurls the large umbrella to cover us from the descending waterfall car drivers gape as we inch forward three millimetres at a time. A warm voice comments from beside us:

'You two guys must be Brits. Only the Brits would carry an umbrella on a motorbike.'

The comment leaves us doubled over and he looks at us completely bemused. Like two escapees from some asylum down the road, the sound feels like an accumulation of all the excitement, stress, worry and fear we have experienced.

Meanwhile, other car drivers use their mobile phones and cameras to photograph the two lunatics as the water rises past Bernard's feet. People continue to smile at and photograph us, as we inch forward to be met by smiling border officials who ask:

'We were just wondering what it sounds like for an English person to speak Spanish?'

'No chance lads,' Bernard answers. 'By the way, was it the umbrella that gave away we're Brits?'

They laugh and ask where we have been (it takes a long time to explain) and where we are going (a very short time) before Bernard declares the only dangerous thing with him is me with my white stick; the twin cause of all his troubles.

'I can pull over there officer and you can pull the whole thing apart but I tell you even the Colombians didn't find anything, and boy did they try. You are more than welcome to give it a go if you want!'

'Naw,' they respond waving us through, 'Welcome to America!'

Twenty minutes later a very nice 90 day visa waiver (because we're British) sits in our passports after we swap fingerprints and a few black-faced photographs with our newfound 30th country friends.

Outside we stand listening to the rain as Bernard puffs away on a cigarette six inches away from a large 'No Smoking' admonishment while across the road a big arrow says 'USA this way'.

Standing, soaked and shivering with the cold, it is hard to realise when you have actually done something that took so long to plan and was such a struggle to do. When a dream is finally realised, as it has been for Bernard throughout his whole life, it is hard to process what the achievement means. The border of America has always been our official Richter scale, a doorway to pass through before being able to say 'Yes, we have done it'.

Waiting for the earthquake of our own recognition to strike, all we experience is the falling rain as noisy splashes fill the air while we stand silently contemplating what it all means.

Lost in my own thoughts arms encircle me to bring me out of my own reverie. A familiar voice whispers in my ear, 'Well done, you are now officially the first blind person to ever circle the world on a motorbike.' I recognise the arms, feeling their gentleness.

They have been with me all along, guiding me through mountains, through areas of the world people told us we should not have been in, nor should even have attempted to go. For me, however, they have been responsible for something far more fundamental, far more important than taking a motorcycle around the globe.

They have repaired the shattered world of my long years alone.

'If you dare to dream,' he tells me quietly, echoing what he'd said so long ago. My arms encircle him as the rain continues to fall.

Merging into one another we stand motionless, each processing the fact that now, truly, we have crossed the world.

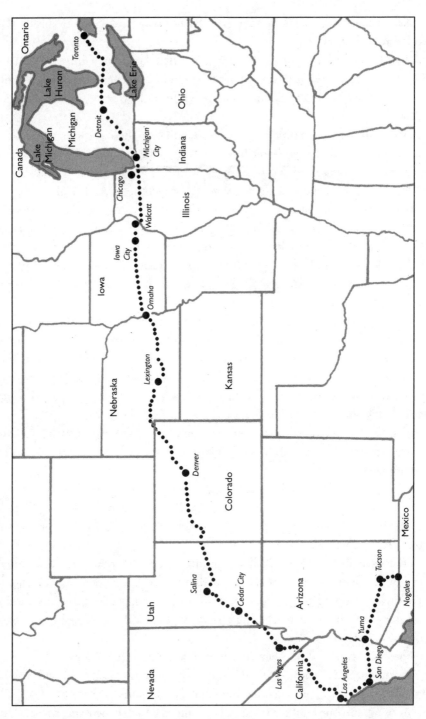

Map of the route through North America. 19 June - 1 July

NORTH

AMERICA

THE UNITED STATES AND LITTLE DID WE KNOW, CANADA

'How far is it?'

(USA) A short ride later I stand under hot showers in a motel room sweeping the coldness from my bones as water drips from bike suits in streams across the floor. As it gathers like little ponds it starts to dawn on me how soon I will be home. Home? It no longer feels the same. It is somewhere else. Somewhere other than I am used to but it's where I want to be, and do not want to be, both at the same time. A confusing kaleidoscope of emotions and images wash through both of us as a short ride to Los Angeles, just 800 km up the road, indicates The End. It feels disconcerting, strange and unreal. As these feelings flit through my mind one factor stands out clearly.

Over recent days my thoughts have increasingly turned to Biscuit, my guide dog, as phone calls wing across the Atlantic to set in motion an event which leaves me nervous. My worry involves meeting her again after so long. With these thoughts come the doubts over how she'll react. Will she remember me? Or will she have become so attached to the home and people she's known for the last year that I am, somehow, 'unwelcome' in a vaguely doggie sort of way? These thoughts leave me unsettled and uncomfortable but there is little else I can do but put them aside; only time will tell.

Over the following days we find that it's easier to arrange motorcycle insurance anywhere else apart from within the most developed country in the world. To be fair, it's easy if you're a Mexican citizen doing a bit of cross-border nipping in a pickup truck, even if the vehicle would be condemned anywhere else. Meanwhile, for a UK (taxed and tested) motorcycle, it proves something akin to finding a solution to the worldwide financial meltdown. The subsequent days pass trawling through American motor regulations in the hunt for an elusive piece of paper which will forestall being hauled off the bike by a mirror-sunglasses-wearing, gun-toting, deeply tanned Highway Patrol officer. We roleplay:

'Insurance, Officer? Do we really need it? Is there some way I can pay you for it here and now?' (nudge, nudge, wink, wink).

We discuss at great length whether American law enforcement officers supplement their income in the same way as their Costa Rican brothers. Do they forward plan, like the Turkish police, for their retirement funds? It does not take us long to discount such an approach. More than likely it would end up with a 'Go directly to Gaol' card from a Monopoly game as we remind ourselves that this is a different world. It is a place operating under familiar, understandable rules generally encompassed in the commandment, 'Thou shalt have vehicle insurance otherwise thou will be at the behest of men in uniforms with big guns.' It takes three days for the matter to be resolved by paying – for one month's insurance – what it would cost an American for a year. It leaves us longing for countries where insurance is considered an optional extra; after all, they seem to get along fine without it.

We come to understand why America is the obesity capital of the world as overflowing planet-sized plates are delivered to our table before we stumble on the 'Over 55's meal' which is much more manageable than even the children's menu. People ask, 'Do you want to Super-size it?' as Bernard responds, 'Good God no, could you possibly downsize it please?' They stand laughing at our bewilderment with the dustbin lid portions as he stares at his first Coca Cola with the comment: 'Good God man that's not a drink, it's a swimming pool.'

Struggling through even the smallest, people waddle back to the dispensers to top up the small buckets they call cups, complete with ten straws. Wandering into a petrol station looking for maps Bernard tells me that, yes, it is true, everything is bigger in America. In nothing like a hushed tone, descriptions flow from him concerning extra large condoms in every colour and size imaginable, apart from small and extra-small he points out. My admonishment of the information he is gleefully, and loudly, imparting leaves him with his innocent hurt little boy voice. After all, he explains, he is merely describing things for a poor blind person.

'America truly is the land of the car, something for the drive home, Sir?' We leave the garage quickly with the heat rising in my face.

Sinking into the morass of trying to arrange shipping Bertha back to London involves ten hours of phone calls complete with emails winging here, there and everywhere. Both lines of investigation reveal the same outcome: the attack on the World Trade Center eight years earlier (2001) has left this country with a serious aversion to anything remotely called 'air shipping'. Having already freighted from such places as Kathmandu our assumption that the land of the free and the brave would not present a particular problem for the shipping of an English bike home turns out to be so wrong. Spectacularly so.

One company wants to put Bertha in a truck and drive her to New York (3,000 or so miles) to overcome what they claim is the inability of the Los Angeles customs officers to stay awake for anything longer than five minutes. The spluttering that greeted the $2,500 price tag convinced them it was not exactly what our now diminished wallets had in mind. Through several conversations with different air freight companies we also find out that the 'Not needed' carnet (according to US Customs at the border and everybody else) is indeed necessary. That is, they tell us, if you want to export a foreign vehicle by air from the USA.

Over the days Vietnam War veterans and salesmen clutching laptops approach us, people from all over the USA who stand shaking their heads (and our hands) at our shipping dilemma. At the same time they proclaim it to be 'amazing' and 'unbelievable' what we have done, on our own 'out there alone' as they put it. Many cannot believe such problems exist in our getting the bike home, as our enforced stay at the motel is now demonstrating to everybody. The land of the free turns out to be, by far, the worst country regarding bureaucracy in terms of getting simple things done.

In Istanbul, Kathmandu, Kuala Lumpur, Sydney and Colombia everything was completed inside three days and often it took only a single day. Here three days pass solving a 'simple' thing like insurance and it seems a whole week will pass before Bertha can be loaded onto a plane back to the UK. Killing time and frustration, lots of 'quarters' are spent at a local car wash scrubbing and degreasing Bertha until she looks pristine. Not since she was given a good going over by four Bangladeshi lads in Kuala Lumpur has she looked so good. Four days eventually pass before we leave on our now shiny clean motorcycle containing her new insurance certificate.

While sitting still, we've made arrangements with a freight shipper in Los Angeles who expects us in two days' time. The 800 km cannot pass soon enough as mentally we are finished, truly finished. With the last few days, grinding to get through and seemingly never ending, we cannot wait for it to end. Strange mixtures of feelings wash over us getting back on the bike and even this is an effort as it's not something we want to do anymore. We do, but we don't.

Irreconcilable emotions drag our psychology around the mental space our heads have become, as the final leg stretches before us. One more barrier, one more effort has to be overcome and it sits in the shape of the Arizona Desert. Consoling ourselves with the fact we have already ridden through India, Pakistan and the heat of Australia, surely nothing can be hotter than the Atacama Desert in Chile could it? Then we found a completely new planetary experience of heat.

Imagine turning on your hair dryer to maximum heat while burning the skin off your face, and every other part of your body. Then turn the heat blast up to 70 mph. Crank up the thought even further to standing behind a 747 jet engine taking off. In that jetstream you stand idly smearing factor-50 sun cream on any exposed delicate part. Now double whatever you are thinking and only then will you have something approaching Arizona on a motorcycle.

Making the Atacama Desert in Chile look like the North Pole, the temperature gauge on the dashboard gives up its unequal struggle with the air at 50 degrees. Running out of puff it surrenders. No more. Thank you very much. The End. Meanwhile, the needle sits straining against the stop with not a flicker of downwards movement. All the time you have no perception of sweat, no sensation of little rivulets marching downwards due to gravity. Even if it does break into the open it is instantly gone. Dangerously so.

Every opportunity is used to take fluids and it doesn't matter if it's only 30 minutes later when another small petrol station, café or bucket of liquid appears. We stop. At one place the staff cannot believe we're riding at midday: it seems bikers always travel at night. During the day they avail themselves of the 'specials', discounted rates on motel billboards between 5am and 5pm. So it is that people sleep during the day and travel at night to escape the heat.

'We're British, we ride in all weathers,' Bernard laughs – when he has enough saliva to get the words out as the staff shake their heads, responding, 'Man, you gotta be careful out there. People don't motorcycle during the day!'

'We're fine thanks, could we have 345 bottles of cold water please.'

Bertha cools down under whatever shade can be found as hands burns on any metal part touched; even the seat is ferociously hot when first climbing back on. Within 15 minutes of moving, thirst reappears and the new water rapidly becomes too hot to drink as it gently simmers in the sun.

Every break leaves Bernard reaching for the sun cream, insisting on applying it to any part of exposed flesh and I can feel the sun's power against my body; the term ferocious does not come close. It's so far beyond ferocious as to be completely on another scale. Another 350 miles and we've had enough with heads bursting as little people inside my skull stab their way out with little sharp axes. The feelings come in nauseous waves, insistent and unremitting. Gratefully pulling into a motel, stumbling off the bike dizzily, people gather saying 'My God, you've ridden through the day?' 'Yep,' comes croaking out of Bernard's throat before two bottles of cold water lubricate him enough to talk properly. Standing in the shade, our body temperatures cool as further drinks are downed while hiding from the sun.

Later on, over the top of plates stacked high with food, we toast our crossing of the hottest place on earth ever encountered. The experience leaves us noting that it would have left even Lucifer reaching for his shades, while turning the thermostat down several notches. A full stomach later, a waiting bed envelopes us in its marshmallow softness as the air conditioner hums its gentle lullaby.

Drifting off to sleep, conversation falls away slowly from our feelings of how tomorrow will be the last day Bertha is to be ridden on foreign soil.

Chomping our way through the continental breakfast in an empty café the next morning it's obvious that people deserted the hotel before the sun came up. It was something to ponder, rising in the dead of night to take advantage of the coolness, but we are not good at early starts. The only time the option was chosen was to escape Indian towns before the level of chaos reached the 'end of the world' Armageddon-like proportions which each day seemed to bring.

Climbing on the bike we settle into the normal routine of petrol stops and liquid intake before pulling off the highway at Pine Springs where whitewashed and painted picket fences greet us. War memorials and people lazily ambling along under the brightness all combine into a quietness, a 'homeliness' reminding us of picture postcard images of America, right down to empty roads and 'have a nice day' responses. The air settles into stillness with the only sound being the occasional vehicle as Bertha is filled with her final tank of 'gas'.

'Where yawl from?' comes from behind the counter in a rich American accent.

'The UK,' the two bookends we have become answer.

'My son went to the UK for 18 months, couldn't understand a word he said when he came back,' the female attendant replies laughing. 'His father used to tell him how funny it sounded when he spoke.'

'Do we sound OK?' Bernard asks with a hint of humour in his voice.

'Yawl sound like the Brits on the TV, so it's OK.'

People listen as we talk of America, Britain, and our journey home. Cooling down under the air conditioning unit, I feel sure there must be steam coming from the two of us as we hog the cold downdraft. 'Yawl have a nice day,' they chorus in unison as we pay for more bottles of water and head back out onto the highway.

The hours pass amid signs flashing past denoting lines drawn on a map long ago where American Indian tribes could now live after centuries of wandering freely; a few square miles in small geographic squares. Nowadays huge juggernauts roll past the boulder-strewn mountains where people once wandered freely while road signs wave in the direction of San Diego. Other signs proudly proclaim altitudes of 4,000 feet, leaving us to reminisce about 15,000 and a small Peruvian girl called Samikai. Small things. Memories of people and places stream through us more now as The End beckons us forward.

Five hours later sees us ploughing through eight lanes of traffic as Los Angeles appears. Street signs bearing famous names flash past as we look for John Wayne Airport while people stream past, on the left, the right, everything moving far quicker than we are used to. Our mental world is unsettled with the speed but the flow makes headway towards our meeting with the agent Rene, with whom we had talked while in Nogales looking for a way home. Reaching his office and climbing off the bike, silence falls as we realise this is it.

The End.

'I can't believe we've made it,' Bernard sighs as he reaches for a cigarette.

'Thanks to you,' I reply quietly, 'Thanks to you.'

'I never thought I'd be able to do it,' he goes on, 'what with the roads, hassles, borders, language problems, breakdowns and everything else. It seems weird to know we've done it.' He stands silent apart from the inhale of nicotine. I squeeze his arm gently before we head for the final round of paperwork, shipping Bertha home.

Rene sits behind his desk and arrangements are made to come back a few hours later to start the paperwork for the way home. The hotel he suggests is within walking distance and once we shower and grab a quick bite to eat Bertha is unloaded. Slipping into our well tried and tested procedure, cameras, laptop and various other bits and pieces are packed into the two pieces of hand luggage to be used for the trip. Meanwhile our heads are chanting 'Home soon'.

Two hours later Rene comes out of his office and is clearly stunned by the size of Bertha and after travelling for two days to get here, he tells us:

'I can send the bike, but nothing else.'

'Yeah, I know, we'll sort out our own tickets for the flight.' Bernard sounds puzzled.

'No, you don't understand; no personal possessions can go with the bike,' he goes on.

We stand in silence as the next question formulates, slowly:

'What do you mean personal possessions?'

'Everything but the bike,' Rene answers.

'You mean the panniers and back box?'

'Can't go with the bike unless they are empty.'

'You're joking!'

'No, since 9-11. Customs will not clear all this stuff to fly in cargo.'

'Clothes?' Bernard asks

'With you,' Rene responds.

'Bike helmets?'

'With you.'

'Tools?'

'With you.'

'Bloody hell.'

'It's also far bigger than I thought,' Rene measures from floor to top of windshield. 'The price will have to alter.'

Bernard cuts in:

'The measurements I gave you are the precise shipping measurements.'

'Can't be done,' our (nearly) newfound friend wisely pronounces.

'It's been done several times over the last year,' Bernard goes on. 'The windshield comes off, the front wheel is dropped, the back box comes off and is packed left side and strapped onto the foot peg. I've done this several times.'

'Can't be done at those measurements.'

Rene dismisses the measurements while measuring back to front, not really listening to Bernard.

'I've just told you it has been done, several times. I know the measurements are correct. It flew from Turkey to Pakistan, from Nepal to Thailand, from Malaysia to Australia, from Australia to Chile, from Colombia to Panama. But anyway, that's not the point right now, how do we get our gear home?'

'Excess luggage,' Rene suggests. 'It cannot go as cargo even as a separate shipment. If it's personal possessions they have to fly with you.'

By now the conversation is telling us that Rene is not interested in providing solutions and/or he seems to have completely gone off the idea of shipping the bike anyway.

'New York?' Bernard queries.

'Same as here, it's nationwide,' shatters this idea despite the 'we'll put the bike in a truck and move her to New York,' shipper we spoke to in Nogales. As the enormity of the information settles in, Bernard's vision of his pipe and slippers, Saturday night premier league football, warm beer, and cold rain, all start to fade away in the bright sunlight. The reunion with Biscuit my guide dog is growing ever fainter as we stand silently with Bernard's brain furiously searching for an answer.

'We need some time to think about this Rene.' Bernard lights another cigarette as Rene disappears back into this office leaving us to ponder. The sun beats down as options are worked through.

Perhaps several huge suitcases could be bought before paying the excess luggage charge but the likely weight would make it prohibitively expensive. Perhaps everything could be ditched in order to empty the bike completely? Not an option really; too many memories, too many treasured possessions have become personal to both of us. Back to Mexico and fly from Mexico City perhaps? On towards Canada?

Bernard thinks Canada would be considerably easier (roads, language and costs) and importantly it suits his mentality; it will be going forward and not backwards. He knows about an option from Toronto, telling me it will be possible to fly overnight whereas it seems it will take nearly two weeks to get Bertha home from here. Several cigarettes later it's 4.30pm and our options have all disappeared, until only one viable option remains. Drive to Toronto.

'How far is it?' I ask dreading the answer.

'About 2,500 to 3,000 miles,' he quietly states, checking maps.

'God,' I mumble. 'How long do you think to it will take us to get there?'

Bernard ponders.

'On these roads? We could do it in five to seven days, maybe five if we do over 500 miles each day. Ten or twelve hour days at an average of 50 taking into account stops, petrol, food and no breakdowns.'

Heading back into the office, Rene is informed of our surrender to the post 9-11 paranoia that has paralysed common sense, how we are heading for Toronto. The news leaves him a little fazed as we share our rough calculations of seven additional days of food, petrol and accommodation; of how it will still be cheaper than shipping from Los Angeles. At this point whatever vague interest he'd shown in shipping the bike disappears as he turns to his computer wishing us 'good luck'.

Back at the hotel we sit stunned as our mood burrows southwards looking for the end to the psychological freefall we both now feel.

Bernard — I walk up and down the stairs carrying everything back down to the bike, repacking into long familiar places. It may sound strange to people reading this as you think, 'Wow, riding across America'. Perhaps you're correct but the clock is beating us into submission and it will mean petrol stations, white lines and hotels; nothing more. It's true that many people get a real kick out of doing 500 mile or even 1,000 mile days, the 'mileage junkies' I call them. They get a buzz out of doing high mileage for the sake of mileage itself. To me it's not what motorcycling is about. I'm not criticising this type of riding, I'm truly not, but it's not for me unless I have to do it.

To us countries are about people and feeling the daily life around you. If all you do is fly past it all there seems little point as the days, to us, are about The Road, The People, and The Differences. Thus one out of three does not work for me as a road is just a road. Without those other factors important things are missing and there's no point going on.

To stand any chance of getting home on time to return to work the whole country must be crossed inside of seven days. Importantly it has to happen with no hitches, breakdowns or problems and it does not bode well considering some of the things that have gone wrong so far.

'America is sneaking up on me'

In the morning Bernard tries to cheer me up with a constant battery of humour but it doesn't work even though I know he's trying to make the best of it, not wanting to drive another 2,500–3,000 miles either. We're still muttering between ourselves over the fact that the 'personal' possessions aspect had not even been considered and, to us, it smacks of the typical over-reactive response to a specific problem. It makes no sense at all when considering Colombia, where they simply pulled everything apart searching every nook and cranny of the bike before pronouncing it 'fit to fly'. At airports, customs posts, borders, and lines all over the world some degree of investigation of possessions has generally occurred. In America they just said no. Perhaps we're missing something that a good search of our goods, or thoughts, would reveal about the logic of it. Then again, perhaps it's just depression settling in heavily upon us.

Leaving Los Angeles, the roads stretch before us like coiled loops of spaghetti in daunting arrays of eight-lane traffic whizzing past on both sides as the long journey north begins. Huge semis thunder past as we gently work our way through the myriad roads, underpasses, overpasses, on-ramps and off-ramps. It takes 45 minutes before the light of day appears and the I-91 quickly comes and goes. It transforms into the I-605 before joining the eastbound I-210, which merges into the northbound I-15. Our mood lifts and feelings improve as the day passes with remembered lines of songs coming through my helmet from him in front, snatching me away from my melancholy thoughts.

'Always look on the bright side of life,' comes through with much gusto, complete with out of tune whistling to accompany numerous other snippets of the famous *Life of Brian* film. Before I can stop laughing it changes to Billy Ocean's 'When the going gets tough', complete with hummed saxophone solos and deep chesty rumblings, exaggerated words conveying themselves through the speakers to my eardrums. I cannot help but feel better as the miles mount and the talk turns to how many people would willingly change places with our 'disaster' of having to ride across America at the drop of a hat. Then off he goes again with his wildly exaggerated voices and snippets of songs all demonstrating every shade of 'we can do this'. The world feels that little bit brighter as the miles mount up.

The 25,000 square-mile Mojave Desert appears in front of us and even though it contains the lowest and hottest place in North America, Death Valley, it doesn't feel as hot as Arizona. No doubt, it's because it's several weeks until the over 50 degree temperatures are expected. The one thing we do know is that it's highly unlikely our umbrella will be required as the gentle pitter-patter of rain rarely ever occurs. Descriptions flow through my helmet of the landscape such as 'burnt', 'desolate' and every shade of beige colour imaginable with signs for the Mojave National Preserve passing us by on our quest for mileage in our new 'mileage junkie' mentality.

The Mojave River tracks us on our right and, suddenly, out in the middle of this burnt landscape we're in Las Vegas and Bertha heads down Dean Martin and Frank Sinatra drive. From beige and gold to green in an instant, as if some invisible line has been drawn across the road. Hotels and casinos flank us as the road cuts straight through the middle of the city showing Caesar's Palace with its Romanesque façade as I tell Bernard of the Formula 1 racetrack meandering its way around the grounds. Trundling through the gaudy town of glitz and tinsel, we lament the fact there is not even the time for our jaws to drop at the OTT buildings.

While people come from around the world to sample the delights of the city, the razzmatazz, the shows, we power through as quickly as possible; it's not a destination for us. It's just in our way and has to be left behind. Pulling over to stop, with 'Vegas' long gone in our wing mirrors, a man leans out of a car saying: 'I thought it was a joke!' pointing to the logo on the panniers declaring 'A Blind Woman, Two Wheels and 25,000 Miles'. 'Then I saw the two of you.'

He asks where we're from and where we're heading, whistling loudly at the answers before asking 'Had any mechanicals?' Reeling off the things that have gone wrong across the months, from starters to alternators, from exhausts to piston rings he notes, 'Nothing serious then,' he concludes, laughing. We have to agree. If you keep everything in perspective then it's true as they've all been fixable, although tedious in the time lost. The man smiles and records the web address on the side of the bike as we stand sipping our ice-cold drinks under the blue canopy of the sky. 'I'll check you two out when I get home for sure,' he says, shaking our hands before setting off back onto the highway.

Sitting in the rest area, Bernard looks back to where Bertha draws crowds of people, all snapping away with their cameras. They clamber off coaches, out of cars, and everything in between to stretch their legs before gravitating towards the bike where they pour over the details etched into her. Hunting shade to settle in, the coolness feels relieving as people stand talking around the bike 60 feet away.

Hours later another petrol station brings a Sikh attendant who notes the India and Pakistan stickers on Bertha and he comes over, pleased we know of Amritsar and the Sikh religion. He goes on to tell us of his six months in the UK before he was driven out by the cold and rain before finding his way here, twelve miles outside Cedar City in Utah, where he's the only Sikh in town.

Several hundred yards down the road Bertha makes horrible noises from below us and our hearts plummet under the weight of the sound. It feels serious, a potential hammer blow to our schedule with all the heavy mechanical grinding pouring into our ears, like several metal parts smashing around in a kitchen blender. The sun beats down as Bernard investigates by placing a screwdriver to his ear, then to engine casings in order to amplify the sound. I too listen, perched on one knee in the dust to hear the whirling, grinding mechanical noises. It sounds like mayhem is about to occur. When the clutch is pulled in it stops and Bertha chugs, rocking happily, but all this tells us is that it's either clutch or gearbox. We decide to head for Cedar City where we'll stay the night and investigate.

Bernard listens to the deep metallic rumbling, which penetrates everything else as we set off. Puzzlingly, it ceases when the engine is accelerating and by the time a hotel appears, everything sounds normal, leaving us both confused and worried at the same time. Keeping our fingers crossed it's some mysterious gremlin which has worked its way through, we're not hopeful. After all, usually such sounds indicate some terminal cataclysmic outcome in terms of whirling mechanical bits.

The next morning comes and the starter is pressed to reveal Bertha having none of the mechanical indigestion indicated the day before. Even more puzzled we keep our fingers crossed and go on. The drizzle descends from the blanket of greyness above us as temperatures fall and it's not what we're used to anymore. Black clouds threaten a torrential downpour in the dry season of Utah but it never materialises.

We ride through breathtaking scenery as canyon after canyon appears with red rock ravines bearing the scars of the stone-cutting machines that forged a path through the landscape. Beautiful rock formations appear left and right and Bertha moves in response to my swivel-headed rider who seeks to find new descriptions for each outcrop. Like 'collapsed packs of playing cards' is my favourite description of one mountain showing huge slabs of rock standing and tilting crazily in the nothingness of the tinder landscape. Massive rock outcrops with folded and pleated cloth-like shapes, tops of Lego block formations complete with missing pieces where collapses have occurred down onto the fold below – descriptions of ever-increasing ingenuity drawing pictures through the words that enter into my mind. Small canyons along the route merge into huge areas with magical names such as 'Devils Canyon' stretching far off into the distance.

The sky clears and waterproofs are peeled off as temperatures rise on perfect roads that we ride at 70 mph. Our mood is elevated as emotional and psychological barriers are breached, coming back from where refuge was taken in the early miles since leaving Los Angeles. Back in 'the zone' even Bertha joins in by not grumbling or rumbling as with the earlier sounds of chaos. Consigning it to our mental list of 'another puzzle for another day', fingers are crossed that the Gods of Motorcycling continue to smile on us. Long may they continue to do so. Please make it so now that we're nearly there.

Other motorcycles start to appear with Honda Gold Wings and Harley-Davidsons being the bikes of choice. Bernard can see them miles before they become distinct as the layers of chrome shine from the reflected sun. First glinting in the distance, they then blast past in the opposite direction with waves and flashing headlights. When they travel in the same direction, passengers take pictures of the two Brits trying to get home as we wave back, smiling in their direction. With their picture taken, a twist of the throttle leaves us to meander onwards.

Petrol stops are now hurried affairs as there is always a need to be further ahead than we actually are. Stopping in Utah an attendant tells us that Colorado is 40 miles away but 'there is nothing there but jack-rabbits', as everybody laughs. New Yorkers had said there was nothing in Arizona but rattlesnakes and lizards and it is easy to recall how each state in Australia said the same about their neighbours. Further afield Turkey was 'dangerous' (according to the Greeks), Pakistan was even more so (according to the Turkish). By the time Pakistan was reached, India was considered the next hotbed of lawlessness. And so it goes on around the world as people warn about the next country or make jokes about their neighbours.

Soon Utah is a memory as Colorado leaves us entranced with its beauty. It finds Bernard, unusually, struggling for words as he tries to describe collapsed mountains and winding gorges with their vertical walls either side of us as the Colorado River rushes past on our right throughout the day. My meandering thoughts around the images are violently interrupted by a huge, sudden Bertha wobble and a piercing yelp from Bernard which leaves me deafened as an Exocet missile has hit him in the face at 80 mph. To the sound of screeching tyres, which nearly leave me sitting on his shoulders we pull over. Leaping off the bike to hop around beside me, he retrieves a long barb from his face complete with nether region still attached. Meanwhile the rest of the critter is probably lying on the road several miles back groaning: 'I can't feel my legs, where's my legs?'

Bernard continues to hop from foot to foot as he seeks to convince me that 'yes, it truly does hurt' as he rips off his helmet to survey the full extent of the damage. 'Imagine how the poor insect feels,' I console him in my feminine way before adding 'Worse than you no doubt.' Less than mollified he comments, 'That'll teach the bugger to run into an English head,' while peering in the mirror to describe how his face is swelling up as he looks at it. 'You'll be fine, you still look good to me, have a cigarette and let's get going.' Sympathy? No, not really.

'I'm deformed!' he grumbles. 'I look like the elephant man and it's hardly comforting that a blind woman tells me I look fine, is it?' After two cigarettes he miraculously feels better. While continuing to insist his head is 'huge and floppy', only fitting inside his helmet with difficulty, we set off as he wonders where the local hospital is, just in case he comes down with some dreaded man version of bug lurgy.

While always knowing America was big, it seems endless as signs start to appear for state capitals involving distances bigger than many of the countries we've passed through. Throughout, however, the weather stays glorious and without those blast furnace waves sitting in the wind waiting to mug all the hydration out of you. Day two of the 'race across the landscape' sees 887 km of the map covered in 10 hours inclusive of stops. Over two days 1,600 km have disappeared behind us.

'Five hundred miles' becomes our signature tune with snatches of the Proclaimer's song occurring as every day a mental and physical shift occurs; aches and pains fade away as the mileage increases. It's like going through a barrier; one minute it hurts and then it does not. People at gas stations often ask where we've come from before we name some distant town and they respond with 'God it's hard enough to drive a car for 500 miles, never mind a bike.' A second person joins in with 'Never driven 500 miles in a day in my entire life!'

Colorado becomes the land of snatches of John Denver songs wafting through my earpieces. 'Rocky Mountain High' changes to 'Grandma's Feather Bed' which merges into 'Fly Away' in his optimistic voice as the landscape drifts past with an urgency even Bertha feels; she smothers all sound of grumbling for another time and another place.

Tilting and gliding our way through the mountains, the Colorado River washes past in its muddy brown way down the hills. Signs for Aspen soon appear but there is no snow on the slopes although it's cold and I'm shivering. Coasting to a halt at an out of season resort at Copper Creek Bernard baulks at the $150 plus taxes (of course) for the night. Moving onto Frisco he jokes with the next Moldavian receptionist how $100 is expensive for a snowless skiing hotel. 'If we had snow it would cost $190' she jokes back in all seriousness. Finding the room has two single beds instead of the regulation huge double, the reception comes to a stop on our return when Bernard points out: 'We actually do like each other so why would we want two single beds? When we hate each other, we'll have two beds or a divorce. For now one will be enough!' Among much laughter, they change the room.

Standing outside unpacking Bertha a family talk to us, asking our thoughts about George Bush. Bernard, the diplomat, thinks that since he does not know the man he cannot really comment. They grudgingly agree before saying they have had enough of 'Eight years of his bullshit'. Bernard amuses them by recounting the question every Pakistani seemed to ask when crossing their country:

'What are your thoughts of George Bush?'

'He's half a brain and his dad had the other half,' he always responded.

Often, when translated, laughter welled from the armed people around us and it was obvious the people of Pakistan liked his answer. Importantly it forestalled any problems that may have occurred by way of our seeming to agree with the decision of the President of the USA to fire missiles into the north of their country. 'When in Rome,' Bernard would mutter in his diplomatic way when difficult questions came at him in situations defined as making us 'vulnerable'.

Leaving our snowless ski resort, Colorado fades in the wing mirrors in the crossing into Nebraska before Iowa appears and the scenery changes profoundly as the mountains lead to huge prairies. Miles and miles of flat green landscapes across which the wind whistles and buffets us as we push on. It's not the gusting battering type but a constant resistance, rather than sideways hammer blows. So many Gold Wings and Harleys pass us in both directions we lose count. Often they come fully kitted with everything that can be squeezed on a bike, including a wave of music as they pass, while passengers recline in luxurious comfort in plush chairs complete with armrests. Behind them twin aerials attached to suitcase-sized back boxes flutter the American Stars and Stripes and many tow trailers behind 1500cc six-cylinder bikes on lawn-like perfectly straight highways.

Three-wheeled trikes are everywhere glistening in the sun with bright glossy paint jobs and murals of figures clutching huge swords or macabre Halloween-type montages. Canary yellow, cobalt blue, deep red all seem to be the preferred colours of choice. It leaves us looking and feeling scruffy in comparison as they thunder past us, trailing their hand out in a sign of greeting.

Waving back in true Brit fashion like two excited teenagers we realise that is what we've become recently. In our urge to get home a simple fact was lost, sadly forgotten when we should have known better: 'Enjoy each day as it comes for it may be your last.'

The land of consideration and politeness (as America now seems to us) extends to hotels and streets where people leap out of our way, apologising if they have not recognised my blindness within a fraction of a nanosecond. Before even getting to the kerb the appearance of the white cane leads cars to stop in the middle of the road. Drivers patiently wait as we cross and Bernard's hand crosses to his heart in thanks as they nod back to him as if to say 'no problem'. Many times over the days spent in wandering from hotels to cafés the same patient consideration is met, even if the traffic lights are green.

Hotel rooms are spacious and wherever we stay voluminous beds and perfect pristine facilities abound. The land of plenty demonstrates itself wandering through a local Wal-Mart supermarket in the move from aisle to aisle where rows and rows of everything are neatly stacked, waiting to be consumed. Walking down an aisle containing everything possible for the American baby, a left turn walks us straight into walls of ammunition stacked high; enough to start WW3. Boxes and boxes of every conceivable calibre of bullet is piled up, or so it seems to the two gun-shy Brits. High-powered catapults, cross-bows and automatic air rifles sit next to the camping equipment for that 'perfect weekend'.

'Bloody Hell,' Bernard exclaims. 'They worry about speeding or car insurance but sell enough stuff here to start a war!' It tickles him when he reads a sign by the boxes of ammunition, declaring: *'In order to be fair to all our customers, each may only buy six cartons per day.'*

By the way, each carton contains 100 bullets. Ah well, that's OK then, we can have 600 today, 600 tomorrow, and so on. Should be enough? What do you reckon, honey?

While all this is true, Bernard admits that America is sneaking up on him even as we stand pondering all the potential firepower on display. I have to agree with him. As the kilometres or miles pass beneath our wheels petrol stations appear with old men talking about hunting, fishing, and all things family. The country is insinuating itself deep into us in a good way with all the little things we encounter. The weather, grandchildren and cars all figure prominently in the conversations as huge cartons of drinks are consumed along with plates of food the size of Everest gradually being whittled down. Then dessert is ordered. Meanwhile our measly one cake is cut in half for the two of us. Perhaps our comfort involves no longer struggling to make ourselves understood. Perhaps it's because familiar things surround us. Maybe it's because of something else? Whatever it is, it's difficult to work out even though we both agree. We like it.

Generally, three tanks of petrol disappear each day with speeds of 112 kph as 800 km come and go. Our average speed is 100 and sometimes India, with its twelve-hour days to cover 160 km, seems so long ago. Thinking of over an hour to cover 6 km in Colombia seems another world as the landscape whizzes past. The Iowa wind soon disappears along with the prairie dust as the boyhood home of Buffalo Bill Cody in the valley of the Wapsipinicon River appears. I-80 runs past the farmhouse built in 1847 by his father (Isaac) and Bernard's teeth can clearly be heard gnashing through the intercom again at not being able to stop.

The wind returns to blow for virtually the whole day as Iowa changes to Illinois where signs are passed with magical song titles such as 'Rock Island Line', which spawned the Lonnie Donegan song in 1955. It doesn't matter to Bernard that the song is actually about the Chicago, Rock Island and Pacific Railroad, quite some distance from where our wheels are turning. Blasts of remembered words come through the headphones:

> The Rock Island Line is a mighty good road
> The Rock Island Line is the road to ride
> The Rock Island Line is a mighty good road
> If you want to ride you gotta ride it like you find it
> Get your ticket at the station for the Rock Island Line.

Every road or signpost seems to trigger a lyric from some song of his past. It does not seem the same somehow in the USA compared to the UK as we try to imagine the latest band in the UK singing about Warrington (where we live), or some small place in the Lake District. Somehow, it would not have the same worldwide chart-topping appeal as singing about New York or Galveston. Passing signs for Indianapolis, with Illinois becoming Indiana, we fly past the location of the famous 500 mile race site as huge warning signs insist you pay attention to a simple message: if you hit a road worker 'you go straight to jail for up to 14 years, without ever passing go'. The same severe penalties exist in Australia and people certainly seem to respond to the imposed speed limits.

Petrol stops lead to the handing over of $2.60 per gallon (about £1.65) and everything is completed with credit cards, apart from we who use cash. Bernard has to trundle off to stand in the queue before handing over $20. Then he comes back to fill up before going back to stand in the queue once again to collect the change. It seems such a nuisance after months of people filling the bike for us.

The newly installed Radar scanner, meanwhile, found just along from the ammunition aisle in the supermarket, sits in the dashboard beeping away at any sign of Mr Policeman's presence. It finds his mobile speed cameras hidden in the bushes or among the myriad advertising hoardings and the strength of the signal determines how close to you the 'problem' is lurking. They're illegal in the UK although you can actually buy them. Now that is British logic for you. It is like saying you can look but not touch, or you can buy a beer but you have to leave it unopened. Yeah right.

The rain comes in downpours the further north we go as roads turn to streams before we enter Michigan and rivers of water are fired at us by passing cars in continuous sheets of spray. Bertha signals her protest at this abuse and stops charging. Again. Bernard finds himself back to Malaysian and Australian riding: gear changing instead of braking, sparing lights and indicators within the grey mush of sheet rain.

Today is our last day before crossing the border to Canada and it's infuriating that, with a single day's riding to go, we have another mechanical problem. Splashing our way onwards nervously pondering the voltmeter readings we're 300 miles from the Canadian border. Stopping for breaks now involves leaving the engine running as each press of the starter motor drops the reading by half a volt. Every single one is now precious to us, leading to hours of careful riding before the bridge spanning the border at Port Heron appears. Canada now sits just out of reach over the St Clair River, at least until the $1.50 toll charge is handed over to enter our 31st and final country.

The tollbooth attendant smiles, telling us all the border formalities are over the bridge and yes, it is true, the Canadian formalities are there. But not the American. Needing Bertha stamped out of America we have to turn around and head back across the bridge again (paying another toll) to re-enter America which, technically, has not been left yet.

The queues are huge to enter the States and Bernard 'innocently' heads for an empty lane due to our rapidly depleting battery condition. The lane he enters declares itself to be the 'Nexus' or rapid entry route and with the voltmeter heading severely south, we certainly do need a rapid entry. The customs official in his booth is not at all impressed at Bertha using the 'pre-paid and pre-cleared' vehicle lane. 'Awfully sorry officer' Bernard innocently answers 'But the sign posting is unclear and we, you may have guessed, are not from this side of the world, never mind the bridge!'

Radio signals squawk between booth and control room before being let through with directions towards a customs post where several officers descend on us before the wheels even stop turning. Surrounded on all sides Bernard asks them to step back so I can climb off the bike without the risk of kicking a federal officer. Warily they comply but when the white stick appears, in a single stroke, we are downgraded from a grade one international threat to two 'Brits' on a bike and one of them blind to boot. Gently shepherding us into the office Bernard is relieved of Bertha's keys.

The keys jangle their way to a board full of similar items belonging to dozens of people being questioned over wanting to enter the good old USA. After some time engaged in the slow shuffle forward to meet more officers, our explanation is eventually heard, including our several forays across the bridge before they start laughing while completing the formality of our exit. Other people in the queue are not so lucky as they are grilled over hot coals and have their finger nails pulled out. Not really. Much harder-toned voices, however, make it obvious that some people are not going anywhere fast.

More officers join the conversation as all the formalities are completed before being led back to Bertha where black-uniformed border staff mill around us (complete with mirrored sunglasses) as our keys reappear. Holding our breath the starter is pressed and slowly the bike turns over and starts. Across the bridge once again, Canadian officials direct us to the immigration office where another round of paper bashing is soon completed with the minimum of fuss.

Bertha starts first time but the end is coming in terms of two or three more attempts before the engine will slowly groan over like the asthmatic old lady she is fast becoming and not for the first time does my friend lament the lack of a kick-starter on a motorcycle. Wondering whether motorcycle headlights are required to be left on in Canada, we set off with none while honing our well-practised ability to act like two innocent Brits abroad. Meanwhile I am placed on standby to wave my white stick for all I am worth to gain the sympathy vote if we are stopped by a police officer with a pointed hat on a big horse.

We're going home

(CDN) Heading for Toronto Airport, a hotel appears just as the systems start to shut down as the battery flattens completely. Within earshot (!) of the flight paths, fortunately it is close enough to be within easy commuting of our final gateway to home. With some prompting from me Bernard asks the receptionist if there is a 'senior' (over 50) rate. 'You certainly don't look it!' she answers as we confirm that, yes, we are. It seems our feeling of decrepitness is not really due to any aspect of visibly advancing old age but more to do with completing over 25,000 miles perched on a motorcycle for a year. Her response leaves us strangely mollified as our knees crack loudly following her towards our room without the aid of Zimmer frames, but only just.

The room is cavernous and as I orient myself the door opens and closes intermittently while Bernard trundles in and out delivering wash bags, clothes, computers and anything else needed for our final assault on getting home. Hopefully it will happen before qualifying for the second level advanced 'severe old age' discount. Taking a taxi to find a solar charger to retrieve poor Bertha's battery from where she's descended ('I'm not starting, I've had enough, and you cannot make me') an hour later we're back at the hotel. Clutching assorted leads and the life-giving panel, everything is connected before praying she will start the following day. Thankfully the sun works its magic by then and she fires up first time.

Phone calls lead us to Air Canada and eight hours later all the paperwork is done and Bertha weights in at 330 kg while a very nice 'Dangerous Goods' certificate is extracted from a lovely man who even comes in on the national holiday of Canada Day (1st July) to sign off the bike. After shipping a bike by air so many times it's apparent we're all talking the same language and he declares himself happy. Meanwhile, our constant companion the carnet is stamped by a customs officer who tells how he has always wanted to take his Harley around the world. Shaking hands with us he comments 'Jesus, you two make it sound so easy,' as he asks about the journey and how we have solved this and that problem. 'It is easy,' Bernard replies, 'If you really want to do it.'

Pakistani and Croatian security staff come over to talk to us as Bertha is readied for her final flight and they ask how we found their countries. Holding my breath I wait for Bernard to say something like 'Head east from England,' but he resists and tells them how much we loved them. The Croatian has not been home for many years and is interested in how his fledgling homeland has developed since the war that finished during the early 1990s. He hears of all the new hotels and of how it is now obviously a tourist haven for Italians who nip across the 160 km watery gap called the Adriatic Sea.

'And Pakistan?' the second officer asks quietly.

Of all the countries visited this one place always presents the most questions from all over the world as people had thought us mad going there. Bernard answers him honestly for the both of us: 'We loved Pakistan, we truly did. The people were lovely and everybody, and I mean everybody, was so helpful.' The officer is pleased with our thoughts on his home country as his voice displays pleasure, coming through clearly as we talk about where, how and when, our wheels had passed through this troubled country. Telling him how we wish the country nothing but peace for the future, Bernard finishes with the Islamic term 'Inshallah' or 'God willing'. It is our wish for the ordinary people of Pakistan, and for people everywhere, in times of trouble.

Three hours later we're standing at Toronto Airport trying to work out how to pay for the 11.30pm flight as our credit and debit cards have been locked out by the UK banks again, the fourth time on the trip so far. In the end a very complicated transaction is done with a Bureau de Change but it was probably in their interest to help us otherwise Bernard may well have destroyed their ATM with frustration. At 11.20pm we're sitting on the Air India flight to London heaving a sign of relief as we settle in for the way home, weeks late, and with a malfunctioning bike (again).

We start to think about The End and of so much that has happened, of the good times, the bad times and every shade in between. As the plane rises into the sky we know it's been a journey of start, stop, go, start, stop, go, involving periods of both intense activity and inactivity as we looked to keep moving ever onwards. Recollections flow of shivering for three weeks in eastern Turkey waiting for the Iranian visa refusal saga (Yes, No, Yes) to be resolved and of how my 50+ friend sitting beside me had, somehow, become a threat to Iranian national security.

From bank lockouts (4), to breakdowns (5), it's easy to recall how each stop caused the leaking of time and funds. The haemorrhaging of finances struck us hard, very hard, as the pound went into freefall with the international financial meltdown hitting the world. It often left Bernard holding his head in his hands as 25% of our budget disappeared in exchange rates while he ruminated on the chance of it happening now, right now, after two years of planning and 30 years of waiting.

My thoughts shift from shocking roads through to all the wonderful people we came into contact with. Sometimes I marvel, no that's the wrong word, I'm left 'incredulous' how it is possible to traverse the planet on a bike, seemingly so simply with barriers broken down as they were encountered.

Sitting in the UK so long ago, it now seems, we wanted to spread the thought that many things are possible if you have the will to face an adventure. Within this journey it cannot be anything else but true that you have to face your own fears, hopes and beliefs. It's also true there can be no sense of adventure without an element of risk, which won't happen in the comfort of security. If I had stayed in this zone then it would never have been possible to show how a blind person, with the right assistance, can have fantastic adventures. The same is true whether or not disabilities are involved as you have to be willing to take a chance, or opportunity, when it presents itself.

Through it all, the assistance I received from the man on my left (who is now fast asleep) is incalculable. It's probably so far beyond most people's perception of what is involved in working with a blind person that it will pass by largely unnoticed. It's the way he prefers it anyway as we both know what occurred and it's probably impossible to truly transmit it by the spoken word. To him, he merely set out to fulfil his own life-long dream, to seek an answer to the question, 'Could I do it?' After all, people can spend their life wondering if they are made of the 'right stuff' for things such as this.

Now he knows.

We've all read about people doing such things and they become something different in the telling of the story, something unique or exceptional. In reality, they too are just like us. Frightened, hungry, cold, wet, insecure, happy, sad, they continue to push their way through what they've set themselves in the best way they can. Like all these people Bernard had read about across his entire life, now he has his own answer to that question. Never again does he have to wonder about the answer. It's my own belief that only a very small number of people would have ever contemplated this venture with a blind woman. Many people did question his sanity for taking me on such a journey and their thoughts simply left him shrugging his own shoulders when he phrased his own question to them, 'Well, why not?'

Over the miles we were to become two people blended into one, in thought, emotion and even written words. Even as he stressed and worried about being able to fix the bike or ride the roads encountered, never once did any thought cross my mind other than 'confidence'. It is a rare state of mind indeed given everything encountered. In all our time spent together, 24 hours a day for a year, the greatest compliment I can remember is how people noticed we liked each other. And more. Much more. Bernard has always said that liking somebody is not the same as loving them as you can love without liking and you can like without loving. We are truly fortunate in that we have both sides of the coin. A year on the road has reinforced these thoughts even further.

My mind replays thoughts and images as I sit beside my now sleeping co-conspirator as the plane flies through the night. Feelings and emotions flow through my mind seeing me climbing elephants in the jungles of Nepal, stroking tigers in Thailand, and cuddling koalas in Australia. It relives meeting wonderful people from all around the world who work with blind and partially sighted people, often under difficult circumstances. From Bruno of Swiss Guide Dogs, to George Abraham in India, from Seeing Hands in Nepal to Vision Australia. They all appear in my mind.

Across the miles many places have become linked to the everyday people we spent time with, from Slobodan in Montenegro to Hector in Peru with his 'Meester Smith' greetings. Glen in Australia reappears in my mind along with the three hours sitting in the dust of the Nullarbor as Bertha was repaired. I think of his upset at the end when he realised I was blind and I wanted to hug him and tell him it was alright. Voices echo through my mind in memory of so many of them, strangers becoming friends with our brief passing through their lives. Indians, Pakistanis, Greeks and people from all over the world settle onto a Scottish wagon driver called Gordon whose advice resounded many times in my head when we were lost: 'follow the wagons'. My legs relive harsh mountain climbs and my body feels events across the world as images continue to flow. The jolt of bad roads, the feel of the bright sun, the dryness of my mouth, the feel of the wind, the noise, the worry, the ecstasy, the fear. All collide in a welter of emotions as I replay and work through what it all means. If ever this is possible.

Our friend Bertha is battered and misbehaving although intact as we wing eastwards on the seven-hour flight. Over the miles only once did we fall off, thankfully without any injuries. I have stood among the clouds at (nearly) 15,000 feet, struggling to breathe and shivering in the snow, before gasping in the heat of the lowlands. Enduring each and every day with humour, roads that were made of mud, gravel, rock and tarmac, sometimes all at the same time. We survived. Clattering and rattling across landscapes for which Bertha was never built, objects were dodged be they cattle, kangaroos, chasing dogs or trees which had fallen and blocked our way. We've encountered routes blocked due to protests, turmoil and political instabilities the likes of which we'd never before experienced. It's small wonder that many people try to come to our own homeland when you understand how they struggle with daily life. While existence is undoubtedly hard in some countries we passed through, it is also a fact that within the poorest we often found the greatest welcome. It seems to be a universal truth.

The kindness often starts at borders of such places where guards helped us through unfamiliar processes while Bernard stressed. The acts of kindness extended to riot police who opened their ranks in Malaysia to let us through as the protesting crowd fell silent as they watched us pass.

When times were hard, or we were frightened, it was a matter of persevering as people often do. Yes, it was frightening at times and Bernard will readily admit to it as, 'Only a fool is not afraid, it's what keeps us alive'. 'Let's get this thing done' was his saying, his motto, his mantra when things had to be done. Over our time on the road, I recall many such sayings as things became physically, psychologically or emotionally difficult. Other mantras such as 'Control the fear or it will control you' is another long remembered voice urging me to tough it out in the crossing of India while his own hands shook long after the bike had stopped. Sometimes he would shout at himself before setting off again, desperately trying to keep us in one piece, alive through each day.

Only twice did he have a crisis in relation to his own abilities: once in the darkness of Lahore in Pakistan and then again on the road to Gorakhpur as we choked on the white dust and chaos of India. Both these times are burned into his, and our, brains. Such is the way when your self-belief and self-image are teetering on the edge of a precipice; you hang on by your fingernails, as you cannot afford to fall. Other people, me, depended on him and he knew this. Times like this, and others, left me like a frightened rabbit for weeks later and it shaped how we both dealt with our fears. Mantras ruled at times as there was little other help, only each other's support to depend on. It was enough and this became even truer as we moved on through time and distance.

My thoughts drift to my late husband Peter, of what he would make of me now. In all probability he would never recognise the person I have become, both with this journey and with the passing of time and life across those lonely years. I like to believe he is sitting somewhere saying:

'Good on you Cath, live life, make each day count.'

I have tried to do just that and nowhere has this been truer than over the last year.

If you are reading this tale of two ordinary people just like you then there is something you should always remember and hold dear to you. You never know when it will all end. It can be so sudden and so unexpected that there is no warning, no further time to say the things you have never said to those around you. This second, right now, is your opportunity to put the book down and correct that omission. Take it now. You may never have another chance. Life is like that.

The hours pass by with all these thoughts of the 26,385 miles eventually covered. Thoughts of life, love, and the people I have known and met. The plane hums and banks across the Atlantic, taking me towards my guide dog Biscuit and everything else that life has to offer me in the years ahead. The knowledge that, truly, each day does count and should be made to count, is my precious gift to you. Some people may well understand this already with startling clarity. They, like me, know the days are not infinite but must all eventually end, much like our own journey through this fantastic world on our friend Bertha.

My reverie is disturbed as Bernard stirs beside me, slowly waking, stretching, taking in where he is. Words are no longer necessary between us as my hand reaches for his. Fingers gently interlock and squeeze to say hello.

It is all we need to say.

We are going home.

EPILOGUE

BY BERNARD SMITH

How do you sum up the achievement of a life-long dream and how is it possible to put into words a suitable response when people ask, 'Well, what was it like?' When I first returned from the journey words would often fail to come beyond 'it was fine'. One person at work had laughed and said to me, 'Only you could reduce going around the world on a motorbike with a blind woman as being fine.'

Many times over the early weeks Cathy would quietly tell me that people wanted to know otherwise they wouldn't ask. She pointed out that if I met somebody who had ridden around the world then I would be disappointed if the totality of their response was 'it was fine'. To her people wanted details, the highs, the lows, the fantastic places I have ridden. They wanted to know about the roads, the problems, the stresses and strains. In detail please, and the more the better.

But, in truth, I found it difficult to talk about.

You see, to me, it felt like meeting a person at a party who then goes onto tell you of all the wonderful things they've done. I've met people like this over the years and it's always left me with an urge to drop kick them as it felt like they were rubbing my nose, deliberately, in the mediocrity of my own life.

It is also true that, while on the journey, many times our paths did cross Western people holidaying in far-flung places and they too asked the very same question of 'well, what is it like?' Sometimes I would try to convey what it meant to be an ordinary person riding in difficult places but the experience always left me uncomfortable. At times, this discomfort came from recounting stories that always seemed to demonstrate the problems we'd encountered. In my own mind, it seemed the problems were caused by my own lack of ability. Sometimes, perhaps, it stemmed from my own insecurities.

You see, it is true that at the start I found it so hard, so tiring. There seemed to be no rest between 'riding and guiding' as I called it. It was also true that I stressed over everything from a bit of gravel in Switzerland to finding somewhere to sleep. Sometimes I even worried about locating the right road itself despite having both map and GPS (global positioning system). However, the true hardship of the motorcycling never really appeared at the start and this is something I now truly understand. It came much further down the line when, in many ways, I was better prepared.

Despite having ridden bikes for the whole of my life, my skills and abilities grew far beyond anything I had imagined across the miles, without ever realising it. When you spend a year travelling two-up on a road bike through mud, gravel and everything in between, only then do you understand what you know. More importantly, you learn what you do not know about riding a bike. This is not something that you can gain from reading a book or watching a video. The only way to understand is to be there. I say this as it is, very much, a psychological world involving the full range of human emotions. Thus it was all these feelings I tried to convey to people whenever they asked the question.

Many times when I did talk about such things it came to me that, for a lifetime, I had read of people who rode the world. Through their words I was privileged to learn, to dream and ultimately to wonder. Once this link came into my mind I understood. The understanding involved knowing that without those people my own dream would have died long ago. Thus this book was born. Consider it a chain, or a single link in an unending story.

As we sat and thought about the writing of our tale we both knew that fears of showing ourselves in positive or a negative way had to be put aside. It was the way it had to be. To us, the printed page had to be real in its reflection of what it felt like to be 'out there' on our own, in our own ways. Inevitably, we both experienced a range of different, and similar, emotions across the miles. Nowhere was this truer than when we had nobody to call on in strange places and we were frightened. After all, the story is about two 'ordinary' people, the same as you. Ordinary people do get frightened, hungry, uncertain and insecure. To say anything else is to deny the facts.

In my own 'ordinariness', the story stretches back across the years to a dark night on a motorway in England. Wet through and riding a misfiring

Norton 850, the sight of a service station and cup of coffee had cheered me up. The heavens had poured water out of the sky for hours and I was cold and very, very, wet in the days before Gore-Tex, heated handlebars and all such things.

Putting off going back out into Noah's domain in case I tripped over the animals, I had squelched into the shop to pass more time and there had stumbled on a book. Many of you may, or may not, know of it. It was Jupiter's Travels, written by Ted Simon. The year was 1980 and I was 24 years old. Ted wrote about something he had done, the same thing I had been already been thinking about for six years.

He rode the world.

Sitting down with another cup of coffee, I opened the first page and my life was to change forever. While I say this you have to understand that Ted was not the first to ride the world. I had already read books of men and women riding through exotic places like Africa in the 30s, along with many other fantastic journeys. What I think he did, fundamentally, was write about it in such an accessible mainstream way. The book kept me riveted with three hours passing as I turned the pages and the roads dried. Thirty-two years later I still have that very same book although now it's dog-eared and battered as it's been read so many times.

I suppose the same 'trigger' could be true for many people reading the tales of more contemporary figures such as Charlie Boorman and Ewan McGregor. In a way, each individual writer forms a line from the previous, adding something, giving something for everybody to enjoy. As with all tales, whether Ted's, Charlie's or Ewan's, it will never be possible to write the definitive story of riding the world. Each book is, in reality, only a reflection of the people who ride certain roads, at a specific time, on a certain bike, in their own way, within their own circumstances and limitations. Much as some people thrive on adversity while others are risk averse, many love riding in various countries while others loathe the same place. Thus, no two people's experiences can ever truly be the same. This is true whether it concerns the motorcycle itself or a country and its peoples. By nature, it must vary. Each is unique.

It took me a long time to sift through my thoughts and put everything into perspective. It was as I was struggling to adapt back into 'normal' life in those early weeks after arriving back that Cathy was diagnosed with cancer. From this point onwards my own petty struggle ended.

If you have ever cared for someone with a life-threatening illness then you will know, without hesitation, what it means. You throw yourself into doing whatever it takes. Over the subsequent months the illness and treatment all made riding the world seem insignificant and unimportant.

Eventually, however, we returned from the darkness of Catherine's illness to enter the twilight world between fitness and ill health. Now she seemed well enough to get back on a motorcycle. For me this was important. I say this as, with such an event, I hoped it would prove to her that there was life after cancer. Everybody needs something to look forward to after all, something to inspire the hopes and dreams we all have. It was a simple thought to reinforce how life stretches out before us no matter how bleak things appear. Thus, my plan involved attending a motorcycle meeting where such dreams are shared.

By now a new bike sat in the garage and it was a link to our journey through Nepal. It was here you will have read of our meeting with another rider and his BMW F800GS. Smaller and lighter than the behemoth 1200s, it rode lightly over the terrible terrain and I knew this was to be my next bike. Originally, I had thought to use one for the trip itself but it had only just been released onto the market. Truly did I agonise until deciding, ultimately, to trust the bike I knew and understood, and could rebuild if necessary. Thus, we set out on an old R100RT that came to be known across the world as 'Bertha'.

With Cathy still weak from her ongoing treatments, we set off for the hundred-mile ride to attend an overlander's meeting on our shiny new bike. Here, 32 years after that dark wet night on a motorway so long ago, I shook hands with Ted Simon. It is funny how life appears to turn full circle. Sometimes the wheels just seem to turn so slowly.

Meanwhile our new bike sat in its anonymity among so many others at the meeting as we blended into the background, listening as others talked of what it means to ride different parts of the world. Eager faces filled each presentation as the 'best' bike for such a journey through to the latest whizz-bang equipment was poured over. Long may it go on as people dream of the possibilities.

We still laugh about pulling up at the front gate to the meeting and waiting for the issuing of our passes. Eventually the attendants noted our brand new (ish) adventure bike and two middle-aged (ish) people. Cathy's blindness was not apparent in much the same way that it seldom is initially. On learning we were staying in a local hotel (due to her illness) rather than in a tent, passes were handed over by a laughing attendant saying, 'Hardly hard core, are you!'

I still find it funny even to this day.

'No, not really,' I'd answered. 'My bum's killing me and I've only come up the road.' You see, sometimes, it's easier to be what people want you to be. The event reminded me of the sun-blasted and much-faded sticker in Bertha's cracked windshield. Its contents had guided much of our thinking as we passed through so many 'dangerous' countries. You see, in white letters on a blue background, it stated:

'What you see mainly depends on what you look for.'

As we travelled those potentially hostile roads, each day that sticker constantly reminded me of how countries can seem so dangerous and physically threatening. At times like that it is all too easy to be misled by what appears before your eyes. Sometimes it will be an armed person on the side of a road or a scowling border guard. Perhaps it may even be two old people attending an 'adventure' meeting on a motorcycle. In that way, people do judge things by what they see, rather than by what they should look for. What happens then is that the truth of the world passes them by. You see, in our experiences set out on the pages of this book, the truth is that the world consists of a wonderful place full of kindness and friends.

Driving off from the gate on that day Cathy had laughed at the way we'd been judged in a way she'd not done for a long time. And it was so good to hear. Her laughter was so loud that, just for a second, I'd thought of turning down the volume on the intercom. But I didn't. I listened. And smiled. As I drove into the meeting I knew I'd been lucky to have the chance to fulfil my dream of riding the world.

As Cathy has written in this book, sometimes it really is simply a matter of timing as rarely in our lives do all the planets line up. Even if they do, you still need the courage to take that final step and it is here that people often falter, falling back into long familiar securities.

For those of you who would ask the question, 'Am I glad I took that step?' I would say yes, absolutely, without any doubt. With no hesitation, no regrets and with nothing but gratitude do I recognise that, for me, all the planets lined up.

Would I do it all again?

In answer – I would say to you that since you have travelled this far through the pages of our journey, only now will you truly understand my response of:

'Would tomorrow be too soon or shall we go right now?'